# SOCIAL VALUE INVESTING

# SOCIAL VALUE INVESTING

## A MANAGEMENT FRAMEWORK
## FOR EFFECTIVE PARTNERSHIPS

### HOWARD W. BUFFETT
### WILLIAM B. EIMICKE

Columbia University Press
*Publishers Since 1893*
New York   Chichester, West Sussex
cup.columbia.edu

Library of Congress Cataloging-in-Publication Data
Names: Buffett, Howard W., 1983– author. | Eimicke, William B., author.
Title: Social value investing : a management framework for effective
partnerships / Howard W. Buffett and William B. Eimicke.
Description: New York : Columbia University Press, [2018] |
Includes bibliographical references and index.
Identifiers: LCCN 2017061568 (print) | LCCN 2018001947 (ebook) |
ISBN 9780231544450 (ebook) | ISBN 9780231182904 (cloth : alk. paper)
Subjects: LCSH: Public-private sector cooperation.
Classification: LCC HD3871 (ebook) | LCC HD3871 .E36 2018 (print) |
DDC 658/.046—dc23
LC record available at https://lccn.loc.gov/2017061568

$\infty$

Columbia University Press books are printed on permanent
and durable acid-free paper.
Printed in the United States of America

Cover design: Noah Arlow

Some images have been enhanced for appearance, for black and white,
or in accordance with nondisclosure agreements.

HWB

To Lili, for her endless support and love;
and Thomas, for the bright future that lies ahead.

———⬥⬥⬥———

WBE

To Karen, Annemarie, Balsam, and Sugar Ray.

# Contents

———— ✦ ————

## PROCESS

## PEOPLE

## PLACE

## PORTFOLIO

## PERFORMANCE

———⊙⊗⊗⊗⊙———

## THE RISKS AND PROMISE OF PARTNERSHIPS

# A Message of Optimism

I am an optimist, a very realistic optimist. You can gain a sense of this by reading Berkshire's annual reports and the op-eds I have written over the years. For one thing, I believe that living standards around the world will continue improving far into the future, as they have done in America since our forefathers discovered the country's secret sauce.

America has led the way with an innovative market system built upon a rule of law and equality of opportunity. This combination has delivered incredible growth during my lifetime—real GDP per capita has increased sixfold since my birth in 1930. And our economy will continue to benefit from a steady unleashing of human potential.

This is never more evident than when I meet with university students. Every year, groups from forty colleges and universities visit with me in Omaha to talk about the world they will inherit and improve. My message is consistent: Despite the difficulties we face, I am confident that their grandchildren will live in a world with far greater abundance than we have today. After we talk, I always come away feeling even more optimistic about the future.

For students like these, this book will be a helpful resource. It is grounded in a well-researched and tested approach, which will serve as a framework for partnership building. As you learn from the strategies pursued in these stories, you'll discover just why I'm so hopeful about the future. You will enjoy this book, and I'll bet you will be inspired, too, by its message of optimism and action.

# SOCIAL VALUE INVESTING

# Introduction

HOWARD W. BUFFETT AND WILLIAM B. EIMICKE

In the middle of New York City is an open and expansive green space—something just as quintessentially Manhattan as its skyline. Every year Central Park welcomes more than forty million visitors from all over the world.[1] Many think of it as a perfectly landscaped and pristinely maintained park, but not so long ago it was one of the most dangerous precincts in what was then the murder capital of the United States. In popular movies—*The Out of Towners, Annie Hall, Six Degrees of Separation*—Central Park symbolized why few people wanted to live in New York, why Europeans were advised not to visit, and why no street smart New Yorker ventured in after dark.

What changed? In the 1980s and 1990s, the neighboring community mobilized to create the Central Park Conservancy (CPC), recruited hundreds of volunteers and millions of dollars in support, hired highly qualified and passionate leaders and workers, and partnered with the city to run the park as if it were their own. The city government still owns the park, and it is open to all for free—but CPC runs it and raises the money to pay most of its operating and capital costs. This was an uncommon approach for its time, but this kind of creative cross-sector partnership is becoming more and more common. It didn't happen overnight, and it required constant, tireless, and visionary leadership from members of the conservancy and the city government. As good as this approach is, the partners are still trying to make it better—and they are helping other parks around the world replicate their success.

Just blocks away in Chelsea, near the previously notorious and highly dangerous Hell's Kitchen neighborhood, is a park built atop the abandoned tracks of an elevated freight train line that once delivered meat, dairy, and manufacturing supplies to the city. A well-organized community organization with inspired leadership convinced the city not to demolish the tracks, and, together, the community and the city built a beautiful park with panoramic views that attracts nearly eight million visitors each year.[2] Similar to CPC, the nonprofit Friends of the High Line manages the park for the city and raises funds from donors to cover most of the rather substantial operating costs.

The Central Park Conservancy and Friends of the High Line are excellent illustrations of cross-sector partnerships: voluntary collaborations between organizations from the public, private, or philanthropic sectors that accomplish mutually agreed-upon goals. Today partnerships are delivering goods and services more efficiently and effectively, and with greater benefit to society, than one organization could ever achieve on its own. The two parks also show how partnerships between different sectors—in these cases, nonprofit organizations partnering with government—often are able to overcome the limitations that constrain organizations in any single sector. Private sector organizations also bring unique contributions to partnerships, generally driving better outcomes for programs that benefit the public in addition to their profit-making purpose.

We explore cross-sector partnerships as case studies at the School of International and Public Affairs at Columbia University, where we teach. Our graduate students are incredibly bright and diverse, and our alumni span more than 150 countries and come with professional backgrounds from government, for-profit, and philanthropic organizations.[3] However, they all come together with a common goal of improving society. In our courses on effective public management, innovation, and philanthropy, we often find ourselves describing cross-sector partnerships as a more effective way to serve the public interest. From the innovative High Line urban park in the heart of New York City to the many other examples in this book—digital transformation of government services in India, economic and agricultural revitalizations in Afghanistan, and so on—organizations from all three sectors are coming together in different ways to meet their individual organization's goals and serve the greater good.

## WHY DO WE NEED PARTNERSHIPS?

The traditional view of how societies manage themselves is changing. Government alone has not been able to handle the growing
responsibilities and costs of the issues it faces in the modern world:
public safety, social welfare, public health, infrastructure, education, national defense, international relations, job creation, housing,
energy, environmental protection, transportation, space exploration,
scientific research, justice, and so on. In addition, most individuals
and local communities do not want these important issues handled
for them without their input, no matter how well-meaning the government may be. A community generally will have better everyday
solutions than officials from their vantage points at city hall or far
away at the capital.

Decentralizing government decision making at the local level may
help, but economic decisions are increasingly influenced by global
developments, which have both positive and negative implications.[4]
On the good side, globalization has improved the lives of billions
around the world, and much of that benefit was made possible
through organizations partnering across sectors and national borders.[5] At the same time, globalization contributed to the financial
crisis of 2008 and its lingering aftermath: displaced homeowners,
drained retirement accounts, limited access to financing, and structural unemployment.[6]

So far globalization seems to have reduced inequality in many countries and exacerbated it in others. The innovations and efficiencies globalization has enabled also has created an uncertain future for many
workers around the world. For example, the coming age of automa-
tion could act as a second industrial revolution in the decades ahead,
with the potential to significantly increase efficiency and convenience.
Simultaneously, millions of workers may be replaced with robots,
worsening already dangerous levels of inequality.[7]

As we discuss in chapter 1, government used to be the leader in
responding to major societal challenges, such as poverty during the
Great Depression. In today's world, however, government bureau-
cracies seem slow, rigid, and clumsy and often are stalemated by par-
tisan bickering and gridlock. Too many people across our country
(and around the world) are underemployed, hurting, and frustrated.

The Brexit vote in Great Britain and the U.S. presidential election in 2016 reflect the pessimism of working-class and middle-income voters, not just regarding their future but also the prospects for their children and grandchildren.[8]

Many around the world believe that our challenges are too great and too complex to be solved. Although these challenges will not be solved by any one country, organization, or even sector of society, solutions to these challenges *do* exist. Leaders from organizations of all types have been developing new strategies and joining together to tackle the most entrenched and intractable problems in our world today—progress that is well documented in economist Steven Radelet's book, *The Great Surge*. In the past few decades alone, extreme poverty has been cut in half,[9] billions more have access to clean water,[10] and under-five child mortality has declined nearly 60 percent.[11] This is undoubtedly incredible progress, and yet much more is needed.

In the following chapters, you will read about how cross-sector partnerships are becoming the most effective method of accomplishing large-scale public good in the twenty-first century—dramatically improving programs by sharing responsibility that governments alone are unable to deliver. However, implementing these new approaches requires unprecedented innovation, inclusivity, and sustainable solutions, and they will only be successful if they focus on creating value for everyone involved.

## CHANGE IS ON THE HORIZON

Major shifts in the characteristics of our populations, their values, and the distribution of wealth are happening all around us. For instance, the baby boom generation has been surpassed in size and influence by the millennials.[12] Simultaneously, roughly $60 trillion of global wealth is expected to change hands over the next 50 years,[13] and 86 percent of future inheritors are interested in sustainable investing[14]—including actions or advancements by businesses that improve our society.[15] According to Deloitte, 2013 marked the first year that millennials began ranking the primary purpose of business as creating social value—not creating profit.[16] Between 2012 and 2014 alone, socially responsible investing grew more than 76 percent,[17] and in 2016, it comprised more than one out of every four invested dollars under professional management.[18] A Pew Research Center study found that 84 percent of millennials report that making a positive difference in the world is more important to them than professional recognition.[19] What these numbers indicate is not a temporary or passing trend but a paradigm shift in how society values itself—value defined by purpose rather than by a relentless march toward profit.

The growing crisis of economic inequality in the United States is a clear example of "success" for some—but possibly becoming disastrous for us all. Nobel laureate economist Joseph Stiglitz agrees, saying that the real solution to the inequality crisis is focusing on community rather than individual self-interest: "Indeed, we are a community, and all communities help those who are less fortunate among them. If our economic system leads to so many people without jobs, or with jobs that do not pay a livable wage, dependent on the government for food, it means that our economic system has not worked in the way it should."[20]

## HOW CAN WE GET BETTER OUTCOMES FOR ALL?

To live up to our collective potential to solve these complex challenges, we believe that a core value of *sharing success*—between organizations, individuals, local communities, and our environment—will enable society to transform how it defines and accomplishes its goals. Professor Stiglitz has outlined policies that could increase economic growth and equality, creating what he calls "a shared prosperity."[21] We agree that society can do better, and in often unnoticed ways we are already accomplishing great things, frequently through new and exciting collaborations. That is really what this book is about. We discuss how important it is for partners to establish clear and mutually beneficial goals, agree on appropriate and feasible performance measures, bring together those who can get the job done, identify the places that want and need help, and implement processes that will lead to success.

Technology and innovation alone will not carry us forward. Economist Robert Gordon has attracted a great deal of attention for his theory that the rate of innovation is slowing dramatically and, therefore, expectations for future improvement in the human race should be lowered.[22] Even if the rate of innovation slows, we can still substantially improve our societies through performance-driven management.

Management expert Peter Drucker believed that leadership and management contribute as much or more to progress as technological innovation does. How well we measure success can dramatically affect our results. As Drucker wrote in the early 1970s, "it is the task of *this* management generation to make the institutions of the society of organizations, beginning with the business enterprise, perform for society and economy; for the community; and for the individual alike."[23]

What Drucker was saying forty years ago is similar to what millennials are saying today: private firms should make money and do good at the same time.[24] Drucker also advocated for cross-sector collaboration with the nonprofit sector to make the world a better place.[25] Over the past several decades, the number and influence of nongovernmental organizations (NGOs), including nonprofit aid agencies, community-based organizations, foundations, and advocacy organizations, have increased almost exponentially in most countries around the world.[26] From tiny neighborhood associations to mega-foundations and global service organizations, these groups are feeding the hungry, housing the homeless, curing the sick, educating children, and promoting sustainability. In many cases, when philanthropic initiatives are taken to scale, they are done so in partnership with government.

Cooperative efforts such as these are not a twenty-first-century phenomenon. Governments have contracted with for-profit and nonprofit organizations to complete projects, supply goods, and deliver services for centuries. What makes current and future partnership models different are the reasons the parties come together, the collaborative manner in which they design and implement their agreements, and how they measure individual and collective success.

## SOCIAL VALUE INVESTING CAN HELP PRODUCE BETTER OUTCOMES

An important message of this book is that we must be smarter in our attempts to make the world a better place. "Doing good does not excuse us from doing better,"[27] and throughout this book, we explore new ways to add or increase value for society through better management, planning, and performance measurement. Ours is not the first attempt to be more analytical about the effects of our public or philanthropic investments, and we hope to build on this quickly developing field. We argue that partnerships combining the strengths of multiple sectors—government, corporations, and philanthropy—can yield the most public benefit, especially when they are structured with integrity and inclusion.

This book presents a framework for creating social value that is modeled after one of history's most successful investment paradigms: value investing. Like value investing, *social value investing* employs a long-term investment strategy that attempts to unlock hidden or intrinsic value, and it focuses on effective management through a five-element approach: process, people, place, portfolio, and performance.

In chapter 2 we introduce this framework and describe its origins, history, and development. The chapters that follow present case studies of cross-sector partnerships, each exemplifying one of the five elements of the framework. These cases are paired with an analysis and the theoretical underpinnings of each element. In all but one case, the partnerships we describe were developed independently and without knowledge of the social value investing approach. While they are not necessarily a perfect adaptation of the framework, we believe this independence reinforces the validity of the broad applicability of the model.

This new management framework begins with the first element: the need for an effective *process* to structure how organizations partner successfully. This is especially important in complex situations that require coordinated action and comprehensive programs. Partners must develop a fully integrated approach, relying on organizations from across sectors, to develop solutions that will outlast their initial investments. To illustrate this element, in chapter 3 we present an initiative in India designed to spur economic growth and opportunity through a partnership led by the national government. The initiative provides official biometric identification for the country's 1.3 billion residents, resulting in a more efficient, effective, and honest distribution of publicly funded benefits. These programs also facilitate savings, investment, and job growth, and raise the standard of living for low-income families. Following the case, in chapter 4 we detail the framework's first element and draw examples from the partnerships in India.

In chapters 5 and 6 we discuss how cross-sector partnerships rely on *people* as their most important asset. Leaders must build teams of diverse human capital and work with other leaders in a collaborative, sustained, and decentralized manner. To understand how well this can work in the real world, we look at the leadership of the Central Park Conservancy and the network of partners that created the High Line. Today CPC is partnering with other conservancies in cities across the United States to bring private resources and expertise to the management of public spaces. CPC has worked with Columbia University and others to design and implement training and certification programs for urban park managers—supporting the next generation of leaders who will help bring the CPC's best practices to parks around the world.

In chapters 7 and 8 we illustrate how successful partnerships empower constituents as co-owners of outcomes by using a *place-*based strategy and cooperative planning mentality. This emphasizes the importance of designing, operating, and implementing a partnership's efforts in support of stakeholder-developed goals. To better assess the opportunities and challenges of applying this element, we explore a cross-sector partnership to strengthen the rural economy in western Afghanistan despite decades of conflict.

In chapters 9 and 10 we discuss ways in which partners from different sectors can coinvest their resources in a *portfolio* to diversify risk and achieve greater impact. To illustrate this aspect of social value investing, we describe the work of an innovative NGO made up of private sector leaders in Brazil called Comunitas. These leaders created a program called Juntos, which brings together corporate expertise and finance, philanthropic donors, and Comunitas staff to partner with willing local governments to improve the efficiency and effectiveness of jointly selected government programs—all in close collaboration with local residents.

Finally, in chapters 11 and 12, we discuss the fifth element of social value investing, which focuses on projecting and measuring *performance* to understand the intrinsic value a program or partnership may create for society. We document how former New York City mayor Michael Bloomberg used performance-based partnerships to revolutionize public safety, saving lives and property and dramatically improving the quality of life in the city. We then present a formula that can help partners—whether in the public, private, or philanthropic sector—compare the predicted positive social impact of different programs that serve the public good. By inputting key variables and a measurable social impact goal (in areas such as fire safety, renewable energy, or smallholder agriculture), partners can calculate an impact rate of return per dollar expended. Enabling partners to compare similar programs seeking to bring about positive outcomes means they can determine which options will achieve the greatest benefit for society. The formula is a starting point and an important step toward an accessible and robust cross sector partnership measurement methodology.

We believe the full potential of the *process, people, place, portfolio,* and *performance* management framework can be realized when applied through cross-sector partnerships. Our case studies and their analyses illustrate how the talents and resources of one partner can complement the others and magnify positive social impact as well as the efficiency of an endeavor.

However, not all partnerships are successful. In chapter 13 we explore a cautionary tale of the complex public-private investments in preparation for the 2016 Summer Olympics in Rio de Janeiro. This chapter examines the government-led partnerships to revitalize the city's dilapidated port area and public transportation system. In this case, a number of elements from the framework were missing, and the results were uneven: corruption ensued, some stakeholders were disenfranchised, and many Olympic venues were virtually abandoned or fell into disrepair.

## HOW DID WE GET HERE AND WHY DOES IT MATTER?

The modern cross-sector partnership model developed over nearly a century of experimentation in how the government engaged with the private and philanthropic sectors, beginning with New Deal programs led by President Franklin D. Roosevelt. The Great Depression left millions of previously self-reliant families destitute, and only government agencies had the size, scope, power, and leadership to partner with private companies and charities to ease their poverty. As many countries deteriorated into anarchy and dictatorship, the U.S. government engaged private businesses and charities to work together toward recovery. World War II boosted the authority of the government to "lead" its private partners and supply the demand for weapons and provisions for all of the Allied forces. However, resulting decades of government-led partnerships bloated the public sector, and public trust in the government's ability to accomplish important work efficiently was lost.

The privatization movement followed. Ronald Reagan and Margaret Thatcher led a growing antigovernment groundswell, and privately run public projects followed. Many of these programs moved faster, cost the government less, and produced visible outcomes. But privatization had its own drawbacks, including a predominant focus on short-term profits over other important considerations, bidders who oversold their outcomes, and contractors who avoided serving hard to reach communities and constituents (who were often in the greatest need). Some scholars argue that, in certain cases, privatization simply replaced an inefficient public monopoly with a private one, offering consumers little more at a higher price.[28]

The reinventing government phenomenon of the 1990s focused on improving how government works rather than replacing it with private companies. This reinvention included some decentralization of decision making, increased community participation, and additional contracting with nonprofit organizations for service delivery. In many ways, it set the stage for the rise of cross-sector partnerships by highlighting successful relationships between governments and community-based organizations, as well as collaborations among federal, state, and local agencies, and occasionally private companies. But reinvention also reinforced the now outmoded idea that government should be the sole source of new policy ideas, of program development, and be the architect of measures of success. Nor did reinvention anticipate the substantial growth in funding and innovative social and public policy solutions that would flow from the philanthropic sector in the twenty-first century.

Today large foundations and nonprofits are leading partnerships with a willingness to provide no-cost and low-cost capital over the long-term and with a keen focus on measurable social impact. Challenges exist here too, as we will discuss, and what these organizations perceive as the desired social value may differ from what community stakeholders want.

---

To solve many of the most important challenges we now face—whether destabilizing inequality, declines in the number of living-wage jobs, degraded soils and food production, damaging climate change, or a shortage of quality, affordable housing and education for all—we must work in partnership. This is because no single sector acting alone is adequately equipped to design the necessary long-term approaches, to deploy the large amounts of required capital, and to catalyze community-led program development.

Partnerships have the potential to maximize the positive attributes of each sector while minimizing their weaknesses. The partnerships that cleaned up Central Park and created the High Line, among others that we discuss in greater detail, provide us with helpful examples of cross-sector partnerships that achieved higher social value than one sector could accomplish on its own. At the same time, in these cases and the others we discuss, it is easy to see that successful partnerships can be difficult to form and maintain.

## BUILDING A BETTER WORLD WILL TAKE TIME

Fundamental problems of hunger, poverty, and inequality cannot be solved with short-term approaches. Meaningful progress on making the world a better place for everyone requires long-term strategies and management frameworks measured by how well we share success. Many of our biggest problems, those most worth solving, may not be solved in our lifetime—*but they can be solved.*[29] It will require investment in all kinds of people to bolster their ability to succeed. It will take thoughtful, contextually appropriate processes that align organizations' goals with local and global needs. It will mean investing time and resources in communities in ways that transform beneficiaries into shareholders of their outcomes. And it will mean putting the right measurement and performance systems in place so that we invest in opportunities that have the highest intrinsic value for society.

---

We live in a postrecession, globalized, collaborative, young, hyperconnected world.[30] More so now than in any earlier time, we have the tools, the science, the best practices, the momentum, and the impetus to bring about positive change on a global scale. Many of us—from baby boomers to millennials—believe our new reality is challenging but that we have the knowledge, technology, resources, and new ways of organizing ourselves to meet our needs more efficiently and equitably. As authors, we each represent one of these two very large and influential cohorts, and we share a strong conviction that we can, in fact, dramatically improve our world. We believe that it begins by coming together and *redefining success*. Our hope is that future generations will focus less on traditional definitions such as wealth, power, or fame and be equally or more interested in making a positive impact on their communities—both locally and globally.

We have developed these observations over a decade of researching, studying, teaching, and working with cross-sector partnerships around the world. We hope this book provides you with inspiration for learning how, by working together, we can make the world a better place.

# CHAPTER ONE

# The Evolution of Cross-Sector Partnerships

HOWARD W. BUFFETT AND WILLIAM B. EIMICKE

During and after the Great Depression, massive, government-led investments reignited economic growth in the United States. Modernization during the twentieth century's World Wars resulted in dramatic improvements in the production and infrastructure capacity of the United States. Subsequently, the privatization movement in the 1980s and the reinventing government reforms in the 1990s sought to redefine and downsize the role of government in society. In the twenty-first century, nonprofit organizations of all shapes and sizes are playing an ever-larger role in what was previously considered the purview of government. Today, cross-sector partnerships are carrying out major infrastructure projects and social programs, sometimes on an international scale. Despite their global reach, much of this partnership activity is a relatively recent, and understudied, phenomenon.

Beginning in the 1980s, public and private sector leaders, politicians, advocates for social change, and academic researchers focused increasing attention on accomplishing large-scale goals through public-private partnerships. These PPPs, as they are widely known, became somewhat "fashionable" and more prevalent in the years that followed.[1] In the simplest terms, public-private partnerships are working agreements between a government and a nongovernment organization to reach a shared objective in line with the legal terms of a contract.[2]

There is a substantial amount of scholarship on public-private partnerships, but only more recently have researchers turned to cross-sector partnerships that include social, philanthropic, and nongovernmental organizations where the primary purpose is to serve the public good.[3] Such cross-sector partnerships focus on a wide range of goals including research and development, local economic growth, poverty alleviation, and public health. In addition, these types of partnerships act as a critical enabling mechanism for accomplishing otherwise impossible objectives, or for addressing previously unsolvable, complex challenges.[4]

Cross-sector partnerships, including those profiled throughout this book, are an important development because they help focus numerous and diverse actors on the pursuit of socially valuable activities.[5] They empower partners and stakeholders alike to overcome collective action problems[6] and to better identify and track the negative and positive externalities of their work.[7] We believe that such partnerships may help society move past the individualistic rent-seeking and free-rider behavior that dominates traditional views of economic self-interest.[8] Although cross-sector partnerships may not be the easiest way to get important things done,[9] we show that they have great potential to leverage resources from all three sectors to meet public objectives efficiently and effectively at a scale not otherwise possible.[10]

## REACHING A GLOBAL SCALE

The emergence and proliferation of cross-sector partnerships is a reflection of the inability of one sector to effectively address many of our most substantial societal challenges. Regardless of such limitations, a number of significant collaborative efforts have made, and continue making, considerable progress. One example is the United Nations Millennium Development Goals (MDGs). In place for fifteen years between 2000 and 2015, this effort represented society's most significant attempt at positive collective action on a global scale. The MDGs and their call to action resulted in "a coherent framework for the entire UN system [which includes governments, private businesses and non-governmental organizations—NGOs] to collaborate toward shared, common goals."[11]

Among the eight MDGs were many goals historically viewed as the primary responsibility of government, including poverty and hunger eradication, universal primary education, gender equality, and environmental sustainability. The UN's subsequent global agenda, the Sustainable Development Goals (SDGs), have expanded this list to seventeen, along with 169 measureable targets.[12] The SDGs also include a goal fully dedicated to promoting partnerships as a means to strengthen society's collaboration for accomplishing the other goals. Even more than before, individuals and organizations of all types are engaging in the SDG agenda and taking remarkably active roles to support one another. For example, Bill and Melinda Gates convened some three hundred participants in late 2017—including activists, journalists, investors, philanthropists, businesspeople, government officials, and more—to raise the visibility of the goals and to broaden public engagement. Called "Goalkeepers," this group is helping to track and report progress on the SDGs annually, advocating for increased government action, and promoting sustained commitment from all sectors.[13]

An inclusive approach is important for many reasons, particularly because there is no one "best" sector for leading major cross-sector partnerships. Nor can any one sector or organization effectively deliver the many diverse goods and services required for meeting important national and global challenges, whether in sustainability, economic growth, or inequality.[14] There is no question that organizations of all types and sizes have to band together, and partnerships will play a major role in reaching complex and large-scale outcomes such as the SDGs.

As cross-sector partnerships increase in size and prevalence, we can draw from some important historical lessons. For instance, the current state of partnerships has been profoundly influenced by the evolution of government-led collaboration in the United States over the past 160 years. Although the public, private, and philanthropic sectors in the United States have been, and remain, independent, there is a long history of formal cooperation between them. We believe this collaboration has helped shape modern partnerships in the United States and around the world, and this chapter touches on major developments in U.S. history since the 1800s.

## PUBLIC-PRIVATE PARTNERSHIP
## EARLY ON

In the early nineteenth century, rugged individualism became the popular ideology of America: pioneers and cowboys "winning" the West through their creativity and the sweat of their brow. In reality, it was the Morrill and Homestead Acts of 1862 and later amendments, plus the public-private partnership to build a coast-to-coast railroad system that connected the nation's people and markets, that enabled the West to flourish. The Homestead Act, although far from perfect, turned over 270 million acres of public land to be claimed and settled by private citizens, including immigrants, single women, and former slaves.[15] The federal government also provided a series of incentives to leverage private capital and labor to build the transcontinental railroad: land grants, direct appropriations to companies involved in the development, waivers and modifications to taxes and regulations, contracts for services, and government backing for corporate bonds.[16]

The public policy to build a national railroad system came at the beginning of what Robert Gordon coined as an era of "Great Inventions" and rapid economic growth.[17] Between 1870 and 1940, the American home went from isolated to connected: electricity, gas, telephone, water, and sewage. The United States was transforming from rural to urban, from underdeveloped to developed. Our life expectancy and quality of life increased dramatically.

Many of these transformative innovations were driven by private finance, entrepreneurs, and the expansive corporations they created. Often known as "robber barons," it was Carnegie, Edison, Mellon, Phipps, Rockefeller, Vanderbilt (and others) and the companies they founded that enabled the modernization of the United States. However, as we learned from the market crash in October of 1929, rapid and monopolized modernization and expansion (along with the investment frenzy that resulted from these world-changing innovations) can lead to disaster.

## "THE ONLY THING WE HAVE TO FEAR IS FEAR ITSELF"

By 1932, the United States was in the throes of the worst economic depression in the nation's history: 25 percent unemployment, runs on banks, businesses closing, and the developing Dust Bowl disaster that left much of the country's breadbasket cropless. President Franklin Delano Roosevelt promised Americans "A New Deal" and used the bully pulpit of the presidency (and the expanding power of radio networks) to encourage hope. As he famously said, "The only thing we have to fear is fear itself."

Elected in November 1932, FDR did a lot more than deliver inspirational speeches and fireside chat radio talks. As former New York Governor Mario Cuomo stated, he "lifted himself from his wheelchair to lift this nation from its knees."[18] Roosevelt assembled a team of the country's best and brightest from all sectors, both parties, and every background (including Frances Perkins as Secretary of Labor, the first woman appointed to a cabinet position in U.S. history).[19] He had them innovate and experiment relentlessly to get the country back on track. Roosevelt sought to save capitalism by reinventing it—putting people's lives back together through an alphabet soup of agencies and the multitude of partnerships they formed with business.

FDR's administration regulated banks much more strictly, but the government also guaranteed savings in private banks and initiated mortgage insurance and purchasing programs that enabled millions of families to own homes and farms. These government-led partnerships with private banks forever changed the country—many of the nation's renters became owners with a long-term stake in the system.[20] During this time, the American public became real shareholders in the U.S. economy.

The federal government financed huge public works projects—dams, bridges, rural electrification, and even the Tennessee Valley Authority (a government-owned economic development corporation)—that created demand for privately manufactured products and stimulated economic growth through cheap power and ubiquitous access to public highways and bridges. Social Security and Unemployment Insurance programs provided mandatory support for the retired and those out of work, were paid by contributions from workers and employers, improved the lives of millions of Americans, and stimulated the economy.

The biggest economic boost came from FDR's commitment to supply the World War II Allied forces in Europe by mobilizing U.S. manufacturing to build tanks, planes, jeeps, and weapons, and produce supplies, which often were financed by loans from the U.S. Treasury. The war effort effectively ended the Depression and simultaneously funded the manufacturing infrastructure that enabled the country to become a global consumer manufacturing powerhouse for decades to come. This connection between national security and domestic economic growth would continue as FDR had showed how large projects with a public purpose could succeed when the private sector was engaged more as a partner than in the limited role of a contractor.

# A MASSIVE AND NEW INTERSTATE PARTNERSHIP

In the two decades following World War II, the next three U.S. presidents initiated major government programs employing the capacity of the private sector to dramatically stimulate the U.S. economy and make life better for millions of Americans. President Dwight David Eisenhower took a job creation and infrastructure development plan of FDR's—a national superhighway—and made it perhaps his most important legacy. The National Interstate and Defense Highways Act of 1956 called for the creation of roughly 40,000 miles of new U.S. interstates crisscrossing the country, with the federal share initially estimated to cost $24.8 billion (about $230 billion in 2018 dollars).[21]

Currently, the system is more than 48,000 miles long and a federal review in 1991 estimated its cost (including additions not originally planned) closer to $58.5 billion in 1957 dollars (about $549 billion in 2018 dollars).[22] From the beginning, the project was a partnership. The federal government authorized the construction and provided 90 percent of the funds to states. States generally paid a 10 percent match for which they were given ownership of the highways within their state lines and the responsibility for maintaining them.[23] The states, in turn, generally contracted with private companies to build the roads. Although national defense is often associated with the act, its primary benefits (and some would say "costs") were economic expansion, spread of the population, and the interconnectivity of the country that it stimulated.

One of the largest public works projects in U.S. history, now known as the Dwight D. Eisenhower National System of Interstate and Defense Highways, our federal highway program not only facilitated the movement of people and goods but also enhanced national security and deepened our national identity. Similar to the New Deal, this government-led partnership, connecting the country in new ways, reminded Americans that we are all on the same team pulling toward a common purpose.

President Eisenhower helped create one of the most successful infrastructure partnerships in U.S. history, but he had concerns about the dangers of partnerships between big government and big business. In his nationally televised farewell address to the nation, Eisenhower warned of the rise of a "military-industrial complex"—a partnership sharing a common interest in the business of war that he saw as a stark and potentially harmful trade-off. "The cost of one modern heavy bomber [could fund] a modern brick school in more than thirty cities . . . we pay for a single destroyer with new homes that could have housed more than eight thousand people."[24]

## THE NEW FRONTIER

With the Cold War worsening in the early 1960s, control of outer space became a key battleground between the United States and the USSR. The USSR took the lead, strategically and in terms of global prestige, with the launch of Sputnik in 1957 and kept that lead as manned space flight began. President John F. Kennedy viewed the situation as so dire that on May 25, 1961, he delivered a special address to a Joint Session of the U.S. Congress[25] requesting up to $9 billion in new funding so that "this nation should commit itself to achieving the goal, before the decade is out, of landing a man on the moon and returning him safely to the earth."[26]

JFK's call to action—and his New Frontier agenda—resulted in the Apollo program of the U.S. space agency, NASA. President Kennedy did not live to witness Astronaut Neil Armstrong proclaim "That's one small step for a man. One giant leap for mankind" from the surface of the moon on July 20, 1969, at 10:56 PM EDT. But his vision was realized because of public-private cooperation, and it was witnessed by more than half a billion people watching on live television.

NASA ran the Apollo program with federal government funds, but fulfilling the mission would not have been possible without a number of private corporation partners including North American Aviation, Grumman, General Dynamics/Convair, and others. The strong national defense rationale of the Apollo program dictated federal funding and a top-down partnership structure that centralized power in the government. Some observers believe this government-dominated partnership neglected commercial technology transfer opportunities. This could have offset costs and perhaps stimulated more innovative approaches, but in the context of the Cold War competition with the Soviet Union, driving down costs was not a priority.[27] JFK's initial estimate of $9 billion expanded to $12 billion by 1963 and exceeded $21 billion by the time Armstrong stepped on the surface of the moon, thereby limiting the future of that era's manned space exploration.[28]

In the twenty-first century, NASA and outside experts now agree that more balanced partnerships are essential in developing a sustainable and successful space exploration program.[29] Private companies such as SpaceX and Orbital ATK are already flying robotic vessels to supply the International Space Station and may soon transport astronauts. SpaceX has developed a reusable rocket, which could dramatically cut the cost of space exploration while making the company a significant profit.[30] Mars, Jupiter's Europa moon (which likely has liquid water), and Saturn are on the agenda of space explorers and entrepreneurs.[31] We cannot predict when this will happen or what we will learn, but we are reasonably certain that cross-sector partnerships will be essential to getting us there. There are also great risks in space exploration, as we learned early in the Apollo program on January 27, 1967, when Astronauts Chaffee, Grissom, and White were lost in the testing of the Apollo I rocket—and learned again in the Challenger and Columbia explosions.[32]

## THE GREAT SOCIETY

Lyndon Baines Johnson was sworn in as president November 22, 1963, following the assassination of John F. Kennedy. Johnson was a skilled politician, particularly at the congressional level, and he seized this opportunity, using the tragedy to enact a number of JFK's initiatives. Johnson then built on that success, embarking on his own ambitious agenda to end poverty, make education and health care more affordable and effective, and put people to work—even if it required federal government subsidies. Johnson referred to it as a war on poverty designed to create a Great Society for all.

Similar to the New Deal, the Great Society comprised dozens of new initiatives; some worked but many did not. The Great Society included several programs that changed the United States forever for the better, including Medicare, Medicaid, Head Start, PBS, and National Public Radio, and a dramatic increase in federal assistance for urban housing and community development. The Vietnam War essentially ended the

Great Society and Johnson's presidency, in contrast to the aftermath of World War II when the New Deal had secured Roosevelt's central objective of revitalizing the U.S. economy.

Johnson's Great Society also marked the end of the era of partnerships directed by "Big Government." Medicare and Medicaid depended on the private health care system to care for its patients, and the Great Society's education and jobs initiatives were generally partnerships among the three levels of government: local, state, and federal. Johnson's programs in housing, community development, and job training relied on nonprofit, often community-based organizations, as implementation partners, which was quite a different approach. The Community Action Program even created community-based agencies to fight poverty and get people into jobs. Many of the Great Society housing programs provided grant funding directly to nonprofit, community organizations to acquire, rehabilitate, own, or manage affordable housing in cities across the United States.

## THE AGE OF DISCONTINUITY

In 1969, Peter Drucker, a professor of management at New York University, wrote that the age of discontinuity was on the horizon. New technologies were already emerging, the international economy was now a global economy, large institutions (particularly the federal government) had lost the public trust, and knowledge would become the most important form of capital in the coming years.[33] Drucker believed that the new world economy was "the one positive achievement of the period since World War II," that it was a creation of business not government, and that it provided a tremendous opportunity for economic growth and a force for global unity.[34]

Drucker wrote that government was never more prominent—the largest employer almost everywhere, "all-pervasive"—but also that it was "sick." After decades of government-led success, Drucker argued that government was big rather than strong and that it had lost the trust of the people, particularly the young. Government was a poor manager, crippled by bureaucracy and red tape, with a reward system based on loyalty rather than performance.[35]

Drucker's solution to this dilemma might surprise you. We believe it opened the door for both the privatization movement of Ronald Reagan and Margaret Thatcher, the alternative "reinventing government" philosophy championed by Bill Clinton and Al Gore, and the cross-sector partnership approach we now propose.

Drucker said government should focus on governing—make fundamental decisions by focusing the energies of civil society: dramatize issues, present choices, and set a course consistent with the will of the people. This is, in essence, a collaborative process in the United States because fundamental decisions require the agreement of a president and a Congress elected by the people, which is designed to represent our diverse population in a balanced way. Implementation of those decisions—execution, operations, and performance—should be handled by nongovernmental institutions such as businesses, universities, and hospitals (which were his examples). In this construct, government sets major objectives, and the private and nonprofit sectors seek to achieve the intended results. Drucker called this approach "reprivatization."[36]

Business is independent of government. It both innovates and abandons because the market forces a performance-based measurement—profit. Profit is easy to understand, clear to see, requires recognizing and taking risks, and provides significant consequences for success or failure. Drucker also believed that non-business organizations have their own rationale for effectively implementing government objectives. For example, he cited the World Bank and the International Monetary Fund (IMF) as successful reprivatizations. These groups were organized and funded by governments and major financial institutions from around the world, but they operated independently in compliance with their mission and sound business and social principles.

Drucker concluded that we need "a strong and very active government," but a government that acts as a conductor of an orchestra, not an "eighteenth-century organ virtuoso that . . . could—and should—play all parts simultaneously."[37] As you will see in the coming pages, Reagan and Thatcher applied an extreme and somewhat distorted version of Peter Drucker's reprivatization theories, which led to the reinvention paradigm created by David Osborne and Ted Gaebler and implemented by Bill Clinton and Al Gore.

# GOVERNMENT IS THE PROBLEM

On January 20, 1981, Ronald Reagan gave his inaugural address to a country weary of a deepening recession, high inflation, and the hostage crisis in Iran. Unlike many presidents before him, Reagan did not see massive government programs and spending as the answer. He said, "government is not the solution to our problem; government is the problem."[38] In that same speech, Reagan said his solution would be to reduce government's burden on private industry, reduce the size of government, and cut taxes. Over time, and often in tandem with Margaret Thatcher, his contemporary and the conservative prime minister of the United Kingdom, Reagan championed what became a global movement to "get government out of the way" and maximize the role of the private sector in society, thereby empowering consumer choice and getting things done more efficiently.

Throughout the 1980s and 1990s, governments around the world sold public assets to private companies, including airlines, telecommunications companies, steel plants, shipyards, ports, power and energy companies, water companies, and even roads, bridges, schools, and prisons. What is now known as the privatization movement dramatically reduced the size of government globally and changed how we all think about providing public services. The movement had a greater impact in Europe where government ownership of major services was far more prevalent than in the United States.

In fact, it was not until 1987 that President Reagan appointed his Commission on Privatization; at that time only Conrail, the national freight rail service, had been sold. Reagan had been more successful in transferring employment from the federal civil service to private contractors (sometimes employing the same people) with a total of 38,000 jobs transferred and a reported savings of $602 million annually.[39] This trend toward contracting out government services accelerated after Reagan left office, becoming a key principle of President Bill Clinton's reinventing government movement.

Privatization also dramatically changed the United Kingdom, the reunified Germany, much of Eastern Europe, and many countries in Asia and Oceania (Singapore, Australia, New Zealand, South Korea, and even China) by moving industries and services from public agencies to private companies. Reagan and Thatcher also led an international movement in support of free trade, which seemed to work as the prevalent pessimism of the 1970s faded and a spirit of optimism and determination grew throughout the 1980s.[40]

Large-scale and often privately driven infrastructure partnerships multiplied throughout the 1980s and 1990s, operating on the middle ground between the government-dominated New Deal and Great Society and the strict antigovernment mantra of Reagan and Thatcher. Massive, well-known examples proliferated during this time. The Eurotunnel launched in 1986 and is one of the largest privately led partnerships in modern history, spanning two countries, ten construction companies, five banks, and multiple insurance companies and government agencies.[41] This contrasts against the often and continuingly troubled development of the Panama Canal from a century before, which failed multiple times as a strictly private initiative, and continues to struggle as a government-dominated enterprise.

In the United States, projects such as the Chicago Skyway and the Indiana Toll Road often are called privatizations, but they were public-private partnerships structured as long-term leases from the government. Other large transportation infrastructure partnerships in the United States include the Denver Eagle P3 commuter rail, the Hudson-Bergen Light Rail in New Jersey, and the AirTrain JFK in New York City. A number of very large partnerships are under way all over the globe, including replacement of the Tappan Zee Bridge in metropolitan New York. This long overdue project failed multiple times over more than a decade for being too costly, but it now seems well on its way to completion through a privately led partnership.

Public-private partnerships are a major category of public works projects that many observers label privatization. Even more widespread are contracts between government agencies, tax rebates to private businesses that advance a policy agenda for infrastructure development, and initiatives for private for-profit and nonprofit organizations to deliver goods and services previously delivered by public servants. These efforts are considered conditional privatizations if they are limited by the length of the contract term and service provisions and if program responsibility is returned to the public sector when the contract concludes.

Other examples of government services that are delivered by private companies now include low-income housing construction and management, child care, elder care, job training, water systems, elementary and secondary education, homeless services, transportation, prisons, and non-combat field support to the military. Some of the most ardent critics of privatization have embraced contracting out government services as a way to make government work better and cost less. In fact, Bill Clinton and Al Gore used this approach to contracting to hold down the cost of the federal government and move decision making and service delivery of social services to local governments and for-profit and nonprofit organizations.

## REINVENTION FOR GOVERNMENT

In the mid-1980s, David Osborne, a journalist and author, was so discouraged by the Reagan presidency's performance on the domestic front that he turned to state governments to evaluate what was being done. To his delight, significant innovation was taking place, including education innovation by a little-known governor in the small state of Arkansas and housing innovation by a better-known governor from the big state of New York, Mario Cuomo.[42]

Osborne expanded his exploration of innovation to local government when he partnered with Ted Gaebler, a city manager who was pioneering new ways of running government more like a business. In 1992, Osborne and Gaebler published an unlikely best seller, *Reinventing Government*, which ultimately had significant influence on the incoming Clinton-Gore administration.[43] The authors disagreed with Reagan and Thatcher that the solution to the world's problems was to get rid of government. Rather, they sided with Peter Drucker, arguing that government was critical to making society better but that government needed to be more efficient, less costly, and partner with other organizations from all three sectors to make the world a better place.

Osborne and Gaebler outlined ten principles of reinvention; the principles were not new then, nor are they surprising today, but taken together they set out a role for government much different from the New Deal / New Frontier / Great Society eras, and equally different from the privatization philosophy of Reagan, Thatcher, and George H. W. Bush. In brief, the ten principles are these: government should steer rather than row (let others "do"); empower rather than serve;

create competition in service delivery; focus on mission rather than rules; fund outcomes rather than inputs; have customers define performance; focus on earning not just spending; prevention over cure; decentralize; and leverage change in the market.[44] Bill Clinton was impressed by this, created a reinvention commission, the National Performance Review, and appointed Vice President Al Gore as its leader. Staffed by federal employees and volunteer outsiders, as well as David Osborne, the commission's report debuted in September 1993 and served as a blueprint for the Clinton administration's operational reform efforts throughout its eight years.[45]

The short-term impact of reinvention in the U.S. government was not much different than prior government reform efforts: budgets were cut, fewer workers were hired, some regulations were eliminated, the hiring and procurement processes were streamlined somewhat, and some layers of management were eliminated. More profound and long-term was the decentralization of authority for many social welfare programs to state and local governments. In turn, those local governments then chose to contract with community-based nonprofit organizations (and some larger for-profit firms). This trend was particularly pronounced in the programs generally referred to as "welfare to work," and often the contracts paid for performance outcomes— job placement and retention—rather than more traditional payments for time and materials.

Another significant innovation during the reinvention era was the theory and practices of then mayor of Indianapolis, Indiana, Stephen Goldsmith. Goldsmith campaigned as an advocate of privatization, but once in office he became convinced that competition between existing public agency providers and interested private contractors might yield the best public services at the lowest cost to taxpayers. During his eight years in office, Goldsmith conducted dozens of competitions, what he called *marketization*, for government activities from filling potholes to sewer billing, wastewater treatment, running the airport, and towing away abandoned vehicles. Sometimes a government agency won back its work, sometimes the private firm won out, but overall the city was able to provide better services at a more efficient cost. Ultimately, the mayor and his union leaders won a Harvard Kennedy School Innovation award for carrying out these innovations while simultaneously making sure workers either kept their jobs or were able to transition to new positions.[46]

The ideas and lessons of reinvention were not limited to the United States. Osborne and his collaborators encouraged others around the world to adopt the principles. In the United Kingdom, Australia, and New Zealand, governments accelerated contracting out of services, increased competition between contractors and government agencies, and set up government agencies as independent "companies," often known as state-owned enterprises. As a philosophy, reinvention-based principles encouraged cooperation and collaboration across sectors and levels of government.

Slowly but surely the principles of reinvention ignited experiments at all levels of government, many of which began to look and act like cross-sector partnerships. Privatization evolved into contracting, then competitive contracting (including government agencies as bidders) emerged, and now we see a culture of innovation and collaboration developing among all three sectors.[47] We believe this is the beginning of a major change in how government interacts with other organizations—moving from director to regulator to partner.

## GOVERNING THROUGH PARTNERSHIPS

Experiments with cross-sector partnerships took place during the administrations of President George W. Bush and President Barack Obama. For example, the federal government aggressively pursued contracts with faith-based organizations (FBOs) to carry out a wide range of social programs, including housing, homeless services, job training, and education. To encourage these partnerships, President Bush established an Office of Faith-Based and Community Initiatives (which President Obama renamed the Office of Faith-Based and Neighborhood Partnerships). The office worked across the traditional agency boundaries to redirect funds from existing federally funded social service and housing programs through the states into contracts with religiously affiliated community-based nonprofits. Even though federal funds could not be used for religious purposes, grant recipients benefited from leveraging other funds, facilities, and the trust of local religious, community-based organizations. The White House made it clear that FBOs were eligible to receive federal funds and worked with them, and federal agencies, to ensure that these organizations applied for competitive grants. Because of this, the number and amount of federal grant awards to FBOs increased by 38 percent (number of grants) and 21 percent (total funding awarded) from five different agencies (Health and Human Services [HHS], Housing and Urban Development [HUD], Department of Justice [DOJ], Department of Labor [DOL], and the Department of Education [ED]) between 2003 and 2005 alone.[48]

The George W. Bush administration also created the Millennium Challenge Corporation (MCC) to improve the outcomes of U.S. foreign assistance programs. MCC uses a competitive process for country eligibility, and prioritizes country-led solutions and country-led implementation. The goal was to achieve transformative progress in governance, economic growth, and social improvement in countries making headway but still facing significant challenges. By early 2018, MCC had invested over $13 billion in twenty completed country-led compacts, had eleven in progress, and had only terminated two projects. More than $3 billion had gone to infrastructure projects, including power generation and transportation (including ports).[49]

MCC differs from many other foreign aid programs. It seeks to reduce poverty through local economic growth, often funding infrastructure-focused public-private partnerships that address local development priorities.[50] MCC also requires performance measures and evaluates the success of projects based on independent analysis, assessing whether or not a project's economic returns exceeded the cost of MCC's investment.[51] Based on publicly available data, reports indicate that more than 90 percent of MCC funds have invested in projects achieving measured economic benefits in excess of the projects' costs.[52] MCC attracted bipartisan support throughout the Bush and Obama administrations, and we believe this results-based, cross-sector partnership methodology could be expanded to other aid programs.

Similarly, President George W. Bush's Emergency Plan for Aids Relief (PEPFAR) has provided more than $7 billion to help people affected by AIDS, particularly in Africa, by channeling the resources through local countries and working through nongovernmental organizations. The themes of these programs—measurement, reward performance, local ownership, achieve scale of impact, efficiency, and partnership—illustrate that the principles set out by Drucker and Osborne continue to resonate decades after they were first articulated.

In 2008, the government took a decidedly expanded role in multi-stakeholder collaborations when it launched the Global Partnership Center at the U.S. Department of State. Initially established by Secretary of State Condoleezza Rice and an advisory committee focused on new forms of transformational diplomacy, this office grew dramatically after the transition to the Obama administration. Their mission was to engage "businesses, philanthropy, and community organizations . . . to advance foreign policy goals and expand the scope and effectiveness of the Department."[53] These early efforts provided important groundwork for the development of future partnership doctrine during the Obama administration, where the Center was expanded into the Office of Global Partnerships reporting directly to the Secretary of State.

In 2009, President Obama established a new White House Office of Social Innovation and Civic Participation. Charged with helping government to do business differently, this office worked to establish new partnerships with citizens, nonprofits, social entrepreneurs, private foundations, and corporations to make progress on the nation's greatest challenges. The office sat at the pinnacle of government reinvention, illustrating that these principles had really taken hold at a national level (we discuss this further in chapter 2).

In fact, members of the national security community also share these views. In 2013, Deputy Secretary of Defense Ashton Carter and Vice Chairman of the Joint Chiefs of Staff Admiral James Winnefeld issued a department-wide memorandum arguing in favor of partnerships between the Department of Defense and nonfederal entities. They called for an increased use and breadth in "voluntary, non-contractual collaborations" with outside organizations of all types in order "to achieve mutually agreed goals."[54] Moreover, U.S. defense Joint Doctrine supports entire divisions or directorates at Defense Department combatant commands focused on partnership development, as is the case with U.S. Pacific Command and U.S. Southern Command.[55] The 2017 *Global Trends* report published by the National Intelligence Council identified "multi-stakeholder multilateralism" as a core driver of changing power dynamics in the coming decades.[56] In it, the intelligence community argues that traditional forms of "material power—typically measured through gross domestic product, military spending, population size, and technology level," will no longer define "the most powerful actors of the future." These actors will be the "states, groups, and individuals who can leverage material capabilities, relationships, and information in a more rapid, integrated, and adaptive mode than in generations past."[57] In other words, power will become more and more decentralized, and success in a globalized world will require the coordinated action of many different types of organizations and people.[58]

## SHARING SUCCESS: GLOBAL CHALLENGES AND GLOBAL OPPORTUNITIES

Many of today's most important public issues are global, crisscrossing national borders: inequality, climate change and severe weather, trade practices and imbalances, conflict and displaced persons, migration and immigration, human rights, poverty, availability of food and water, transportation, natural resource management, and natural disasters. Not only do these issues cross national borders, but national borders can be part of the problem. Global challenges require global solutions. Institutions such as the United Nations, the World Bank, the IMF, the International Finance Corporation (IFC), the G-20, and regional organizations such as the Inter-American Development Bank (IADB) and the Association of Southeast Asian Nations (ASEAN) can and do lead global initiatives.[59] However, these multilateral, government-led partnerships can be easily bogged down by bureaucratic procedures and regulations. Fortunately, many of today's NGOs and businesses also are global, and they are leading new partnerships and driving solutions in ways not previously possible. Great challenges are facing us as a global community, and we see government, business, and the social sector partnering in new ways to meet our current challenges efficiently and effectively.

Throughout this book you will see examples of how organizations from all three sectors can accomplish major public objectives that might otherwise be unattainable. Each type of organization brings natural advantages and certain limitations in addressing national and international issues, but today's new forms of partnership can amplify those advantages while minimizing the limitations.

We have seen an evolution of partnership structures over the past few decades, and we believe there is enormous potential in how current and future public, private, and philanthropic capital can be deployed to solve society's problems. This type of *social value investing*, as we describe in the coming chapters, provides opportunities for organizations to create more inclusive and comprehensive approaches to global challenges. As our world continues to transform, so too will our organizations and institutions. Through better collaboration and by sharing success through cross-sector partnerships, the next progression of this evolution will lead to significant improvements in the quality of life for billions of people around the world.

# CHAPTER TWO

# Social Value Investing

## A Personal Narrative

### HOWARD W. BUFFETT

*This chapter presents the author's personal narrative
to describe the history and development of the social value
investing framework.*

The federal government's role in building and shaping public policy and infrastructure through partnerships with the private and philanthropic sectors has evolved significantly over the past few centuries. So, too, has the scope, scale, and approach of philanthropy itself in the United States.

The so-called Gilded Age philanthropists, or scions of industrial wealth—Rockefeller, Carnegie, Eastman, and others—made unprecedented charitable gifts during their lifetimes.[1] These gifts launched an era of modern, otherwise known as professional, philanthropy that continues to influence giving today. In the past thirty-five years, successful businesspeople and entrepreneurs, including Paul Newman, Ted Turner, and Mark Zuckerberg and Pricilla Chan, have committed vast portions of their private wealth to philanthropy.[2]

A particularly notable event took place on June 26, 2006, at the New York Public Library. My grandfather, Warren Buffett, made a seminal announcement that he would leave almost his entire fortune, valued then at approximately $44 billion, to the benefit of humankind.[3] Not only did this announcement shock the world of philanthropy—news outlets heralded it as the beginning of a new era of mega-foundations[4]—it also stunned the world of finance. My grandfather represents the pinnacle of success in the field of investing; his is an achievement built in a capitalist economy that measures success by how much wealth you accumulate—not by how much you give away. In taking this step, he set an example for others that will continue to have unforeseen ripple effects for years to come.

In a well-known story, my grandfather built his fortune through the business operations of Berkshire Hathaway Inc., utilizing the principles of value investing. Value investing was originally developed in the 1920s by Professors Benjamin Graham and David Dodd of Columbia University.[5] In the fall of 1950, my grandfather attended a course titled Investment Management and Security Analysis, taught by Dodd, and the following semester he attended a small seminar taught by Graham.[6] These courses, and books by Dodd and Graham—*Security Analysis* (1934) and *The Intelligent Investor* (1950)[7]—provided the necessary framework for engaging in what became one of the most enduring and successful investment paradigms of all time.

Although the approach is based on a complex and rigorous securities analysis framework, many of the main tenets of the value investing methodology are straightforward. For example, when allocating capital, look for investments that are "on sale"—investments that have an intrinsic value beyond what appears on their balance sheets. Assume that the market's supply and demand curves are often misinformed for investments; investors must establish a minimum size discount, or margin of safety, before they consider making a purchase. Furthermore, investors must resist the temptation to react to media hype or market hysteria. Finally, and perhaps most important, the approach relies on a long-term investment strategy.[8]

Following these and other principles, my grandfather built one of history's most successful investment holding companies and amassed what was at one time the largest fortune in the world.[9] With his decision in 2006, that fortune became one of history's largest gifts.[10] Traditionally such a donation would go to a namesake foundation under the donor's close and personal control. However, my grandfather chose a different approach, announcing that he would make annual distributions of Berkshire Hathaway stock to five separate charitable foundations. The bulk of the contributions go to the Bill & Melinda Gates Foundation, and other significant commitments go to the Susan T. Buffett Foundation and foundations for each of my grandfather's children.

My grandfather's gift caused each of these foundations to face a new and important challenge: given significant resources to accomplish something great in this world, what should be done? The 2006 gift did not come with strict guidelines or overly burdensome stipulations, but my grandfather provided a set of strategic suggestions for the foundations in a letter accompanying each gift.[11]

The letters encouraged the foundations to focus their new funds and energy on relatively few activities and to take a broad view when evaluating where they could make an important difference in the world. The letters also suggested a concentration of resources on needs that would not be met without the foundation's specific efforts, which acknowledged the unique and flexible role that philanthropic capital can play in addressing pressing challenges. In light of that flexibility, these letters also encouraged making mistakes, stating that nothing important in life is accomplished with only "safe" decisions. Finally, the recipients were encouraged to focus on the impact they could make while alive and actively involved in the operations of their foundations, so that they could learn from their mistakes, adapt, and carry the lessons forward.[12]

These suggestions served as informal guidance for the foundations, including my father's, the Howard G. Buffett Foundation (HGBF). The ideas my grandfather conveyed were important, especially the last one, which encouraged a sense of purpose and urgency in the foundation's work. In line with this suggestion, and almost unheard of among foundations, my father had instituted a sunset clause to put his foundation out of business roughly forty years after the 2006 announcement.[13] Knowing his foundation will not operate in perpetuity has encouraged my father to take smart risks, to learn as quickly as possible, and to operate in a way that seems to maximize the impact of every dollar the foundation distributes.

I have been very fortunate that my father involved me so closely in his foundation's work. Over the course of twenty years, I traveled to more than seventy countries—almost all with my father for the work of the foundation—to learn directly from people and communities we visited. I have observed many of the world's challenges firsthand, and I have witnessed my father's dedication to being the best steward he can be of the resources his father gave to him. I also have observed that he is as strongly driven by this sense of duty—the effective stewardship of philanthropy—as my grandfather is by his duty to Berkshire's share-holders. I know of few individuals who exhibit a stronger commitment to their self-described missions, and I have gathered many lifelong insights as a witness to their somewhat parallel approaches in the worlds of finance and philanthropy.

Until 2006, the business operations of the foundation were somewhat limited. HGBF had a relatively small team equivalent to roughly two full-time staff; it distributed about $6 million in grants in 2005.[14] Grant making increased almost tenfold by the year following my grandfather's announcement, to nearly $60 million.[15] The influx of funding and increased activity prompted some significant and immediate organizational changes. Almost overnight the foundation's annual distributions rose dramatically. It added staff capacity to meet an immediate increase in grant making, diligence, operations, and program supervision. It needed additional office space and began exploring new management processes to handle quickening work flows. Most important, it needed to identify additional grantees, high-reward opportunities, and long-term challenges to address, encouraged by the suggestions my grandfather had provided in his gift letter.

A number of programmatic shifts took place between 2005 and 2007 as well. In its early years, a portion of the foundation's grant making had been funding programs to protect against environmental degradation and to save threatened wildlife species. Many grants were in the form of individual gifts to single organizations, and they were small in scale and in their ability to solve widespread problems due to the limited size of the foundation's annual grant making budget.

In 2006, my father developed detailed internal position papers on each of the foundation's main programmatic areas, supported by research, lessons learned from past activities, and input from previous and existing grantees. He also explored a deep analysis of the web of underlying causal relationships, where he saw ways that one problem made another worse. The foundation's increased giving enabled my father to take a more comprehensive perspective, and new funds focused almost entirely on humanitarian efforts, water conservation, and global food security programs. Perhaps most significant, this widening view led to three main shifts in the organization's overall operational approach.

First, the foundation began deepening its view of grantees as partners in its overall philanthropic mission, with roles going beyond that of contractors or the recipients of gifts.

Second, to have lasting impact my father decided the foundation needed to work collaboratively with partners and to encourage them to incorporate and prioritize local community ownership of the projects the foundation supported.

Third, the foundation began looking at opportunities to fund larger initiatives or groups of organizations working toward common goals rather than one-off or isolated projects. This allowed the foundation to develop a more robust strategy over time, refocusing its mission and activities on the individuals whose lives it hoped to improve. It also enabled the foundation to better define its target issue areas and look at mitigating root causes of challenges, such as causality between conflict, poverty, and hunger.

Many of the organizational shifts following the increased funding in 2006 subtly mirrored particular operational values that had made Berkshire Hathaway incredibly successful. For instance, in 2007 the foundation launched a $150 million, multiorganization effort called the Global Water Initiative (GWI).[16] The goal was to improve water management policies, research, investment, and knowledge resources for sustainable agricultural production and improved food security—mainly in Africa and Latin America.

At the foundation's invitation, senior managers from leading water nongovernmental organizations (NGOs) and other funders came together from around the world to jointly develop a strategy that aimed to be both comprehensive and flexible.[17] The organizations the foundation eventually worked with were selected based on their competencies and track record and on their complementary skills and assets for solving the web of problems involved in improving water quality while conserving it as a limited resource. The group found ways for the comparative strengths or experiences of one organization to offset risks created by gaps or shortcomings in another and vice versa.[18] The foundation established a portfolio of NGO partners, hoping to unlock value through a belief that their coordinated efforts would be worth more than the sum of their isolated activities.[19]

Because of HGBF's increased funding, it was able to develop and finance multiyear implementation plans such as GWI. In doing so,

HGBF could take a relatively long-term investment focus, which was in contrast to typical nonprofit sector time horizons that can be as brief as the next round of fund-raising. These new strategies, which were developed in tandem with a variety of stakeholders, prioritized the inclusion of local communities in the design and development of solutions so that they could better assume co-ownership over the philanthropic investments.[20] Furthermore, the foundation instilled a great deal of trust and autonomy in the leadership at these organizations. By recognizing that these managers would be the stewards of the philanthropic capital, HGBF sought ways to incentivize them to work together to accomplish everyone's shared goals rather than to approach fund-raising with a zero-sum mentality.

Although this may not initially seem analogous to Berkshire's value investing style, my father was following a playbook similar to that of his father. The key ingredients were there but were applied to philanthropy rather than business, using an investment approach focused on the long-term that attempted to unlock hidden or intrinsic value through its allocation strategy. More important is how HGBF's methodology mirrored a broad application of many of the management principles that made Berkshire Hathaway so successful through its operating strategy.

Consider the following key elements of Berkshire's operational paradigm that have led to such successes.

1. *Berkshire is a partnership of diverse yet complementary businesses that collectively contribute to its creation of long-term value.*[21]

   In other words, Berkshire's operating *process* expands and aligns its subsidiaries' efforts in a mutually collaborative manner, often drawing on comparative strengths.

2. *Berkshire's team is a network of decentralized managers who operate its independent subsidiaries—they comprise a range of varied strengths but are aligned toward shared goals.*[22]

   In this way, Berkshire invests in and empowers one of its most important assets—its *people*, the managers operating its businesses—and supports their collective ability to lead and succeed.[23]

3. *Berkshire incorporates shareholders as owner-partners of the company—not just investors—by building their trust and prioritizing their best interests.*[24]

The company's operating manual invites investors to stay with it forever, just as if they "owned a farm or . . . house in partnership with members of [their] family." This concept of permanent community, or *place*-based co-ownership, is apparent in the unique relationship between the company and its shareholders.[25]

4. *Berkshire draws from a combined set of financial tools, assets, and liabilities that diversifies risk and increases its balance sheet over time.*[26]

In other words, Berkshire blends different types of financial capital—including equity, cash on hand, deferred taxes, insurance float, debt, and so on—spanning a versatile and coordinated *portfolio* of investments.

5. *Berkshire identifies and invests in opportunities with comparatively high intrinsic value (especially in comparison to book value) that are in line with the company's principles.*[27]

Through this approach, the company predicts the relative future *performance* of a given set of investments and allocates capital based on its priorities and goals.

This outline provides a basic description of Berkshire's value investing approach through five aspects of its management methodology. These five elements—*process, people, place, portfolio, and performance*—are also the basis for the framework I call *social value investing*.

In the coming chapters, we explore ways in which this framework combines the principles of value investing with the intentions and goals of philanthropy and the public sector to create partnerships that provide a meaningful and positive impact for society. In the remainder of this chapter, I briefly explore how the social value investing framework evolved over the course of a number of distinct phases.

The five elements of social value investing.

## THE ORIGINS OF SOCIAL VALUE INVESTING

My early thinking about social value investing began while attending Columbia University's master's program in Public Policy and Administration, studying under the tutelage of my coauthor, Bill Eimicke. Bill and I spent many hours outside of class discussing management theory, interesting cases such as Central Park, and ways that successful management practices from one type of organization could be modified and adapted to other organizations. Although we did not know it at the time, these conversations informed the early development of the social value investing framework.

I arrived at Columbia more than fifty years after my grandfather had attended and almost immediately after his 2006 announcement. Around this time, philanthropies and NGOs alike were grappling with the challenges of how to increase the scale of their impact and how to measure that impact and determine, in quantifiable terms, how effectively donor's dollars were being used.[28] During my master's program, I worked on a customized, flexible, and expandable analytical framework for defining and comparing the potential social impact of philanthropic grants. Much has changed since its first iteration as I have refined the tool into what is now the Impact Balance Sheet.

The Impact Balance Sheet provides a uniform way to analyze and compare the expected quality of impact that a project or program may deliver, based on a customized set of constraints and preferences. In one sense, the framework provides insights into the potential intrinsic social value of a program, defined by one's intended goals. In addition, the underlying principles and analytical structure of this tool helps partners define success in a common language using similar methods of measurement. This enables partners with diverse goals to better plan activities, allocate resources, and improve their impact-related performance. This tool is part of the social value investing measurement methodology and is incorporated into a new formula I call Impact Rate of Return (see chapter 8).[29]

Living in New York City while pursuing my degree provided me with an opportunity to work with and learn about a wide range of organizations spanning the public, private, and philanthropic sectors. Many of the leaders I worked with seemed to be asking a common question, "How can we combine our resources with other organizations to better accomplish shared goals?"

One individual I worked with was Amir Dossal, then the executive director of the United Nations Office for Partnerships (UNOP).[30] Dossal and I had connected through a somewhat chance meeting, and he invited me to join his office as a partnership advisor. The UN Secretary General established the UNOP to serve as a gateway for partnerships and to leverage external resources in support of the UN's global agenda.[31] Among other programs, it oversaw the United Nations Fund for International Partnerships and facilitated cross-sector collaboration in support of the $1 billion gift Ted Turner announced in 1997.[32] Dossal and his team looked for ways to combine private sector programs, philanthropic capital, the assets of the UN family, and other government donors toward coordinated and aligned objectives. This type of blending of assets from different organizations and sectors resulted in a coordinated portfolio approach.[33] (We discuss this aspect of social value investing in chapter 7.)

## DESIGNING A PARTNERSHIP BUILDING PROCESS

Many aspects of the process component of social value investing were expanded and formalized during my work in the federal government following the 2008 presidential election. This may seem oxymoronic because the U.S. federal government is usually regarded as an ineffective collaborator—frequently mired down in rules or regulations preventing it from successfully working across organizations and sectors. However, the financial crisis of 2008 sent a clear message to the incoming presidential administration: be prepared to do more with less and involve a broad spectrum of stakeholders. From the outset of his election, President Barack Obama made it a priority for his administration to find new ways for the government to collaborate with public and private organizations alike in solving the country's challenges.[34]

This collaborative mind-set started in the very early days of the Obama administration. Following the 2008 presidential campaign, I joined the presidential transition team's efforts to help prepare for the government's turnover and develop the president's 100-day agenda. The transition team was also charged with authoring innovative and inclusive strategies to respond quickly to the Great Recession, even as it was still unfolding. This ultimately contributed to the American Recovery and Reinvestment Act, known as "the Stimulus," which was signed into law less than one month after President Obama took office.[35] Woven throughout these policies was a common thread: the importance of engaging in meaningful cross-sector partnerships across the administration and across the country.

Also during this time, the transition team's Technology, Innovation, and Government Reform Policy Working Group (TIGR) was charged with developing specific ways in which the White House and its executive departments could better partner with nonprofits, foundations, philanthropists, corporations, and social enterprises of all kinds and sizes.[36] To advance the president's Innovation Agenda, this group established a set of objectives that would eventually make up the priorities for the only newly created office in the White House— the Office of Social Innovation and Civic Participation (SICP)—where I served as a policy advisor under Sonal Shah, its inaugural director.[37]

During the first eighteen months of the administration, SICP developed a variety of programs and government-wide initiatives prioritizing and relying on meaningful partnerships for success. For example, SICP established the government's first Social Innovation Fund, created to finance partnerships in support of the administration's key domestic policy priority areas.[38] The office also hosted a series of Energy Innovation Conferences, bringing together dozens of organizations and agencies, where the Department of Energy announced

$60 million in new funding for Small Business Clean Energy Innovation projects.[39] Further, SICP launched a Next Generation Leadership initiative focused on fostering collaborative partnerships between millennial leaders all across the country.[40] Internal to the Executive Office of the President, SICP advanced the president's partnership agenda by establishing an interagency working group on the subject, titled Partnerships for Innovation. This group shared information across fifteen executive branch agencies to develop new cross-sector partnerships and innovation strategies to enhance collaboration between the White House, federal departments, agencies, for-profits, nonprofits, and foundations. Through my role in these initiatives, I assembled relevant knowledge and guidance from a variety of perspectives and gathered lessons learned regarding the development of effective cross-sector partnerships.

With key input from agencies such as the State Department and the Small Business Administration, the SICP team codified these new practices and lessons into the president's internal policy framework for engaging the executive branch in a coordinated, cross-sector partnership strategy. This effort and the work it led to inspired many of the principles, definitions, and models related to partnership development that are reflected in my social value investing framework. We explore some of these principles in chapter 4, which outlines the process by which partners create a comprehensive strategy for addressing complex challenges.

## DEVELOPING PLACE-BASED
## OWNERSHIP STRATEGIES

Following my work in the White House, I joined a unique economic development team based in the Office of the Secretary at the U.S. Department of Defense (DoD). Much of DoD's efforts at the time focused on the conflict areas of Afghanistan and Iraq, and this team's mission was to promote diverse economic stability operations in regions across both countries.[41]

As the head of the team's agricultural development program, I further refined the principles of the social value investing framework. One focus area was creation of community-led economic development strategies in Afghanistan's western Herat region. Following the food price crisis of 2007–2008, the government prioritized investment in Afghanistan's agricultural systems as a direct way to alleviate unemployment and hunger and promote security and stability in the region.[42]

The agricultural development team worked hand in hand with each of the local communities engaged in the initiative and with their *shuras* (which are similar to community councils). We established or supported creation of women owned local enterprises linked to new farmer cooperatives developed in the region. We engaged the local city and provincial governments to garner their support and to develop policies and resources needed for the initiatives over the long term.[43] Ultimately, every program dollar expended, capital project constructed, and piece of equipment procured was in consultation with and led by local guidance. Herat University, farmer cooperatives, and local NGOs and associations took legal ownership over our investments, with the goal of transforming "beneficiaries" into true shareholders of the program's outcomes. The cross-sector partnerships we developed among the DoD, external funders, local communities and NGOs, and universities also put in place a permanent training infrastructure and knowledge base required for the long-term success of the program.[44] This led to important capacity development and infrastructure for the agricultural sector across the region.

The third element of the social value investing framework— supporting local community ownership in the places where partners are working and investing—is discussed in detail in chapter 8. We dive into this subject by establishing cooperative principles for developing place-based strategies so that organizations and communities can coinvest their resources toward an intended outcome. A set of best practices for sharing success across organizations is outlined in the chapter, as well as ways to balance decision-making authority between funders, implementers, and local communities. Furthermore, we discuss how partners can plan and sequence activities strategically and build collaborative evaluation models for allocating shared resources.

## DEPLOYING NEW INVESTMENT IN PEOPLE

After my time at the Defense Department, I began serving a two-year term as the Executive Director of HGBF. During this time,

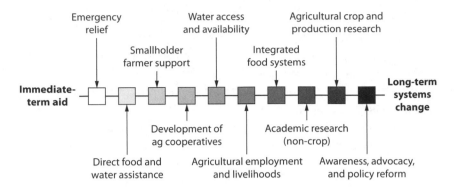

*Figure 2.1* The Howard G. Buffett Foundation's Global Food Security Spectrum illustrates a range of interconnected activities and programs falling within the organization's mission.

the organization went through a brief strategic planning process as I worked to incorporate principles of social value investing into its programming and operations. The foundation's team discussed ways it could restructure objectives into a more comprehensive approach and developed what we called our Global Food Security Spectrum to provide thematic guidance for programs (figure 2.1).

The left end of this range represented immediate-term relief and aid, and the right end represented long-term systems change. Various types of activities or initiatives filled the spaces in between, such as water resource management or the development of integrated food systems. The team ordered these activities based on longevity of program impact, complexity, and the foundation's experience with the given type of work.

At the far right end of the range we listed activities such as awareness and advocacy, topics the foundation had been exploring with increasing frequency. We observed that large-scale impact requires the coordinated efforts of numerous funders, the government, influencers, and support from the general public. In addition, we considered ways to elevate the visibility of issues the foundation had prioritized.[45]

Also during this period, we spent a great deal of time reflecting on the foundation's work from the past decade and the experiences we had learned from the most. We eventually decided that these experiences could serve to drive public awareness on global hunger challenges, and the foundation began working on a book to chronicle insights and lessons learned about the complex problems our world was facing.

My father and I wrote *40 Chances: Finding Hope in a Hungry World* to create a conversation on what was and was not working, particularly in the development and aid community. This was an opportunity to share our observations and our failures over the past decade, but we also hoped it would inspire increased public engagement in local and global issues that could encourage important policy changes in the United States and abroad. Also, this presented an opportunity for me to discuss some aspects of the social value investing approach.[46]

As we organized the book's chapters, it became clear that we were telling the stories of people from around the world where the foundation had made major investments. These people were the real heroes. Throughout the years, we had built a network of successful "managers" who were dedicated to achieving goals shared by the foundation and who put their missions and their altruistic hopes ahead of themselves.

One standout example is Kofi Boa, a Ghanaian farmer and environmental conservationist who has dedicated his life to advancing Africa's sustainable agricultural practices. Boa is a soft-spoken but tireless advocate for improved production techniques, and the foundation recently partnered with him to launch Africa's first Center for No-Till Agriculture. Because of our trust in Boa, we structured a unique cross-sector partnership designed to improve the productivity and sustainability of smallholder farmers through conservation-based techniques—first in Ghana, and later, we hoped, across much of Africa.[47]

The objectives of the partnership with Boa are complex because the agricultural issues it addresses are multifaceted and tough to solve. For example, the World Bank estimates that nearly 80 percent of the world's poor live in areas where agriculture is the primary economic activity—areas that often need investment throughout the agricultural value chain.[48] However, if done well, these investments can be very fruitful. The World Bank approximates that agricultural sector development is up to 4 times more effective at lifting the income of poor individuals than investments in any other sector.[49] Moreover, this effectiveness jumps to as much as 11 times more effective for sub-Saharan Africa.[50]

Working closely with Boa and the smallholder farmers in his community, HGBF orchestrated partners to develop a suite of context appropriate tools (such as a new model of small-scale, conservation-based planters manufactured by John Deere), resources (such as customized seed and cover crop recommendations based on soil types and topography), and agriculture-sector-related infrastructure improvements. The program has taken work that goes beyond what many traditional development projects require, but it has endured because of HGBF's partners, the collective group's commitment, and especially Boa, who understands that the success and scalability of this partnership could have far-reaching implications.[51]

Boa and his team lead all aspects of the program's design and the center's programs and operations, only seeking input from the foundation as needed. Another central aspect of this partnership is to reach and influence farmer behavior in meaningful but everyday ways to encourage them to adopt conservation-based practices through in-person workshops and radio broadcasts. Because of Boa's reputation with farmers throughout Ghana, he is uniquely positioned to capture their attention and speak with authority on the subject. Boa's work and his personal story is told in chapter 35 of *40 Chances: Finding Hope in a Hungry World*.

---

In 2012, halfway through my time at the foundation, there was yet another announcement—the funding provided from my grandfather's 2006 gift to his children would be doubled.[52] My father began looking for opportunities to further increase his investments and expand his impact, and for new partners to help deploy the capital. The foundation's reliance on its managers became more important than ever. By 2014, the foundation's total giving increased to more than $150 million per year, and its capacity to take on new and exciting challenges increased as well.[53]

This example illustrates the importance of human capital and how leaders can invest in and empower the people both on their staff and in a partnership. In chapter 6 we discuss a leader's role in working effectively across decentralized partners and teams. We also discuss the importance of diverse leadership qualities and of understanding the underlying emotional and intellectual influences that motivate teams. Finally, we discuss ways that leaders can inspire their team's energy and momentum throughout the life cycle of a partnership.

# THE SOCIAL VALUE INVESTING FRAMEWORK

The coming chapters further illustrate the social value investing framework, and how it reflects principles from the value investing approach. This adaptation is apparent at the most basic level of the framework, as outlined in the process / people / place / portfolio / performance paradigm. At the same time, many of the parallels vary significantly due to the obvious nature of the adaptation—it is a translation of principles from a purely financial construct for building monetary value to one providing guidance on effective ways to collaborate for the creation of social value.

The framework sets out a series of preconditions for planning and building effective partnerships between organizations of all types. However, it is not a comprehensive list, nor will all aspects of the approach apply to every partnership. This is a generalized framework on purpose, and the principles outlined are broad so that they are widely applicable. The cases discussed and their accompanying course companions and video documentaries demonstrate how these lessons apply, but the principles and observations are not the end result.[54] Instead, we hope they provide a starting point for others to expand and improve on our ideas, to establish sets of common goals, to create a more inclusive and community-driven vision for the future, and to begin exploring new and more effective ways for investing in social value.

# PROCESS

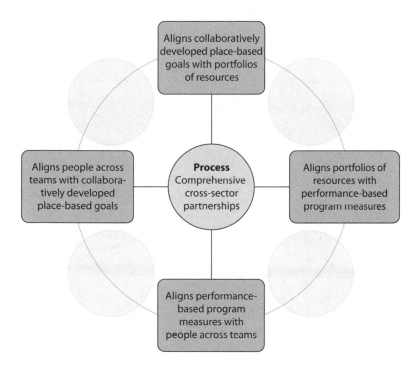

Aligns collaboratively developed place-based goals with portfolios of resources

Aligns people across teams with collaboratively developed place-based goals

**Process** Comprehensive cross-sector partnerships

Aligns portfolios of resources with performance-based program measures

Aligns performance-based program measures with people across teams

# CHAPTER THREE

# The Process Case

## The Digital Revolution and Telemedicine in India

### WILLIAM B. EIMICKE

Across India several expansive partnerships are under way to connect citizens with important government services. In return, citizens are receiving high-quality health care and access to bank accounts, which is simultaneously stimulating the economy of India and reducing corruption often referred to as "skimming." One set of partnerships is widely known as Digital India, a suite of related initiatives to provide every one of India's more than 1.3 billion residents with a secure identification card through which they can access a national network of public and private services.

The government is working with numerous partners on significant up-front investments in a long-term strategy that will take many years to fully implement. These programs will unlock significant intrinsic value over time by making government more efficient and honest, and by providing citizens with direct access to essential public services. For example, using biometric security, residents can conduct banking and access important personal records, such as proof of identity, voter registration, deeds and permits, driver's licenses, and automobile registration. All of this can be delivered through a relatively inexpensive smartphone, serving citizens across income levels and from even the most remote rural areas.

Building on these investments, the government is also working closely with the private sector to provide advanced, high-quality health care services to poor and working class citizens. Through cross-sector partnerships, the government is providing residents across India with access to low-cost medical care in clinics and local service centers using the Internet and advanced medical technology and practices. The government is partnering with private programs, such as Apollo Telemedicine, as well as with local entrepreneurs to collaboratively develop a strategic plan and deploy complex programs. This chapter discusses how Digital India and Apollo Telemedicine used a well-structured, highly decentralized process to serve a huge and very diverse population across a country as large as a small continent.

## INDIA RISING

Independent since 1947, India is a relatively young democracy established after several centuries of tumultuous relations with Great Britain. Britain effectively ruled large parts of India from 1600 to 1857 through the independent East India Company and directly as a British Colony from 1858 to 1947, a period often referred to as the British *Raj*.[1] Imperialism and colonialism are largely discredited and vilified in the twenty-first century, but the Indian democracy, its well-respected (and frequently criticized) civil service, and even two of its greatest modern leaders, Gandhi and Nehru, were shaped by the experiences of the Raj.[2]

Today's India reflects its past as it seeks to transform itself into a leading nation for the twenty-first century.[3] India is the world's second most populous nation, with more than 1.3 billion people, and ranks as the world's third largest economy.[4] The number of very poor people in India is declining, and its ranking in the Gini Index—a ranking of relative inequality—is improving, but it remains a poor country with huge disparity between rich and poor. India's Gini score (lower is "better" or "more equal," higher less so) is 35.2 compared to 26.8 for Norway, 45 for the U.S., and 49.7 for Brazil.[5] India currently has less income inequality than the United States or Brazil; however, more than 21 percent of the population still lives on $1.90 a day or less.[6] Hundreds of millions of Indians remain extremely poor, representing about one-third of the poor in the world.[7]

There is good reason to be optimistic about India's future, however. Over the past three decades, India has transformed its agricultural sector, becoming a net exporter of many agricultural products instead of a net importer. India is now the world's sixth largest net exporter, particularly of rice, cotton, sugar, and beef (buffalo). Its export growth was the highest of any country in recent years, with twice as many exports as the EU-28, and India is second only to the United States in cotton exports.[8] India has become a global player in health care, pharmaceuticals, data processing, and space technologies and is a world class "back office" for call centers, credit card processing, legal work, and radiology, among other areas. In addition, India will soon have one of the largest and youngest workforces in the world.[9] In 2014, India elected a new prime minister, Narendra Modi, who had great success at the state level using public-private partnerships to jumpstart economic growth and reduce poverty. As prime minister, Modi promised to use the successful state-level techniques at the national government level to integrate public-private partnerships through programs such as Digital India.

## DIGITAL INDIA

Building on the groundwork developed by his predecessor Manmohan Singh, Modi developed Digital India, founded on the Aadhaar ID, through which India can deliver an ever-expanding portfolio of complementary services over time—income subsidies for heating and cooking gas, records and record-keeping through DigiLocker, health care through telemedicine, and more to come. Key ingredients of the social value investing framework run consistently throughout the Digital India case. For example, the partnership has a long-term investment strategy—building the country's broadband network and local services centers, and connecting all citizens to it through Aadhaar. Digital India is unlocking hidden or intrinsic value through programs such as the health partnership with telemedicine. These methods are aligned with the social value investing framework because they integrate local stakeholders in program design and delivery. The programs use local banks to provide a broad range of financial services to even the poorest citizens in the most remote communities through cell phone and smartphone accounts. These networks of organizations provide potentially world class health care for everyone from private companies such as Apollo Hospitals Enterprise Ltd., as well as a full range of work-based benefits such as pay, insurance and pensions, and government services directly to employees and citizens through their mobile devices.

Digital India[10] is a series of related initiatives created (or rebranded) in 2014 by Prime Minister Modi that are designed to reinvent the country's public sector using state of the art information technology.[11] Modi's vision is to transform India into a connected, knowledge-able and information-based society through broadband "highways," universal access to mobile connectivity, electronic delivery of public services, dramatic expansion of access to quality health care, and banking—even to rural and remote areas—and IT-related employment opportunities (including electronics manufacturing).[12] A key element in achieving this vision is Aadhaar,[13] a twelve-digit random number identification "card," or ID, issued by the government's Unique Iden-tification Authority of India.[14]

Voluntary and free of cost, any resident of India can obtain a unique Aadhaar number. Security and veracity are ensured by demographic information—name, verified date of birth or declared age, gender, address, optional mobile number, email, and biometric information—that includes all ten fingerprints, two iris scans, and a facial photograph (figure 3.1). Available online, Aadhaar can potentially provide residents with a wide range of services and benefits from virtually any location securely, and with much lower risk of skimming and fraud.[15]

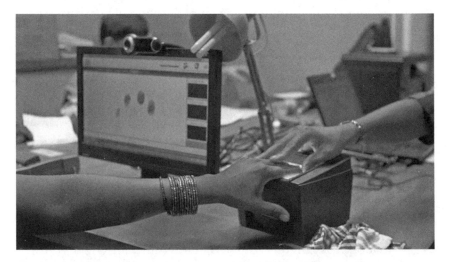

*Figure 3.1* Voluntary biometric registration of Indian citizens at an Aadhaar processing center. Photo by Richard Numeroff, courtesy of SIPA Case Collection.

Proof of identity is an important and long-standing challenge in India, particularly for the poor, in a country of 1.3 billion, mostly Hindu (80 percent) and Muslim (14 percent) but also with significant numbers of Christians, Sikhs, Buddhists, and Jains. Between them, Indians speak twenty-two official government-supported languages and live across twenty-nine states and seven territories.[16] Many people have insufficient documentation to conduct business, create bank accounts, or access government programs. Many different IDs could be used for individual purposes, but until recently only passports and tax IDs (PAN cards) were widely recognized, and few Indians carry those.[17] As recently as 2015, 57 million had passports, 170 million had PAN cards, 600 million had voter ID cards, 150 million had ration cards, and 173 million had driver's licenses.[18]

One of the main reasons the Indian government pushed forward with a unique identification card was to combat the problem of "leakage." This kind of corruption or skimming diverts a portion of government social welfare program benefits, often to ineligible recipients (such as local government officials charging "fees," tribal leaders, or family members) or through duplicate claims. Government officials estimated suspect beneficiaries amounted to 10 to 15 percent of social welfare, totaling as much as half a billion dollars or more annually.[19] A World Bank report in 2015 estimated the potential leakage of savings in one government cash transfer program now covered by Aadhaar at $1 billion annually.[20]

Aadhaar evolved out of a series of initiatives by the Indian national government to provide its residents with a single, multipurpose, verifiable identification card. This began in 1993 with the Election Commission issuing photo ID cards. In 2003, the government approved the creation of a Multipurpose National Identity Card (MNIC). It wasn't until 2006 that the government began the pursuit of a *unique* identification card by executive order through the India Planning Commission. This new initiative overlapped with work of the Registrar General of India on the National Population Register and the issuance of a Multipurpose National Identity Card.[21] Then prime minister Dr. Manmohan Singh created a multiagency committee to recommend a plan to align the two related projects.

Based on recommendations of the committee, the government created the Unique Identification Authority of India (UIDAI) to be responsible for implementation of Aadhaar.[22] The National Population

Register (NPR) remained responsible for creation of a national database of all citizens and residents of India under the provisions of the Citizenship Act of 1955. This information is then sent to UIDAI to make sure there is no duplication and UIDAI issues (or documents) the Aadhaar number.[23]

Despite its visionary appeal, Aadhaar faced substantial opposition for many reasons and from many quarters. There was opposition based on privacy concerns, fear that it would be used to deny government benefits not extend them, and that it would benefit illegal residents/immigrants. Other institutions, particularly NPR, but also Congress, feared a loss of control and authority among each other and vis-à-vis their "customer-citizens."[24]

The prospects for Aadhaar changed dramatically for the better when billionaire technology businessman Nandan Nilekani was appointed as UIDAI chair in July 2009 (figure 3.2). He decided to partner with a broad array of private sector partners for everything from infrastructure to more than seventy thousand street-level enrollment contractors. UIDAI partnered with private companies, state governments, banks, and insurance companies to scan biometric data and store it.

*Figure 3.2* Prime Minister Narendra Modi with Nandan Nilekani, private sector technology business leader recruited to make the Aadhaar partnership a success. Narendramodi.in.

Even UIDAI management and staff comprised a mix of civil servants and loaned executives from the private sector.[25]

HCL Infosystems Ltd. (HCL), India's giant computer systems management and outsourcing firm, was chosen to help build and manage Aadhaar's hardware, networking, and software, beating out international competitors Accenture and Wipro—even IBM and HP dropped out before the final round. HCL would build the central ID repository and manage the database. HCL also ensured Aadhaar was interoperable with existing government systems and emerging new applications in the banking, agriculture, and legal system. Aadhaar staff took responsibility for verification, security, maintenance, and the helpdesk.[26]

As enrollment increased, the Indian government began to offer programs that worked with Aadhaar members' IDs. Beginning in late 2012, the national government initiated a cash transfer program linked to Aadhaar for cardholders eligible for cooking gas, food, and fertilizer subsidies. After a successful pilot phase in 2013, the program was made available nationally in 2014. Initial research on the gas program indicated that the more efficient corruption-resistant cash transfers to Aadhaar-linked bank accounts was saving the government between 11 and 14 percent[27] (as of 2015, the savings were estimated at $2 billion in this program alone).[28] Another study of the cumulative impact of all the subsidy programs converted to cash transfers through the Aadhaar ID bank link was estimated to exceed $11 billion in efficiencies annually.[29]

Noted economists and India experts Jhagdish Bhagwati and Arvind Panagariya strongly support the shift from in-kind benefits. They observed, "Significant gains in efficiency can be achieved by replacing the public distribution system by cash transfers. . . . The advantage of cash transfers is that they would greatly minimize the leakage along the distribution chain and also eliminate the huge waste that characterizes the public distribution system."[30] Indian governments subsidize a wide range of items—rice, wheat, sugar, water, fertilizer, electricity, rail transport, and cooking gas—so the potential efficiencies and increased welfare to those in need could be tremendous. Leakage in the subsidized kerosene for home lighting program can exceed 40 percent.[31] Cumulatively, these subsidies total more than 4 percent of India's GDP, enough to raise the consumption levels of the nation's poor above the poverty line if distributed through this more efficient process.[32]

———— ✐✐✐ ————

In addition to the successful partnership process used, Digital India illustrates underlying fundamentals of social value investing: investment in programs over a long-term time horizon that unlock intrinsic social value. These aspects are accelerating Indian's modernization and helping to raise the standard of living for the world's largest concentration of people living in poverty. Long-term public infrastructure investments are building a nationwide "digital highway" connecting local service centers, government agencies, and banks to residents through Aadhaar. Once connected, citizens are able to benefit from a new electronic cash transfer system that ensures they receive the full amount of their government program payments, virtually eliminating related corruption. As noted, such a reduction in corruption would have significant impact on the consumption levels of the nation's poor. The partnership process reflects multiple elements of the social value investing approach by integrating local leadership into program operations and using local banks to provide a broad range of financial services, in turn building community wealth and supporting economic stability and prosperity.

## JAM

In 2014 a team from Columbia University visited India to film our case study on these partnerships (figure 3.3). Since that time, the scope and impact of the programs organized under the Digital India umbrella have increased. Social programs tied to Aadhaar are often referred to as JAM—Jan Dhan, Aadhaar, Mobile. Jan Dhan is Modi's initiative to provide banking services to Indians: accounts, credit, and insurance. Mobile is the cash transfers directly to beneficiaries on their mobile devices. By early 2016, the number of Jan Dhan bank accounts exceeded 210 million, with more than 70 percent actively transacting. Over 170 million are linked to debit cards, and participants are beginning to make their own deposits, apply for loans, and buy insurance.[33]

*Figure 3.3* Prime Minister Modi (*center*) with economist and Columbia Professor Arvind Panagariya (*left*). Panagariya served as Modi's vice chairman for the National Institution for Transforming India, the government agency responsible for Digital India. Photo by AP, courtesy of Arvind Panagariya.

By 2018, the number of Aadhaar IDs issued was over 1,200,000,000,[34] and the number of mobile phone subscribers in India exceeded 1 billion, with 350 million of them smartphone users.[35] By early 2017, India had become Facebook's largest market of users.[36] Some analysts also see a direct connection between smartphone growth and economic growth.[37]

Challenges to maximizing the potential of JAM continue. Matching a wide array of national and state means-tested benefits to the eligible Aadhaar cardholders and then connecting those eligible to bank accounts accessible on mobile devices is a work in progress. Extending those bank networks to extremely rural India is also under way but not yet a reality.

In 2015, Prime Minister Modi announced a series of new initiatives to expand Digital India and reach more people in many ways, creating a national digital highway.[38] Taken together, the initiatives should make more government services available online, expand connectivity and digital access in rural areas, and expand the nation's electronics manufacturing sector. In a speech to Silicon Valley technology executives in San Jose, California, in the fall of 2015, Modi said Digital India would make governance "more transparent, accountable, accessible and participative," and that it would "touch the lives of the weakest, farthest, and the poorest citizens of India and also change the way our nation will live and work."[39]

As the communications minister phrased it, "if the Atal Bihari Vajpayee government is remembered for laying down national highways, the Narendra Modi government will be known to have laid the digital highway of the country."[40] Specifics of the initiative included a new data center, eight new software technology parks, and "digital villages" in rural areas that provide telemedicine facilities, virtual classes, and solar-powered Wi-Fi hot spots. More broadly, Modi has pushed to expand access to high-speed Internet connections across much of India.[41]

The Modi government is also committed to using Aadhaar to make a DigiLocker available to all citizens to safely store important documents such as driver's license, car registration, education certificates, and deeds. Similar to cloud storage provided by companies such as Microsoft, Apple, and Google, DigiLocker has the twin advantages of being linked to the Aadhaar ID and being protected by multiple levels of security.[42] It is easily accessible from a mobile device—no need to hand over a driver's license or car registration to a police officer or other government official.[43] DigiLocker saves documents in PNG, JPEG, and PDF formats so they are easy to share, and it is linked to government services and financial benefit accounts. DigiLocker provides state of the art security measures including 256 Bit SSL encryption, Aadhaar authentication-based document access, hosting an ISO 27001 security certified data center, data redundancy backup, timed log out, external security audits, and data sharing only with explicit consent of the user.[44] By early 2018, DigiLocker had 9.5 million registered users, 14 million user uploaded documents, and access to 2 billion other related documents—just a beginning, but a very impressive start.[45]

Taken together, JAM is following a particular cross-sector partnership process. It has created a system that connects a massive number of users and recipients to essential public and private services over a huge geographic area and uses the best of the private sector's cutting edge technology as its implementer. As the primary funder, the government provided regulatory authority and expansive financial resources, and each sector engaged a very large number of local entrepreneurs and other stakeholders throughout program delivery.

## FIGHTING CORRUPTION

Prime Minister Modi also sees Digital India as a means to fight corruption by putting the competition for public contracts up for bid online, openly and transparently.[46] Alleged favoritism in awarded telecommunications and coal licenses by the government prior to Modi's election are estimated to have cost the taxpayers more than $70 billion.[47] Aadhaar protects low-income workers from leakage by local bureaucrats who deduct a "certification and payment fee" typically equal to one-third of the worker's wages. Under the Digital India innovations, these workers can claim their wages through an app on their cell phone, payable at a local grocery or local center, with a fixed commission equivalent to approximately sixteen cents.[48]

Digital India is thereby serving the interests of many different stakeholders. It provides a more level playing field for those bidding for government contracts and increases transparency. It also makes government more efficient by helping to ensure that the full amount of income and benefits reach low-income citizens, and it creates an opportunity for many Indians to access banking services for the first time.

## BUMPS ALONG THE DIGITAL HIGHWAY

Aadhaar, the linchpin of Digital India, is not without its critics, and there are lingering obstacles to its universality and long-term success. Although well on the way toward universal participation—over 1.1 billion of the country's 1.2 billion residents registered by the fall 2017— there is currently no strategy to serve those hardest to reach, including millions of homeless people.[49] Officially, both the Modi government and the Congress want to require an Aadhaar ID for access to a number of public benefits. But, several Supreme Court decisions have ruled in the special cases before them that an Aadhaar ID cannot be required.

Can biometric data make Aadhaar a unique, reliable identifier? Experiences in the United Kingdom, Australia, France, Argentina, and Kenya indicate that those with medical conditions, the elderly (the iris may change over time), and manual laborers might encounter verification issues.[50] UIDAI Director Ram Sewak Sharma told our team in 2015, "experts say our ID can achieve an accuracy level of 99.99 percent. Unfortunately, 0.01 percent off from 1.2 billion is 102,000."[51] Director Sharma went on to say, "from a public policy perspective, even in the current situation where Aadhaar is voluntary, where a large [segment of the] population has Aadhaar, I am left with a much smaller subset to monitor."[52]

UIDAI leadership is focused on using Aadhaar to improve the lives of India's low-income workers and their families and the very poor. At the same time, UIDAI shares the concerns raised by privacy advocates and has therefore resisted information demands from other government agencies, particularly law enforcement organizations. A 2014 Supreme Court ruling decided in favor of UIDAI's position that it could not be forced to share Aadhaar data without the individual's consent. The decision also reaffirmed the court's prior rulings that Aadhaar must remain voluntary.[53] Nevertheless, in 2015, a Delhi court ordered that Aadhaar records could be accessed to identify hit-and-run accident victims.[54]

A large data repository of valuable identity information on more than a billion people poses serious security concerns, particularly in light of the major hacks into large public and private databases all over the world, including the U.S. government's Office of Personnel Management, Internal Revenue Service, and National Security Administration. Data breaches have also hit the Democratic National Committee, and private sector companies such as Target, Yahoo!, Home Depot, and others. UIDAI has strict policies and multiple protocols to protect Aadhaar and has a good track record so far. Yet, in 2013, the UIDAI Maharashtra office lost the data of 300,000 applicants. Although no evidence of damage has been identified, the affected individuals had to reapply—and faith in the system was shaken. As UIDAI deputy director general Ajay Bhushan Pandey explained to our team in 2015, "people will always find ways to commit fraud with Aadhaar. Nothing is foolproof. There's always some ingenuity where someone figures out how to game it. But we have given Aadhaar to more than 850 million people and we haven't come across any significant number of cases where people have been able to beat the system."[55]

The Modi government continues to press forward with Aadhaar as a critical interface between citizens and their government. In 2015, public sector businesses such as Air India and the state steel and oil companies were directed to require employees to register for an Aadhaar ID to serve as the basic identification for company attendance, payroll, insurance, and benefit systems.[56] As we have seen in numerous examples, public and private databases are vulnerable to criminal and political cyberattacks and government overreach, which present real threats to an individual's right to privacy. In the case of Aadhaar, it is encouraging to see that the Indian courts have been active in this area to protect the rights and security of all Indians and that the government has worked closely with its corporate partners to maximize the security of the Aadhaar database.

## APOLLO TELEMEDICINE: PARTNERING TO BRING QUALITY HEALTH CARE BEYOND THE URBAN CENTERS

Modi still had broad public support in 2018. Although his BJP political party lost some key elections at the state level in 2015 and 2016,[57] in early 2017 Modi's BJP won an important electoral victory in India's largest state, Uttar Pradesh, dramatically strengthening his political position.[58] A Pew Research report found that more than 80 percent of Indians viewed the prime minister favorably, and even a majority of the opposition party members surveyed viewed him positively.[59] This widespread popularity is no doubt related to India's economic growth rate of 7.1 percent for the quarter ending in June 2016 (compared to 6.7 percent for China), making India the fastest-growing large economy in the world.[60] And it could well be that Aadhaar and the Digital India infrastructure that the Modi government and its private sector technology partners are building will spur private sector innovation. Furthermore, it will put money directly in the hands of low- and moderate-income Indian consumers to buy the goods and services that the innovation created, thereby growing the economy at an even faster rate.

Emerging cross-sector partnerships in India's public health sector could enhance the societal infrastructure by making what will be one of the largest and youngest workforces in human history healthier and thereby more productive. For example, to advance health care services in the country, the government (through Common Service Centers) partnered with Apollo in 2013. The partnership is aimed at providing state of the art health care to Indians living outside the major cities via telemedicine (figure 3.4).[61] Apollo operates a for-profit hospital chain and one of the largest organizations of its kind in the world, with

*Figure 3.4* (*a*): Apollo medical experts conduct a remote telemedicine consultation. (*b*): A village Common Service Center (CSC) where telemedicine consultations are offered to the community. Photos by Richard Numeroff, courtesy of SIPA Case Collection.

45 million patients from 121 countries and 9,215 beds across sixty-four hospitals.[62]

Common Service Centers (CSCs) is a division of the central government's Department of Information and Technology. Created in 2006, CSCs expand the availability of web-based e-governance services throughout the country, particularly to rural areas. Based on a partnership model, CSCs are staffed by Village Level Entrepreneurs (VLEs) and representatives from the national and state government. Services include agriculture information; payment of electric, water, and telephone bills; banking; government forms and certificates; printing; and Internet access.[63] The Modi government sees CSCs as a cornerstone of Digital India because they provide access points to every corner of India and to the increasing number of services and assistance the government hopes will create a much more inclusive society and will improve the quality of life for India's very large population of poor families and individuals.[64] Apollo sees the program as an opportunity to do good while simultaneously attracting new customers and perfecting a new way of delivering medical services. The government also hoped to serve the public interest by illustrating how Digital India could help make a real difference in the lives of its most needy and isolated citizens.

Both partners realized that the potential was great but that this initiative was complex and expensive, with a relatively high risk of failure. Apollo built its business by providing high-quality health services to middle-class and wealthy Indians and international patients at a much lower price than U.S. and European providers. As early as 2000, Apollo experimented with telemedicine as a pro bono enterprise serving India's rural areas using satellite technology provided by the Indian space research organization. Later the Internet, Skype video, electronic records, Bluetooth stethoscopes, and wireless sensors enabled Apollo to expand its market-rate health businesses through tele-radiology and clinics in large housing developments in India, the Middle East, and Africa, totaling more than one hundred centers in twelve countries.[65]

Developing a telemedicine public health service partnership primarily to serve India's rural poor is an ongoing challenge. Apollo wanted the enterprise to be a for-profit business with a positive social impact. The government's CSC leaders envisioned a free, public service. After much discussion, the partners agreed to charge patients a low fee of 100 rupees ($1.60) for primary care and 900 rupees ($14.40) for specialties such as neurology and cardiology.[66] The fees are split 40 percent to Apollo, 40 percent to the local Village Level Entrepreneurs that facilitate the examination at the local center, and 20 percent to the government CSC. Even at these very low fee levels, Apollo's leadership believed the organization could at least break even on the initial service because of the large number of patients. In the long run, they also expect that once access is established and relationships are built, use of services covered by state-subsidized insurance would make telemedicine a viable business in India.[67]

Indian telemedicine continues to face ongoing technical challenges: unreliable electrical supply, inadequate Internet bandwidth, video distortions, and software malfunctions. Even so, Apollo reports that telemedicine examinations provide reliable diagnoses for 80 percent of patients, including the more complicated neurological and craniological cases. Telemedicine examinations are generally videotaped (with the permission of the patient), providing the physician with an opportunity to review or "see" the patient again several times, to make sure the initial diagnosis was correct and that no important information was missed.[68]

The prospects for the telemedicine partnership remain bright, but the rollout has taken some time. The program—National Telemedicine Network (NTN)—was officially launched by the Ministry of Communications and Information Technology and Apollo Hospitals on August 25, 2015.[69] Initially, services were provided in 60,000 CSCs across the country with a focus on reaching underserved remote regions. The government also announced that the CSCs would collaborate with the Bureau of Pharma PSU of India (BPPI) so that telemedicine patients could order generic drugs online through the CSC network.[70]

The Modi government's commitment to telemedicine remains strong in 2018, although it is now supporting a new modified approach to its rollout. The original model begun in 2015 and the CSCs remain in place, but the Indian government has now supported a new project involving 164 eUrban Primary Health Centers in the state of Andra Pradesh. The technology for delivery remains the same as with the CSC model, but each local center is a fully functioning and professionally staffed local community health clinic, rather than a privately run office offering a variety of services. Apollo uses remote telemedicine to deliver expert care from its specialists in the central hospitals, but it can rely on more fully trained local staff for support. The government, whose role in the original CSC model was more limited, is now providing full funding for each center's operating costs, and Apollo is responsible for all local staffing and service delivery. Remote telemedicine remains a core component of the plan, allowing most services to be delivered by trained registered nurses and telemedicine technicians. As a network of organizations and communities, this initiative has developed into a comprehensive and complex cross-sector partnership providing expansive, world-class health care.

## LOOKING FORWARD

Although challenges remain, Indian government telemedicine initiatives clearly show the powerful results of a successful government funded, private-sector operated, and community supported and engaged partnership. There is a convergence of interests between the partners to expand affordable health care to the very poor, sharing the financial risk and potential reward. Each partner is making resource investments and working together to secure a reliable, sustainable revenue stream without pricing anyone out, and they are working to have a greater positive impact on health outcomes for the poor than would be possible without the partnership. They also have a comprehensive strategy for long-term program sustainability, a plan that has been modified several times since Apollo first ventured into telemedicine in 2000.

Achieving financial viability for programs serving the poor is improving as the government expands the number of services covered and develops relationships with health insurance providers. Clearly, long-term investment in building an infrastructure backbone is essential to success, and both the government and Apollo have invested in its construction. In the case of telemedicine, increased involvement by Apollo in the implementation phase has yielded much better results.

For the Digital India and JAM initiatives, government legislation, regulations, and funding have been crucial to progress. Building the infrastructure and implementing and connecting the system to services for residents has been run by private companies. Significantly, Aadhaar's unique biometric identification system, on which Digital India and JAM rest, achieved a new level of permanence and legitimacy on

March 26, 2016, when Lok Sabha (House of the People, the Indian Congress) passed The Aadhaar (Targeted Delivery of Financial and Other Subsidies, Benefits and Services) Act, 2016. The law entitles every resident to obtain an Aadhaar card but does not require it. Any public or private entity can accept the card as proof of identity, but it is not a proof of citizenship or domicile. The law is important because it enables the government to link the card to additional benefits and for banks to use it to eliminate fake accounts.[71]

In many respects, Digital India, JAM, and Apollo Telemedicine are partnerships that exhibit multiple elements of the social value investing framework. Having the right *people* has been crucial. Without the leadership of Prime Minister Modi, billionaire technology businessman Nandan Nilekani, and one of Apollo's leaders, Dr. Krishnan Ganapathy, it is unlikely that Digital India or Apollo Telemedicine would have been nearly as successful as they have been to date. These partnerships illustrate how important the partnership *process* can be when planning and designing complex cross-sector collaborations.

These examples also exhibit the other elements of the social value investing framework, which we describe in the coming chapters and cases. Numerous organizations made coordinated and tangible investments in individual communities—very much a *place*-based approach—that were informed by local residents and entrepreneurs. Each partner had something unique and important to contribute, sharing various aspects of risk as well as potential reward from the outcomes of the initiatives—resembling a *portfolio* strategy. Although program delivery was decentralized and partners came from different sectors, they were able to share success by maximizing the public benefit generated for citizens across India through measurable *performance* indicators.

In the next chapter we use the cases of Digital India and Apollo Telemedicine to illustrate our cross-sector partnership process. Combined with other's extensive related research, we include formalized definitions and descriptions of partnership functions and partner roles. We also discuss tools partners can use to assist in comprehensive planning to achieve their shared goals.

# CHAPTER FOUR

# The Process Framework

## Effective Partnerships Across All Sectors

HOWARD W. BUFFETT

Large-scale, complex challenges facing society cannot be solved by organizations acting alone. When groups decide to work together, using the best *process* is critical.[1] How organizations develop comprehensive partnership strategies is just as important as their willingness to engage in work with others.[2] When companies in the private sector partner, collaborative arrangements are straightforward and use well-established legal structures and precedents. Companies may align their activities through acquisitions or mergers, joint ventures, product or service contracts, and so on.[3] In most cases, private sector organizations collaborate to attain higher returns on equity by improving operating efficiency and reducing either short-term or long-term costs.[4] Such improvements may be seen directly in ways that are reflected on the balance sheet, or indirectly through factors such as customer satisfaction and loyalty, strategic planning, or workforce retention.

When businesses partner or consolidate, they can draw from their comparative strengths. Partnering businesses are usually governed by similar laws, operate under similar principles, and focus on creating value for similar stakeholders—a parent company, private owners, or shareholders. Effective private sector partnerships align the objectives of top-level strategy and capital allocation with the operations of subsidiaries or business divisions, as well as with the interests of shareholders. But how does collaboration work when addressing more complex, societal challenges where the alignment of activities or the compatibility of private and public interests may be less straightforward?[5]

In the cases of Digital India and Apollo Telemedicine, the makeup and delivery of programs evolved and expanded over time. The government of India allocated capital through investment in training and infrastructure, and it established high-level goals for the country. Private sector partner Apollo Telemedicine focused on medical service delivery through a geographically diverse network of Common Service Centers (CSCs) funded by the government. The CSCs were staffed by local Village Level Entrepreneurs (VLEs) who shared in fees for services that were affordable for low-income residents in the community. Those residents—stakeholders in their government—received access to critical human services, including basic health care. This mutually collaborative partnering process, based on distributed operations, enabled the program to expand to more than 60,000 community-level CSCs fairly quickly, and eventually led to more than 160 new, major eUrban Primary Health Centers.[6]

This process for partnering describes the India case in general terms. However, the observations and lessons herein apply to cross-sector partnerships quite broadly, particularly when those partnerships include a diverse array of participants. Funders or investors in these partnerships provide financial capital, implementers or operators carry out partnership activities, and stakeholders or shareholders provide principled direction and guidance for the partnership and receive benefits from its outcomes.[7]

When organizations from the public, private, and philanthropic sectors decide to collaborate, not only will legal structures and operating principles differ but so, too, might each group's end goals, interim objectives, or stakeholder interests.[8] My grandfather observed yet another important differentiating factor. In a letter he wrote to Bill and Melinda Gates, he said that "success in philanthropy is measured differently from success in business or government."[9] This difference defines a key challenge in developing effective cross-sector partnerships: how you measure success is based on how you define it. Organizations from across sectors define success using different terminology, develop different planning procedures to work toward success, and deploy different methods for delivering organizational or operational strategies to achieve success.[10]

This chapter discusses how potential partners can overcome these differences, especially when considering the needs and interests of the public good. It begins by outlining a formal definition of what it means to enter a cross-sector partnership, and the key characteristics and advantages of doing so. Next it examines the primary function of a partnership, the three main partnering roles, and how a partnership can be modeled. Finally, it addresses the issue of comprehensive strategy development through two analogous tools: a theory of change process for planning at a program level and a value chain analysis for identifying gaps and weaknesses at a system level. Each of these aspects is an important early step toward building a partnership of diverse yet complementary organizations working in alignment.

## DEFINING A CROSS-SECTOR PARTNERSHIP

In recent years, *partnership* has become an expansive term with a wide range of interpretations.[11] In some cases the word carries legal implications, such as when each partner "contributes money, property, labor or skill, and expects to share in the profits and losses of [a] business."[12] An example of this is a joint venture.[13] In other cases, groups may use the term more informally when they announce a political alliance, are awarded a services contract, or receive a grant. This lack of consistency and formality creates challenges at the very start of partnership development, particularly when two very different organizations try to collaborate—such as a global for-profit technology company and a local, community-based nonprofit human services provider.[14] So what do we mean by a *cross-sector partnership?*

Fundamentally, a cross-sector partnership is a collaborative working relationship between two or more entities, and in our examples these entities span two or more sectors.[15] Our work and research is concerned with significant or complex challenges facing society, so many of the cross-sector partnerships described here are led by public or philanthropic organizations, or serve to benefit the public good. Our definition of a cross-sector partnership arises from the belief that many of society's challenges cannot be addressed by any single sector or organization alone; coordinated action is required to achieve collective, positive social impact.[16]

Given this context, we define a cross-sector partnership as a *voluntary collaboration between organizations from two or more sectors that leverage their respective teams and resources to achieve mutually agreed-upon and measurable goals.*[17] This definition is as much a mind-set as it is a process, and it requires further clarification.

- By *voluntary*, we mean that partnering organizations enter the collaboration by choice (not as a result of punitive or compulsory action). Partners often begin with clear agreements that guide the development of their engagement. Some partners may prefer nonbinding documents, particularly in the early stages of cooperation.[18] That said, most cross-sector collaborations are governed by a formal structure, such as a letter of intent (LOI). Others may use a memorandum of understanding (MOU) for general terms, or a memorandum of agreement (MOA) to spell out activities and resource sharing.[19] Later, this chapter outlines seven partnership models that illustrate possible structures for collaborative engagements.

- By *collaboration*, we mean the engagement goes beyond straightforward fee-for-service or product procurement between organizations.[20] Unlike traditional contracting or PPPs, collaborative, cross-sector partnerships involve multiple types of partners in the design, planning, and progression of the overall effort.[21] Partner roles and functions are well defined, as discussed in this chapter, and the partnership strategy is developed jointly across teams (using tools such as a theory of change and value-chain analysis outlined later).

- By *teams*, we mean the collective knowledge and leadership experience of the people operating the organizations in the collaboration. Teams in a cross-sector partnership represent their organization's distinct perspectives and resources. Furthermore, teams are responsible for advancing their organization's objectives and maintaining progress while also accomplishing the partnership's goals. Leaders across teams contribute critical skills-based capital (see chapter 6) that complements other resources invested toward shared outcomes.[22]

- By *resources*, we mean a broad range of different types of assets or capital. This can include a coinvestment in a portfolio of blended financial capital (see chapter 10). Or, this can include access to physical assets, infrastructure, intellectual property, technology, or natural or environmental resources.[23] Alternatively, coinvested resources may include important, yet intangible contributions that create intrinsic value for participants or that advance the partnership's goals.

- By *mutually agreed-upon goals*, we mean that partners and stakeholders work together to develop and prioritize specific objectives, milestones, and the long-term desired impact of the collaboration. Together, these groups determine individual and shared responsibilities within the overall scope of the partnership.[24] They also codevelop time lines and priorities for resource allocation based on common terms and operating standards (see chapter 8).

- By *measurable*, we mean that partners are able to discretely define success using clear and relevant metrics tied directly to their mutually agreed-upon goals. Specific objectives may vary significantly when organizations from different sectors are partnering. Therefore, the partnership will require a consistent, yet flexible methodology to outline and measure the performance of its collaborative programs.[25] We recommend using a customizable approach that combines quantitative and qualitative measures into the analysis (such as the Impact Rate of Return methodology described in chapter 12).

The more a partnership meets or exceeds the various aspects of this definition, and the preconditions outlined throughout the book, the better positioned its participating organizations will be for success. Other definitions of similar types of partnerships vary,[26] but they typically share overlapping terms or provisions.[27] Terminology aside, engagements under the social value investing cross-sector partnership rubric exhibit a number of important characteristics:[28]

- They are based on the convergence of interests between the partners that advance the objectives of each respective organization. These interests must be clear, fair, well thought out, and can be amended as needed;[29]

- They share both risk and potential reward for all partners through the mutual investment of various types of resources. Thoroughly planning on, agreeing to, and coordinating shared investment throughout the collaboration helps reduce potential conflict between partners;[30] and,

■ They rely on leveraging partner skills and assets, producing outcomes with higher measureable impact than could be achieved
independently. This requires an up-front evaluation of each partner's strengths and weaknesses, as well as key resource constraints.[31]

## ADVANTAGES OF PARTNERING

We believe that partnerships following this definition and exhibiting
these characteristics will enjoy distinct advantages.[32] Such partnerships
can produce significant collaborative value for all participants.[33]

1. *These partnerships enable participating organizations to accomplish
   more than they could on their own.*[34]

   By combining efforts, partners can leverage their respective
   resources. From a financial perspective, this aspect of partnering
   appeals to organizations confronting budget deficits, government
   sequesters, or volatile market fluctuations. Partners also benefit by
   gaining access to others' physical assets (such as meeting space),
   intellectual property, or the ability to share information widely
   across social groups. In the Digital India case, for example, the
   government had legal authority and national scope, private companies had technology and expertise, and community entrepreneurs
   provided local places of access for potential Aadhaar enrollees
   spread across the Indian subcontinent.

2. *These partnerships enable participating organizations to build on
   each other's expertise.*[35]

   Organizations in a partnership benefit from the core competencies and unique capabilities of each other's teams. This provides
   partners with access to leadership skills and knowledge they may
   not otherwise possess. Partners can build off each other's experiences operating specific types of programs or delivering particular services, share past lessons learned, and avoid repeating the
   mistakes of others. In the case of Apollo Telemedicine, Apollo
   had medical staff with specialized expertise as well as technological
   experience operating the delivery platform. The government had

administrative systems and staff in place who were well equipped to handle the partnership's financial resources and to help operate the initiative's local clinics and multiservices centers.

3. *These partnerships enable organizations to draw from cooperative and coordinated activity.*[36]

By bringing together new coalitions of public and private actors through an interactive process, partnerships can generate activities with a wider reach and larger scale than any single organization can alone. This especially matters when accomplishing the partnership's goals depends on the cooperative action of multiple partners across wide geographic areas or between diverse communities. This was apparent in the success of both the Digital India and Apollo Telemedicine cases in which numerous decentralized teams carried out similar programs throughout the country.

4. *These partnerships can drive improved performance for each organization.*[37]

Partners must agree on specific and clear milestones. Coordinated activities should draw on the comparative strengths of each partner and focus on tracking and advancing progress. For example, aligning activities with external stakeholders who are more agile can improve the speed of accomplishing shared objectives, especially if partners work in harmony toward the same milestones. In other cases, some partners may be able to advance common goals because they are governed under less burdensome rules or regulations. In the case of Digital India, Prime Minister Modi established aggressive time lines and ambitious goals that the government would have been unable to meet on its own. He also used his "bully pulpit" to encourage all members of the partnership to work together, to make progress quickly, and to provide mutual accountability.

5. *These partnerships benefit by including a broad range of diverse actors.*[38]

Partnerships that prioritize diverse and inclusive participation in their program design and deployment are more likely to result in long-lasting outcomes. Collaborative planning creates opportunities for individuals, communities, and small- and medium-sized organizations to participate in larger-scale problem solving. Stakeholder inclusion opens access to critical domain specific information and important cultural nuances that otherwise may be inaccessible to other partners.

In both cases, Digital India and Apollo Telemedicine needed the participation of a wide variety of organizations and communities to succeed. The large, nationwide federal government and partners in the private sector provided highly sophisticated technology and administrative services but designed their programs to meet the needs of both big cities and rural villages across the country. The VLEs in the Apollo Telemedicine example acted as an important linkage between their communities and the CSCs, thereby providing local context for program outreach and delivery.

These features apply in many settings beyond the ones discussed in India, as you will see throughout the book. Cross-sector partnerships come in all shapes and sizes, but these five core advantages are seen across each of our examples.

## THE PRIMARY FUNCTIONS
## OF A PARTNERSHIP

With common definitions established, and an outcome-oriented process in place for organizations to chart their intended goals, partners must identify the "bottom line" objectives driving their motivations for partnering. Three core functions serve as a baseline for establishing a common understanding of what organizations hope to achieve through the partnership process:[39]

*Coordination of resources.* Partnerships often form so organizations can combine or leverage resources. One organization may have a resource that another organization does not and cannot easily acquire, such as unrestricted funding, technology, expertise, or distribution networks. By coordinating efforts, partners draw on key sources of capital from each other and benefit from their comparative advantages as part of a coordinated partnership plan.[40]

*Enhancement of visibility or reputation.* Some organizations partner for the explicit purpose of raising their public profile or that of their cause. The actual partnership may focus on charity, education, or community development, for example, but a primary purpose relates to the visibility or perception of a brand, group, or specific social outcome.[41]

*Shared policy goals.* Organizations across sectors work toward specific policy objectives; this can mean more government funding, reduced reporting burdens, creation of behavioral incentives, elimination of taxes or penalties, and so on.[42] Policy agendas are relevant to every organization, whether they act on them or not. Agendas may include maintaining a status quo, increasing a policy oversight or available funding, or decreasing a policy or program restriction.[43]

## THE PRIMARY ROLES WITHIN A PARTNERSHIP

To carry out these functions, organizations within a partnership typically take on one of three roles. *Funders* are donors or investors who finance the activities of the partnership or the capital expenditures. *Implementers* or operators carry out or manage the activities and programs of the partnership. *Stakeholders* are those who receive a benefit from or who have a highly vested interest in the partnership's outcomes. Stakeholder groups often include communities at a local scale where the partnership's investment of resources is focused.

### Funders

Funders may be foundations (family, corporate, community, or operating foundations), governments (local, state, or national), bilateral organizations, multilateral organizations (such as the United Nations), corporations and other private sector actors (ranging from multinational companies and global financial institutions to venture capitalists and entrepreneurs), university endowments, pension funds, or sovereign wealth funds.[44]

In the Apollo partnership in India, the country's government acted in the role of funder, and it facilitated program oversight, delivery, and some financing through its network of Common Service Centers. In this instance, the CSCs acted as a bridge between the funder and the implementation partner, which is common in larger or more complex cross-sector partnerships—particularly ones that span a broad geographic region.

## Implementers

Implementers are typically contractors, nonprofit nongovernmental organizations (NGOs), academic institutions, external advisors or experts, faith-based organizations, or other private or government-funded aid agencies or collaborative initiatives designated with carrying out the activities identified in the partnership's theory of change (outlined later in this chapter).[45]

With Digital India, the Apollo program and its hospital network acted as the primary implementation partner. However, the government's CSCs acted as delivery mechanisms for the services being provided. Local VLEs helped operate the CSCs and acted as a bridge between the primary implementation partners and the communities where the CSCs were located.

## Stakeholders

Finally, the stakeholders of a partnership may include locally engaged management, place-based experts, any number of community-based institutions, universities or schools, churches and other places of worship, neighborhood associations, or a community's individuals. In some partnerships, stakeholders may be defined as taxpayers, voters, constituents, members of a neighborhood, or participants of a specific project or program related to the collaboration.[46] In most cases, collaborative engagements derive from the active leadership or participation of stakeholders with a highly vested interest in the outcomes of the partnership.[47]

Stakeholders in the Apollo partnership were many. Not only did this include residents in all the communities where the CSCs were delivering new Apollo health services. This also included the VLEs, who were local area residents, and who received an equal cut of the program fees as Apollo. This benefited the local community in numerous ways—not least of which were improved health outcomes and cost savings from preventative care. It also supported the overall climate for small businesses in each area and boosted local wealth creation.

Oftentimes organizations overlap between these descriptions. For instance, an NGO may serve as an implementer in one partnership and a cofunder in another. Or an implementation partner, such as a VLE, may operate a community-based organization with local stakeholder interests. However, these generalizations hold true when groups are categorized based on the primary activities they undertake and their responsibilities relative to other participants in the partnership.

## HOW PARTNERS STRUCTURE THEIR COLLABORATION

Organizations working together to form partnerships must structure activities in ways that coordinate their respective strengths and provide an environment for sustained, collective impact.[48] Because the functions of a partnership may vary, and because there may be multiple partners across roles, structuring a collaboration can be incredibly complex. Funders, implementers, and stakeholders can model partnership engagements in diverse ways. The following set of examples, written by and adapted from findings and analysis of the 2009 Collaboration Prize, represent distinct models for how organizations can work together and advance their common goals.[49]

### Joint Programming

Funders, implementers, or community-based organizations frequently partner to deliver new or improved programming, which may occur in one of two ways (figure 4.1).[50] They may combine otherwise separate programs into one, especially if those programs have significant overlaps and would benefit from economies of scale. Groups forming a joint programming effort to eliminate duplicative activities or operating expenses will benefit from coordinated action toward a common goal. For example, a community food bank and a nearby health clinic might separately conduct nutrition-related programming—including conflicting or competing educational outreach. Although their core missions remain distinctly different, these groups could be more effective

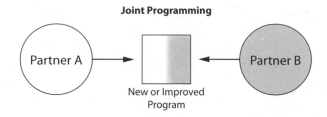

*Figure 4.1* Joint programming allows partners to benefit by reducing duplicated efforts or by leveraging complementary activities for new or expanded programs.

if this aspect of their programming were jointly developed and executed in concert.

Alternatively, this model may be used when partners work together to form new programming based on their strengths rather than combine already existing programs. This was the case in the Apollo Telemedicine example when the CSCs partnered with the VLEs to deliver Apollo's new health services.

## Affiliated Programming

Some organizations may be engaged in programming that is complementary but not as duplicative as the previous example.[51] These groups may engage in a type of joint affiliated programming, working together to develop shared projects (figure 4.2). This can be effective when there is an existing overlap in programming or the delivery of goods or services or when there is a natural hand off between groups. For example, a community youth development nonprofit and a local government job placement agency may jointly develop programming

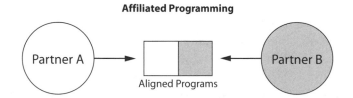

*Figure 4.2* When partners engage in affiliated programming, they maintain independent operations but coordinate activities to better accomplish their missions.

*Figure 4.3* With a joint advocacy partnership, organizations work to elevate awareness of issues of shared interest, particularly as they relate to policy changes.

for the same stakeholders at different stages in their life. Such a partnership may result in a conveyer belt approach, providing services for constituents as they age or progress through their education and training.

## Joint Advocacy

Multiple organizations may choose to work together and form a partnership for joint issue advocacy (figure 4.3).[52] This may be done when groups collaborate to raise awareness about a topic of shared importance, such as economic development in a low-income community. This type of collaboration may be a relatively short-term engagement when there is a need for concentrated visibility on a specific subject or impending policy change. For example, a hybrid-energy car manufacturer and an environmental nonprofit may work collaboratively to pass a ballot measure supporting tax incentives for purchasers of low-emission vehicles.

## Independent Spin-Off

Another form of partnership is when organizations combine resources into an entirely new, independent entity (figure 4.4).[53] This can happen when a joint programming office or a partnership for joint issue advocacy matures or grows significantly and would benefit from having its own streamlined operations. This is also true if the founding organizations cannot or do not want to take on additional activities internally, or if a joint program evolves outside of the scope of the

*Figure 4.4* Organizations may jointly form an independent entity when doing so enables them to support related or complementary activities while remaining focused on their core missions.

founding organizations' missions. For example, a foundation and a university might work jointly to raise awareness about the importance of science, technology, engineering, and mathematics (STEM) education. In this case, programming and mutually contributed staff time grow to a point where the program's mission would benefit if it were an independently operated nonprofit organization.

## Combined Administration

With a combined administrative or back office partnership, two or more organizations identify overlapping resource needs or excess capacity (figure 4.5).[54] This could include underutilized operations staff, excess office space, or access to prohibitively expensive technology or other infrastructure. These groups may come together to share resources without creating new programs or separate legal entities, and in doing so, they may benefit from reduced costs or overhead. For example, a university and a group of small companies may coinvest in advanced

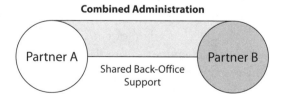

*Figure 4.5* Even when partners do not create new or expanded programming, they may benefit operationally by combining or streamlining certain administrative or back office activities.

research and laboratory equipment to support similar research and development needs. Or two nonprofits may simply decide to share backend accounting and legal services that they cannot otherwise take full advantage of independently.

## Formal Confederation

Through a formal confederation structure, a parent organization or umbrella entity provides services and support to a group of member partners (figure 4.6).[55] Although structures vary widely, member groups may pay fees or otherwise finance the operations of the coordinating organization. In return, all members receive benefits, including leveraged resources and visibility. On a global scale, the United Nations functions as a form of confederation, providing diplomatic services (among other things) to its sovereign nation-states. Alternatively, a membership organization may bring together companies, nonprofits, and foundations all working in a similar field, such as health care, and provide services to enhance knowledge sharing, workforce development, and public policy.

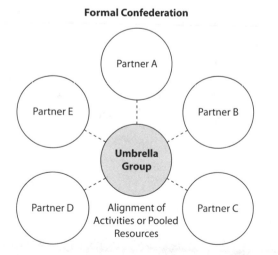

*Figure 4.6* A formal confederation enables organizations to partner directly or indirectly through a parent or umbrella group that provides collective services or benefits to members.

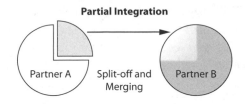

*Figure 4.7* Through a partial integration, organizations partner by merging certain programs or activities while maintaining their separate brand identities and operational independence.

## Partial Integration

Finally, two organizations may choose to partner through a partial integration, either at the organization or the program level (figure 4.7).[56] In such a case, the majority of one group's programs may be absorbed by the other partner in a way that leaves the brands of both groups intact but with a new partnership story. This can provide distinct strategic advantages to each organization while eliminating duplicity and competition. One organization may voluntarily spin out a specific program that is adopted or acquired by another organization. For example, imagine a small community-based organization that focuses mainly on preventing the spread of sexually transmitted diseases. One of the group's benefactors wills them a home to be used as a halfway house. After a year of struggling to operate the house as a new program, the organization decides to partner with a larger nonprofit that already successfully operates multiple similar facilities. The first group officially transfers ownership of the house to the new partner but continues to provide their prevention services. This is the least typical example of the types of cross-sector partnerships discussed here, but it does take place.[57]

## DEVELOPING A THEORY OF CHANGE

Once partners have established common definitions, goals, and functions, and an understanding of each other's partnering rationale, the focus shifts to the partnership's program strategy. This section will discuss two considerations for developing outcome-driven solutions across a set of diverse organizations working toward common goals.

Through our work, we have observed a surprising number of organizations that fail to adequately (or collaboratively) define each aspect of a proposed partnership's strategy or scope. Frequently used in the philanthropic or nonprofit community, a *theory of change* is a comprehensive outline and visual depiction of a desired set of outcomes.[58] Although these frameworks can vary widely depending on complexity, preference, and need, the process for developing a collaborative theory of change should begin at the end: partners must define their common goals and intended long-term societal outcomes for the engagement.[59]

As a next step, partners then work backward to map out which intermediary steps stand between the present situation and their hoped-for outcomes, often accompanied by measurable outputs from a set of activities. These activities must be defined, along with appropriate indicators, and assigned ownership responsibilities. More thorough theories of change articulate prerequisites for success, organized thematically, such as the necessity for knowledge development, policy change, or infrastructure investments. Finally, partners should create a comprehensive list of the resources and inputs required for the activities and identify which of those resources are available and which are missing among the partners. Figure 4.8 illustrates the logic flow for

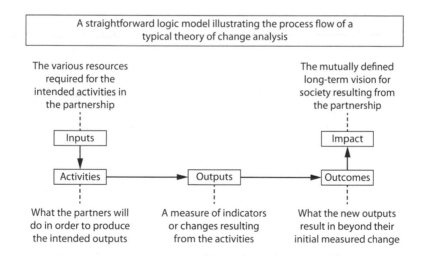

*Figure 4.8* A theory of change logic model provides partnering organizations with a planning process resulting in an overview and logic flow of inputs and activities required to reach a desired set of outcomes and impact.

a theory of change model. Although many organizations undergo a similar type of strategic planning for their individual missions, it is vital for multiorganizational partnerships to plan like this as well.[60]

In the Apollo Telemedicine case, for example, the partners undertook a fairly comprehensive planning analysis. They recognized that the partnership would be both complex and expansive and would carry a relatively high risk of failure, especially given the extensively decentralized nature of the service delivery. Building on the previous model, figure 4.9 illustrates what a simple theory of change might include in the Apollo Telemedicine case study. In practice, the logic model used by partners in cases such as Digital India are far more multifaceted and in-depth and should include a detailed time line (likely in the form of a Gantt chart) linked to the various actions and stages in the theory of change.

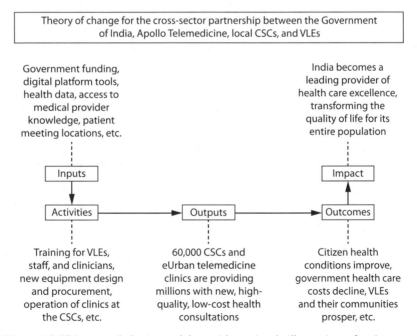

*Figure 4.9* This example logic model provides a simple illustration of various elements in a theory of change applicable to the Digital India partnership profiled in the chapter 3 case study.

Developing long-term, permanent solutions to complex challenges will not typically occur without a collaboratively developed and integrated approach that allows partners to test each other's assumptions, thoughtfully plan activities, and establish pathways to success.[61]

## COMPREHENSIVE PLANNING THROUGH VALUE CHAIN ANALYSIS

Completing a theory of change process alone is not enough to develop a comprehensive partnership strategy. As a program-focused model, it outlines resources for inputs and the various stages or steps needed to reach a given outcome. A similarly important process charts the overall system of organizations and, frequently, the flow of goods or services related to the inputs, activities, and outcomes outlined in the theory of change. This may include how various programs interact with one another, or dependencies between programs and services. It may require an understanding of different economic and contextually relevant variables in a particular place or geography and mapping of *value chains* related to the partnership's goals.

Value chain analysis was originally developed as a tool for looking at an organization's "strategically relevant activities" across supply chains and how that process ultimately brings value to customers.[62] We broaden the value chain analysis to include wider systems in which societal challenges are being addressed or a public good is being supported through a partnership. This includes the various interactions and operational functions that go into a partnership's development and the production and delivery of relevant products or services that support shared goals. Expanded definitions may include research and development, workforce training, competitive environment analysis, marketing and sales, and other industry or sector-relevant support over the long term.[63]

Many of our examples of partnerships deal with complex systems, and the pathway to system-level change may not be immediately "linear, predictable or controllable."[64] Comprehensive planning requires a thorough understanding of the context, interconnectedness, and dependencies between organizations relevant to the partnership's goals and activities.[65]

Many complex challenges in global development are sustained by similar factors: immediate resource constraints, lack of appropriate regulations, rule of law considerations, or economic market failures. Organizations themselves may be resource-constrained, focusing on single or isolated portions of a given challenge or "intervention" taking place within the context of a larger system's failure. This type of siloed approach is arguably a root cause of organizational failure or project dysfunction, and it exists across all sectors despite being a long-recognized problem.[66]

One major challenge is that few funders are excited about financing expensive and time-consuming up-front research. This can include field surveys to analyze existing activities, studies on economic and regulatory conditions, and reviews of academic literature. It also may mean conducting informed theories of change processes alongside other funders, local organizations, community members, and city or provincial governments.

This is even more challenging if past attempts at in-depth planning have failed. Partners may be reluctant to invest time and energy in this type of analysis if past work has gone unnoticed or unused. They may have produced reports that went nowhere—gathered dust on shelves, unread and unstudied. In rapidly changing environments (such as conflict zones or during immediate postdisaster recovery efforts), any kind of in-depth studies may be outdated before they are even completed.

Despite these challenges, concerted analysis must take place if a multiorganization effort, implemented over a long period of time, hopes to be successful. Many multiyear, complex initiatives require distinct research and planning phases, beginning with problem definitions and the identification of root causes.[67] This kind of early analysis is even more important in underdeveloped geographic areas because a systems analysis may challenge partners' assumptions and provide unexpected insights. Furthermore, a single break in a value chain can disrupt an entire collaboration's efforts. Not addressing gaps identified in this analysis means that resources invested upstream or downstream of that disruption might fail to have a sustained impact.[68]

For example, consider a three-year rural development project in a poor country with an agrarian economy. The project hopes to improve smallholder farmer productivity, with an end goal of increasing a farmer's crop output, thereby increasing income and improving the farmer's livelihood.[69] In this example, a donor aid program (run by an NGO) receives funding to provide new seeds and fertilizer to a group of fifty farmers and provides them with technical assistance and advice. In this example project, the farmers see a nearly instantaneous increase in yields, and the donor agency deploys vehicles and staff to help transport that season's bumper crop to regional markets and food processors. The farmers produce more, sell more, make more money, and invest in their families' livelihoods. For example, farmers may purchase livestock to produce additional products and diversify their revenue streams.

Figure 4.10 outlines a simple generic version of an agricultural-based value chain, including the example activities of the NGO donor aid program.

Based on the goals of this isolated program, they will achieve success for the fifty farmers and their families. The implementer will likely write a report for its funder reflecting the program's accomplishments and lessons learned, and they will consider their project complete. But some obvious questions arise:

- What happens in the fourth year when the NGO program ends and new seeds and fertilizer stop coming?

- Even if farmers have another plentiful crop, how will they transport it to market without the NGO vehicles or staff support?

- What happens if the farmers do not produce enough extra crop to feed their livestock, or the livestock get sick?

- What if a new monetization program starts nearby and destroys local sales prices for the farmers?

Questions such as these arose during partnership development for our Afghanistan case study later in the book. In chapter 7, you will see this type of value chain analysis in practice.

It is challenging to have a permanent and lasting effect when working in difficult operating environments. Furthermore, organizations

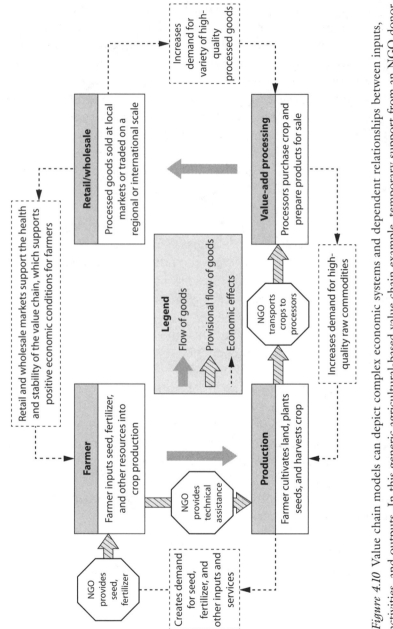

*Figure 4.10* Value chain models can depict complex economic systems and dependent relationships between inputs, activities, and outputs. In this generic agricultural-based value chain example, temporary support from an NGO donor aid program illustrates the problematic nature of short-term solutions when long-term, system enabling investments are required.

working in isolation cannot face the challenges that require a systems scale solution, especially if there is not an entire economic support system in place to pick up when aid money runs out.[70] Long-term solutions cannot fail to address market linkages, resource waste, labor shortages, contract enforcement, disaster mitigation, and a host of other potential roadblocks.

Planning with a comprehensive approach in mind may sound like common sense, and it is certainly nothing new, but many programs suffer without systems thinking or fail to address gaps in the value chain—especially when those gaps fall outside their core funding or programmatic areas.[71] Hence, planning and analysis are important components in the social value investing approach.

## OVERCOMING OBSTACLES

Engaging in effective partnership development is difficult work, and it presents numerous challenges.[72] Leaders of some organizations simply do not understand the potential benefits to partnering or value what may come of the work. Some leaders or administrators may be indifferent. In many cases, an organization simply lacks the resources or human capacity required to meaningfully engage in partnership development. Or they may not have the mandate to do so from their funders or a parent organization. Some groups will have tried before and failed, and others lose interest when attempting new partnerships. Building out long-term, cross-sector collaborations is complex and time consuming. Ensuring that partners begin with a similar understanding of the intended objectives through a collaborative design process is an early prerequisite for success. Incentives and motivations for stakeholders within a partnership can be very different; aligning these is not easy and should be addressed as early as possible in the collaborative process.

Public, private, and philanthropic organizations working to develop a comprehensive partnership strategy must survey the complete value chain of a given industry or set of objectives in a given place and combine this analysis with appropriate logic models to cover critical enabling factors needed for sustained positive impact. Such planning allows partners to chart the interdependent web of organizations required to work together for an entire ecosystem of solutions to flourish.[73]

In the case study in chapter 3, we described collaborative efforts to modernize the way the government of India delivers social services to the poor. We described how a diverse set of partners, coordinating their efforts throughout the value chain of health care services, could unlock intrinsic value worth more than the sum of their individual and isolated activities. We believe these types of strategic, comprehensive partnerships can bring about new and important emergent processes that are critical for success—and for solving many of our world's most persistent and pressing problems.

# *PEOPLE*

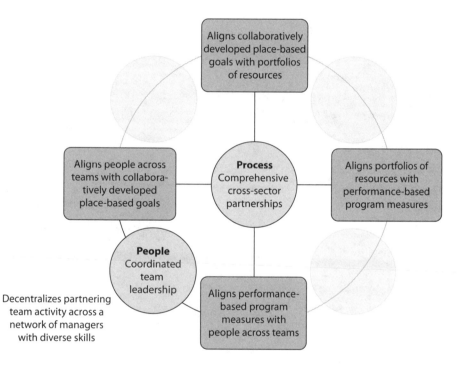

Aligns collaboratively developed place-based goals with portfolios of resources

Aligns portfolios of resources with performance-based program measures

Aligns people across teams with collaboratively developed place-based goals

**Process**
Comprehensive cross-sector partnerships

**People**
Coordinated team leadership

Decentralizes partnering team activity across a network of managers with diverse skills

Aligns performance-based program measures with people across teams

# CHAPTER FIVE

# The People Case

## Improving Big City Life
## Through Urban Parks

WILLIAM B. EIMICKE

We began this book with the story of Central Park and the High Line because they so dramatically and visually demonstrate how cross-sector partnerships can achieve amazing results simply not possible under a more traditional single sector, hierarchical, organizational structure. These stories demonstrate the power of partnerships led by *people* with collaborative leadership skills. Were it not for a handful of committed, experienced, and focused leaders, Central Park and the High Line might still be dangerous eyesores, as they both were not so long ago. In each case, a nonprofit organization formed to rescue or create these iconic parks. In partnership with New York City government and businesses and community organizations, the Central Park Conservancy (CPC) and Friends of the High Line operate and maintain these public spaces primarily with their own funds and free of admission charges to visitors. As important, and mirroring many elements of the social value investing framework, these two partnerships have led to a new way to create, rehabilitate, and operate public parks that can be replicated in cities across the United States and around the world.

In chapter 3, we saw effective partnership processes operating through Digital India and Apollo Telemedicine. These partnerships succeeded under the strong, collaborative leadership of the Modi administration in partnership with India's major technology companies, the global Apollo health care organizations, and local entrepreneurs. In this chapter, we look at how Gordon Davis of the New York City Parks Department and Betsy Rogers of the fledgling Central

Park Conservancy built a partnership, slowly and methodically over time, through motivational leadership and a relentless commitment to a shared vision. Later, under the collaborative leadership of Doug Blonsky, the Central Park Conservancy implemented an innovative Zone Management System and more effective ways to manage turf, care for trees and plants, remove trash, and reuse biowaste. Applying many aspects of the social value investing framework—a formal partnership structure, mutual operations, and a comprehensive strategy—the decentralized zone park maintenance system is operated by forty-nine diverse teams across Central Park, each with the necessary experience, skills, and autonomy. In addition, CPC created a subsidiary education and training institute to help its partner, the New York City Parks Department, successfully apply these innovative techniques in dozens of parks run directly by city employees.

Comparable to CPC is the success of the High Line, which is largely attributable to another decentralized team approach implemented by an equally extraordinary, collaborative, but somewhat different style of leadership. Joshua David and Robert Hammond came from the community and formed the nonprofit Friends of the High Line to preserve and reuse what they perceived as a potential community asset. David and Hammond also sought the broadest possible public participation and acted as community advocates throughout the partnership (in line with the place element of social value investing, which is discussed in chapters 7 and 8). They also recruited John Alschuler, a nationally recognized real estate expert and consultant, to help define and quantify measurable indictors of success. Using the CPC as a model, they developed a portfolio of funding, securing risk capital from a number of high-profile philanthropists and working closely with influential and powerful members of New York City Mayor Michael Bloomberg's team, including Amanda Burden, chair of the City Planning Commission, first deputy mayor Patricia E. Harris, deputy mayor of economic development Dan Doctoroff, and parks commissioner Adrian Benepe. The city leaders brought the power of zoning, substantial capital dollars, political expertise, and parks knowledge. The Friends of the High Line brought the vision, the community support, philanthropic dollars, and the willingness to sustain the project over the long haul.

Both the Central Park restoration and creation of the High Line were made possible by effective cross-sector partnerships led by collaborative leaders who were in touch with their team's needs and motivations. These leaders clearly and mutually established measurable indicators (by freely sharing data and information between organizations) and defined success around their shared goals. It is important to recognize that in both cases these organizations do much more than raise a great deal of money for the maintenance and operations of the parks. They run the parks with their own staff and equipment, using innovative management techniques developed with their partners, and they have subsequently helped the City Parks Department apply these techniques widely.

## THE QUINTESSENTIAL NINETEENTH-CENTURY PARK

Most people flying into New York City over Manhattan are amazed by the size of the green space in the heart of the most densely populated city in the United States, a city often referred to as the City of Skyscrapers. Central Park is huge for an urban park: 843 acres, 2.5 miles long, and half a mile wide. It stretches from 59th Street—bookended by Columbus Circle on one side and the Plaza Hotel on Fifth Avenue on the other—all the way up to 110th Street in Morningside Heights, just south of Columbia University and Harlem. It is open every day of the year from 6:00 AM to 1:00 AM.[1]

Central Park was designed in 1858 by Frederick Law Olmsted, its superintendent of construction, and English architect Calvert Vaux. The site was set aside for a public park by the government, and Olmsted and Vaux were chosen to design it through an open competition. Built out to its current dimensions in 1873, the original land area is largely intact to this day.[2] In addition to the trees and open green spaces, the architects designed footpaths, bridle paths for horses, and carriage paths, along with four sunken transverse roads, enabling cars to pass through the park without disruption. Most of the park is relatively free of cars and buses to this day.[3]

The uses of the park have changed somewhat over the past 150 years to reflect "the most important values held by the society of the day."[4] Built as a quintessential nineteenth-century park for peaceful thought and joyful celebration of nature, in the twentieth century the park dramatically expanded recreational opportunities, including more than twenty playgrounds for children, skating rinks, a swimming pool, tennis courts, and ball fields. Today the park is an important component of urban infrastructure. It serves as a major tourist attraction, a place for cycling and jogging, and as the backyard and "view" for some of the world's most valuable residential properties. These views help generate hundreds of millions of dollars in taxes for the city government, as well as tax revenue from visitors coming from all over the world.

## CYCLE OF DECLINE AND RESTORATION

Great vision and tremendous effort made Central Park possible. Maintaining and protecting it from politics, opportunism, progress, and underfunding over its entire history has proven equally difficult. Olmsted applied for the position of superintendent of Central Park in 1857 and was hired by a park board appointed by a Democratic administration and run by a corrupt political machine widely known as Tammany Hall.[5] Nominally a Republican, Olmsted was highly qualified for the job, and the board viewed the appointment as an opportunity to satisfy Republican demands for a share of the patronage controlled by Tammany Hall.[6] It was Olmstead's visionary and inspirational leadership, professional expertise, and ability to navigate the politics of the board and the city government that enabled him to keep the park in good condition for as long as he did.

Olmsted sought to manage the park professionally, but he was constantly caught in the crosscurrents of New York City and New York State politics. Between 1870 and 1883 he was forced out, reinstated, resigned, came back in a lower position, was let go, and was retained as a consultant. Finally, in 1883, he relocated to Boston and worked on building their park system.[7] The permanent departure of Olmsted and the death of Calvert Vaux in 1895 marked the beginning of a slow but steady decline in the condition of Central Park.[8]

Under the control of Tammany Hall, the city parks became "fiefs for private gain."[9] As a result, the parks, including Central Park, became "scabs on the face of the city."[10] Between 1900 and 1934, the park's great lawns turned to weeds, then to dirt and mud holes when it rained. The paths and walkways were littered and broken. Buildings, fountains, statues, and walls were filled with graffiti, vandalized, and, in many cases, literally were falling down. The city park workers "complemented the scenery" with their appearance.[11] The condition of the park worsened with the onset of the Great Depression when homeless men constructed and lived in more than two hundred shacks behind the Metropolitan Museum of Art.[12]

The depression era also marked the beginning of the restoration of Central Park, with significant assistance from New York State and the federal government. In 1933, Fiorello H. La Guardia, a reformer and liberal Republican running on the Fusion ticket, was elected in a three-way race with only 40 percent of the vote. According to historian Robert A. Caro, it was the last minute but passionate endorsement by the widely-known and influential Robert Moses that put La Guardia over the top. In return, La Guardia supported state legislation drafted by Moses that consolidated the city's five borough parks departments into a citywide department and enabled Moses to simultaneously hold the positions of state and city parks commissioner as well as several other commissions and authorities concerned with parks and roads.[13] Moses pulled together important financial support to accomplish the parks restorations and engaged numerous federal, state, and local agencies to get the necessary work done. He was a strong leader but hardly a collaborative one, as his many very public battles and reputation attest.

On January 19, 1934, Moses became New York City Parks Commissioner, and he began what would be twenty-six years of restoration and innovation for Central Park. Between 1934 and 1938, he used federal Civil Works Administration (CWA) and Works Progress Administration (WPA) dollars to fund architects, engineers, and thousands of laborers working in three shifts, 24/7, through even the most severe winter weather, to bring Central Park back to its former beauty.[14] He planted trees, flowers, and bushes; fixed roads and bridges; restored paths and modernized playgrounds, ball fields, and the landscape of the "Great Lawn"—he even reinvented the Central Park Zoo. Moses was often hailed in the press for these achievements—"dynamic," "brilliant," "Moses' New Deal for Parks," "Moses made an urban desert bloom"—and by the general public as well.[15]

Moses is sometimes criticized for changing the original look of the park, replacing many of the original materials with red brick. Some of his new structures blocked important views designed by Olmsted and Vaux.[16] On the positive side, Moses restored Central Park and ushered in an era of professional management and maintenance. He also initiated a wide range of free entertainment and programs for children and their families, including a Winter Carnival, dance competitions, puppet shows, an entire children's district (including a musical clock, the zoo, sculptures, the boat house, and concessions), and the very popular Shakespeare in the Park produced by Joseph Papp.[17] Ironically, it was a very public battle with Papp over the future of Shakespeare in the Park that contributed to the end of the Moses era in Central Park.[18]

Moses resigned as City Parks Commissioner on May 23, 1960, to accept the presidency of the 1964–65 World's Fair in Queens, New York.[19] Many of Moses's hires remained in the Parks Department, and Moses himself continued to exercise some behind the scenes influence, but his departure marked the beginning of nearly two decades of severe decline in infrastructure, cleanliness, and safety in the park.

The social movements and upheavals of the 1960s and 1970s often used the park as a site for gathering and demonstration. Lax management permitted heavy use of high-impact sports, with and without permits. Lawns were turned to dust and mud, and clogged catch basins resulted in frequent flooding of open spaces, paths, and walkways.[20] The simultaneous decline of New York City's fiscal health was unfolding—the city nearly went bankrupt in 1975, and local tabloid headlines announced that then President Ford told New York it could drop dead.[21] The loss of the city's manufacturing industry to the lower-cost southern states and the massive exodus of the city's middle class (over highways and bridges built by Robert Moses's public authorities), combined with a national recession, put the city budget in severe imbalance. Banks cut off the city's credit and, ultimately, a financial control board and state assistance were put in place. The price for the city was severe, and budget cuts resulted in the loss of 6,000 police officers, 6,000 teachers, and 2,500 firefighters.[22]

The consequences for parks in general and Central Park in particular also were severe. The City Board of Estimate had approved a $7 million Central Park rehabilitation fund, but newly elected Mayor Abraham D. Beame chose to use that fund for other parks around the city. Shortly thereafter, in 1975, the fiscal crisis put all parks restoration projects on hold.[23] For Central Park, this led to vandalism, graffiti, piling up of garbage, and deferred maintenance.[24]

Broken benches, playground equipment, and lights that were never fixed created an environment that invited crime, as is often described in the broken windows theory of policing.[25] As recent Central Park Administrator and Central Park Conservancy President and CEO Doug Blonsky described the situation, "the bridle path had more rats than people, the Great Lawn had become the Great Dustbowl, Turtle Pond was filled with the stink of dead fish, and the Castle was covered in graffiti, surrounded by razor wire, and inaccessible to the public."[26] Central Park became so dilapidated (figure 5.1)

*Figure 5.1 (a):* Belvedere Castle with graffiti before its renovation in 1984; (*b*) the dilapidated Great Lawn. These images illustrate conditions in the park before the partnership between the New York City Parks Department and the Central Park Conservancy. Photos by Sara Cedar Miller, courtesy of CPC.

that major feature films including *Annie Hall* and *Six Degrees of Separation* used it as a symbol of New York City's physical decline and dangerously high crime rate.

Despite the city's ever-worsening fiscal condition, the New York City Parks Department workforce swelled to more than three hundred on the government payroll assigned to Central Park. Without a leader with the strength, dedication, and command of Olmsted, Moses, or Blonsky, and without performance measures to hold those workers accountable, the parks continued to decline.[27] Perhaps the low point in the history of Central Park was the beating and rape of Trisha Meili—known as the Central Park Jogger case—which filled the world's tabloid headlines in the spring of 1989.[28]

For many outsiders, Central Park is a very visible symbol and a barometer of the state of the city, and in the 1980s and early 1990s New York City was a very dangerous place. In 1990, 2,245 people were killed in New York City, an all-time record and up 17.8 percent from 1989. Then police commissioner Lee Brown blamed the absolutely frightening totals on drugs and guns.[29] To put this in perspective, 2015 was a year in which murders spiked nationwide: New York City had 352 murders, and Chicago, with a third of the population of New York City, led U.S. cities with 488 murders. Today the media often represents Chicago as a very dangerous city, which gives you a sense of how really unsafe it was in New York City in 1990.[30]

These tragedies created fear across the city and around the nation. Central Park is located in the heart of Manhattan, easily accessible to residents, commuters, and tourists alike.[31] Because of its beautiful, pastoral setting in midtown Manhattan, some of the most expensive and exclusive high-rise residences, hotels, and office buildings surround its perimeter. This location and its influential neighbors made the sad and dangerous state of Central Park in the 1970s and 1980s a very visible, much discussed, and very troubling state of affairs.

The wealthy occupants and owners of the buildings surrounding the park view Central Park as their backyard—and its condition has a material impact on their quality of life and the value of their substantial real estate investments. The danger and violence in Central Park was danger and violence in their backyard, the backyard of the "rich and famous." To combat the decline, several voluntary organizations and friends of the park groups formed to try to restore the park to its former glory.[32]

# PARTNERING TO BRING THE
# PARK BACK

One such group, the Central Park Community Fund, led by two wealthy financiers, George Soros and Richard Gilder, commissioned a study of the park's management in 1974. Published in 1976, it became known as the Savas Report, after its author, then Columbia Business School professor E. S. Savas (who subsequently became well-known as one of the intellectual forces behind the privatization movement).[33] The report made three major recommendations: first, create a Chief Executive Officer for Central Park (and the city's other flagship parks) with full responsibility for parks operation (which emphasized collaborative leadership); second, establish a Central Park Board of Guardians responsible for developing a strategic plan (or comprehensive strategy) for the park and for ensuring its implementation; and, third, promote civic engagement (and community ownership) through the planning process, including private fund-raising to realize the strategic plan.[34]

In 1978, newly elected New York City mayor Edward I. Koch was rightly focused on restoring the city's fiscal health: balancing the budget and establishing a sustainable, long-term fiscal plan while keeping the city livable and thereby growing its economy. His mantra to the agency commissioners he appointed was the same, repeated ad nauseam: "Do more with less!"[35] To head the Department of Parks and Recreation, Koch chose Gordon Davis (figure 5.2), a Harvard-educated attorney with prior New York City government experience under former mayor John Lindsay.

Gordon's response to Koch's "Doing more with less" was, "Give me a break!"[36] What Commissioner Davis meant was that funding for parks had already been cut dramatically. The Parks Department staff was down from 8,000 during the Moses years to 2,500 in 1978, so there would be few savings and much potential danger in further cuts. Davis instead developed a multidimensional strategy founded on decentralization, collaboration, and partnerships, very much in line with our social value investing model.[37]

Internally, Davis advanced a decentralized team approach for managing the city's parks by creating the new position of Borough Parks Commissioner, who acted as a chief executive for all of the parks

*Figure 5.2* New York City Parks Commissioner Gordon Davis (appointed in 1978) recruited Central Park's first Administrator, Betsy (Barlow) Rogers. The two led the park's revitalization by establishing the Central Park Conservancy partnership. Photo courtesy of CPC.

in each of the city's five boroughs (otherwise known as counties). He also appointed an administrator for each large park, which proved to be critical to the future of Central Park. To deal with the staffing crisis, Davis leveraged complementary federal Comprehensive Employment and Training Act (CETA) funds to create new parks jobs that were paid entirely by CETA for the first eighteen months for positions qualifying for federal job training funds under the act.

He also worked with the mayor's office to obtain authorization for a new job classification, Urban Park Ranger, which was outside the department's existing civil service titles and enabled Davis to bring in young, well-educated, dedicated individuals with management skills and a customer service attitude. New uniforms and young, friendly professionals as a visible presence in parks, particularly in Central Park, helped project the reality that things were getting better.[38] One of those rangers, Adrian Benepe, later became the Commissioner of Parks and Recreation under Mayor Michael Bloomberg. This parallel structure to the traditional Parks Department organization and staffing would continue to expand as the management of Central Park shifted from direct city operation to the cross-sector partnership that runs it today.

## BETSY ROGERS AND THE CONSERVANCY

Perhaps the important innovation of Commissioner Davis was his decision to hire Elizabeth "Betsy" (then Barlow) Rogers—a young Yale educated urban planner, writer, and Olmsted expert—as the first Central Park Administrator in 1979. Prior to her appointment, she was the director of the Central Park Task Force's program for summer youth interns, which worked closely with the Parks Department.

As administrator, Rogers was directly responsible for all aspects of the daily operations, exactly what the Savas Report recommended. Upon taking the job, Rogers asked some logical questions: Where is my office? What's the budget? And what are my responsibilities? Davis told her that he didn't know if there was an office, there was no budget, and they would figure out her responsibilities as they went along.[39]

A self-described "zealous nut" about the importance of Central Park to the future of New York City, Rogers (figure 5.3) loved the mission of restoring the park to its former greatness.[40] It was Rogers (with full support from Commissioner Davis) who developed the

*Figure 5.3* Betsy (Barlow) Rogers, the first Central Park Administrator and first President and CEO of the Central Park Conservancy (positions she held simultaneously). Photo courtesy of CPC.

vision of a cross-sector partnership to restore and maintain Central Park primarily with private dollars. She acquired and used a small gift from the Vincent Astor Foundation to hire a horticulturist, summer interns with some horticulture training, and an environmentalist, and she completed several small but visible restorations to show the public and potential donors that Central Park was on the way back.[41] From the very beginning, Rogers used a collaborative leadership approach as she brought together the city administration, the Parks Department, outside funders, community leaders, and volunteers with a passion to help restore Central Park.

A year later, Rogers became president of the newly created Central Park Conservancy, merging two existing and important advocacy groups: the Central Park Task Force and the Central Park Community Fund (an organization similar to what the Savas Report recommended). Rogers masterfully leveraged private donations to add to city tax dollars to help the government run the park; she continued on as Central Park Administrator while simultaneously serving as president of CPC. Some advocates suggested she couldn't criticize the city when necessary and appropriate if she also sat on their side of the table. Her response, "I don't want to be critical. I want to work with the city."[42] In that spirit, Mayor Ed Koch assured the Conservancy that he would not reduce the city's financial commitment to Central Park as more private dollars were raised and contributed to the Park from CPC. By sharing success in this way, the CPC built credibility with donors, knowing that their gifts would accelerate the park's restoration, not just provide general budget relief to the still-stressed New York City finances.

Initially, the city government provided virtually all of Central Park's operating funds, and the Conservancy—which had fewer than thirty employees as late as 1985—focused on funding the design and preparation of major shovel-ready capital projects such as the restoration and renovation of the Sheep's Meadow, the Dairy, the Cherry Hill foundations, and Belvedere Castle.[43] The team knew they needed a big, visible success early on to show there was reason to believe the park could be rescued, and Davis wanted Sheep's Meadow to be that symbol. This project, however, cost well beyond an amount they could dream of raising at the time. It just so happened that New York City governor Hugh Carey was also looking for a highly visible project to signal hope for the city's future. To Davis's surprise, Carey also settled on Sheep's Meadow and secured state funds for the restoration.[44]

Commissioner Davis and Administrator Rogers recognized from the beginning that they were forming a cross-sector partnership that could transform Central Park for decades to come. They also recognized that there were great risks: conflicts between the two workforces, significant differences over priorities and policies, and real and perceived issues regarding private entities having any kind of control over public spaces, particularly such an important public space as Central Park. Partnerships, even more traditional PPPs, were somewhat uncommon in the United States at the time and virtually unheard of for the operation of large public parks, so Davis and Rogers kept the relationship as informal as possible, "No lease . . . no license agreement."[45] Although they consistently acted as collaborative leaders with complementary yet diverse teams, they delayed formalizing the partnership until they had achieved sufficiently broad public participation and support.

Rogers also trod lightly on issues regarding location of the two groups of workers, differences in training, and equipment. She found many of the civil service workers poorly trained and unmotivated, and there was resentment. As Rogers recalled, initially the Conservancy workers were not welcome in the City Parks building and were forced to use a small pesticide shed as their "headquarters."[46] Rogers preferred to hire new workers through the CPC, without civil service red tape and negotiations with citywide public employee unions. Nevertheless, she worked hard to maintain integrity and respect; and over time, the two workforces came together.

## CPC AND BLONSKY TAKE THE LEAD

Doug Blonsky, a landscape architect, joined the Conservancy's Capital Projects office in 1985. His technical expertise and passion for being hands-on in the field, along with his coordinating skills, propelled him up the organization's management ladder—from supervising construction projects to chief of operations, then to Betsy Roger's title of Central Park Administrator. His intimate knowledge of park management and maintenance provided him with critical leadership skills for success. Since 2004, he also has held the title of president of the Conservancy and CEO, responsible not only for the park's management and operations but also for fund-raising.

Like Rogers, Blonsky supervised both Conservancy and City Parks Department staff. It is a real challenge to create diverse teams of workers from two very different cultures and to establish a unified set of standard operating procedures, job descriptions, and roles and responsibilities. By listening, learning, and then leading, Blonsky established a common culture of professionalism and innovation that characterizes the CPC-Parks Department combined staff to this day.

Blonsky implemented a comprehensive management strategy (an important partnership process) at CPC called Zone Management, which divides the park into forty-nine geographic zones for managerial purposes. Each zone is headed by a zone gardener, who supervises grounds technicians and volunteers. Each is held accountable for his or her area, according to maintenance standards set out in a management and restoration plan. Throughout the late 1980s and early 1990s, the Conservancy used strategic planning and measurable performance indicators and accountability to define success. They also used ongoing fund-raising to eventually create a formal partnership with the City Parks Department. As Blonsky commented,

> We were very good at having projects truly shovel-ready and prepared. We would do the designs, have the plans complete, and then at the end of the fiscal year, City Hall would go to the Parks Department and say, "We have this pot of money, do you have any projects ready to go?" We did, and it became a really great way for us to get City money invested into the park, leveraged by the private dollars we used for the designs and plans.[47]

In 1987, the Conservancy launched its first capital campaign, which raised $50 million. Although significant improvements in the park had been achieved throughout the 1980s, an economic slowdown in the city economy led to major cuts in Parks Department staff and maintenance. There were delays in capital projects, and it became more difficult to raise private donations. In 1990, Rogers said, "These are the hardest times we've seen in 10 years. The Great Lawn is a dust bowl [again] and the pond is almost completely silted up."[48]

In response, Richard Gilder created a challenge grant in 1993 to support the Conservancy and the city in their second "The Wonder of New York Campaign." That campaign reached its goal of $51 million—$17 million from Gilder, $17 million from the city, and $17 million raised by CPC from other donors. From this point forward, the Conservancy would provide at least two-thirds of the capital budget for the park and an ever-larger share of the operating budget and staff.[49]

Although crime in the city continued to rise until 1990, the work of the Conservancy in beginning to reclaim and rebuild Central Park provided a very visible symbol of hope for the city overall. Then mayor David Dinkins secured state funding to significantly increase the number of NYPD police on patrol through his "Safe Streets, Safe City" initiative. In 1994, NYPD Commissioner Bill Bratton's CompStat innovation (see chapter 11) started to significantly reduce crime and restore the quality of life in what would become the safest big city in the Americas. In many respects, CPC's work in Central Park and the NYPD's work on the city streets were mutually reinforcing efforts to make New York City livable again.

The collaboration between CPC and New York City became a formal, structured partnership in a contract signed in 1998. Under the eight-year agreement, the Conservancy, led by Central Park Administrator Doug Blonsky and CPC Chair Ira Millstein, reported to the Parks Department Commissioner Henry Stern under then mayor Rudolph Giuliani. The city would contribute up to $4 million annually (it averaged $3.7 million over the term of the contract), up from about $3 million under the informal relationship. In return, the CPC would take full responsibility for operation and maintenance of the park, including operating expenses in excess of the city's contribution, and nearly all capital costs would come from CPC fund-raising.[50] Blonsky was okay with the deal because he really thought of the park's budget as one big pot. CPC did not own the assets. For him, creating and maintaining a great park was a combination of capital restoration and maintenance, cutting the grass, pruning the trees and bushes, a lot of picking up of garbage, security, and customer service. To Blonsky it was one big job with one big budget.

Even back then, some were concerned that CPC's reliance on (and success at) fund-raising would drain public and private resources from the rest of the parks in the system. Those concerns persist today, but the true sharing of success and the smooth operation of the partnership continues to attract much more praise and support than criticism. From the city side, as NYC Parks Deputy Commissioner Robert Garafola said, the city still owns and controls the park. They have a contract with CPC to run the park, and the Parks Department ensures contract compliance and mutual operations.[51]

CPC and the New York City renewed the contract to operate Central Park in 2006 for a second eight years, and in 2013 for a third eight years, for what will be twenty-four years of formal partnership and nineteen years of informal collaboration (1979–1998). By 2017, CPC provided approximately 75 percent of Central Park's $67 million annual operating budget. Since 1980, CPC has invested $950 million in the park.[52]

## MAKING SURE THE IMPROVEMENTS ARE SUSTAINABLE

CPC leadership stressed a long-term strategic approach from day one. A 1985 report commissioned by the CPC, "Rebuilding Central Park: A Management and Restoration Plan" became the foundation of a comprehensive strategy to revitalize and maintain Central Park. That strategic approach, combined with project-by-project success and superior ongoing maintenance, encouraged more and more private donors, foundations, and corporations to invest in rebuilding and restoring Central Park (figure 5.4).

Following the first two campaigns in 1987 and 1993, the Conservancy launched its third one, the Campaign for Central Park. That campaign concluded in 2008, raising $120 million, which enabled CPC to fund the continuing implementation of the 1985 restoration plan.[53] In addition, the Conservancy created an endowment that it is hoped will permanently end the history of cyclical decline and restoration.[54] On October 23, 2012, John A. Paulson (a hedge fund manager) announced a $100 million gift to the Central Park Conservancy, the largest donation in the history of the city's park system. Half of the gift went to long-term operating support and the other half to capital improvements.[55]

In the summer of 2016, CPC announced an ambitious ten-year, $300 million plan, "Forever Green: Ensuring the Future of Central Park."[56] The new campaign will help fill the ongoing and growing need for maintenance in a huge park that also now has the challenging reality of over forty million visitors, often 250,000 in a single day. Among the projects to be funded from the new campaign are

*Figure 5.4* The Great Lawn (*a*; photo by Sara Cedar Miller) and the Belvedere Castle (*b*; photo courtesy of CPC), have been fully restored due to the success and sustainable operations of the partnership between New York City Parks and the Central Park Conservancy.

restoration of Belvedere Castle, dredging and repairing the Ravine in the North Woods, replacing and revitalizing much of the Naumburg Bandshell, restoring the badly deteriorating Dairy, and many other pressing infrastructure needs such as upgrading the irrigation and drainage systems. Less than a year into the campaign, the goal was raised to $500 million, with approximately $300 million planned for capital projects and $200 million for operating support and the endowment. By design, the capital budget schedule can be accelerated or stretched out, depending on the size of the endowment and the demands of the operating budget.[57]

## HELPING OTHER PARKS AROUND THE CITY AND AROUND THE WORLD

Over the past several years, CPC created and expanded a new program, the Institute for Urban Parks, to share the knowledge and tools developed over nearly forty years of restoring and maintaining Central Park. The institute educates and trains urban park users and managers on how to care for urban parks in New York City, across the United States, and around the world, through more than a dozen management seminars and webinars annually. The institute also develops educational programming and experiences for children and their families on the importance of urban parks, how ecosystems work, and how to become responsible users and urban park stewards.[58]

Additionally, the institute offers apprenticeships, internships, and fellowships to aspiring park managers. Consulting services, including detailed manuals and training sessions on trash management and recycling and turf management, are given to park managers and workers throughout the city and across the region. The Conservancy's Five Borough Crew program supports fifteen city park sites around New York City, including direct services, training programs, and management plans. In 2014 alone, the Conservancy spent more than $2.6 million in services to other parks.[59]

In 2015, CPC's Institute for Urban Parks began working with students and faculty from Columbia University's School of International and Public Affairs and Columbia's Earth Institute to pilot a Certified Urban Park Manager (CUPM) education, training, examination, and certification program. Three successive capstone classes worked on building out the pilot program, and in the spring of 2016 CPC committed to launch a pilot test class for certification during 2017–18.[60]

In June 2016, the CPC and Forest Park Forever of St. Louis hosted a National Forum on Urban Park Sustainability and Public-Private Partnerships in New York City. Seven conservancies, one alliance, and a foundation came together to explore how they could work collectively to protect and improve their own parks over future generations and to share their learning with public and private urban park managers.

## REDEFINING SUCCESS FOR NEARLY FOUR DECADES

Since 1979, the New York City Department of Parks and Recreation and the Central Park Conservancy have partnered to rescue, restore, and enhance Central Park for the people of New York City and millions of visitors from all over the world. In 1978, Gordon Davis took over as Parks Commissioner when he and Betsy Rogers were perhaps the only people who could envision what we enjoy today. Working together as visionary, coordinated, and collaborative leaders, Rogers and Davis forged what has become a model for outstanding cross-sector partnerships like those profiled and analyzed in this book.

The success of the partnership goes beyond the boundaries of Central Park. The city's economy stimulates restoration of the park every day, and the benefits are much greater than those generated by the spending of tourists visiting the park during their stays. A 2007 study found that the revitalized Central Park added $17.7 billion to property values around the park, an 18 percent premium, or about 8.1 percent of the total property value for all of Manhattan.[61] Estimates of annual economic activity and revenues generated for the city by Central Park exceed $1 billion.[62] By 2015, an updated economic impact study estimated that Central Park had added $26 billion to property values around the park, and the taxes and fees paid to New York City government attributable to the Conservancy and related Central Park enterprises totaled more than $1.4 billion for 2014 alone. The Conservancy itself employs over 450 with a payroll of $21.4 million.[63]

CPC and the revitalized Central Park do much more than generate additional taxes and increase property values in the area, as important as that is to New Yorkers. In 2014, the 41.8 million visitors to the park included 8.3 million from outside the United States and 13.7 million from outside the metropolitan region, supporting nearly 1,900 full-time job equivalents and over $200 million in economic output. As important, New York City residents made approximately 27 million visits to Central Park in 2014 for exercise, recreation, cultural, and entertainment activities, and the quiet appreciation of nature.[64]

Today Central Park is treasured by everyone, a space that is both a respite from the city that never sleeps and a free and open space enjoyed by many from around the world. Despite the heavy use, the Conservancy's zero tolerance for both garbage and graffiti has changed the way people behave in the park. In the words of the Conservancy, "the American ideal of a great public park and its importance as a place to model and shape public behavior and enhance the quality of life for all its citizens once again defines the measurement of a great municipality."[65]

Through the efforts of the Institute for Urban Parks, CPC is sharing its recipes for success with parks departments, conservancies, and aspiring parks professionals and volunteers from all over the world.[66]

## THE HIGH LINE

Just across town and a few blocks south "a pair of nobodies . . . undertook [an] impossible mission":[67] use the Central Park Conservancy playbook to create a new urban park atop an abandoned elevated railroad track in what was then a rough neighborhood on Manhattan's West Side (figure 5.5). A few years later there is now a public park known as the High Line, free and open to all. Already visited by millions from around the city and around the world, the High Line is a partnership between the New York City government and the Friends of the High Line. Similar to Central Park, the High Line is operated by the Friends of the High Line and most of the operating funds come from private donations.

The West Side Line was once a very active commercial railroad line on the west side of Manhattan, serving the factories, meatpacking, dairy, and food stuffs businesses in the area. Western Electric built

*Figure 5.5* The High Line as an active rail line in the 1930's (*a*; photo by Fred Doyle); and abandoned and overgrown in the 1980's (*b*). Photo courtesy of Friends of the Highline.

telephones beside the rail lines, and later Bell Telephone Laboratories conducted research there until 1966, when they moved to New Jersey. As trucks replaced rail as the primary distribution method in the 1950s and 1960s, traffic on the West Line declined precipitously. By 1960, the southernmost section of the West Line was demolished. In 1980, Conrail ceased using the remaining half of the line.[68]

During the 1970s, an attempt to reuse the line for passenger rail failed, and support for demolition of the elevated rail structure grew. At the same time, residents in the neighborhood started to become interested in the wild natural "garden" growing along the line. By 1999, the New York City government was ready to sign off on the demolition of the elevated tracks running from Gansevoort Street north to the 34th Street rail yards through Chelsea and the West Village.

A group of neighborhood residents, preservationists, naturalists, and artists had another idea. Led by residents Joshua David, a freelance magazine writer and editor, and Robert Hammond, who worked for a variety of entrepreneurial start-ups, they formed a nonprofit organization called Friends of the High Line.[69] In almost every respect the creation and maturation of the Friends of the High Line reflects important aspects of collaborative cross-sector partnerships and leadership, which we analyze in chapter 6.

Initially, David and Hammond were focused on just preserving the railroad structure. Using the Central Park Conservancy as the model, the group determined that the best way to preserve the structure was to raise private and public funds to convert and operate the space as a linear, elevated park, not unlike the Promenade Plantée in Paris (also constructed on an abandoned railroad line).[70] A federal program would permit the CSX rail company to transfer the property to New York City for park purposes.[71] If the city chose to do so, it could work with Friends of the High Line to develop a revitalized residential and commercial neighborhood around the new public park.[72]

Fortuitously, there was a personal connection between Friends of the High Line and CPC—the families of Robert Hammond and Betsy Rogers were friends from previous days in San Antonio, Texas. As Robert Hammond said, "Betsy Barlow Rogers and the Central Park Conservancy had always been models for us. Theirs was an existing park, but a group of private citizens had come along, saved it from ruin, and then gone on to manage and operate it, raising the majority of funds to do so."[73]

To persuade the city to go along with their vision, Friends of the High Line would need to find a way to finance both construction and ongoing operations and maintenance. John Alschuler, a nationally known and well-regarded real estate consultant (who later became board chair), advised the Friends team on how to structure the project.

Designing it as a cross-sector partnership could deliver the park and open space at a lower cost than the city could do on its own and, over time, would make a significant "profit" for the city financially in terms of the incremental increase in real estate values, economic development, tourism, and higher income, sales, and property tax revenues. This would be the same Central Park effect that a similar study of Central Park found.[74] Specifically, Alschuler's study found that, while the High Line would be costly to build (his first estimate was low, predicting only $65 million), it would generate significant additional tax revenues to the city over its first twenty years of operation.[75] Originally, this increase in revenue was estimated at $140 million, and was later revised to $900 million, indicating the amount of unexpected value unlocked through the partnership.[76]

Alschuler was a strong believer in the power of cross-sector partnerships to build and maintain great cities. He noted that the New York City subway system and regional commuter rail systems were both built with private capital and are now maintained and operated by public authorities. Central Park was originally built and maintained with public capital and was restored and now maintained and improved primarily with private capital and managed by a nonprofit entity. He believed the High Line could follow that same proven plan for sustainable success.[77]

The New York City government under Mayor Rudolph Giuliani did not favor the Friends' vision for the High Line; in fact, the city had already begun plans to demolish the elevated structure. Friends of the High Line filed a lawsuit to block the action, but the city government never moved forward. The attacks of September 11, 2001, occupied the attention of Mayor Giuliani and his staff for the remainder of his term.

In January 2002, the new mayor Michael Bloomberg took office with the revitalization of Lower Manhattan one of his top priorities. As a successful businessman, he was already aware of the potential benefits of cross-sector partnerships, and he was and is a strong supporter of the Central Park Conservancy. Even as a candidate, Bloomberg had expressed support for the High Line.[78] Beginning in 2002, Bloomberg, his first deputy mayor Patricia E. Harris, his deputy mayor for economic development Dan Doctoroff, Amanda Burden, chair of the City Planning Commission, and Parks commissioner Adrian Benepe all became active and supportive of the High Line project.[79]

## "OUR GENERATION'S CENTRAL PARK"[80]

To capture public attention, in 2003 Friends of the High Line launched a light-hearted competition for the best ideas to reuse the old rail line. First place for the best idea went to building a lap pool along the entire length of nearly two miles; second place went to a roller coaster of the same length. Although many of the ideas were silly, the main objective—to bring attention to the High Line and engage the community—succeeded. A formal design competition in 2004 selected James Corner Field Operations, Piet Oudolf, and Diller Scofidio+Renfro as project leads and landscape architect.[81] The team essentially had a blank—but challenging—canvas on which to work.

According to Amanda Burden, the city considered la Promenade Plantée in Paris as a model and sent the design team to visit it.[82] The Promenade Plantée runs along the former path of the Vincennes railway line, which linked the Bastille station to Verneuil–l'Étang until 1969, after which it was replaced by a commuter rail line. In the 1980s, the entire Promenade Plantée area was redeveloped, and the Bastille station was demolished and replaced by the Opera Bastille. Landscaper Jacques Vergely and architect Philippe Mathieux designed the park to reuse the abandoned rail line between Bastille and the old Montempoivre gate to the city. The shops below the park were renovated in the late 1980s, and the Promenade Plantée was officially inaugurated in 1993.[83]

The Plantée was an interesting approach for the High Line development. The New York City government took a number of steps to make the park feasible and to ensure that the redevelopment had a major, positive economic effect for the city overall and would create a vibrant and diverse neighborhood. Previously zoned for light industry (the southern end is widely known as the Meatpacking District), the new Special West Chelsea district (from 16th Street to 30th Street, between 10th and 11th Avenues) allowed for a mix of manufacturing and art galleries and residential and commercial development. To gain the support of private owners under or adjacent to the proposed elevated park, those owners would be able to sell their development rights to properties on 10th and 11th Avenues, enabling developers to go higher and thereby make more money.[84]

This aspect of the project was crucial and substantial. Zoning changes to permit greater density and more profitable development uses attracted significant private investment, as well as fees and property taxes on higher property valuations, which made the High Line financially feasible and sustainable. Furthermore, there was a zoning bonus to exceed the zoning height limits, provided the developer pay a fee of $50 per square foot to the High Line Improvement Fund. This was attractive, as the market rate in the area was several hundred dollars per square foot. For the city, the fees and taxes from increased property values would help finance the long-term capital costs of the park. The owners of a large development in the area—Chelsea Market—convinced the City Planning Commission to expand the district north to include them. In return, the developer agreed to pay about a third of the $19 million fee for affordable housing and education programs for public housing in the neighborhood.[85] Overall, the High Line financing plan led to an important portfolio of substantial, complementary investments necessary to help overcome common fiscal limitations on "public" projects.

## BUILDING A SPECIAL PLACE

Development of the project was complicated by the number of partners involved. Superficially, it was a partnership between Friends of the High Line and the New York City government; in practice, New York City involved four different agencies—the New York City Department of Parks and Recreation, the Department of City Planning, New York City Economic Development Corporation, and the Mayor's Office. Despite the challenges of five sign-offs on every significant design issue, such as whether market-rate new buildings should have private entrances to the park, and many not-so-significant issues (such as twelve-inch versus eighteen-inch bench seat widths), a groundbreaking for the first section occurred in 2006. That first section, from Ganesvoort to West 20th Street, was opened to the public in 2009.[86]

Also in 2009, Friends of the High Line signed a formal partnership license agreement with the City of New York. Under the agreement, the city would own the elevated structure in exchange for fully

*Figure 5.6* Friends of the High Line founders Joshua David and Robert Hammond on the High Line before its transformation began. Photo by Joan Garvin, courtesy of Friends of the Highline.

funding the three phases of construction and restoration. Friends of the High Line agreed to raise funds from private sources to cover 90 percent of the park's annual operation and maintenance costs, public programming, and community outreach.[87] It is not surprising that the agreement mirrors that between the city and the Central Park Conservancy.

Even in 2009 New York City did not have the resources to adequately fund and manage the parks it already had (figure 5.6). At the same time, many of the donors who had helped sustain the project from the beginning would continue to contribute only if the vision and commitment of the Friends organization had a major role in its operations. So, as Joshua David said,

> Neither Robert nor I ever felt that we would stand off to the side. But ultimately to occupy the central role, like that of the Central Park Conservancy, would mean stepping up and being the park's primary funder—forever, basically. . . . We were setting up an organization that was aiming to run a public park in New York City.[88]

The second section of the park, from West 20th Street to West 30th Street opened to the public in 2011. Together, construction of the first two sections of the park cost a little over $152 million,[89] nearly 75 percent provided by the city and roughly half the remaining covered between the federal government and private sources (New York State contributed $400,000).[90] The third section, known as the Rail Yards, opened in September 2014 and runs from West 30th Street to 34th Street and cost about $75 million to construct.[91] As *New York Times* critic Michael Kimmelman said, "Phase 3, like the rest of the High Line, cost more per acre than probably any park in human history."[92] At the same time, he also said, "If the newest last stretch of the High Line doesn't make you fall in love with New York all over again, I really don't know what to say."[93]

What he did not say is that more and more of the cost of creating and maintaining the High Line was coming from private contributions raised by the Friends of the High Line. Encouraged by Alex von Furstenberg, a member of the Friends of the High Line board, his mother, Diane von Furstenberg, and her husband, Barry Diller, visited an exhibition on the High Line on display at the Museum of Modern Art (MoMA). A proposal for funding soon followed. Before the end of 2005, von Furstenberg and Diller pledged $5 million in support.[94] In 2008, despite the onset of the world economic crisis (and charitable contributions drying up for organizations across the city), the Diller-von Furstenberg family made a $10 million challenge gift.[95]

In 2011, Mayor Michael Bloomberg announced that the Barry Diller-Diane von Furstenberg Family Foundation was making a $20 million gift to pay for the design of the third phase and build the endowment for the park (this was on top of their previous gifts).[96] It was the largest gift given to New York parks at that time, prior to the $100 million gift to Central Park by John Paulson. In addition to raising substantial funds for capital expenses and an endowment, the Friends of the High Line continues to cover nearly all of the park's annual operating budget.[97]

Similar to Central Park and CPC, city officials and developers from all over the world—Rotterdam, Hong Kong, Jerusalem, Singapore, Chicago, Memphis, and Atlanta, just to name a few[98]—are coming to see the High Line, as much for its partnership model as for its innovative and spectacular design. The formal partnership between the city and Friends of the High Line is extremely important and is a key to the huge success of the High Line. Emeritus Friends board chair John Alschuler also stresses the importance of community involvement: "The most important partnership here is between engaged and passionate citizens and their government. These partnerships are economic. They're legal. They're civic. They are ways for the passion of citizens to be engaged in the democracy that reflects their values."[99]

## ALL THINGS TO ALL PEOPLE?

The High Line has already attracted over twenty million visitors from all over the world and the Friends organization has worked hard to be a good neighbor, as demonstrated in part by over 450 public programs and events hosted annually. Nine seasonal food vendors serve tourists and daily meals for people who live and work in the community. Over 120 artists from all over the world have exhibited in the park. It is also a public garden, with over 350 species of perennials, grasses, shrubs, vines, and trees, with plenty of spaces to walk, sit, read, chat, people watch, paint, take pictures, or just think. Due to the strong public-private efforts it took to create and sustain the High Line, today it is a free and public park owned by the City of New York.[100]

Just as Alschuler predicted, the High Line is proving to be a very good financial investment for the New York City government and its taxpayers (figure 5.7). City officials estimate that the first two sections alone have generated more than $2 billion in planned or new development.[101] In 2016, the *Wall Street Journal* reported that the High Line was having a "halo effect" on properties along the park, with resale prices 10 percentage points higher than properties only a few blocks farther away.[102] In 2016, when resale prices were softening throughout Manhattan, prices near the High Line (and Central Park) continued to rise. More restaurants and shops are serving the neighborhood, but the area retains its image of "hipness."[103]

Twenty apartments in the High Line neighborhood have sold for $10 million or more since 2009, and the median price for condos has risen from $1,000 a square foot in 2009 to between $2,000 and $3,000 in 2016. In 2016, there were eleven projects with 155 apartments under

*Figure 5.7* The High Line as it appears now, following its complete renovation. Photo courtesy of Friends of the Highline.

construction and nine more with 751 apartments planned.[104] Interestingly, the High Line park area has developed a reputation as family-friendly, and developers are building family-sized apartments to meet their needs. According to real estate experts, families that previously focused their home searches on the traditional family neighborhoods in the Upper East and Upper West Sides are also looking at the High Line area as a preferred location.[105]

Real estate development in New York City is often controversial and political. Before the High Line, the surrounding Chelsea neighborhood provoked images of a place where prostitutes were a familiar sight on the streets at all hours of the day, drugs were dealt openly and often accompanied by violent crimes, and the infamous Westies crime gang often ventured in from neighboring Hell's Kitchen. The neighborhood continued to improve as the High Line was constructed and completed, and many observers worried about rising prices, higher densities, and gentrification. John Alschuler saw it another way,

> One of the great things about New York is, we all coexist as part of a diverse neighborhood. It's one of the reasons why public housing is so essential, [so] that when neighborhoods such as West Chelsea do transition, there are important blocks of housing that will be perpetually devoted to low and moderate income people and their future in a diverse neighborhood.[106]

Even as the neighborhoods around the High Line continue to attract new housing and commercial investment (some would call it gentrification), the High Line neighborhood remains the permanent and longtime home to three major New York City Housing Authority low-income developments with a total of two thousand apartments. Chelsea Houses has two twenty-one-story buildings on 1.71 acres, opened in 1964, and is located on Ninth Avenue between West 25th and West 26th Streets. Chelsea Houses Addition is a fourteen-story tower for seniors completed in 1968 on a one-acre parcel bordering Chelsea Park at West 26th Street and Tenth Avenue. Elliott Houses, four high-rise buildings, opened in 1947, covers 4.70 acres between West 25th Street, Ninth and Tenth Avenues, and Chelsea Park, and is named after John Lovejoy Elliott, who was passionate about one of the city's worst neighborhoods and became a major force in getting the Elliott and Chelsea developments built. He was the founder of the Hudson Guild, which operates a summer camp program for young children in the area. Fulton Houses, eleven buildings between six- and twenty-five-stories tall, opened in 1965 on 6 acres located at Ninth Avenue between West 16th and West 19th Streets. The project is named after Robert Fulton who produced the first practical steamboat, the "Clermont"; its first successful voyage was from New Harbor, up the Hudson River, to Albany.[107]

Although the neighborhood now has one of the greatest levels of inequality in the city, the large number of public housing units in the community also makes it one of the most economically diverse. Due to vigilant civic engagement and responsible public policy, the public housing locations have never been seriously threatened with relocation, nor is there any imminent threat. A study in 2015 found that public housing residents in the area are benefiting from safer streets and better schools, and incomes of the residents are rising, probably due to better job opportunities in the neighborhood. Residents also enjoy the many free entertainment events organized by the Friends of the High Line. Nevertheless, longtime residents miss the many locally owned and operated stores whose spaces are now occupied by higher-end retailers and restaurants. Many residents must travel well outside the neighborhood to shop for lower-priced groceries and find more affordable restaurants.[108]

On balance, it seems that most people feel that things are better for the residents of public housing as a result of the High Line and the development it has spurred. As the vice president of the Elliot Houses tenants' association (and president of the Hudson Guild advisory committee) told the *New York Times*, "I'd rather have Chelsea as it is today. There's more people. It's brighter, it's beautiful, it's more inviting than it used to be. We're very lucky to be able to stay in housing that hopefully will not disappear."[109]

## BETTER PARKS THROUGH COLLABORATIVE LEADERSHIP

The renaissance of Central Park and the creation of the High Line are successes brought to fruition by cross-sector partnerships and exceptional, collaborative leadership. Neither park would exist if it weren't for enlightened government officials (and the citizens that support them) such as Parks Administrator Frederick Law Olmstead, Mayor Fiorello La Guardia, Parks Commissioner Robert Moses, Parks Commissioner Gordon Davis, mayors Ed Koch, David Dinkins, Rudy Giuliani, and Mike Bloomberg, and parks commissioners Henry Stern and Adrian Benepe. Despite best efforts though, even well-funded cities such as New York simply do not have the resources to sustain great parks consistently, and support from private partners and donors has proven indispensable.

Partnering with the Central Park Conservancy and the Friends of the High Line saved one great park and built a new one, thanks to a large number of consistently generous donors and a number of visionary and tireless collaborative leaders, particularly, Betsy Rogers, Doug Blonsky, and Ira Millstein for Central Park, and John Alschuler, Joshua David, Robert Hammond, and Phil Aarons for the High Line.

The city did not, could not, and would not have done it on its own. The same could be said about Battery Park, Prospect Park, Brooklyn Bridge Park, Bryant Park, and many other great parks from Forest Park in St. Louis to Golden Gate Park in San Francisco.

With the majority of the world's population living in cities (and expected to reach 66 percent by 2050),[110] the world will need more and better urban parks—and it will take partnerships like those of Central Park and the High Line to meet the growing demand.

In recent years, New York City mayors Mike Bloomberg and Bill de Blasio significantly increased the public funding for parks, stemming decades of cuts in public dollars. Bloomberg spent hundreds of millions of city capital dollars to help create the High Line, the new Brooklyn Bridge Park, and parts of the Hudson River Park.[111] Mayor de Blasio created three programs to help parks that have not yet attracted significant private investments. Five large parks, one in each borough, will get $30 million each between 2016 and 2020, and projects in the parks will be chosen in collaboration with the local communities. The second program, the Community Parks Initiative, will invest $285 million to improve sixty smaller parks around the city. And the Parks Without Borders program will spend $50 million to make parks more accessible and inviting by opening them up to the neighborhood streets and taking down high fences.[112]

Current Parks Commissioner Mitchell Silver (figure 5.8), an active partner of the Central Park Conservancy and the Friends of the High Line, recently won a significant increase in Parks Department staffing, which had not happened in some time. We believe that the success of the Central Park and High Line partnerships has raised public consciousness about the importance of urban parks for all New Yorkers. That, coupled with the budget relief to the city government provided by all the private dollars flowing to the flagship parks with private partners, has enabled and encouraged city officials to provide significantly more tax dollars to the other city parks without access to private support.[113]

---

Success in cross-sector partnerships is best accomplished when everyone coordinates their efforts to achieve the maximum benefit for the people and the communities they serve. It also works best when each

*Figure 5.8* Graduates of the Community Parks Initiative Gardener Training Program in 2017. Attending the ceremony were New York City Parks Commissioner Mitchell J. Silver (*third from the left*), CPC Institute for Urban Parks Chair Ira Millstein (*center*) and Central Park Conservancy President Doug Blonsky (*far right*). Photo courtesy of CPC.

partner contributes its fair share of resources and effort to reach the partnership's goal. And that is exactly why so many parks in New York City are better than they have ever been—and why millions of people from all over the city and all over the world enjoy them every day.

In chapter 6, we analyze how partnerships work best when leaders act collaboratively and their organizations operate as decentralized teams, each with its own expertise and areas of responsibility. Keeping partner organizations in alignment so that they are working efficiently and effectively toward common objectives and goals is a key responsibility of leaders. This is a complex and difficult task, and we outline how leaders can operate effectively when encountering unexpected challenges and opportunities.

# CHAPTER SIX

# The People Framework

## Leadership for Successful Partnerships

HOWARD W. BUFFETT

Cross-sector partnerships are well suited for addressing complex societal challenges, but only if the *people* leading them are highly effective in coordinating their team's efforts across partnering organizations.[1] In many of the partnerships we discuss in this book, collaborations work in similar ways. Partners function as a network comprised of decentralized teams, each with diverse abilities, expertise, and responsibilities. Each leader is empowered to manage his or her team without much interference from the other partners, which allows leaders to do what they do best—operate their organizations based on the knowledge and insights they are uniquely positioned to provide. Synchronizing distinct organizations and teams in a decentralized manner presents one of the more complex and difficult tasks when building effective partnerships.[2] This chapter highlights common observations and important characteristics of how teams and leaders align their efforts and focus on shared goals.[3]

Decentralized team management under a shared decision-making authority is relatively common in the business world.[4] This structure often characterizes the relationship between a parent company and its subsidiaries, and it is representative of a multiproduct or multiservice corporation operating distinct business divisions. In these cases, the lines of authority and communication between an organization's governance, executive, and management teams are usually clear, as are relative degrees of operational independence.[5] Effective decentralization requires shared authority for decision making between these different levels of leadership, as well as an ability for teams to take on new or unfamiliar responsibilities in an operating environment that is not overly restrictive.[6]

There are many benefits to this approach, which also apply to teams in a cross-sector partnership. Due to its resulting autonomy, decentralization fosters individual team motivation and creativity.[7] It allows for large, independent groups to focus multiple and diverse perspectives toward a common challenge. The structure provides for flexibility in how teams problem solve, and for distinct approaches to idea development.[8] Many of these advantages were apparent in our case example (see chapter 5). Leaders from across sectors inspired their teams to successfully partner around common goals and visions to improve New York City's parks. This was even the case internally within Central Park, where Doug Blonsky implemented an innovative Zone Management System. Under Blonsky's leadership, the Central Park Conservancy decentralized park maintenance systematically across forty-nine teams, each with the necessary experience, skills, and autonomy to manage and restore the park successfully.[9]

In our examples of cross-sector partnerships, we find that leaders exhibit similar characteristics across management styles. These characteristics are prerequisites for highly successful partnership building,[10] and they include vision, drive, integrity, admirable ambition, emotional intelligence, and empathy.[11] These all contribute to a leader's predisposition to collaborate with others.[12] Leaders who display this combination of characteristics are well suited to motivate their teams, to work well across partnering teams and with other leaders, and to understand key resource and operational constraints—and benefits—of different kinds of organizations.[13] As successful partnership builders, they combine these leadership characteristics with an awareness of their team's needs, the patience and perspective needed to understand partnering teams' dynamics, and the resilience required to maintain their team's momentum toward a partnership's goals.[14]

Leaders of effective partnerships continually inspire their team to carry the partnership forward, regardless of difficulties or challenges.[15] They must motivate buy-in throughout their entire organization, just as Betsy Rogers and Gordon Davis did in the case of Central Park. Leaders must communicate their vision internally and externally and effectively engage community stakeholders. In addition, they must establish measurable outcomes, be willing to learn and modify strategies, and set and follow realistic expectations for their teams and themselves.

These activities and leadership qualities are discussed in further detail throughout this chapter. The analysis begins by describing roles and resources that different kinds of organizations and their leaders can contribute to a partnership. The chapter then outlines five types of leadership skills that may be represented by the leaders in a partnership, as well as a set of programmatic leadership experiences relevant for effective collaboration. Next is a discussion of core group identities of a team and why leaders must know and understand them. Finally, the chapter explains how leaders can motivate their teams and maintain a partnership's momentum. This chapter is not meant to serve as an assessment tool for organizational capacity, impact, or individual leadership—many of those exist already.[16] Rather, it provides broad guidance on important leadership perspectives in a decentralized team environment, and some strategies necessary for sharing success across organizations in a partnership.

## ADVANTAGES THAT DIFFERENT PARTNERS BRING TO THE TABLE

Chapter 4 described the types of organizations that engage in cross-sector partnerships and the roles they typically assume. Foundations, government agencies, or private sector entities often serve as donors or investors in a partnership. In the Central Park and High Line cases, the funders were both private donors, such as John Paulson, and decision makers at government agencies, such as the New York City Parks Department and the Mayor's Office. Contractors, NGOs, or services firms often serve as a partnership's implementers. This included the Central Park Conservancy as well as the Friends of the High Line described in chapter 5. Each organization was founded to improve the parks and coordinate development activities, and their leaders worked hand in hand with funders, going far beyond a standard contractual or grantee relationship. Finally, partnerships have groups of stakeholders—such as the residents and neighborhood associations surrounding each of the parks—around which a partnership is focused or where a partnership's efforts are invested.

Partners across organizations bring unique perspectives and resources to a partnership, regardless of their role. However, for leaders to work well with counterparts in a decentralized team structure, they must understand the ways in which different partnering organizations contribute value. For example, a state government agency delivers its mission and operates programs much differently than a small-business management consulting firm. Yet each organization has particular capabilities and specific advantages it can apply toward a partnership's goals. The following section outlines a number of organization types related to collaborations profiled in this book, discusses their strengths at a general level, and how those strengths apply to partnership building.

Leaders in the public sector usually create legal and policy conditions necessary for long-term systems or community change, and the government agencies they operate have the power to regulate markets and market actors.[17] Government agencies at any level can draw on relatively large-scale budgets, and their leaders can use prestige or power to attract attention to drive progress in a cross-sector partnership.[18] These leaders also engage in diplomacy and the development of international trade agreements that may be applicable when building multinational partnerships. Many government agencies have access to significant amounts of data that may be relevant for partnerships ranging from the community level to the global arena. Furthermore, each branch of government plays a role in enforcing policy change or altering legal frameworks, which has the potential to enhance other organizations' ability to serve the public good.

In the private sector, leaders can contribute to cross-sector partnerships in a wide variety of ways. They may provide business acumen or access to physical capital necessary to achieve the goals of a partnership.[19] These leaders have valuable experience focusing on product or service innovation and customer satisfaction and retention. Private sector leaders are uniquely positioned to nurture and sustain economic markets related to their business practices.[20] This can create demand for jobs, support employment growth throughout related value chains, and help build individual and community wealth. The private sector also invests in significant research and development, which may be relevant to a partnership's goals. However, the resulting knowledge or technology usually is limited to the products or services the company produces and may be locked up through intellectual property protections.[21]

Leaders of philanthropic organizations, such as foundations or grant-makers, have experience thinking strategically about effective ways to work with multiple stakeholders to improve social conditions.[22] They can direct patient (or long-term) capital to a partnership, or their assets can serve as first-loss capital for a partnership's coinvestment. In doing so, philanthropic capital can offset short-term risk and encourage long-term private sector investment that might not otherwise occur.[23] Furthermore, the leaders of foundations face fewer external forces of accountability (they have no direct shareholders or public elections) and can more easily attempt efforts that have a high probability of failure.[24] Although most foundations have yet to tap into the full suite of financial tools available to them (see the examples outlined in chapter 10), their structure affords important flexibility for cross-sector partnerships.

The heads of community-based nonprofits, such as food banks or religious organizations, typically have significant on-the-ground experience in a given area or region. Due to the nature of their work, these leaders build and maintain community relationships beyond those of less locally focused leaders.[25] Their organizations can be effective at service delivery, and they often innovate to accomplish significant social good with little or restricted funding. These organizations and their leaders have to be flexible to respond quickly to changing community needs and resources. Leaders of these organizations tend to have a deep understanding of local challenges, an awareness of important historical context, and know what cultural nuances must be taken into account so that a partnership's investments make a lasting difference.[26]

Academic and research organizations present their own set of strengths and capabilities.[27] Many are well-established institutions, with leaders focused on long-term knowledge development and idea dissemination. These organizations might partner with others, such as think tanks or foundations, to help develop institutional capacity for a given field or practice.[28] Universities and community colleges are engaged in workforce training and readiness through their degree and vocational programs, and are well equipped to develop new and useful technology for society and effectively transfer that technology externally so that it may be scaled to serve the needs of many.[29]

This is not an exhaustive list of all types of organizations, nor does it capture the full scope of advantages, skills, or resources they may bring to a partnership. But it serves as a representative outline for considering the potential levers that leaders across decentralized teams can pull to contribute to a partnership's overall goals.

## LEADERSHIP SKILLS THAT CONTRIBUTE TO A SUCCESSFUL PARTNERSHIP

Leaders work more effectively with their counterparts in decentralized teams when they can identify and understand the leadership skills possessed by their peers. Our examples of successful partnerships are run by teams with leaders who have diverse backgrounds, experiences, and expertise.[30] Research on what makes a good leader, on the quality of leadership, and on effective team management is expansive, and this chapter does not summarize or replicate that work.[31] However, the leadership skills observed in our examples can be distilled into five categories, which are outlined in this section. Leaders with skills in each of these areas also benefit from corresponding *skills-based capital*,[32] which describes associated leadership strengths they can draw from to contribute to the success of a partnership.[33]

### Intellectual Leadership

*Intellectual* leadership skills are typically associated with leaders who have an innate or highly developed ability to understand important or complex ideas or concepts.[34] These leaders draw on or leverage intellectual or knowledge-based capital through their deep awareness, expertise, or experience regarding a specific issue area, system, or process innovation. They also may be viewed as thought leaders in a field and may have the ability to influence the views of others. In the High Line example from our New York City parks case, John Alschuler, the nationally known and well-regarded real estate expert, provided critical guidance and insights on how to establish the Friends of the High Line partnership. Not only did he advise on the complex structuring of the initiative, he also helped to communicate the vision and worked with community representatives, such as the newly elected mayor Michael Bloomberg.

## Representative Leadership

*Representative* leadership skills are exhibited by leaders who are effective at representing the needs or preferences of a specific constituency or group of individuals.[35] They may leverage political capital through their role, or through access to local, state, or national individuals who are elected, hired, or appointed to positions that can influence or better inform policy, regulation, or management of public resources.[36] In the Central Park case, one of New York City mayor Edward Koch's important leadership decisions was to appoint Gordon Davis as head of the Department of Parks and Recreation. Koch gave Davis key direction: focus on the city's and the park's financial sustainability through your role as a steward for the public. In his appointed position, Davis built a multidimensional strategy focused on collaboration and partnerships that led to significant success for Central Park.

## Transactional Leadership

*Transactional* leadership skills are associated with leaders who are effective at negotiating, especially when bargaining for or structuring access to resources for a partnership.[37] These leaders may have control or influence over significant financial capital that can be directed toward or coordinated for a partnership's goals, or they may bring a keen understanding of or access to key markets. Consistent across both New York parks cases was the importance of external or private funding to support each park's partnerships. In the case of the High Line, Mayor Michael Bloomberg's experience, leadership, and relationships helped inspire significant financial contributions. This leadership continued through the final phases of construction and supported the establishment of an endowment (funding more than 90 percent of the park's annual operating budget).[38]

## Inspirational Leadership

*Inspirational* leadership skills are found in leaders who inspire trust and action across their teams, partners, or groups of stakeholders.[39] These leaders often possess significant social capital, such as a deep reach into a community, or a broad reach between communities, through traditional or innovative networks.[40] These leaders have well-regarded reputations and may be considered a reliable voice for their peers.[41] This was obvious in the case of Betsy Rogers, who was an effective and inspirational leader for the Central Park efforts. Through her vision and demonstrated passion, she was entrusted by the city and its residents to steward resources in support of critical improvements to the park.

## Organizational Leadership

*Organizational* leadership skills are exhibited by leaders who understand processes that better coordinate physical or human capital, or sequence planning and activities toward common partnership goals.[42] These leaders can activate or access significant operational or infrastructure resources at local, regional, or national scales, and may have expertise in logistics, information systems, strategic planning, or facilities management, for example.[43] This quality was apparent in the leadership efforts of Doug Blonsky in establishment of the Conservancy's Institute for Urban Parks.[44] He was the first executive to manage both the Conservancy and the City Parks Department staff, which required him to establish a unified set of standard operating procedures and to align the efforts of multiple teams, organizations, and departments around a common vision.

## LEADERSHIP EXPERIENCES ACROSS DECENTRALIZED TEAMS

Planning strategies for developing cross-sector partnerships, including a theory of change model to outline desired outcomes from a collaboration, are discussed in chapter 4. The *activities* portion of that model describes what actions partners undertake to produce intended outputs in support of the partnership's goals. Partners will have varying degrees of experience conducting different types of programmatic activities. Therefore, leaders working in decentralized teams will benefit from understanding the scope and types of experiences represented by their counterparts. The following is a typology for identifying and categorizing experience sets relevant to partnerships discussed in this book. This typology was developed by, and is adapted from, a joint McKinsey & Company and Annie E. Casey Foundation analysis on best practices for advancing social impact programs.[45]

*Knowledge Development.*[46] This may include experience with "discovering, developing, interpreting, or sharing" new information or data to solve challenges.[47] Knowledge development activities may seek to identify root, underlying causes of a challenge, or improve existing methodologies for scientific research or data interpretation related to the goals of the partnership.[48]

In the case of Central Park, the effort began with a commissioned study of the park's management in 1974, known as the Savas Report.[49] The knowledge developed through this study translated into key management recommendations, and partnerships, necessary for the future prosperity of the park.

*Policy Change and Implementation.* This may include experience with activities that promote or resist "a change in government, multi-lateral, or corporate policy"[50] or regulation.[51] Partnership activity may focus on early stage engagement, such as the clear articulation of the implications of a proposed policy change, or may support grassroots campaigns, lobbying efforts, or litigation on the subject matter.[52]

As we saw with New York City's High Line, the partnership benefited significantly by working with developers and city teams to establish new zoning regulations. The policies led to financing for the High Line Improvement Fund, which supported capital costs for construction and led to new affordable housing and education programs in the area. Former New York City planning director Amanda Burden was able to bring city officials and Friends of the High Line leadership together in a collaborative way to solve some very complex and contentious zoning issues.

*Platforms and Enabling Systems.*[53] This may include experience working with organizations or government bodies to create common standards, networks, or physical infrastructure.[54] Examples of these activities may be partnerships that develop a significant public works initiative, the creation of requirements or specifications for a new technical service or technology, or some other advancement or framework that meets the needs or demands of the general public.[55]

The ongoing development of Central Park and construction of the High Line serve as examples of infrastructure development. Beyond that, the team for the Central Park Conservancy's Institute for Urban Parks focuses on working with other parks and conservancies around the world to share best practices on urban park sustainability.[56] Through this, they are working to grow a network of potential public, private, and philanthropic partners with shared missions.

*Organizational and Individual Improvement Programs.*[57] This may include experience working with individuals or organizations to expand their educational or professional capabilities or to encourage behaviors that result in positive gains for society.[58] Partnerships may support activities ranging from job training and technical assistance at the individual level, to development of new programs or executive training for staff at the organizational level, to community-wide public service campaigns for issues such as neighborhood safety, energy efficiency, or recycling.[59]

Thanks to Doug Blonsky's leadership, the Central Park Conservancy now offers internships, fellowships, service learning activities, and workforce development training. This is also apparent through the Conservancy's Institute for Urban Parks and subsequent Certified Urban Park Manager education program, which drew from the expertise of teams at Columbia University's Earth Institute.

*Basic Human or Community Services.* This may include experience providing new or improved community-based services, or it may be the delivery of basic goods, such as food or medical supplies, "to fulfill unmet needs of constituents."[60] This activity may serve broader community enrichment, such as supporting the performing arts or programming at a children's museum.[61] In any case, a partnership exists to provide or produce some set of outputs where expertise in service or product delivery will be relevant.[62]

Under Betsy Rogers's leadership, the Central Park Conservancy restored and created new community services early in the partnership. The Conservancy renovated Central Park's Sheep Meadow, Wollman Rink, Cherry Hill, and Belvedere Castle—providing important cultural and recreational services to the community.

Cross-sector partnerships may include activities falling outside of this list; however, these categories describe a range of typical core experiential sets relevant across teams and leaders. A given leader's knowledge and familiarity will vary widely across these activity groups. Therefore, other team leaders in a partnership should be equipped to identify critical experience gaps and supplement their teams accordingly.

# HOW DOES A LEADER DEVELOP A
# PARTNERSHIP TEAM'S IDENTITY?

Effective leaders know how to look outward across a partnership to understand the advantages other partnering organizations can provide. They also know what skills and experiences their counterparts can contribute to complement their own. But leaders must also look inward at their own teams and understand what drives and motivates team member commitment to a partnership's success.[63]

We saw this with the development of the Central Park Conservancy partnership under the leadership of Betsy Rogers. Rogers's management style allowed for a hands-on approach to her team's activities. As a self-described "zealous nut" about the park, it helped that she worked tirelessly to strengthen its mission and refine its programs.[64] Her focus on park maintenance and the creation of new restorative processes resulted in an almost ritualistic pride among her team. She tapped into her staff's loyalty—to both herself and the park—to inspire previously unaccomplished advances in the park's complex operations. Rogers articulated a new vision for the park's future, establishing new and exciting values for the organization and its employees. Finally, Rogers was able to build meaningful shared experiences for her team members—not only through her management style but also by celebrating critical fund-raising successes, lauding visible improvements, and highlighting the efforts of her team.

Each of these examples represents different ways that Rogers built and tapped into her team's underlying *core identities*. Described in Daniel Shapiro's *Negotiating the Nonnegotiable*, core identities represent the "spectrum of characteristics that define you as an individual or as a group."[65] Understanding how to develop and nurture these core team identities enables leaders to support their team's efforts in ways that are critically important. It allows leaders to better motivate their teams, reassure them when facing challenges, or avoid conflict between members. It can provide context for when leaders should help teams emphasize certain identities over others. And it can assist leaders in situations where clashing cultures or differing norms between partner organizations are slowing progress toward goals.

The following list of core identities, adapted from Shapiro's work, describes the emotional and intellectual foundation from which many groups and teams react to a challenge, process their response, prioritize their needs or requests, or make decisions regarding a new course of action. It is important to recognize that a group's identity is not the same as the sum of its parts; rather, an organization can foster its own team character based on team dynamics, operational norms, management history, or governance priorities articulated through a values statement—any of which can be healthy or unhealthy. To create healthy team identities, leaders must focus on developing the following five attributes:

*Beliefs* make up the collection of "convictions, principles," or ethics held by all members of the team that provide broad behavioral guidance.[66] Team beliefs may be articulated in a charter, codified in an organizing document or mission statement, or described as a set of philosophies framed and displayed on a wall.

*Rituals* are a team's "meaningful customs" or repetitive acts. This could include celebration of an individual milestone reached, welcoming of a new team member, or recognizing significant progression toward a goal.[67] This could be a ribbon-cutting ceremony, a party in someone's honor, traditions of eating lunch together, or how a team ends their workday together.

*Loyalties* are dedications, or strong senses of commitment. They could be toward the organization, the team itself, other members of the team, a team leader, or a collaborative partnership. Loyalties also can extend to a particular idea, goal, or purpose, or to an organization's brand identity.[68]

*Values* are a team's ideals, such as integrity, honesty, justice, or freedom. They describe or articulate what a team believes is worth holding in high regard. Values often represent a set of standards the team hopes to uphold through its actions or choices, such as ethical conduct, providing good customer service, or excellence in a work product.

*Shared emotional experiences* are "events, positive or negative," that affect a team's identity. This could include the resignation of a critical team member or team leader, the resolution or accomplishment of a team's goal or purpose, or a particularly difficult or uncertain time in the group's existence. These experiences contribute to a sense of common history or camaraderie among group members.[69]

Each of these core identity attributes provides a basis or rationale from which a team leader can better understand the team's behaviors and inspire team action.[70] Given this knowledge, what discrete steps can leaders take to motivate their teams?

## HOW DOES ONE START—AND CONTINUE—LEADING A PARTNERSHIP?

Recognizing that partnerships inherently bring about some kind of change or inflection affecting an organization's culture, leaders must constantly reinforce the goals, vision, and efforts related to the partnership's intended outcomes.[71] Decentralized team leadership is complex; it requires significant effort in team design, in team member recruitment, in building and maintaining team momentum, and in anchoring successes along the way. Achieving a partnership's outcomes can take a significant amount of time—many months, years, or even longer. Because these processes can be drawn out, leaders across partners must engender team ownership throughout the life cycle of the partnership, especially during incremental progress.

In considering the chapter 5 case, many important aspects of maintaining a partnership's long-term momentum are apparent throughout the early history of Central Park's revitalization. When New York City mayor Edward Koch assumed office in 1978, he instilled an important sense of urgency in Gordon Davis, directing him to quickly bring about significant improvements throughout the park system.[72] Realizing that Central Park may soon suffer further setbacks, Davis recruited Betsy Rogers as the first Central Park Administrator in 1979, and they set out to save park operations from an already shrunken staff and dismal resources. Rogers quickly rallied her team around a newly communicated vision, and she established coalitions of community, government, and private sector support.

At the same time, Davis worked with the government to clear hurdles for expanded park staff by creating new job positions that would qualify for federal job training funds.[73] He anchored this progress through an Urban Park Rangers program, which brought in fresh, young, and well-educated individuals to improve park operations.[74] He and Rogers also made subtle yet noticeable changes to organizational culture, including new uniforms and a customer service–oriented mentality for park employees. Taken together, this all became part of Central Park's new brand story.

The following strategies outline ways to inspire team member engagement and buy-in throughout the time line of a partnership's implementation, and to help team leaders realize significant goals along the way.

1. *Establish a clear need or sense of urgency.*[75]

   In some cases, this requires leaders to issue a strong call to action, building on independent indicators that a sense of need or urgency exists and is appropriate given the circumstances. In other cases, this can be done by effectively communicating the consequences of not engaging in a partnership (or what will happen if a partnership fails to achieve its goals). In either case, leaders need to address why the particular effort being proposed is essential, and consider its overall compatibility with their team's *core identities.*

2. *Build internal and external support.*[76]

   Leaders assemble team members with sufficient resources and influence to develop and sustain the life cycle of the partnership. They identify advocates whose *beliefs* align with the partnership's goals. They also recruit champions with strong *loyalties* from throughout the organization, ranging from the base up to the board of directors. Leaders must garner support from key external stakeholders, which may include clients or customers, and focus on ways that support can mitigate potential obstacles for the partnership.

3. *Communicate the new reality.*[77]

   Leaders develop a communication plan that builds on team *values* and articulates a clear image of what is possible in terms of end goals. They provide access to relevant information and engage in open dialogue. It can be difficult to build real commitment unless teams realize what the partnership is intended to accomplish. Staff may need to internalize what success means to them, and how the partnership's work may or may not affect their role in the organization.

4. *Clear the path for necessary change.*[78]

Leaders work with their governance team, such as a board of directors, to eliminate or modify rules or policies that would prohibit the success of the partnership. They work with management to procure technology and the equipment the partnership needs. Similarly, organizations must dedicate space and time to focus on the partnership's efforts, sometimes through new team *rituals,* and must consider necessary organizational shifts to support the goals. Finally, leaders encourage an appropriate risk-taking mind-set in testing and proposing changes that benefit the partnership's goals.[79]

5. *Celebrate team member accomplishments.*[80]

Leaders must plan activities around milestones to illustrate visible and practical progress made by their teams and by individual members. Leaders should work to recognize and reward those who are responsible for reaching milestones, and they can use new or existing team *rituals* to build *shared emotional experiences.* Such recognition should champion progress with public statements, appearances, and high energy. In doing so, leaders will more effectively reinforce the progress made during a partnership, and the shortened distance toward its new vision.[81]

6. *Anchor the team's progress toward goals.*[82]

The progress of partnerships can easily be reversed, particularly when a partnership is still new or if it challenges the previously embedded culture of an organization. Milestones must be anchored, for instance through changes in technology, updates to standard operating procedures, or improvements to organizational structure in support of the partnership's goals.[83] Leaders should consider their team's *values* and work to highlight and positively frame changes for team members based on those values. At times, anchoring may require tangible shifts to the organization's human capital structure: promotions, changes in job descriptions, or new hires.

7. *Create the partnership's new brand story.*[84]

Partnerships tell a story of how organizations come together to accomplish something new. This story can be one of the most compelling tools a leader has to build and maintain momentum throughout the development of a new or difficult partnership. The story and the *shared emotional experiences* it reflects reinforce a team's *loyalty* to the partnership. It can help team members conceptualize how a shift in operations fits within the culture of the organization itself. Functionally, leaders should include team members formally and informally in the development of the narrative, and consider important brand elements, such as a dedicated logo, color schemes, and marketing for the partnership.

8. *Align the partnership's vision with the team's vision.*[85]

The goals of a partnership describe a new reality, and the brand story conveys how that reality fits with the culture, but leaders must also align a partnership's mission with their team's *beliefs.* Overall, both the new vision and each step throughout the partnership time line must support all aspects of a team's core identities. Outcomes must lead to higher satisfaction among team members and to a new culture of success built around the overarching narrative of the partnership.

Central Park's long-term narrative, for example, began with the partnership between New York City and Frederick Law Olmstead and Calvert Vaux, the landscape architects who envisioned a design for the park that led to its opening in 1858.[86] Every Parks Commissioner and Administrator since then has built on the strength of that foundation, allowing for today's modern park services, and underscoring every partnership and private donation that continues supporting the park and its success. Doug Blonsky, for example, worked continuously and tirelessly to support the CPC staff over the past thirty-two years, and focused on creating a positive work environment for the entire team during his tenure.[87]

Throughout the stages of partnership engagement, leaders recognize the need to build and nurture a team's cross-sector identity.[88] They do so by defining core mutual beliefs and by developing shared rituals. They also delineate common values across teams, and create shared emotional experiences by instilling a sense of achievement and pride over the quality of the collective work. Finally, leaders cultivate loyalty to the partnership's vision and to each other. When leaders are effective at doing this, all members of their organization will be positioned to share in the partnership's success.

## OVERCOMING OBSTACLES

Employing an effective decentralized leadership strategy is a challenging process. Sometimes a team lacks specific leadership skills or experiences and may be unable to make up for those deficiencies. Cost and time can be barriers to working across teams representing a multitude of partners.[89] Some organizations face regulatory restrictions governing their staff size or composition—this is particularly true in certain government situations, where additional human capital may be needed but cannot be hired or contracted due to statute.[90] Team member or leader attrition, especially during lengthy partnership time lines, can significantly complicate or hinder success.

Decentralized teams in a cross-sector partnership may not be balanced or representative across the five leadership skill sets discussed in this chapter. This is one reason the Central Park Conservancy built and continues to expand a multifaceted training program, codified through detailed program guides, to maintain and upgrade the skills of all team members working in Central Park.[91] However, strengthening teams from within is not always a plausible course of action and depends on the goals and activities of the partnership. Leaders may have to build trusted coalitions outside their senior team members to offset skills gaps or shortcomings. This may add additional stress between executive leadership and senior management, or it may result in an unevenness in contributions between partnering teams at different phases of the partnership.[92]

## CONCLUSION

Team leaders are responsible for facilitating a partnership's ongoing success and must commit significant time and energy to the partnership-building process. Leaders must be cognizant of their team's emotional health, especially if a partnership is causing difficult or stressful experiences. They must model the partnership's goals or agenda in their actions and public speeches, and when addressing their teams. And they must constantly strive to inspire trust and confidence.

When working with their counterparts, leaders must ensure that the design and composition of the partnership itself supports an effective decentralized team structure. When operated successfully, partnerships will support collaborative environments that:[93]

- Convene leaders representing organizations across sectors that contribute distinct advantages to the partnership, and who exhibit the necessary leadership skills for developing a comprehensive partnership strategy;

- Coordinate planning with partners who represent diverse and extensive experiences required for the partnership's theory of change activities, and who possess a range of skills-based capital relevant for accomplishing goals shared across organizations; and

- Catalyze the collective action of partners with leaders who develop and nurture their team's core identities, who inspire and guide their teams to actively seek solutions to shared challenges, and who facilitate engagement with additional partners throughout the life cycle of the partnership.

Leading a partnership toward a unified vision of success can be extremely difficult; it is time consuming and requires balancing many factors.[94] Even the most successful leaders find this challenging. However, doing so effectively helps teams avoid duplicated efforts, enables teams to learn from one another and generate new or unexpected ideas, and allows teams to develop and share best practices. When partnering leaders understand and employ decentralized team management, they are better equipped to advance mutual goals, share success, and achieve the partnership's intended outcomes.

# *PLACE*

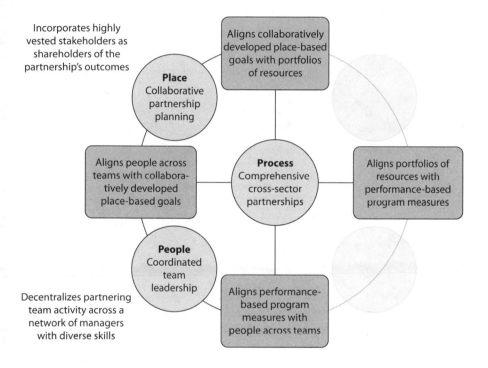

Incorporates highly vested stakeholders as shareholders of the partnership's outcomes

**Place**
Collaborative partnership planning

Aligns collaboratively developed place-based goals with portfolios of resources

Aligns people across teams with collaboratively developed place-based goals

**Process**
Comprehensive cross-sector partnerships

Aligns portfolios of resources with performance-based program measures

**People**
Coordinated team leadership

Aligns performance-based program measures with people across teams

Decentralizes partnering team activity across a network of managers with diverse skills

# CHAPTER SEVEN

# The Place Case

## Economic Stability in Afghanistan

### HOWARD W. BUFFETT

By 2009, the U.S. Department of Defense (DoD) was deeply entrenched in military conflicts across Afghanistan. That same year the U.S. government released an updated multiagency Counterinsurgency (COIN) Guide aimed at creating a "blend of comprehensive civilian and military efforts designed to simultaneously contain insurgency and address its root causes."[1] In line with this approach, the Secretary of Defense called on an economic development team to work in tandem with military command in theater to promote stability programs and business development throughout Afghanistan.[2] Relying on military assets for the mission was critical, but the team's combined civilian and military efforts were not combat-related, they were in support of economic stability goals.[3] As the COIN guidebook stated, "Non-military means are often the most effective elements, with military forces playing an enabling role."[4] This multipronged approach was also in line with certain Afghan perspectives. In 2008, former finance minister (and future president) of Afghanistan Ashraf Ghani wrote that "collaborative partnerships across state, market, and civil society boundaries" were required to stabilize and rebuild economies in countries such as Afghanistan.[5]

The mission of the DoD economic development team spanned multiple industry sectors, numerous programs, and many provinces. The team brought together experts and investors from diverse backgrounds to consider "private-sector strategies to create a sustainable Afghan economy."[6] The agriculture sector in Afghanistan quickly became an obvious focus for the team, a perspective that senior military officials also supported at the time.[7] This chapter outlines the strategy and project development that supported the DoD's economic stability efforts in Afghanistan's agricultural sector, specifically in Herat Province. The importance of cross-sector partnerships between the DoD and a number of private and public sector organizations is also explored.

The DoD's initiatives addressed underlying economic and infrastructure challenges that led to improved agricultural output and employment in rural areas. This strategy was built on an early iteration of social value investing, with a primary goal of transforming beneficiaries of the programs into shareholders of the initiative's outcomes.[8] Specifically, the management approach and resulting programs treated the people of Herat as co-owners of the investments, with a sense of *place*-based permanence. Four closely linked and interrelated projects were initiated in the Herat area. These projects (1) increased a community's production of agricultural commodities and (2) expanded nearby food processing capacity and job opportunities. The initiative also (3) organized large groups of farmers into more prosperous and stable cooperatives and (4) built a new agricultural college and related program capacity to serve important educational and research needs for the country.

## AGRICULTURE IN AFGHANISTAN

Afghanistan is an agrarian economy: agriculture is its most important economic activity. Nearly 80 percent of Afghans live in rural areas,[9] producing wheat, rye, rice, potatoes, fruits, and nuts.[10] However, Afghanistan's agricultural production faces significant challenges. Fewer than 12 percent of the country's 161 million acres are arable,[11] and a majority of farmers engage in subsistence or near-subsistence irrigated or rain-fed agriculture, cultivating only a few acres or less (figure 7.1).[12]

In the twenty-two years following the 1979 Soviet invasion, Afghanistan's agriculture sector grew by only 0.2 percent annually.[13] This compares with 2.2 percent growth during preconflict between 1961 and 1978.[14] In 2010, the World Bank estimated that an annual rate of 5–6 percent growth (or more) would be required to support the country's employment and economic needs.[15] In addition, approximately 90 percent "of Afghanistan's manufacturing industry and most of its exports" rely on agricultural production.[16]

*Figure 7.1* An Afghan village surrounded by subsistence farming. Smallholder plots such as those seen here characterize agricultural production throughout the country. Photo © Howard G. Buffett.

Shortly after the DoD launched its economic development team in Afghanistan, it engaged the Norman Borlaug Institute for International Agriculture (the Borlaug Institute), centered at Texas A&M University. Borlaug Institute personnel traveled to Afghanistan to assess and identify ideal locations to develop new agriculture-based programs. These assessments, outlined later in the chapter, illustrated that investing in Herat Province's agricultural sector would be an effective way to employ Afghans and improve food security and stability.

## FOOD INSECURITY AND POVERTY IN HERAT

Herat Province suffers from pervasive food insecurity and malnutrition. At the time of the economic development team's first assessments in 2009, one-third of Afghans lived below the minimum healthy daily caloric intake.[17] Such chronic malnutrition diminishes physical and mental development for children and limits work productivity in adults.[18] Herat's food insecurity was largely the result of cyclical poverty perpetuated by decades of war and conflict.[19] Researchers have documented the link between poverty and recurring conflict in many poor countries. For example, Oxford professor Paul Collier found that 73 percent of the world's poorest citizens suffered a civil war during the ten-year period between 1993 and 2003.[20] Afghans understood this well: in a 2009 survey, 70 percent of those interviewed perceived poverty and unemployment as the major causes of conflict in their country.[21]

Rural or remote areas often magnify the effects of poverty and conflict because residents lack access to advanced health and human services, wholesale or retail markets for commodities, or steady employment.[22] In 2009, over 70 percent of the nearly two million residents of Herat Province were living in rural areas.[23] DoD research estimated that approximately two-thirds of these residents were unemployed and that 300,000 additional jobs would be required by 2020 just to maintain the status quo.[24] Reports also estimated that this unemployment would spike to as high as 90 percent of residents during winter seasons when reliable agricultural jobs disappeared.[25] The Borlaug Institute estimated that 46 percent[26] of the residents of rural Herat Province earned less than $2 a day, or about $600 per year.[27] Without reliable employment and livable wages, most of Herat's residents could not purchase nutritious food throughout the year. According to Afghanistan's Ministry of Rural Rehabilitation and Development, this situation threatened security and stability throughout the province.[28] Because of economic instability and unemployment, and because control of the district shifted frequently, the military classified Guzara district,[29] a focal point for the development team's efforts in Herat, as "amber" (transitional conflict).[30]

The region's insecurity exacerbated already poor living conditions for its most vulnerable residents. Recurring hunger and limited economic opportunities disproportionately affected women and children in the area, which contributed to a worsening cycle of instability.[31] To achieve successful and sustainable development, particularly in areas such as Herat, U.S. government efforts had to consider this. Therefore, the DoD strategy prioritized collaboration with women-focused organizations on economic empowerment programs—with investments going beyond typically funded prenatal, child health, and nutritional projects.[32] In fact, engaging and empowering women through agriculture provides the best protection against the long-lasting effects of child malnutrition, according to the United Nations Special Rapporteur on the right to food.[33] Connecting these facts from a policy perspective, the Afghan government and the United Nations recently developed a countrywide strategy on women in agriculture. The strategy stated, "Empowerment of women is fundamental to reduce poverty, hunger, and improve food security," arguing that successful agricultural projects require gender equity and greater economic integration across gender lines.[34]

## A FOCUS ON AGRICULTURAL INFRASTRUCTURE

Food insecurity can corrode social cohesion and prolong conflict around limited natural resources. Agricultural productivity gains in the early stages of development can be indispensable, especially if they demonstrate a visible and meaningful impact on local communities.[35] Because of this, Herat's development plan had to take into account economic, social, and environmental realities, and its strategy had to focus on long-term sustainability rather than short-term assistance. The DoD economic development team determined that one of the most effective ways to do this was to invest in the agricultural sector value chain. As discussed in chapter 4, a value chain typically encompasses the various inputs, activities, and business functions that go into a product's development, production, and delivery.[36] It can be customized to include industry or sector-specific attributes. For example, stability and development programs that aim to support an agricultural value chain must consider year-round access to adequate nutrition as a core component of food security, and as a foundational aspect of prosperity, particularly in rural parts of the world.[37]

At the time of the DoD's assessments, Herat's agricultural sector faced several structural deficiencies: seasonal shocks (such as drought), limited skilled labor, dated scientific knowledge, and market failures along a broken and unpredictable value chain.[38] Typically, during the traditional harvesting season from May through October, rural families in Herat produced sufficient staple crops of vegetables and grains.[39] During peak season, processing capacity usually could not keep pace with production, nor was there adequate cold, cool, or dry storage for excess crops. Because there were few opportunities for processing, preserving, or storing raw goods, rural families did not have enough food for the entire year. In a province home to tens of thousands of malnourished children and adults, crops rotted in the fields during peak season.[40] The need to alleviate market disjunctions in the food supply chain was obvious. The top priority of the project team was to support links between agricultural production and processing to ensure more consistent food availability in Herat and develop a steady source of income for families.

## ASSESSING WHAT COULD AND SHOULD BE DONE

Because of the importance of agriculture in Afghanistan, the DoD economic stability team launched a dedicated group focused on agricultural development (the DoD Ag team). The DoD Ag team settled on a broad mission for its agricultural strategy: improve food supply and agriculture-related infrastructure to promote security, stability, and rural development throughout Herat. Because it was relatively secure, Herat was an attractive area for investment. Using counterinsurgency language, the DoD felt it could develop the region as an expandable "ink blot" of stability, which could spread to adjoining, less stable areas.[41] As the economic benefits spread, they hoped Herat could drive commercial integration and intracountry trade throughout more of Afghanistan.

The DoD Ag team engaged the Borlaug Institute to identify and assess specific, actionable opportunities for agricultural development across Afghanistan.[42] This study identified several important attributes of Herat Province, including its inexpensive and somewhat dependable electricity in the capital, suitable climate for crop growth, soil that was comparably rich, and relatively limited insurgent violence. The assessments also identified some isolated agricultural activities, including fruit and vegetable production, which were promising given the local conditions. These assessments reviewed potential areas for investment, as well as specific projects, using four categories (and a number of subcriteria):

- *Impact*: the amount of revenue, employment, and political effect a successful project in the area would generate;

- *Feasibility*: the condition of the existing supply chain, including reliable electricity, human capital, and financial investments;

- *Sustainability*: the presence of clear and consistent market demand, and dependable logistics necessary for commodity trade; and

- *Speed*: the time required to create a desired effect. In an unstable environment, projects that take too long often run the risk of disruption by insurgent actors or by funding interruptions. Therefore, timing was an important consideration to ensure that local communities actually benefited from successful project implementation.

The first four potential project evaluations were for a poultry hatchery, a wholesale market, expansion of a grape farm, and development of a vegetable packaging and processing operation. Between the four, the vegetable packaging initiative received the highest score, in part because it supported and built on other investments in the value chain. The team conducted a preliminary analysis of external activities required to support the vegetable packaging initiative. Figure 7.2 illustrates a rudimentary list of partners and their functions relative to that analysis.[13]

## INFORMING STRATEGY DEVELOPMENT

Following the research and assessment phase, the team developed a strategy centered on improving farm outputs, filling gaps in agribusiness processing, and driving demand for agricultural sector jobs. Further, these efforts strengthened the production, agribusiness, processing, livestock, crop, and horticulture subsectors of the broader agricultural industry throughout other parts of Afghanistan.

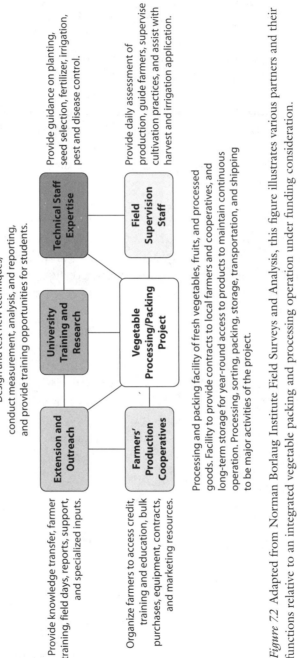

Design and test new techniques, conduct measurement, analysis, and reporting, and provide training opportunities for students.

Provide guidance on planting, seed selection, fertilizer, irrigation, pest and disease control.

Provide daily assessment of production, guide farmers, supervise cultivation practices, and assist with harvest and irrigation application.

Provide knowledge transfer, farmer training, field days, reports, support, and specialized inputs.

Organize farmers to access credit, training and education, bulk purchases, equipment, contracts, and marketing resources.

Processing and packing facility of fresh vegetables, fruits, and processed goods. Facility to provide contracts to local farmers and cooperatives, and long-term storage for year-round access to products to maintain continuous operation. Processing, sorting, packing, storage, transportation, and shipping to be major activities of the project.

*Figure 7.2* Adapted from Norman Borlaug Institute Field Surveys and Analysis, this figure illustrates various partners and their functions relative to an integrated vegetable packing and processing operation under funding consideration.

Many of the programs aimed to help farmers cultivating between one and five acres of land (figure 7.3). This group's support would be valuable for rural long-term stability efforts because these farmers were often members of prominent local governing councils. They accounted for 60 percent of the population, farmed 80 percent of the land, and

*Figure 7.3* A smallholder farmer cultivating land in central Afghanistan.
Photo © Howard G. Buffett.

produced more than 80 percent of the agricultural output.[44] When income increased for these farmers, so would the demand for rural nonfarm goods and services, which would create economic multiples and drive employment for many of the poorest citizens. Research indicated that this type of "middle market" farmer would more than double agriculture employment growth in Herat's economy between 2010 and 2020.[45]

Strategy development benefited from hundreds of in-field missions for data gathering, farmer interviews, and relationship building. Time in the field is particularly important when working with rural communities because it allows for consistent contact and for collaborative working relationships to develop. The team engaged local agribusiness and learned about the state of quality assessment and quality control, food safety, processing capacity, and product sourcing. Regional military commands were making their own investments in local agricultural development, which factored into the strategy, as did the existing capacity of farmer support services and programming at Herat University, especially as it related to cooperatives in the area.

The strategy also had to align with the broader military missions and the preexisting objectives and resources of U.S. and NATO forces in Afghanistan, which included:

- Supporting operational needs of commanders in the field;

- Maximizing measurable results in the early months of operation; and

- Prioritizing opportunities for market-driven solutions.

The DoD Ag team strategy led to four mutually supporting projects in areas around Herat Province. The first project helped a group of rural farmers improve their access to underground water so they could irrigate their crops and expand their food production. The second project built nearby food processing centers, allowing expanded crop production to undergo value-added processing (turning tomatoes into tomato sauce, or wheat into flour for cooking). These centers also provided jobs, equipment, and training for underemployed women and increased local demand for raw agricultural commodities. The third project focused on forming cooperatives for large groups of farmers who were further out from the city of Herat. By pooling their resources, farmers could get bulk discounts and diversify their risk.

The final project included construction of a new agricultural college at Herat University, along with staff resources, training, and laboratories for critical agricultural research.

## MAKING THE STRATEGY WORK

The team developed its plans in line with the State Department's recommendations in its "Afghanistan and Pakistan Regional Stabilization Strategy."[46] In broad terms, the strategy had four focus areas with objectives and implementation methods for each.

### Strategic Area 1: Regenerate Agribusiness Value Chains

The team facilitated infrastructure and equipment investment to spur business creation and fill gaps in local supply chains by addressing market failures. Objectives included:

- Improve crop production and inputs;

- Prevent postharvest loss (through cold, cool, or dry storage);

- Increase processing capacity and market access;

- Enhance water usage and irrigation; and

- Deliver resources and appropriate mechanization to cooperatives.

Agribusiness development in this strategic area relied on joint civilian-military efforts to connect farmers and farmer associations to markets through trade corridors, and it supported transborder facilitation.

### Strategic Area 2: Invest in Farmer Development

The second strategic area supported farmer access to improved extension services. Extension programs, often operated as partnerships between local governments and universities, provide farmers with applicable scientific knowledge through non-formal education and training (by *extending* research and the classroom to the field).[47] Improving extension would improve technical assistance to farmers through better procedures, curriculum, information delivery, and outreach services. This also supported a secondary goal of regaining rural support for the local Afghan government.

DoD partnered with leading U.S. agricultural extension universities (including faculty at Texas A&M University and the University of Nebraska-Lincoln) to gain their expertise.[48] DoD also partnered with a new initiative, the Center on Conflict and Development, to add staff and research capacity focused on agricultural development in conflict regions, with an initial focus on Herat.[49]

## Strategic Area 3: Grow Demand for Ag Sector Jobs and Cooperatives

The team prioritized increases in agricultural production through support to cooperatives. The main objectives were to create jobs and increase rural household income and prosperity. This also led to support for labor-intensive programs, such as watershed rehabilitation and rebuilding irrigation infrastructure, to help reintegrate former combatants into the economy. The team cooperated with initiatives already under way, such as the U.S. Agency for International Development's Local Governance and Community Development program[50] and the Commander's Emergency Response Program (CERP) operated by the military.[51] The team could then influence preexisting strategies and direct funding and support into related programs. Overlapping with existing government programs through interagency collaboration meant agribusiness activities and stability operations would be better coordinated and better resourced.

## Strategic Area 4: Expand Agricultural Education and Research

The team's final strategic area focused on the development of long-term national agricultural education, including infrastructure, curriculum, and both practical and advanced research capacity. The team worked with existing faculty and staff at Herat University's College of Agriculture, as well as with the district office of the Afghan government's Ministry of Agriculture, Irrigation, and Livestock (MAIL). Specific objectives for this strategic area included:

- Expand the overall knowledge base for the agricultural sector through instruction and research;

- Improve the quality of technology transfer from university research to producers;

- Increase extension and outreach services provided by staff of the university and the Ministry of Agriculture; and

- Provide linkages between farmers and local and regional sales markets, including capability for international exports.

## INTEGRATING SOCIAL VALUE INVESTING

The DoD Ag team's strategy used an early version of the social value investing framework described previously. Specifically, programs closely aligned with the framework's people, process, and place elements.

## People

By partnering with the Borlaug Institute, the DoD Ag team accessed world class talent, broad skill sets, and deep knowledge bases. The Borlaug team provided leadership and expertise needed for effective local capacity building and for identifying outside resources to support the program. Team members had training and advanced degrees in numerous agronomic subjects relevant to the strategy: agronomy, horticulture, marketing, quality control, value-added processing, cooperatives, extension, university education, and livestock. The team operated in a decentralized manner, conducting field visits throughout the villages and, at times, provinces around Afghanistan. They worked with local communities on a daily basis to identify opportunities to unlock intrinsic value that would have otherwise gone unnoticed by outsiders.

## Process

The team's partnership process resulted in an expansive cross-sector approach, organized as a holistic value chain solution for the local community in Herat. The team recognized that a single break in the value chain would likely mean that funds invested upstream or downstream of that disruption would fail to have a sustained impact on a community. This collaborative approach required equipping and empowering people and institutions throughout the province, and it required new mechanisms to get products and services to market and create sufficient return on stakeholder investment. The team developed a simple value chain analysis mapped against the initiative's key strategic areas (see figure 7.4).

## Place

The team's place-based strategy focused on investing in regional ownership and management to integrate local context into the design, development, and deployment of all aspects of the initiative. Stakeholders (including community groups and local political leadership) were involved in decision making from the beginning. These stakeholders were willing to coinvest their time, energy, and expertise in building a functioning, long-term, and healthy economic system that engaged the community in addressing its own challenges and maintaining long-term solutions. The DoD Ag team partnered with local institutions—both cooperatively and privately owned—as coinvestors in the projects. As articulated at the time, this strategy intended that the population receiving the benefit would become shareholders of the project's outcomes rather than remain reliant as dependents on foreign assistance or donor aid.

The people, process, and place elements of social value investing were all represented by the initiative. Furthermore, financing for the program followed many of the principles of the portfolio element of social value investing. However, the programs relied heavily on the place-based aspects of the framework through locally driven project development and economic ownership for the communities.

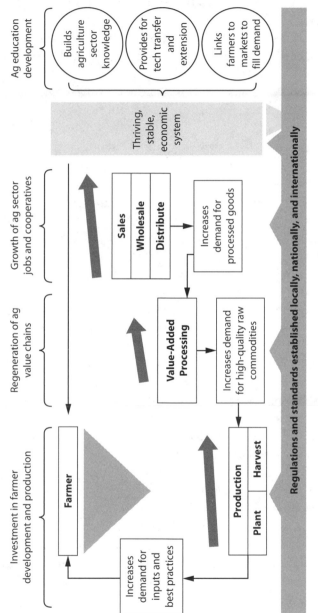

*Figure 7.4* Value chain analysis helps partners develop a comprehensive overview of program activities and gaps to fill in a region's economic system. This diagram maps out aspects of Herat's agricultural value chain within the context of the DoD economic development team's four strategic areas.

## HERAT'S PLACE-BASED INITIATIVE

Following the assessments and evaluation of proposals, the DoD Ag team identified four program areas for Herat's place-based initiative.

### Increase Community Production

Creating an economically sustainable model requires a comprehensive suite of solutions to fill gaps along the value chain. One critical gap in Afghanistan's agriculture sector is access to water and irrigation infrastructure for crops. Herat is a semiarid climate, and irrigation is required for most crops during the dry season.[52] Afghanistan once had an elaborate system of wells and belowground irrigation canals (called *karez*), but much of it was destroyed by decades of war and conflict.[53] Conflict also hampered modern water management, resulting in inefficient resource use upstream (through methods such as flood or furrow irrigation) inadvertently harming farmers downstream by depriving their crops and livestock of water. Flood irrigation requires very little infrastructure, but it is incredibly wasteful and inefficient.[54] Modern irrigation applies water through a long line of sprinklers that pivots in a circular pattern over large areas of land, often 160 acres. Such pivots apply water relatively slowly, can use low-pressure nozzles, and can reach as high as 98 percent water application efficiency. By comparison, flood irrigation is only 40 to 50 percent efficient.[55] However, pivots typically require large fields and specialized maintenance, and they are capital intensive.

During the assessment phase, the Borlaug Institute spent time in a district east of Herat City, in the Rabāṭ-e Pīrzādah village.[56] The head of the local governance council (called a *shura*), Ghulam Jalani (figure 7.5), welcomed the DoD Ag team into the community to consider how the village could be more prosperous. Members of the community, as well as the Ag team's assessments, identified the lack of irrigation as a chief constraint for crop production.[57]

Some community members had seen a small demonstration irrigation pivot in Kabul and proposed the system as a solution for their farms. Jalani, a local farmer himself, knew that this project could make a significant difference for his village, and he worked closely with the

*Figure 7.5* Ghulam Jalani with a center pivot irrigation machine, installed in 2012, outside of the Rabāṭ-e Pīrzādah village. Photo courtesy of Saboor Rahmany.

DoD team to develop ideas. At first, it was unclear how a center pivot covering a large area could meet the needs of many individual small-scale farmers. The community proposed that its farmers coordinate their production cycles, adjust field boundaries, and grow complementary crops in specific zones under the pivot.

With community approval, the DoD Ag team evaluated well sites and tested water availability.[58] They then managed procurement, delivery, and construction of new pivots, as well as maintenance and operations training programs with Herat University. Project success depended on a long-term and substantial commitment from the governor of Herat, who provided additional electricity infrastructure to power the pivots. Local government officials were continuously engaged to maintain their support for the project and to build support for similar projects based on lessons learned. In addition, the Borlaug Institute arranged for new varieties of crop seed to be available for sale to the farmers, so that they could take advantage of the improved water supply.[59]

Previous experience and contacts with global irrigation companies expedited the design and shipment process for the pivots, and the local community was eager to deploy the systems and benefit from better access to scarce water resources. By providing high-efficiency moisture application, these farmers could significantly increase yields for their wheat and double crop plants such as melon, cucumber, onion, eggplant, or tomato.[60] This was especially important during the low rainfall months.

Near Herat city is the Urdu Khan Research Farm (a government-sponsored demonstration farm and research facility).[61] Researchers at the farm were similarly interested in deploying a center pivot to conduct field research and rigorous data collection and analysis. Urdu Khan, the DoD team, and Herat University partnered on a research program to inform expanded use of irrigation systems in Herat and potentially elsewhere in Afghanistan. This included adaptive and comparative research on varieties of corn, cereals, and other vegetables and plants.[62] Following this project, the World Bank issued a tender for improved crop inputs and capacity development at Urdu Khan through its Afghanistan Agricultural Inputs Project (AAIP) initiative.[63] As of 2016, the Afghanistan government's Ministry of Agriculture, Irrigation, and Livestock was actively working to expand this project and its research at the Urdu Khan facilities.[64]

## Build Community-Based Value

Increases in crop production meant increases in raw produce as well. It was critical that additional output from the pivots be met immediately with expanded value-added processing capacity. Otherwise, local prices could suffer, and excess production might spoil.[65] The DoD Ag team worked concurrently on new, women-owned cooperative food processing centers. These centers were reasonably straightforward to develop with short start-up times, they increased living standards for employees, and they helped stabilize local food supplies. New jobs and improved food security also created positive visibility in the communities, which yielded additional direct short-term benefits.

Simple food processing activity was already taking place in communities neighboring the center pivot projects. A local Afghan NGO, for example, focused on providing jobs for women by supporting in-home, rudimentary operations. However, these activities were limited in scope and had little or no quality control (figure 7.6a). The DoD Ag team hoped to leverage the preexisting relationships and experience in place and collaboratively established new Women's Food Processing Cooperatives (WFPCs).

The team conducted a thorough planning process, integrating the full range of stakeholders. In line with the social value investing framework, the team ensured that local Afghan community members played a leading role in designing each processing center and collaboratively developed marketing and distribution plans. These plans integrated local production and logistics information and provided a clear path for market expansion to Herat city and other rural towns. The team worked with technicians and employees at the centers to differentiate their product lines and expand processing operations from the current crop-dependent schedule of six to eight months to a more consistent schedule of nine to ten months. With proper training and equipment, the centers' employees learned to meet quality and control standards (which was necessary for exporting), and the rural processing centers became profitable, self-sustaining, and scalable (figure 7.6b).

Local residents worked with the team to build small-scale hot houses fitted out with the necessary supplies and equipment. This allowed local growers to jump-start production for the first growing season and provide high-quality produce to the food processing centers very quickly. By allowing farmers to grow fruits and vegetables throughout much of the year, the hot houses extended the time line of income-generating activity for farmers and employees at the processing centers. Developing the WFPC program included the training of technicians to assume responsibility for the full-spectrum of business and processing operations as well as creation of a maintenance fund for the building and equipment.[66]

Upon completion, the WFPC immediately led to new full-time jobs for local women, with a strong prospect for additional jobs as operations expanded. More goods and capital were exchanged between local farmers and the rural processing centers, and the production of pastes, sun-dried fruits, jams, and jellies processed from locally grown and harvested vegetables and fruits showed a significant increase.

This all led to a successful agricultural development model that was transferable, sustainable, and scalable for other parts of rural Afghanistan, especially other communities with similar demographic,

*Figure 7.6* (*a*): In-home preparation and sale of processed goods in 2010 before project investments into the community. (*b*): A thriving cooperative store in the Herat area selling the community's processed goods in 2017, years after the cross-sector partnership concluded. (*a*) © Howard W. Buffett, (*b*) courtesy of SIPA Case Collection.

economic, and political characteristics. The DoD Ag team focused on this effort because the early agricultural assessments indicated that fruit and vegetable processing had a high potential for success. Over time, the team continued to provide expertise, capital, and infrastructure to develop more fruit and vegetable cooperatives, also run by women.

Project team leaders for the WFPC adhered to two critical guidelines. First, they ensured buy-in from the local stakeholders every step of the way. Second, they maintained consistent stakeholder communication to ensure that funders and implementers were delivering a project that met local needs. The team engaged local stakeholders from the outset of the project, investing the time and energy to develop trusted relationships. Furthermore, the team did not develop the project until invitations for the initial assessments were received from the local shura and from the preexisting NGOs.

The community also assisted by helping to secure a location for the team to work while they oversaw the project and by maintaining frequent communication during program development. It was a truly balanced partnership; each group brought their own skills, expertise, and resources, and the project team coordinated outside private sector capital to construct the processing centers. Collaborative planning and open communication in the early stages of project implementation proved critical for success.

Ultimately, the program established stable, women-owned and -operated cooperatives that sourced, processed, and marketed local fruits and vegetables in Herat and the surrounding region. One of the processing centers, in the village of Ziaratja, prospered very quickly (figure 7.7). A year after the center opened, Afghanistan's minister of agriculture named the center's leader, Zainab Sufizada, the best commercial farmer of Herat Province.[67]

## Establish a Community-Centered Cooperative Model

Rural farmers' associations existed in Herat long before the DoD Ag team began working in the area. However, farmers often struggled because their operations were small and they had rudimentary equipment, usually limited to hand and animal power.[68] In rural areas, food from locally produced crops was readily available only during the growing season, but farmers frequently had to sell or eat what they

*Figure 7.7* (*a*): Zainab Sufizada's in-home processing operation in early 2011 before the cross-sector partnership. (*b*): A cooperative food-processing center operated by Zainab in late 2011, around the time of the project's completion. (*a*) © Howard G. Buffett, (*b*) courtesy Mark Q. Smith.

grew immediately because there were few ways to store, package, or ship crops after the harvest.[69] Farmers' associations could not adjust production to changing market conditions, and income levels varied wildly throughout the year. Without better production and marketing capacity, the agriculture value chain remained disjointed, and rural citizens faced food insecurity and hunger throughout much of the year.[70]

To address these challenges, the DoD Ag team worked with the Borlaug Institute to establish a large farmer-owned group of cooperatives, the Herat Cooperative Council Growers Association (Cooperative Council). The project organized more than fourteen hundred farmers across several districts into "producer associations." These associations connected farmers to processing facilities so they could access more reliable markets. This project complemented other projects implemented by the regional military command, which was in charge of security forces in the Herat region. This, in turn, supported more secure conditions for sourcing food, more equitable market prices, a more stable rural economy, and, most important, a sense of hope for a better life.

The Cooperative Council helped organize business activities and provided technical advice to fruit and vegetable grower's associations in each active district. This initiative served three primary functions. First, it provided assistance to the coalition forces and Afghan communities through security, stability, and economic investments that would encourage conditions for reconstruction and development. Next, it assisted the adoption of effective business models among rural farmers and agribusinesses that were open, transparent, and reliable. Finally, it developed a comprehensive farm-to-table approach for small fruit and vegetable growers.

The DoD Ag team worked with Afghanistan's Ministry of Agriculture and Herat University's College of Agriculture to enhance the university's applied research for improved fruit and vegetable cultivation. It also provided technical assistance including field inspection staff, crop variety selection, advice on planting and harvest dates, evaluation of soil fertility and water use, integrated pest management plans, and diagnostics on fruit and vegetable growing problems.[71]

In turn, the Cooperative Council supported adoption of new methods and technologies to compete with products from other countries (such as imported wheat from neighboring Iran). For example, the Council was better able to identify market demand fluctuations and forward pricing, and schedule increased or decreased processing capacity as a result. It also improved brand identity for local products. Jointly with the DoD Ag team, the group trained farmers in the cooperatives on how to develop business plans, including distribution, advertising, and overall market growth. Furthermore, the group identified supporting customer services that would increase market share for its raw goods and for the food processing center's products.[72]

The Herat Cooperative Council Growers Association aimed to reduce hunger, poverty, and conflict by increasing economic well-being and food security in Herat's rural communities. The initiative worked to coordinate on-farm planning, assist in the timely production of vegetables, and develop skills that Herat's subsistence farmers needed to operate their rural fruit and vegetable farms. It also developed programs to provide literacy and technical skills these farmers did not have. The projects used or augmented existing agricultural infrastructure, which made them more likely to succeed. Moreover, the strategy developed small- and medium-size farms and strengthened local value chains, including the weak links, such as research and development, production, processing and preservation, and distribution.

In the first year of operations, funding from the development team provided base salaries for Afghan field consultants to work on quality control issues with participating farmers. In addition to providing a framework that would create new rural jobs, the field consultants advised the Council on operations critical to each surrounding community: crop planning, marketing, weed and pest management, and equipment maintenance and operations. From a trade and sales perspective, the training focused on developing marketing channels and on logistics such as shipping and payment processing. These activities increased participants' professional and technical skills, bolstered the long-term economic viability of each village, and reduced the need to migrate from rural areas to city centers.

The program worked quickly to engage the fourteen hundred small-scale farmers identified across key villages and added new extension staff who could support agricultural efforts.[73] University staff and students were involved in a collaborative exchange of data and information. The Council supported financial instruments for contracts and cooperative planning for more efficient product delivery. The DoD Ag team hired local staff as technical field personnel who could resolve issues the farmers faced, and this staff developed training for self-directed leadership based on improved and more accountable business practices.

In the end, the Cooperative Council initiative was a co-ownership model truly emblematic of the social value investing framework. By design, the model was directly applicable to other regions across Afghanistan. It was immediately scalable to twenty-seven thousand small-scale farmers in four surrounding districts to support the larger area's development into a reliable source of products for wholesalers, processors, and exporters.[74] The Council helped stabilize the region and improve the perception of Afghanistan's military security there. The partnership also strengthened relationships between the government of Afghanistan and coalition forces—and support for the U.S. presence among local Afghans.

## Invest in Long-Term Stability: Herat University

In addition to supporting a resilient end-to-end agricultural supply chain, an integrated development model requires investment in place-based institutions to advance human capital, conduct research, and translate academic expertise into value for farmers. To this end, the DoD Ag team worked on construction of a new agricultural college at Herat University. Agricultural colleges are one of the most important building blocks of a thriving, stable, productive agrarian economy. As institutions of higher education, they are committed to the long-term development of agricultural sciences, horticulture, and related subjects.

Plans for a new agricultural college at Herat University began years before the DoD Ag team arrived. The framework of a partially constructed building stood on campus for years, incomplete due to a lack of funding and political support.[75] The DoD Ag team obtained the original blueprints for the building's construction and worked with the university, the Borlaug Institute, and local contractors on cost and time estimates to complete the facility. The team had experience with this kind of project, having previously coordinated construction of the Dr. Abdul Wakil Agriculture College building at Nangarhar University in eastern Afghanistan.[76]

Once complete, the new agricultural college at Herat University was able to house thousands of students studying in existing agriculture-related departments as well as new departments created by the program (figure 7.8).[77] The college was fitted with advanced laboratories for commodity and soil testing, and 130 students were able to learn from laboratory instruction at a given time.[78] The DoD Ag team also coordinated equipment procurement, greenhouse construction, supplies for current and future operations, and provided technical expertise.

*Figure 7.8* (*a*): Herat University's agricultural college building sat partially constructed for years. (*b*): It was completed in 2013 as a result of the collaborative efforts of numerous partners. (*a*) courtesy of Lou Pierce, (*b*) courtesy of Richard Ford.

New programs provided the training and technical capacity for farmers in the area to increase production, meet advanced processing needs, and gain the skills and knowledge to access markets. By building an institution centered on enhancing agricultural productivity for years to come, the team anchored the other agricultural projects in the region—creating a truly comprehensive partnership process for one of the largest long-term stability challenges in Afghanistan.

As a first step, the team established a research-training program to train agricultural faculty to use the new laboratory facilities. This program was also open to regional agricultural ministry personnel, local staff of the UN's Food and Agriculture Organization, as well as workers from a local flour processor.[79] Prior to this program, neither the agriculture faculty nor the regional government staff had access to this type of advanced laboratory or the requisite training in analytical methods.[80] The community benefited directly as the quality of teaching and research at the university improved significantly, as did the value of the government's services to farmers. Rather than an academic research lab for a limited few, this project emphasized the importance of teaching and extension efforts to engage many in the agricultural community. The university developed a uniform curriculum of twelve classes that covered basic statistics and laboratory practices, lab work, and exams.[81] It opened the course to all students, regardless of their gender, religion, background, or area of study.

Although some of the students failed the initial assessment test required to enroll in the course, these students worked with the instructors to develop a special independent study program outside of normal business hours. Fifty-five students enrolled in the first one-month program, of which fourteen were from outside the university (nine from the regional government).[82] During interviews, the instructors spoke highly of the motivation of the students, especially because many of them were taking the course in addition to their normal employment or academic obligations. The class demographic was unusually diverse, attracting both men and women.

## WHAT CAN WE LEARN FROM THE AFGHANISTAN INITIATIVES?

The development team's community-driven approach created a comprehensive and complementary set of place-based solutions for farmers in Herat. Each project aligned with the implementation strategy's four strategic areas:

- *Investment in Farmer Development and Production* was supported by the Herat center pivot irrigation systems, which allowed for more quantity and consistency of production.

- *Regeneration of Agribusiness Value Chains* was supported by establishment of the Women's Food Processing Centers, which provided new processing capacity to meet the increase in production from the center pivots.

- *Growth of Agricultural Sector Jobs and Cooperatives* was supported by the Herat Cooperative Council Growers Association, which organized farmers for economies of scale, broader distribution and wholesaling of food, and a reduction in unemployment.

- *Expansion of Agricultural Education and Research* was supported by the new College of Agriculture at Herat University, which provided support for the entire agricultural sector through extension, workforce readiness, technology transfer, cooperative advancement, and technical staff.

The Herat initiative was the most comprehensive set of place-based projects undertaken by the DoD's economic development team, and it was an invaluable field test for the social value investing framework.[83] This initiative was the team's most ambitious effort to build cross-sector partnerships for agriculture in Afghanistan, and it engaged stakeholders across the entire agricultural value chain. The development team's experiences in Herat were unique given the complexity of the setting, the resources brought to bear, the challenges, and the partners involved. Nevertheless, some of the lessons learned may be applicable to agricultural development projects elsewhere.

To succeed, these projects required local buy-in and the commitment from community residents to contribute what they were able to, such as the specialized labor for the women's cooperatives. Building local buy-in may take time and is challenging in high-risk environments, but it was a significant contribution to the on-time and on-budget delivery of services—particularly the equipment installation and training at the women's cooperatives and the successful implementation of the center pivots and the university training and development programs. The Herat team built productive working relationships with the military, USAID, and foreign government entities operating in the province, which further strengthened the programs.[84]

The working relationship between the U.S. and Afghan governments, private investors, and public institutions was a uniquely appropriate military-civilian collaboration for stabilizing the local environment. NGOs and the private sector often can move quicker and with more flexibility than government. Millions of investment dollars from public and private funding poured into Herat in alignment with the U.S. government's objectives for regional agriculture and stability operations.[85] Furthermore, funders would not have had the opportunity to survey these initiatives without support from the military for transportation and security. We have found only limited instances of cross-sector partnerships with military-civilian collaboration in conflict settings that combined private sector investment and philanthropic support for stability operations.[86]

Significant cultural barriers between the military, private sector, and the NGO community remain, but a clear and coordinated plan to facilitate cross-sector partnerships can overcome organizational differences. Under such difficult operating conditions, this was important for developing effective programming that did not solely rely on traditional fee-for-service contracts. The DoD Ag team acted as a broker for efforts in the region; in future partnerships, a similar secretariat could provide clear communication and manage various activities, relationships, and cultural nuances that develop throughout the partnership.

The Herat project looked comprehensively at the entire agricultural environment, well beyond isolated aspects of the agricultural industry. Addressing only one dimension of agricultural development could lead to more harm than good. Focusing on farmer production alone may serve a rural population's needs for a short time, but failure to link those farmers to broader market opportunities could be disastrous.[87] The assessment team saw this in parts of Afghanistan when farmers had a bumper crop but faced bottomed-out market prices. Some five thousand farmers in a district the Borlaug team evaluated planted tomatoes with the promise of later selling them to a development-aid-funded processing plant. However, these farmers were told four years in a row that the local "market disappeared" when they went to sell, and they were left with excess production and struggling incomes.[88]

The team's assessments in Afghanistan relied on an expansive, context appropriate value chain analysis that looked at various links between training, crop production, processing, and marketing. The assessments informed key investment and resource allocation decisions such as focusing on vegetable and fruit processing and cooperatives. But the Herat project went beyond business supply chain analysis by factoring in the physical and human costs and benefits of the project. By implementing programs to improve human capital, cultivation methods, and the capability of agricultural institutions, the Herat team created a framework to strengthen the links in the value chain and create a healthier economic system that included support structures for agribusiness that have prospered in other places.

The teams focused on engaging experienced local management, and on fully integrating local preferences into strategic planning and program implementation. The team's early assessments ensured that the necessary local capacities were in place to create effective partnerships. This was a productive collaboration between the government, private sector, philanthropic organizations, local NGOs, and the community, and everyone involved shared in the program's successful outcomes.[89]

# CHAPTER EIGHT

# The Place Framework

## Collaborative and Inclusive Partnership Planning

HOWARD W. BUFFETT

Debate between scholars and practitioners over the need to shift broad economic development policy and implementation toward regionally contextual, *place*-based strategies has intensified over the past decade.[1] Interest and investment in place-based initiatives among funders, ranging from economic development institutions,[2] to private and family foundations,[3] to U.S. government agencies,[4] has helped fuel this debate. Neither the concept nor practice is new, but the financial crisis and great recession of 2007–2009 prompted reexamination of traditional economic development models.[5] As a result, place-based initiatives received greater attention, including new research and expanded dialogue by think tanks[6] and academic institutions.[7]

Initiatives are often considered place-based when they bring together multiple partners and stakeholders to develop long-term, comprehensive strategies that support or revitalize a defined geographic area[8] such as a neighborhood or a community.[9] These initiatives attempt to improve social conditions by integrating contributions from funders, implementers, and stakeholders. They form and interconnect programs and services in the given place, often using a common analysis framework for defining and evaluating measures of success.[10] In effect, place-based initiatives are intended to concentrate and coordinate resources, and when designed well, they empower local stakeholders and engage them in the design and implementation of how those resources are deployed.[11]

The programs in the Afghanistan case exhibited many of the characteristics of a place-based approach. Partners coinvested their time, energy, and resources in a set of interconnected programs in and around the city of Herat. Stakeholders in the area worked together with government agencies, foundations, NGOs, and others to design, plan, and carry out the overall partnership. Local entities, ranging from community councils to the public university in Herat, took ownership of the projects, determined program governance, and codeveloped priorities and time lines with the other partners. The initiative's funders and implementers entered the partnership with a specific mentality, treating the community and other stakeholders as true shareholders, or permanent co-owners of the investments being made.

Overall, the approach was supported by an important sense of place, it built on a disposition of longevity, and it engendered stewardship among all partners over shared resources.[12] The management approach of this particular case, and the resulting collaborative attitude between partners, may have been somewhat unusual, but we believe the lessons from its stakeholder focus are important.[13] This focus built trust and encouraged cooperation between community members and local organizations, and it prompted partners to emphasize programs and investments that would yield positive results over the long run. Each of these aspects, fundamental to the social value investing approach, was critical to the initiative's overall success.

In this chapter we will explore ways in which funders, implementers, and stakeholders can work together in partnership through commitments to candid and open dialogue, accountability, and active participation between teams. We discuss ways to support inclusive engagement and consensus building through a joint scoping exercise, and the need for principles that reinforce collaborative ownership. Finally, we outline a process for partners to mutually determine how they prioritize projects through a scoring methodology based on partners' preferences and priorities. This common analysis framework, called the Impact Balance Sheet, is a tool that helps partners cooperatively evaluate program options and plan activities throughout the life cycle of a partnership.[14]

## INCLUSIVE PLANNING REQUIRES
## INTENTION

Cross-sector partnerships involve participants from numerous organizations differing in size, scope, and mission, and with differing timetables and priorities.[15] These participants have to collaborate under diverse leadership styles, and they have to balance their organization's respective objectives, requirements, and resources while working toward common goals. However, few organizations have adopted norms, guidelines, or standard operating procedures for how they will plan and interact with other participants in a cross-sector partnership.[16] This is especially important when collaborative efforts involve neighborhoods, community-based organizations, or individual stakeholders with a highly vested interest in the activities or outcomes of the partnership.[17] The absence of widely established principles for stakeholder inclusion in place-based development can result in stakeholder disenfranchisement, can lead to harmful unintended consequences, or can create resistance to a partnership's objectives.[18] Not only does this present moral considerations,[19] it is also problematic when solutions to complex societal challenges require the willful, active, and coordinated participation of many diverse individuals and organizations.[20]

Almost by default do investors or donors enter a partnership in a position of power or control because they can stipulate requirements for their funding.[21] Often this allows them to set the agenda, determine the goals, unilaterally make major capital allocation decisions, and even micromanage the activities of other partners.[22] As a result, funders may end up imposing their approaches or beliefs on the cooperating organizations whether or not those views are accurate or appropriate for a given context.[23] This means a partnership's goals may be overly "top down," may fail to account for stakeholder preferences or customs, or may fail to identify a problem's root causes.[24] Similarly, when implementation partners respond to requests for proposals or tenders, it positions them to prioritize the wishes and perspectives of the funder above all others. In these cases, delivery of a partnership's programs could be based on misperceptions, uniformed assumptions, or biases rather than on a community's true needs or interests.[25]

For cross-sector partnerships to be effective at providing lasting solutions to problems facing society, funders, implementers, and stakeholders alike must be involved in a partnership's decision-making process.[26] As was done in the Afghanistan case, leaders and participants across organizations should view partnerships as a long-term coinvestment of their time and resources, and stakeholders should be treated as co-owners of the partnership's outcomes.[27] Partners should mutually design the scope of the partnership, develop and follow cooperative principles, and determine agreed-upon responsibilities between participants.[28] Doing so will result in an effective partnership strategy that guides the goals, implementation, and outcomes of the engagement, as well as its governance and the resolution of conflict.[29]

## COOPERATIVE PRINCIPLES FOR PLACE-BASED COLLABORATION

Teams in a partnership have unique underlying core identities, and what goes into developing and strengthening those identities is outlined in chapter 6.[30] For example, teams often engage in important rituals that maintain team cohesiveness, and they hold loyalties toward their organization, fellow members, or leaders. Teams strive toward ideals and values, and team members all go through a variety of shared emotional experiences together. Finally, teams often share a set of common principles that guide their thinking and the execution of their work.

Similarly, partners working collaboratively must share a set of common principles to guide their cooperation throughout the partnership. Funders, implementers, and stakeholders will have diverse preferences and priorities that may come into conflict, and cooperative principles are critical for supporting ongoing work at challenging times. As collaborative efforts become increasingly complex, cooperative principles can help guide ongoing program development and support effective teamwork between partners. The following principles are relevant to cross-sector partnerships engaging in place-based strategy deveopment:[31]

*Inclusive Engagement.* Effective planning of place-based strategies includes as many stakeholders as possible who have a vested interest in the activities and outcomes of the partnership. Partners should conduct exercises to assist with stakeholder identification, mapping, and assessment to help develop engagement strategies. Partners also may conduct scoping exercises to outline programs and help guide decision making early in the partnership. The scoping method (discussed later in this chapter) can assist partners in understanding partnership activities and outcomes in relation to stakeholder preferences and priorities. This is especially important due to the imbalance of power among partners; funders and implementers must embrace inclusive participation and allocate time and resources for consensus building. Doing so benefits the partnership by helping to avoid barriers and opposition to program selection.[32]

*Committed Leadership.* Organizations and stakeholder groups working together must have leaders committed to the goals and outcomes of the partnership. These leaders must establish teams responsible for specific activities and outputs throughout the time line of the partnership, otherwise the collaboration itself is unlikely to survive. Each partner should identify the individuals, including representation from their organization's senior leadership, who will support inclusive engagement and advance partnership goals. Leaders should invest time outside of their partnership teams as well so the goals of the partnership are fully understood and embraced by the entire staff of participating organizations.[33]

*Mutual Accountability.* Initiatives must articulate methods of accountability between partners' respective ownership teams and the stakeholders or members of the local community engaged in the partnership. Partners must mutually develop a set of high-level guidelines to support one another during partnership development and to help establish appropriate expectations regarding program activity. These guidelines may govern conduct between members or outline specific responsibilities undertaken by the partners. The resulting responsibilities must take into account the differing roles, strengths, and activities of funders, implementers, and stakeholders within the partnership.[34]

*Recognition of Progress.* Designing, building, and managing cross-sector partnerships is complex and difficult work that requires ongoing effort. Sometimes partnerships occur over protracted periods with lengthy program time lines that can suffer from stagnation or lead to partner disengagement. Teams and communities alike benefit when milestones are celebrated, partners are brought together frequently, and progress is recognized toward the partnership's goals. Continually recognizing progress is self-reinforcing—it encourages ongoing participation, supports consensus building, and encourages participants to constantly build on relationships and reinforce mutual commitments.[35]

*Participatory Decision Making.* Inclusive partnerships use open and transparent processes to guide governance; this is particularly important for program selection criteria. Effective place-based strategies draw from evaluation models developed cooperatively across partners and stakeholder groups. Similar to the analysis framework outlined later in this chapter, these models help partners customize measures of success, analyze program options, and revise objectives as necessary. To avoid inadvertently excluding stakeholders, the funders and implementers in a partnership must actively support necessary participatory decision-making activities. Initiatives must incorporate ways in which participants can constantly share information and engage in open and honest dialogue.[36]

*Continual Improvement.* Partnering organizations must support methods for continual process and program improvement throughout strategic planning and partnership implementation. Resources will be required to develop tools and methods to monitor, evaluate, and report the progress of programs. Partners must ensure there are opportunities for communities or individuals to contribute ideas, viewpoints, and commentary throughout the life cycle of the partnership. Furthermore, initiatives must use effective feedback loops to capture lessons learned, share insights across organizations and individual stakeholders, embrace best practices, and avoid unnecessary activity or the duplication of efforts.[37]

This is not an exhaustive list, and partners are encouraged to expand on these principles in ways that are relevant for their specific programs and working environments.

Creating an effective and collaborative environment for participants in a cross-sector partnership relies on principles with a common theme: stakeholders must be proactively engaged throughout the design, development, and deployment of place-based strategies.[38] Funders and implementers must be inclusive and welcoming of stakeholders ranging from community individuals to local political leadership to community-based organizations to neighborhood associations and beyond.

## ESTABLISHING THE SCOPE OF
## A PLACE-BASED PARTNERSHIP

Including multiple partners and stakeholder groups in partnership planning and engagement helps align their activities and goals around a common mission and set of shared objectives. Partners who understand each other's preferences and priorities are more likely to respect differences, overcome potential conflict, and appreciate diverse viewpoints.[39] Knowing each partner's perspectives regarding the type and scope of programs that align with their mission means that partners will be better equipped to plan inclusively.[40]

A value chain analysis identifies gaps that a partnership can fill, and the logic flow model outlines inputs, activities, and outputs required to accomplish a partnership's outcomes (see chapter 4). Both should be developed in a cooperative manner; however, neither tool includes elements of partner preference (such as ideal program scale) or operational or mission-related priorities (such as program time lines) in the planning process. Engaging funders, implementers, and stakeholders in a scoping exercise can add those dimensions and provide commonality for exploring respective viewpoints.

In our examples of partnerships throughout the book, initiatives show a higher degree of success when partner's preferences, priorities, and collective actions are harmonized across participants. The thoroughness and inclusivity of partnership planning often governs this harmony and affects whether partners remain engaged, programs meet objectives, and partnerships provide lasting outcomes over time.[41] In particular, funders and implementers in our examples support stakeholder-led development of program plans, or ensure program alignment with existing plans, so that activities reflect stakeholder needs and desires.

Figure 8.1 illustrates the scope of activities in a place-based partnership. These partnerships have a defined geography, or place (the *y* axis), have defined program time lines (the lower *x* axis), and are comprised of programs with differing degrees of impact (the top *x* axis). This chart shows the generalized relationship between those factors and enables funders, implementers, and stakeholders to collaboratively plot their activities within the scope of the partnership regardless of their respective role, sector, or mission. Partners may begin by outlining the

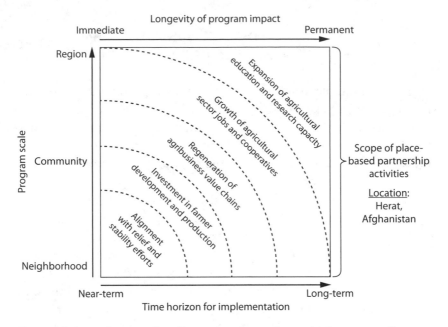

*Figure 8.1* A scoping exercise allows partners to plot multiple aspects of a place-based partnership, as seen in this example based on the Afghanistan case. Strategic focus areas falling further along the right of the *x* axis generally require more time to implement but have a higher potential longevity of impact. The *y* axis delimits the potential or targeted geographic scale of reach, and these values can be exchanged for varying scales (for example, a range from city block to citywide, or from province to multinational).

partnership's goals or objectives on the chart. This example includes strategic and program focus areas from the place-based strategy in the Afghanistan case.

In Afghanistan numerous organizations worked alongside one another. These groups operated programs meeting different needs, and their preferences and priorities are represented by different areas in the figure. For example, food aid and relief efforts were operated by the United Nations World Food Programme located at small primary schools. The administrator overseeing those school-level programs, or a leader in charge of a nonprofit providing similar programs, may prioritize how many hungry mouths get fed in a given day and the next. They may prefer working at the individual school level due to local logistical constraints and the ability to cluster other services on site.

Activities such as these provided an important quick-response stabilization function in our case and fall into the lower left area in the chart.

The Department of Defense (DoD) team worked closely with communities of farmers at the village level on training and the installation of irrigation infrastructure. Local governance councils were most interested in program options that would have a fairly quick and direct impact on their crop production, therefore leading to increases in income and village-level prosperity. The team also worked with small groups of women entrepreneurs whose preference was to serve a broader population than that of the farmer-based programs. In tandem with the governance councils, these entrepreneurs formed cooperative food processing centers to provide the community with access to value-added food products. These centers were supplemented by somewhat limited-use, but important hot houses that extended growing seasons for processed crops. Overall, these activities fall higher on the chart's program scale than the school feeding programs, but they took longer to implement. As reflected in figure 8.2, the depth of the effect of the food processing centers on the community was expected to be similar to that of the farmer irrigation projects in their respective villages.

A collaboration between Afghanistan's Ministry of Agriculture and Herat University led to the development of multiple farmer-owned cooperatives, which were organized under the Herat Cooperative Council Growers Association. The association reached across multiple communities in the area, and over time it improved the quality of crop production and supported more stable local commodity markets. Program participants received training and new knowledge through increased university extension services and access to research conducted at new university greenhouses. Furthermore, partners worked closely with the city and provincial government in Herat, which increased political support for the university's new programs and the village- and community-level initiatives. For example, a local politician committed resources for new electricity supply and infrastructure serving the partnership's projects east of the city of Herat. Not only did this deliver improved services and assistance to his constituents, it provided the official with a widely visible "quick win," which is plotted in the upper left area of figure 8.2.

Finally, partners made numerous long-term investments in agricultural research and educational capacity at Herat University's College of Agriculture. The university and the Ministry of Agriculture both had

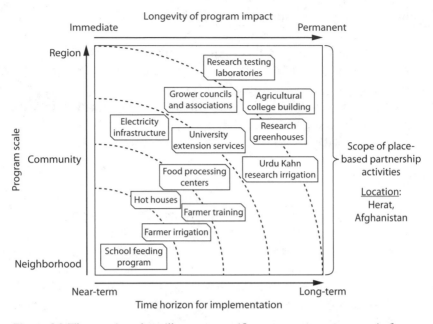

*Figure 8.2* The scoping chart illustrates specific programs across strategic focus areas, as seen with this mapping of activities depicted in the Afghanistan case.

an interest in supporting knowledge development that would span a multiyear time horizon. This interest included long-term, advanced research needs and new opportunities for students in relevant areas of study. High-tech laboratories for commodity and soil testing provided services to local farmers and cooperatives and led to important advanced research data for improving crop production at a regional level.

Based on this outline, we can plot Herat's place-based programs and activities across figure 8.2.

In the Afghanistan case, all partners worked well together, but this type of seamless integration is more often an exception than the norm. A frequent challenge in partnership building is conflicting implementation schedules and objectives for desired outcomes between teams.[42] Because of differing preferences and priorities, teams must work collaboratively to ensure that early or small-scale activities support strategic objectives and the resiliency of the partnership's programs over time. Concurrent programming should be considered throughout the continuum of short-, to medium-, to long-term planning efforts, ranging from actions that meet immediate needs to ones that coordinate community resources, address policy changes, or expand enabling systems or infrastructure. Engaging in inclusive planning helps groups look beyond individual constraints—such as limited resources, information, influence, or time—and illustrates how coordinated action supports the accomplishment of a partnership's goals and outcomes.

## MUTUAL ACCOUNTABILITY AMONG PARTNERS

Partners in a successful place-based strategy maintain mutual accountability to one another and support ongoing cooperative action among participants.[43] Effective place-based partnership strategies establish high-level expectations regarding important conduct that is representative of the partnership's scope and in line with its collaborative principles. This conduct can be governed by operational standards and responsibilities agreed on by the partners, and may be customized and expanded so it is relevant to the nature of specific programs in a given partnership. These standards and responsibilities should be mutually developed and accepted by all participants involved in the engagement, whether they are funders, implementers, or stakeholders.[44] We have found that the following list of accountability practices, grouped by partner role, has led to successful partnerships.

### Funders

Organizations assuming the role of investor or donor in a partnership (such as foundations, corporations, or government entities) should consider the following practices:

- Allocate funding for or make up-front investments in the development of human capital in implementation partners or stakeholder groups if needed. In some cases, this may take a significant amount of lead time and may include training or knowledge transfer for partnering teams or team leaders. Or it could include local or regional capacity building, infrastructure investment in academic or research institutions, or the development of a new knowledge base necessary for making informed decisions.[45]

- Ensure that ample time is spent on the alignment of missions and priorities between partnering organizations. Although a seemingly straightforward task, this requires a concerted effort to give a voice to all partners during partnership planning.[46] It also requires frequent or consistent revisiting of plans and procedures to ensure that necessary course corrections are made throughout the partnership's time line.

- Support linkages between team leaders, program and project managers, external advisors, and other participants across the funders, implementers, and stakeholders in the partnership. Investors or donors often are well positioned to allocate resources to coordinate these linkages, which can help keep otherwise disparate activities aligned.[47]

- Provide guidance and insight on the principles of operation, performance metrics, and the desired long-term goals of the partnership—and how these factors can build on or benefit from other programs or initiatives falling outside the scope of the place-based strategy. Funders can draw on analogous experiences and provide access to advisors or other teams who can introduce new information and fresh perspectives in the development of a partnership's strategy. However, this must be done collaboratively with other partners, and not by directive.[48]

The Defense Department followed many of these practices in the Afghanistan case. The DoD team prioritized contextually appropriate proposals by investing in months of preliminary research and by supporting hundreds of field visits during program design. The team also set clear expectations for stakeholder engagement; implementation partners were both empowered and required to integrate local perspectives and preferences in program planning and development.

## Implementers

The implementers in a partnership (such as contractors, NGOs, or publicly funded aid agencies), should consider the following practices:

- Identify and recruit world class talent, as needed, to support the development of the partnership strategy and the delivery of programs and operations.[49] This is particularly important when there is a need for specialized capacity building, or when partners are operating in difficult or challenging environments. Outside expertise must be brought in with the intent of supplementing existing team experience and stakeholder knowledge rather than supplanting it.

- Assess available resources and key resource constraints required for the partnership to succeed. Implementers must have an understanding of what place-based capacities will be necessary for an effective collaboration, and whether or not those capacities exist.[50] Implementers may need to encourage funders to invest the time and resources required for a proper survey and analysis before full program deployment.

- Create feedback loops for sharing information about partner expectations, program implementation, and stakeholder satisfaction throughout all stages of the partnership. This function is particularly important for maintaining communication between funders and stakeholders, especially at the individual or community level where resources often are deployed. This is frequently a critical missing link in the development of projects, leading to a mismatch between donor or investor intent and community or stakeholder needs and preferences.[51] Without this link, there may be few other means by which to enable effective accountability between the participants in a partnership.

- Improve on or develop new solutions by identifying outside resources not otherwise available to a community or stakeholder group.[52] Implementers may have team members with experience working across wide geographic areas or networks that can be tapped into for innovative ideas. Team members may be able to draw from similar project experiences and responsibly integrate new capabilities or fresh knowledge into the strategy. Implementers also may have access to important political capital relevant to specific program barriers or to the broad scope of the partnership.

In the Afghanistan study, both the Norman Borlaug Institute of International Agriculture and Herat University were key implementation partners. In each case, these implementers oversaw daily project activities and were in constant contact with stakeholder groups throughout the program's planning and operational phases. Because members of the DoD team moved frequently between initiatives in various provinces, and were back and forth between the United States and Afghanistan, the implementation partners provided essential continuity and consistent feedback. They conducted frequent stakeholder interviews and worked with regional partners, including military programs, to acquire additional funding and equipment to support the projects.

## Stakeholders

Stakeholders with a highly vested interest in a partnership's outcomes (which may include community members, local experts, community-based institutions, neighborhood associations, and others) should consider the following practices:

- Supply domain knowledge and local expertise for identifying program opportunities with the greatest potential effect in a given geography or for a given population.[53] Locally engaged organizations and community members are well positioned to provide input on whether or not approaches and proposed solutions are contextually and culturally appropriate or welcome.

- Participate and remain fully engaged in the strategic planning and development of as many aspects of program design and implementation as possible.[54] Stakeholders and implementers should collaboratively plan meetings at times and locations that allow for broad and inclusive participation, taking into account the conditions and constraints of various stakeholder groups. Some stakeholder groups may need to rely on an independent consensus process and self-select members to represent their interests or participate by proxy.

- Develop diverse community support and foster ongoing engagement throughout the life cycle of the partnership to provide practical and constructive input to the partners.[55] Local leaders or representatives must communicate goals effectively and accurately, collect feedback and suggestions, and integrate community perspectives throughout the deployment of the partnership's activities.

- Provide insight on community history and background, social and group identities, and collective beliefs or norms that would otherwise be unknown to outsiders.[56] Every community is made up of unique tangible and intangible attributes, nuanced culture, and shared emotional experiences that help define the character and energy of its stakeholders. These fundamental aspects all contribute to a community's preferences and priorities and cannot be overlooked when developing a place-based strategy.[57]

Local communities were heavily engaged in all aspects of the Herat initiative in the Afghanistan case. One of the village shuras coordinated farmer participation and crop planning for the center pivot irrigation project. This was a delicate matter requiring some field boundary adjustments and updated cultivation practices. In another instance, the head of one of the food processing centers was heavily involved in the design, sizing, and layout for the center. She corrected some preliminary assumptions around the building's overall square footage and staffing capacity, and the implementation partners adjusted plans accordingly.[58]

In the case of the cross-sector partnerships in Afghanistan, funders and implementers made program and infrastructure investments in locally or publicly owned entities—Afghan NGOs, the public university, community cooperatives, and so on. However, in some partnerships, a funder (such as a government entity) may maintain ownership over an investment rather than transfer direct ownership to an implementer or community-based institution. In these cases, partnerships involving public assets should be structured so that stakeholders benefit regardless of ownership or control, such as the arrangement with the Central Park Conservancy profiled in chapter 5. There are many sources of further information on partnership models where the government maintains asset ownership. For example, the United Nations Economic Commission for Europe published a relevant typology in its *Guidebook on Promoting Good Governance in Public-Private Partnerships*.[59] Regardless of the model used, successful and collaborative place-based partnerships should exhibit and follow a well-established set of operational standards and responsibilities.

## Cooperatively Designing an Analysis Framework

When collaborative principles and mutual responsibilities are established, partners will be better equipped to design the partnership's program analysis framework. Numerous tools exist on which to base the design of the framework.[60] Given the complexity of decision making in cross-sector partnerships, tools drawing on multiattribute utility theory may be most applicable.[61] For example, a Pugh matrix analysis[62] may be well suited when partners engage in multiple criteria decision making.[63] Regardless of a framework's specific attributes, the analysis helps illustrate the alignment of participants' respective priorities and preferences with the partnership's strategy and intended outcomes. In effective place-based strategies, these frameworks are developed cooperatively across all partners, and partners work together to use the information to analyze program options and guide decision making.[64]

In the case of Afghanistan, the DoD, the Borlaug Institute, and Herat University collaboratively developed an evaluation tool that was used to analyze proposed programming early in the partnership. This tool included evaluation categories such as "expected impact" and "complexity of program implementation." Each category included project-specific measures such as "employment generated," "safety and security" in a given project's location, and "speed or time required" for project completion. Measures for each criterion were divided into a range from one (the lowest score) to five (the highest score), and all projects were evaluated using this standardized scoring. Figure 8.3 is an excerpt from a project evaluation in Herat.

Evaluation tools can be highly flexible and as multifaceted as required based on the complexity of a partnership and the preferences of funders, implementers, or stakeholders. Although the structure of the initial Defense Department tool was fairly straightforward, portions of it were similar to a more complex model described in the next section.

## The Impact Balance Sheet

We assume that partnering organizations have established a collaborative logic flow model and have surveyed various value chains relevant to the partnership's goals. Partners have leaders with diverse skills and

|  | 1 | 2 | 3 | 4 | 5 |
|---|---|---|---|---|---|
| **Additional revenue ($MM/year)** | <$.100 MM | $.100–500 MM | $.500–1 M | $1–10 MM | >$10+ MM |
| **Employment** | Less than 100 FTEs created/restored | 100–250 FTEs created/restored | 250–500 FTEs created/restored | 500–1000 FTEs created/restored | >1000 FTEs created/restored |
| **Non-economic impact (political)** | Counterproductive to stability (e.g., indirectly supports extremists) | Little political importance, may strain some local relationships | No political impact | Positive local political impact or highly likely to reduce incidents | Positive national political impact and highly likely to reduce incidents |
| **Required investment** | >$5 MM | $1–5 MM | $.250–1 MM | $0.100–.250 MM | <$.100 MM |
| **Facilities and equipment** | Nonexistent, irreparable damage | Old-dated equipment, damaged, etc. | Developing world standard, little damage | Modern facility, little/no damage | State of the art facility and equipment |
| **Human capital availability (management and skilled labor)** | Complete lack of management skill; significant gap in labor skills | Minimal management and labor competence, unreceptive to outside assistance | Minimal management and labor competence, receptive to outside assistance | Capable management and labor, in place, receptive to outside assistance | Managers and labor meet international private sector standards |
| **Power gap** | >15 MW required | 7–15 MW required | 1–7 MW required | 0–1 MW required | No additional power required |
| **Security** | Unsafe, dangerous for personnel or high likelihood of physical damage | Risky for locals, reasonable probability of physical damage | Safe for locals, not safe for outsiders, some likelihood of damage | Safe for locals, non-locals require security support | Safe for all personnel, low probability of being damaged |
| **Reliability of inputs** | Poor access, unreliable inputs | Continuous unreliability of inputs expected | Minor disruptive shortages of inputs expected | Minor input volatility unlikely to disrupt operations | Completely reliable flow of inputs |
| **Distribution network** | No distribution options | Must overcome significant obstacles to make viable | Correctable obstacles in 2 of the 3 parts of the supply chain | Readily addressable obstacle in 1 part of the supply chain | Established, secure distribution networks |
| **Market attractiveness/ competitiveness** | No demand | Local market/import substitution | National or provincial market/ import substitution | Middle Eastern export potential | Strong demand/ export potential |

Impact

Complexity of execution and sustainability

*Figure 8.3* A simple weighted project evaluation excerpt conducted by partners operating in the Herat region in the Afghanistan case. Measures for specific project attributes (the rows) and assigned scores (the columns) are indicated by the shaded boxes. In this example, the evaluated project is expected to generate $1–10 MM of additional revenue, therefore scoring four points in that category.

experiences in place and have a plan for maintaining team momentum throughout the life cycle of the partnership. We also assume that partners understand each other's strengths, constraints, priorities, and respective time lines, as discussed previously.

Partners also need to formalize how they analyze program options for the partnership and what aspects of analysis will be most helpful and relevant to collaborative decision making. The Impact Balance Sheet forms the basis for the place-based program analysis framework outlined here, and derives from an analytical tool codeveloped with the Bill & Melinda Gates Foundation.[65] Furthermore, it is an integrated component of the Impact Rate of Return (iRR) formula presented in chapter 12—specifically, it contributes to iRR's Impact Multiplier variable.

Effective frameworks for place-based partnerships provide funders, implementers, and stakeholders with a model consisting of the following attributes:[66]

- A set of evaluation criteria reflective of each partner's preferences and priorities regarding options for program implementation. These criteria should be context relevant within the place-based strategy and are used to score or rank program alternatives within the partnership. In the Herat assessment tool, one criterion was the amount of time required for project completion.

- An assessment platform that allows for customized weighting between different criteria—depending on the importance of those criteria to the partners—and yet provides a consistent scoring structure across partners' frameworks and between program analyses. One partner may view the safety and security in a given project location as a more important criterion than the project's expected time to completion. In such a case, that partner would assign a higher numerical weight to its preferred criterion (safety).

- An ability to adjust weighted criteria scores based on the confidence the partners have in assigning scores. There may be varying levels of uncertainty across criteria and between projects, and this acts as a discounting factor. For example, if partners have a high level of uncertainty about the amount of time required to complete a project, they may discount that score by a relatively high amount.

■ An analytical output that is meaningful, comparable between program alternatives, easy to communicate, and can be plotted in different ways (for example, the time required for project completion relative to a project location's safety, or the size of the population reached relative to the expected economic impact).

Analysis frameworks vary from partnership to partnership, and the specifics of a given place-based strategy will influence which evaluation criteria are used to score the different program options. Although individual criteria may differ between frameworks, we suggest that the criteria categories generally include the following groups:[67]

1. *Program Alignment.* This aspect of the framework evaluates the extent to which a given project or program aligns with high-level goals or parameters established by the partners' leadership teams. When developing cross-sector partnerships, there may be many options for allocating resources. Taking into account that a full assessment of all options against all criteria could take considerable effort, cost, and time, this section acts as a stage gate for the overall process. If a project or program alternative does not achieve a minimum alignment score, as mutually determined by the partners, it will not be considered further within the analysis.

   This category may include line items related to the size of funding for a project (relative to the overall partnership's budget), the type of program activity (for example, product or service delivery, knowledge development, or policy change), how well the project fits partners' missions, the degree of alignment with community-led plans, and so on.

2. *Program Objectives.* This aspect of the framework evaluates how well a given project or program aligns with the partnership's defined objectives. The program objective score may include line items such as the size of population reached, depth and longevity of impact, sustainability of a project, or cost efficiency of a program. Other factors that may be considered include the uniqueness of the opportunity for the given partnership and the time horizon within which the given program or project can be implemented.

This category helps determine what aspects of program impact are most important to the partners, and how effective a given opportunity may be at delivering such impact. This category often includes criteria representing the operational factors making up the $x$ and $y$ axes of the scoping chart (see figure 8.1).

3. *Program Risk.* The final aspect of the evaluation framework looks at types of risk related to program options, such as the risk that a set of activities will not result in the intended outcomes or that a program will lead to unintended consequences that cause harm or disrupt the partnership's time line. It also questions whether the partners can properly implement the project being evaluated.

This category may include criteria that account for risk to the partnership or partners' reputation, risk based on a project's overall complexity, or whether or not there is a risk that significant amounts of unexpected or unavailable follow-on funding could be required.

These categories help partners define the overall areas they will evaluate, and line items in each category address how the partners will evaluate specific programs. Partners also determine how they will score the valuations across the categories and criteria and how they will assign weighting depending on outcome preferences. This will answer what specific metrics the analysis framework will use to measure opportunities against each other and how important each metric will be.

As an example, one of the program objective categories may be allocated 200 points. A line item within that category, say, the predicted *breadth of impact* of a given project, may be weighted with 25 percent of the overall points in that category relative to the other line items. This would yield a possible 50 points for that line item.

Criteria within the line item help define what partners mean by *breadth of impact.* This can be customized depending on program specifics, but may include the *number of people reached directly* and *indirectly* by a project, as well as the *likelihood a project can build off of other projects* already taking place in the program area. Each of these criteria are subweighted within the possible 50 points for that line item. The criterion *people reached directly* may receive 50 percent of the 50 possible points allocated, or 25 possible points.

Performance ranges define the evaluation ratings for each of the criteria, and these ratings determine what percentage of possible points the project actually receives. Continuing with this example, if a project is predicted to reach more than 10,000 stakeholders, it may receive a rating of 3. If it will reach between 1,000 and 10,000 stakeholders, it may receive a rating of 2, and so on.

In our example, a rating of 2 is only 75 percent as good as a rating of 3, so if that criterion is rated a 2, it receives 75 percent of 25 points, or roughly 19 points. Figure 8.4 shows a few line items from a simplified version of the Impact Balance Sheet analysis framework and illustrates this calculation across category line 2.1, criterion 2.1.a.

The evaluation rating portion of the model helps partners describe, in a quantifiable way, how they differentiate scales or qualities of impact across their line items—something central to the Impact Rate of Return formula (see chapter 12). This example uses a simplistic three-step rating scale, in which an evaluation rating of 3 equates to "high quality impact," a 2 equates to "medium quality impact," and a 1 equates to "low quality impact." Fully customizing a model of this type provides partners with a means to define their joint priorities and to collaboratively determine what metrics and ranges should be used to evaluate many possible projects in a consistent manner.

In more complex evaluation models, each of the scores can be adjusted based on the partner's perceived level of confidence in assigning a given valuation (for example, the partner's level of confidence that a given project will reach the claimed scale of population, or succeed in time). A discounting factor can be applied based on levels of uncertainty, which is particularly helpful when projects use untested methods or partners operate in locations with instability, unreliable infrastructure, or other constraints.

These categories combine to provide an overall project evaluation score, discounted appropriately based on the confidence ratings. The results can be plotted on a scoping chart to illustrate how the methodologies work together visually. This is a useful tool showing an easily understandable relationship between projects and user-selected variables (such as program cost and implementation risk). For example, figure 8.5 plots scoring criteria representing a subset of consolidated projects from the Afghanistan study.

**Step 1: What to evaluate**

**Step 2: How to evaluate**

**Step 3: How to score**

| | Evaluation line item | Sub-weight | Total points | Criteria # | Evaluation criteria | Sub-weight | Sub-points | Evaluation rating key — Impact scale (1 = low, 3 = high) | Eval. rating 1,2,3 | Score rate 50,75,100 | Score pts × % |
|---|---|---|---|---|---|---|---|---|---|---|---|
| 2.0 | | | 200 | | | | 50 | | | | |
| 2.1 | **Breadth of impact:** At what scale will this project reach people? | 25% | 50 | 2.1.a | Assuming project success, how many people would be reached *directly* through this project? | 50% | 25 | 3 = over 10,000<br>2 = between 1,000 and 10,000<br>1 = fewer than 1,000 people | 2 | 75% | 19 |
| | | | | 2.1.b | How many people would be reached *indirectly* through this project? | 24% | 12 | 3 = more than five times as many<br>2 = between 2x and 5x as many<br>1 = 2x as many or fewer | 1 | 50% | 6 |
| | | | | 2.1.c | How much potential is there for positive ripple effects with other projects or community organizations? | 26% | 13 | 3 = High potential<br>2 = Moderate potential<br>1 = Low potential | 3 | 100% | 13 |

Program objectives

*Figure 8.4* The Impact Balance Sheet tool allows partners to develop complex evaluation models for program selection. In this example excerpt, line 2.1.a illustrates how a given partner may assign weights and scoring to a specific criterion regarding the number of people directly reached by a program under consideration.

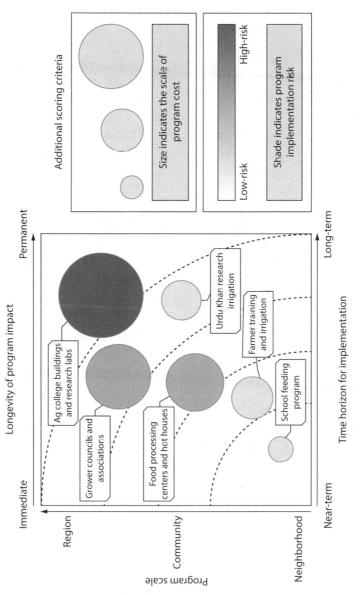

*Figure 8.5* Plotting program evaluation scores on the previously outlined scoping chart provides a visually useful output illustrating the relationship between projects and partner selected variables. This example includes operational variables such as the scale of program cost and program implementation risk.

## OVERCOMING OBSTACLES

Co-creating a comprehensive strategy between organizations from different sectors must account for their different strengths, motivations, time lines, and cultures. This is a challenge, particularly when it is time for organizations to prioritize their activities. Partnerships often offer a positive-sum result, yielding successes far greater than any one organization could achieve alone.[68] But it is not unusual for partners to fall into a negative-sum mind-set and worry about how and where to allocate finite resources. This is ironic because it is often the case in resource constrained environments that "cooperation is not merely a luxury but a necessity to address complex societal problems."[69]

Developing an effective place-based strategy requires funders to involve other partners in making decisions about budgets and goals. They must be willing to consider new, and perhaps less exciting, ways of allocating funding over longer time horizons or in ways that support transitions between short-, medium-, and long-term programs. It is likely that funders will need to consider making up-front investments in preliminary work that supports the development of local and regional capacities.

In general, funders and implementers must be willing to do something that has been traditionally difficult for them: engage stakeholders at the community level, involve them in project development and decision making, and provide them with the opportunity to shift the course of programs during the life cycle of a partnership.[70] Furthermore, implementers must constantly ask themselves how they can do a better job facilitating open communication between funders and stakeholders and how they can provide feedback loops between the two.

Challenges at a local level also may impede a successful place-based partnership strategy:

*Stakeholder Rejection.* A community or group of stakeholders may not wish to engage in partnership building if that group has developed mistrust in outside partners, or if there is a track record of failure. This could be because a funder or implementer did not develop plans inclusively or follow a set of cooperative principles in the past.[71]

*Challenging Conditions.* Certain locations may lack a degree of governance, rule of law, or enforcement mechanisms (for contracts,
for example) that are necessary for effective engagements between
funders, implementers, and local communities or community-based
intuitions.[72] This can be particularly difficult for organizations
without experience operating in such environments.

*Foundational Needs.* The absence of basic services (such as quality
health care or education) or enabling infrastructure (such as roads
or Internet access) can be prohibitive for successful partnerships.[73]
This is especially true if funders are unable or unwilling to take on
the responsibility of making up-front investments to address these
needs or to invest in local capacity building.

*Partner Mismatch.* A funder's intentions and a community's needs may
be incompatible, or a funder or implementer may misunderstand
stakeholder preferences. Staff of an implementation partner may
believe their experiences working in one environment will translate
well to another—and be mistaken. Implementers may find that
they are unable to deliver on a project, leading to unfulfilled commitments or partnership stagnation. Any of these may result from
a lack of early and inclusive planning, quality discussion, or the
alignment of partner preferences and priorities.[74]

These are just a few of the potential difficulties. Other possible
obstacles include coordination complexity, the prevalence or persistence of corruption, unanticipated resource constraints, and more. We
will illustrate some of these challenges in the case outlining partnerships
delivered for the Olympics in Rio de Janeiro, Brazil (see chapter 13).

## CONCLUSION

The recommendations outlined in this chapter may not be universally applicable or practicable. Every partnership is unique, constantly
changing, and dependent on each partner's willingness to work collaboratively through conditions both positive and challenging. It is critically important for funders and implementers to engage stakeholders
thoroughly in partnership planning and development.

As we saw in the case of Afghanistan, a strong connection between
funders, implementers, and stakeholders was a vital component of

the initiative. In any partnership, success relies on the delicate relationship between all groups involved, as well as their commitment to work together over time regardless of the difficulties that present themselves. Open, honest, and frequent communication is important, as is the partnership's emphasis on building community and the partnering team's familiarity and camaraderie with its participants.

The set of operational responsibilities and cooperative principles described in this chapter can guide these engagements, helping to conceptualize and encourage a long-term sense of place and inclusion in support of a partnership strategy. By incorporating these principles, we expect that partners will be more willing to act in the interests of all who are involved, and funders and implementers will treat stakeholders as they would want to be treated themselves, working collaboratively through setbacks and sharing in the partnership's success.

# PORTFOLIO

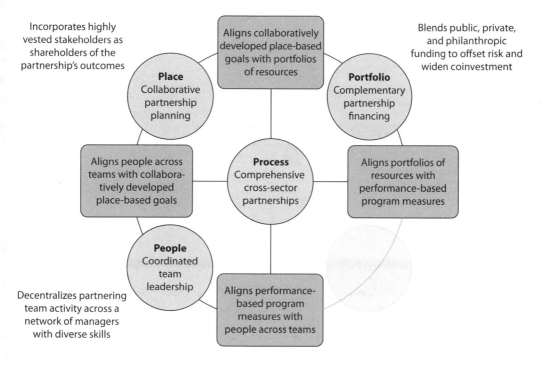

Incorporates highly vested stakeholders as shareholders of the partnership's outcomes

Blends public, private, and philanthropic funding to offset risk and widen coinvestment

Aligns collaboratively developed place-based goals with portfolios of resources

**Place**
Collaborative partnership planning

**Portfolio**
Complementary partnership financing

Aligns people across teams with collaboratively developed place-based goals

**Process**
Comprehensive cross-sector partnerships

Aligns portfolios of resources with performance-based program measures

**People**
Coordinated team leadership

Aligns performance-based program measures with people across teams

Decentralizes partnering team activity across a network of managers with diverse skills

# CHAPTER NINE

# The Portfolio Case

## Increasing Government Effectiveness and Accountability in Brazil

### WILLIAM B. EIMICKE

Previous chapters provide diverse perspectives on a variety of cross-sector partnerships. We explored collaborative planning and the partnership process through India's expansive public service programs. We saw how collaborative leadership in the Central Park and High Line cases created and maintain two of the most iconic and visited public parks on the planet. And we learned how stakeholder-focused program development led to improved and sustained prosperity for rural agricultural communities in Afghanistan.

This chapter describes a cross-sector partnership in Brazil, led by a nonprofit organization called Comunitas.[1] Comunitas is known for their work as a convener of conferences in Brazil focused on best practices in local government. They also provide full fellowships for local officials in Brazil, enabling them to earn master's degrees in public policy and administration. Comunitas's membership and board includes many of Brazil's most successful private corporate leaders, who focus on improving the performance of city governments throughout the country. All of the organization's work is funded by voluntary contributions from members. Recently, Brazil has gone through very difficult economic times, with several major corruption scandals affecting federal, state, and local government officials as well as corporate executives. Public faith in the effectiveness and honesty of government has fallen.

In response to these challenges, Comunitas launched a program called Juntos, designed to bring greater efficiency, integrity, and transparency to local governments in Brazil. Although designed and developed independently of the social value investing framework, Juntos delivers its mission in ways that are analogous.

Juntos has developed formal, cross-sector partnerships with cities through expansive processes and comprehensive strategies. It also relies on decentralized, collaborative leadership across diverse teams, with organizational values that emphasize integrity and respect. Through Juntos, Comunitas members provide philanthropic capital and private sector expertise to help their city government partners. Juntos helps cities revise their financial practices, increase community outreach, and better use their public dollars to improve and expand critical community services, such as public health and education. They also employ place-based strategies to enhance local economic development so these cities can sustain new innovations and improvements with a growing tax base. By mixing social, corporate, and individual investment into a blended portfolio, they are offsetting implementation and political risks, expanding pools of available capital, and aligning financial and social goals to increase public program efficiency. Although Juntos is a relatively new program, it has already achieved measurable success in several Brazilian cities, as you will see in the coming pages.

## GOVERNANCE CHALLENGES IN BRAZIL

Brazil has been a boom and bust economy for most of the twenty-first century. Between 2003 and 2012 Brazil enjoyed prolonged economic growth. The boom attracted substantial international investment and helped raise millions of Brazilians out of poverty as the government used higher tax receipts (particularly from oil-related taxes) to fund substantial increases in government cash transfer payments and other social programs. When the global rise in commodity prices ended and oil prices fell, cities across Brazil had to raise taxes on individuals, property, and local businesses to sustain themselves.[2]

As Brazil's economy continued to decline, the federal, state, and local governments also cut programs, leading to massive protests across the country. Millions of Brazilians took to the streets, demanding more affordable public transportation, better education, improved infrastructure, as well as greater transparency, more honesty, and less corruption from lawmakers. Many officials were criticized for imposing high taxes yet failing to provide basic city services.[3] Responding to legitimate complaints about tax levels and tax fairness would not be easy.

Brazil's tax system is widely considered one of the most complex and bureaucratic in the world. A 2014 study by PricewaterhouseCoopers (PWC) in cooperation with the World Bank and the International Finance Corporation (IFC) found that business tax compliance in Brazil was the most burdensome tax system of the 189 economies included in the study.[4] PWC found that the worldwide average for tax compliance was 268 hours, with United Arab Emirates at the lowest (12 hours) and Brazil as most burdensome, requiring more than 2,600 hours to comply with tax codes.[5] In 2018, the World Bank Group rated Brazil 125th of 190 countries in the ease of doing business overall, 139th in trading across borders, and 176th in starting a business.[6]

Not surprisingly, these high barriers to access a rapidly developing market of two hundred million people enabled a relatively small group of local companies and large multinational corporations to do very well. For all its complexities, Brazil's legal and tax systems remain stable and consistent, and the World Bank ranks Brazil relatively well in protecting minority investors (43 of 190) and enforcing contracts (47 of 190).[7] Some of the most successful companies include Jereissati Participacoes (shopping centers and telecommunications) and Kieppe Patrimonial Ltda. (construction services, oil, and gas). Kieppe is controlled by the Odebrecht family, who played a major role in construction for the Rio de Janeiro Olympics, including the Porto Maravilha (see chapter 13).[8]

Some of the leaders of these companies and some leaders of other smaller, successful enterprises recognized that Brazil's growth and development was constrained by overly complex and often inefficient and corrupt governments. They share a sense of corporate social responsibility for the harm this poor governance had on the country's large population of low-income families and the inequality that characterized most cities in Brazil. In 2000, several of these private sector leaders came together to form a social organization called Comunitas, which combines philanthropic and private sector investment to improve management of the public sector.

## COMUNITAS PARTNERS WITH AND INVESTS IN LOCAL GOVERNMENTS

Comunitas's mission is to drive private sector participation and investment in the social development of Brazil.[9] Comunitas is founded on the belief that a better future for Brazil requires more effective local governments and that public-private partnerships, including private sector expertise and investment, can achieve that. Research by Comunitas indicates that private companies are willing to make that investment; its 2014 study found private firms invested R$2 billion (roughly USD $620 million) in education, health, environmental protection, public safety, and other social development projects in that year alone.[10]

Originally focused on researching best practices in corporate social investment and on its Annual Leaders Forum (which is an ongoing program), in 2012 Comunitas created a cross-sector partnership called *Juntos Pelo Desenvolvimento Sustentável* (Together for Sustainable Development), widely known as Juntos. Comunitas director and president Regina Siqueira (figure 9.1) explained that Juntos created a network of private sector leaders and companies deeply committed to

*Figure 9.1* Regina Siqueria, director and president of Comunitas. Siqueria runs the Juntos program, which works with cities to improve their effectiveness and their accountability to citizens. Photo by Adam Morrell, courtesy of SIPA Case Collection.

corporate social responsibility, particularly focused on improving local governments' financial practices, increasing government outreach to the public, enhancing local economic development, and improving community services. Juntos seeks to accomplish these objectives through cross-sector partnerships of leaders from the private sector, civil society, and local governments, with a primary objective of combining social, corporate, and individual investments to increase public program efficiency.[11]

Through this combined capital approach, board members such as José Roberto Marinho and Carlos Jereissati, and Comunitas President Siqueira, sought to develop a new strategy for investing in local governments. Rather than support individual gifts to local organizations such as a hospital or school, Comunitas would create a large fund for concerted action and focus on a range of medium-sized cities. The group identified cities as the level of government most in need of help and whose improvement would have the most direct impact on local businesses and residents. The group would provide a package of services, and selected cities could choose options from the package, such as independent financial consulting, leadership coaching, and digital platforms to facilitate citizen engagement.

The initiative is funded by a group of approximately forty donors, including several Juntos board members and other Brazilian business leaders, who together raised more than USD$23 million for the first four years of operation.[12] These business leaders believe that a more effective and efficient public sector will improve the lives of all Brazilians and thereby improve the business climate. They also believe that through Juntos they could transfer the best practices of private sector management to local governments across the country, particularly in financial management, customer service, strategic planning, innovation, and communication.[13]

Juntos board members and senior staff agreed that the most pressing issue facing most local governments in Brazil was recurrent budget deficits. In Brazil, most of the power to tax is at the federal level, but most of the responsibility to deliver key public services such as education, health care, and public safety is handled locally. Federal aid to localities usually falls short of the amount needed to provide quality services. Poor local management, bad planning, fiscal mismanagement, opaque government, poor communication with the public, outdated technology, and corruption exacerbate the impact of the funding shortfalls. All of this is made worse by the pressure of the four-year election cycle for local mayors. Strategic planning and fundamental reform is difficult when you must prepare for the next campaign no more than two years after you are first elected.

Professor Thomas Trebat, director of Columbia University's Global Center in Rio de Janeiro and an economist and former bank executive, commented, "To build a culture of taxation . . . requires a lot from local managers. If they are seen as asphalting roads, building a hospital or school [they hope that] voters would somehow reward them for that, but a lot of that spending turns out to be aimed at winning re-election, rather than providing the services that citizens really need and want at prices that are sustainable."[14]

To overcome these obstacles, Juntos looked for cities where the mayor and local officials were in their first term and would commit their professional staff to the effort. They followed a similar playbook to that of the social value investing framework: they used formal agreements to enter and structure their partnerships, established mutual operations, and developed comprehensive strategies for city projects. They also developed diverse, decentralized teams, including members from Comunitas, city officials and staff, and private consultants. Programs are place-based by nature due to their focal areas, and the partnering mayors work to include broad community participation and a willingness to operate transparently and share important financial information with Juntos staff, consultants, and the public. With all of the elements in place, a formal contract is signed, and Comunitas, city leaders, and constituents collaboratively select projects for reform and innovation.[15]

## JUNTOS BEGINS IN CAMPINAS

Juntos leadership pilot tested their model in the city of Campinas, located ninety minutes from São Paulo, the largest city in South America, and in Brazil's most affluent state. The population and wealth of Campinas grew rapidly during Brazil's boom years, and it became home to major companies including Samsung and Honda, as well as to some important universities. It is connected to the rest of Brazil and to much of the Americas through an international airport and modern highways.

The city government of Campinas was well known for its recurrent budget deficits, inefficient and complex bureaucratic procedures, and corruption. To many of those dealing with the city, it seemed that the only way to get an approval or move paperwork along was to pay a bribe or make a political contribution. Decades of bad behavior reached a breaking point in 2011 when then mayor Hélio de Oliveira Santos was arrested and charged with accepting illegal payments for city water and sewage contracts.

A reform candidate, Jonas Donizette, ran and was elected on a promise to bring fiscal reform, transparency, and responsiveness to Campinas city government. Taking office in 2013, Mayor Donizette and Juntos agreed to partner in the reform. The first step in the process was balancing the city's budget. To do so, with the city's approval, Juntos hired a well-respected management consulting firm, Falconi, to conduct a comprehensive financial assessment and audit. The city agreed to open all its books and records to Falconi and then, to broaden community participation, Falconi would present their findings in meetings open to the public and the media.[16]

Instead of a quick and easy fix by cutting major programs and laying off city employees, Campinas and the Juntos team focused on measuring, monitoring, and reforming government processes to balance the budget in a sustainable manner while improving public services (so citizens would be more willing to pay the taxes they owed). The first step was to set monthly targets for revenues and expenditures that would bring the budget into balance. Second, the city focused on collecting taxes already due that were unpaid or underpaid. By the end of the 2013 fiscal year, for the first time in several decades the city had an operating surplus.[17]

This strategy reflects aspects of a cross-sector portfolio approach similar to that of social value investing: offsetting financial and implementation risk by blending resources from different sources. The mayor and his team understood that their financial management practices could be improved and, if they were, that the city would likely collect more revenue and reduce expenditures. However, hiring an expert private consulting firm for the analysis and for identifying the appropriate reforms would be politically controversial, and the procurement process would take a long time. Moreover, the winner of procurement might be the least costly consultant rather than the most talented, and there was also the risk that once implemented the reforms might not improve the city's finances enough to justify the cost of the consultants—at least in the near term. Through the partnership, Comunitas could quickly hire one of the best financial consultant firms in Brazil and pay their fees, protecting the city from significant political and financial risk. With the expertise of Falconi consultants, the city's implementation risk was also reduced. The city covered the costs of implementing the recommendations, but also reaped the benefits of significantly higher revenue collections and lower expenditures.

The next step for the city and the Juntos team was to show Campinas taxpayers that the city could work better. To illustrate this visibly and meaningfully, the reform team focused on the building permit process. The existing process was extremely complex, very slow, and often corrupt. Typically, granting a building permit required the approval of dozens of bureaucrats in eleven separate agencies, which took an average of more than three and a half months. For local builders and small projects, the cost of the permit process in time and money was high, and the payment of small bribes was often required to move the paperwork along.[18]

The consultants found that all projects were subject to the same rigorous and complex analysis, regardless of whether it was for constructing a major new factory or a minor home modernization project. In fact, more than 75 percent of all applications were for small projects. Their solution was radical for Brazil (but practiced in many cities around the world): put the process online and allow small projects (up to five hundred square meters for residential projects and up to one thousand square meters for commercial projects) to be "self-certified" by the licensed engineer or architect supervising the construction.[19]

Average approval time for small projects dropped dramatically to less than a month, and some approvals happened in a matter of days, a very significant and measurable performance improvement. Now city experts and officials could focus their time on large, complex, and potentially higher-risk developments. The new process communicated a basic trust between citizens and their government.[20] Here, again, the financial risk of hiring an expert consultant was mitigated by Juntos choosing the firm and paying their fees (figure 9.2). The city continues to bear the implementation risk—the new process might not work—but that risk is partially mitigated as the city relied on experts at Juntos and Falconi to design and implement the new process. To date, the process is working well.

*Figure 9.2* In Campinas, Brazil, a team works on the Colab platform provided by Juntos. Colab engages citizens by giving them a voice in setting city priorities and providing feedback on how well the city is functioning. Photo by Adam Morrell, courtesy of SIPA Case Collection.

Enhancing citizen participation in municipal decision making was next for the Juntos collaboration with Campinas. Using an existing online platform called Colab, Juntos helped Campinas engage its citizens digitally through the Colab mobile application and website. Citizens use the application to alert the city government about roads or buildings in need of immediate repair, such as potholes or a crumbling cornice. Citizens can propose a new initiative or rate an interaction with a city agency or official. The new link gives citizens a voice in city decisions, and city officials have a chance to rebuild their credibility in the wake of a major corruption scandal and discover firsthand information about the public's priorities. Mayor Jonas Donizetti signed a contract with Colab in 2015, and a recent count showed over nine thousand Campinas citizens actively using the platform.[21] The use of Colab in Campinas is an important step toward supporting increased community ownership over city programs.

Based on the success in Campinas, Juntos helped the cities of Pelotas and Santos adopt the Colab platform. Juntos worked with each city's in-house IT staff to customize the platform and integrate it with existing hardware, software, and other communications channels. Juntos ensured that the three cities could operate and maintain their system without expensive outside consultants or ongoing subsidies from Juntos. By blending various sources of capital, Juntos paid for creation of the Colab application and platform and customized it to work with each city's existing IT hardware, software, and staffing, which allowed the three cities to reduce their financial risk.

Our team visited Campinas in 2016 and observed the progress of the Juntos-Campinas partnership. We spoke to them about their comprehensive strategic plan and next steps in moving the government of Campinas toward long-term success. We met with Mayor Jonas Donizette, the Juntos Leader Partner, Campinas department heads and staff, citizens, and local business leaders. Although the visit was relatively short, we saw much of the city, met many residents, and were impressed with the professionalism and commitment of the government and Juntos. It was clear from the many people we met there that citizens in Campinas wanted to make their city a model for other cities throughout Brazil and even around the world.[22]

## JUNTOS PARTNERSHIPS SPREAD ACROSS BRAZIL: PELOTAS

Building on the success of the Campinas pilot project, Juntos launched similar initiatives in small and medium-sized cities across Brazil. The popularity of the Colab platform in Campinas encouraged Juntos to use technology to improve management and services in other places. The city of Pelotas, in Brazil's southern state of Rio Grande do Sul, provided Juntos with an opportunity to work with a young, newly elected, energetic mayor, Eduardo Leite (figure 9.3), who was known for his intelligence and integrity. These collaborative leadership attributes contributed to the choice of Pelotas as a Juntos partner. Mayor Leite believed the private sector could help government manage more effectively and efficiently. Acting on this belief required political courage because partnerships between the government and private entities were generally viewed unfavorably in his region. Mayor Leite (elected in 2012) said he welcomed a partnership with Juntos because they had the financial resources and management expertise that could help his city deliver better services to its citizens at a lower cost.[23]

*Figure 9.3* Mayor Eduardo Leite at a city health clinic designed collaboratively with local residents and completed through the Juntos-Pelotas cross-sector partnership. Photo by Caco Argemi / Valor Econômico / Agência O Globo, courtesy of Comunitas.

Juntos agreed that the city should choose which services to improve with their help. Based on public surveys and meetings with his constituents, Leite focused on improving public health by refocusing the municipal health care system on primary care. Leite hoped that by doing so the city would not only improve the health of its citizens but also save money.[24]

With financial assistance from Juntos, Leite hired Falconi, the same consultant firm used in Campinas. The city also partnered with the Tellus Institute to rethink and redesign the city's public health program. The redesign process began with a dialogue between citizens and frontline health care workers, which continued throughout the implementation phase. The top priority for the participants was to make the system and the facilities more welcoming and the approach more holistic.

Ultimately, they created a new system called *Rede Bem Cuidar* (Well-Cared-for-Network) in the Bom Jesus Basic Health Care Unit. The facility includes not only health care services but also an educational kitchen to promote a healthy, well-balanced diet, a community garden, an outdoor exercise space, a playground for children, and green space for quiet contemplation and relaxation.[25] The city could afford to pay only about 15 percent of the capital costs for a new facility, so Juntos provided a capital grant for the rest and construction began immediately. This approach was an effective blending of capital in which the initial risk was offset from philanthropic contributions, making it possible to kick-start these public service upgrades.[26]

Like Campinas, Juntos funding helped mitigate the city's financial risk in choosing the private sector consultants (Falconi and Tellus) for the health care reform initiative. Juntos also helped the city reduce its implementation risk by paying 85 percent of the capital costs of redesigning the first holistic clinic. Subsequent surveys indicate that the people of Pelotas are very pleased with the new facility they helped design. Today the clinic is much more than a place for the sick: citizens come in regularly to learn how to cook healthy meals, how to exercise more beneficially, and to watch their children play. Based on this initial success, Pelotas has financed the redesign of two more clinics, with partners making substantial complementary investments.

Using the Colab model from Campinas, Juntos helped Pelotas create a digital platform called Click Health (*Clique Saúde*). Click Health shows its users the most convenient health care center or emergency room and lists the services provided and the medications available—it can even schedule vaccinations by location. Click Health also sends out health care alerts and public health information from the city.[27]

Mayor Leite commented that the Juntos partnerships with local government are extremely important in improving Brazil's public management. He said Juntos gave his city access to the best experts in financial management, strategic planning, and design, substantially mitigating the city's financial and his own political risk of adopting more innovative management practices. Juntos also helped expedite the implementation of the innovations by paying for some of the capital costs of rehabilitating the first new health clinic and of setting up the Colab communication platform. The Juntos network also connected Mayor Leite with the Lemann Foundation, experts on education innovation in Brazil. With Lemann's help, Leite brought the well-known and well-respected Khan Academy to Pelotas to help improve elementary and secondary education in the city.

## CURITIBA: BUILDING ON A HISTORY
## OF PLANNING AHEAD

In the 1970s, the leaders of the southern city of Curitiba sought to emulate the futuristic, well-planned new Brazilian capital of Brasilia. Brasilia was based on the now world-famous vision of Oscar Niemeyer and Lucio Costa and was built from scratch in four years. Brasilia was designed to be modern and beautiful and was carefully and rationally organized. The buildings are widely viewed as beautiful, but the city is huge, designed for the automobile, and lacks the "street life" we often associate with great cities such as New York or Paris.[28]

Curitiba embraced the Brasilia concept of a modern, well-designed and beautiful city but with a very different vibe, greatly influenced by architect and former Curitiba mayor Jamie Lerner. Lerner sought to design a city that would welcome working, shopping, recreation, diversity, and art, and one that would not depend on the automobile.[29] Building on these principles, Curitiba is becoming a model for other sustainable cities, particularly for its innovative and expansive express bus-based transit system (BRT)—essentially an aboveground subway. In the 1980s, Curitiba expanded the system to the entire metropolitan area and subsequently the model was copied by Bogota, Colombia's TransMilenio, and in other cities around the world from South Africa to China.[30]

Entering the twenty-first century, Curitiba's commitment to innovation through strategic planning was slowing. The tremendous growth in population—from 360,000 when the commitment to planning began to more than 1.8 million today—put tremendous pressure on the system. Despite the continuing success of the BRT, new housing developments were less carefully planned, and car use increased significantly, adding traffic congestion and air pollution.[31] As the population grew, planning became more top-down, less collaborative, and less effective.

In response, during the early 2000s, the city introduced a new plan—Curitiba 2030—but it was only partially implemented and then shelved. City officials believed the problem with Curitiba 2030 was that key stakeholders and the public were not engaged enough in its formulation and implementation. Therefore, Juntos and Curitiba decided to partner in an effort to recapture the community's spirit of cooperative planning and innovation.[32]

Working with Juntos, the city began to reinvent the 2030 plan as Curitiba 2035, using aspects of a place-based approach (see chapter 8). Juntos provided technical assistance on network management to engage key citizens and civil society. Overall, thirty stakeholders and more than 250 technical experts contributed to the strategy. A series of lectures, panels, meetings, and communications expanded participation and knowledge about the new plan. In late 2016, the opposition party won the municipal elections, so the future of Curitiba 2035 is unclear.[33] Nevertheless, the partnership between Curitiba's government and Juntos developed a new city planning engagement platform that can be replicated elsewhere. And, the new Mayor seems to be embracing the partnership with Juntos.

Here again, Juntos helped mitigate the financial and implementation risks of innovation in Curitiba by providing technical assistance to design a networking system that would effectively connect key stakeholders. The system also enabled a very large number of experts to contribute to the plan itself, and it provided substantial transparency by communicating the substance of a series of meetings and discussions regarding what the plan should encompass. Because the plan has not yet been implemented, it is uncertain whether the Juntos investment will mitigate the city of Curitiba's implementation risk.

## A GROWING NEED FOR THE JUNTOS MODEL

Beginning in 2015, a wide-ranging set of corruption scandals enveloped Brazil, starting with the revelation of kickbacks and payoffs around the oil and gas giant Petrobras and spreading to the construction projects for hosting the FIFA World Cup in 2014 and the Rio Summer Olympics in 2016. Hundreds of politicians and company executives have been accused, and many convicted. A former president (Lula) and the current president (Temer) stand accused, another former president (Rousseff) was removed from office, and trust in the Brazilian government continues to erode.[34] A 2016 Gallup poll found that a mere 15 percent of Brazilians trusted their country's leadership, a record low. The study also indicated that perceived corruption was at a record high of 78 percent.[35] A poll in April 2017 found that over 90 percent of Brazilians felt the country was on the wrong path, and President Temer's September approval rating was at 3.4 percent.[36]

For Juntos and the leadership of Comunitas, these national events make their work at the municipal level even more critical and challenging. Juntos and its partner cities have sought to overcome the public's general skepticism and understandable anger at their government by providing positive results. Working locally, Juntos is helping to improve services that matter to the citizens through a partnership process that engages the public and operates with a full commitment to transparency. So far, the public seems to recognize the difference. In the 2016 elections, public officials in Juntos network cities were reelected at twice the rate of the national average. In the eight partner cities in which the mayors were up for reelection, six were reelected and one, Eduardo Leite of Pelotas, chose not to run for a second term, leaving office with a 60 percent approval rating.[37]

## JUNTOS: TODAY AND TOMORROW

Since its initial 2013 pilot project in Campinas, Juntos has partnered with the cities of Pelotas, Curitiba, Paraty, Juiz de Fora, Teresina, Santos, and Itirapina to facilitate improvements and innovations in local governments across Brazil. In 2017, Juntos initiated new partnerships with larger cities, including São Paulo, Porto Alegre, and Salvador. Juntos also continues to host an annual meeting of its network of public officials and its expert members for discussion and debate on important issues and problems facing local governments in Brazil. The 2017 meeting, for example, focused on cross-sector partnerships. Comunitas sought to spur new thinking by inviting representatives from outside Brazil to speak about their experiences with partnerships as a tool for innovation, including the Mayor of Medellin, Colombia, whose city has been called a model for twenty-first century urbanism.[38] Juntos also hosts special forums on critical municipal challenges.

At Juntos governance meetings, local business leaders, mayors, cabinet secretaries, and technical partners gather to discuss expectations, challenges, and opportunities for the program itself.[39] Also in 2017, Juntos took its knowledge-sharing and government-improvement initiatives beyond its network of partnerships by offering an open online learning and training platform called Rede Juntos, which provides information, digital tools, and private sector expertise to anyone.[40]

Going forward, Comunitas and the Juntos initiative face significant challenges. Whether the network can be sustained and expanded in the economic and political malaise that currently envelops Brazil remains to be seen.[41] Additional funds must be raised to add new cities to the network. A very important and positive Juntos rule (but significant fund-raising challenge) is that private donors cannot have a financial interest in Juntos partner cities. Also, new projects need to have medium to high initial investment costs (covered by Juntos private members) and low ongoing maintenance costs, so that the cities are able to sustain the innovations over the long term.

Evaluating the performance of the initiative, internal studies by Comunitas found that partner cities benefit ten dollars in program savings or increased revenues for every dollar Comunitas invests through Juntos.[42] Clearly, the investment of private capital and expertise produces a major benefit to the people of Brazil. By offsetting program, cost, and implementation risk for its partners, the Juntos program engages in a blended capital approach aligned with the social value investing portfolio element (see chapter 10). Although the Juntos portfolio represents investments broader than the set of financial tools outlined in chapter 10, the overall principles are the same— combine different types of capital, especially from less risk-averse sources such as philanthropy, to create a coordinated strategy that finances the programs in a cross-sector partnership.

# CHAPTER TEN

# The Portfolio Framework

## Blending Capital for Social Good

HOWARD W. BUFFETT

In previous chapters, we outlined the benefits of cross-sector partnerships and important methods and considerations to ensure they succeed. We provided common definitions and discussed the need for comprehensive program planning. We also described human capital coordination across teams, and crucial aspects of collaborative program ownership between funders, implementers, and stakeholders. In chapter 8 we discussed ways for partnership participants to evaluate and select programs cooperatively to ensure that place-based development strategies focus on long-term stakeholder-driven needs. This chapter outlines how partners from across sectors can combine resources into a blended *portfolio*—with a particular emphasis on philanthropic capital—to finance activities throughout the life cycle of the partnership.

Developing and deploying a blended cross-sector portfolio brings together funding from public, private, and philanthropic partners collaboratively to address challenges that require the coordinated activity of many participants. It focuses the efforts of decentralized teams and leaders across funders, implementers, and stakeholders and drives improved performance toward mutually developed programs and common goals. By including financial market mechanisms, it opens partnerships to for-profit sector knowledge, resources, and expertise that might otherwise be isolated from activities that provide a social good.

The blended cross-sector portfolio approach allows partners to draw from diverse capital pools to affect or offset risk and, in turn, to unlock coinvestment opportunities. This chapter begins with a brief discussion of investment-related risk and then introduces concepts of a blended finance portfolio. We then describe the potential role for philanthropy and detail ten types of philanthropic capital allocations relevant to a cross-sector strategy.

## THE ORIGINS OF A PORTFOLIO APPROACH

The 1950s saw the emergence of a new mathematical framework for investors to analyze the trade-off between financial risk and reward. The technique looked beyond an individual investment's risk/reward profile and focused on the interactions of many investments across asset classes when combined into a diversified portfolio. This approach, *modern portfolio theory*, suggested that investors analyze and take into account how assets are interrelated rather than consider them in isolation.[1] Because assets can share similar volatility, diversifying investments in a portfolio can reduce risk and lead to more predictable or profitable returns.[2]

Blending diversified investments to influence the risk/reward profile is central to the theory.[3] Investors can analyze groups of investments based on this relationship and select those with the highest levels of return at given levels of risk. Plotting the ideal trade-off points between risk and reward illustrates the *efficient frontier*—a series of portfolio configurations with optimal investment allocations (figure 10.1).[4]

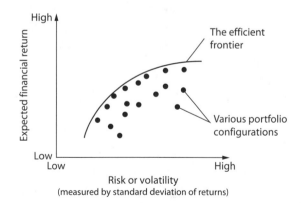

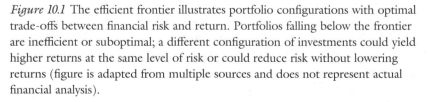

*Figure 10.1* The efficient frontier illustrates portfolio configurations with optimal trade-offs between financial risk and return. Portfolios falling below the frontier are inefficient or suboptimal; a different configuration of investments could yield higher returns at the same level of risk or could reduce risk without lowering returns (figure is adapted from multiple sources and does not represent actual financial analysis).

Portfolios falling below the efficient frontier are combinations of investments that are suboptimal. If they were configured more efficiently, they could yield higher expected returns at the same level of risk, or the same expected returns at a lower risk.

## EXPANDING THE FRONTIER

The efficient frontier as originally conceived focused on the field of traditional finance. It likely did not account for the inclusion of grants or concessionary investments through cross-sector partnerships. For example, consider how public finance, charitable contributions (as first-loss capital), or instruments comprised of philanthropic dollars might change the composition of a portfolio.[5] In the context of cross-sector partnerships, could traditional portfolios move beyond a given frontier by blending nontraditional forms of capital into the mix to drive down risk or drive up return?

This question, and the topic of blended finance more broadly, is the subject of a recent joint project between the World Economic Forum and the Organisation for Economic Co-operation and Development (OECD).[6] Called the ReDesigning Development Finance Initiative, this project focuses on increasing the amount and flow of development finance and philanthropic capital to enable private sector investment.[7] This blended cross-sector approach is meant to facilitate funding for international economic development in riskier frontier[8] and emerging markets.[9] The OECD has also made recommendations specific to policymakers for mixing and then mobilizing new forms of capital to these types of markets, and in support of the United Nations Sustainable Development Goal agenda.[10] A blended finance portfolio, from this perspective, mitigates risk and supports commercial risk-adjusted returns for private sector partners.[11] Similar to the way investors mix assets to reduce risk in their portfolios, blending financial and philanthropic capital attempts to provide analogous results.[12]

The social value investing framework goes one step further and considers the contribution of philanthropic dollars to a blended cross-sector portfolio as more than a mere subsidy to other investors.[13] Funders following this approach actively collaborate with private sector partners, other implementers, and stakeholders in the selection and development of projects. Funders also have a vested interest in the positive social outcomes of the collaboration as it relates to their charitable mission and the long-term viability of the projects in the partnership. From this perspective, funders can leverage private capital to deliver larger projects with greater impact than they could using their dollars alone.

Imagine a scenario in which an investor is considering some set of high-risk investments in small-scale manufacturing in an emerging market. A foundation working in that same region could provide first-loss capital for loans to small enterprises in the same value chain to support the overall business climate.[14] It also could partner with local NGOs to provide critical training and education programs so more members of the community are eligible for loans and employment.[15] By coordinating activities and goals and blending programs and investments, this type of cross-sector partnership can offset risk or improve returns in ways that traditional finance can not or will not.[16] In this scenario, philanthropic capital may have the effect on portfolio configurations marked A, B, and C in figure 10.2.

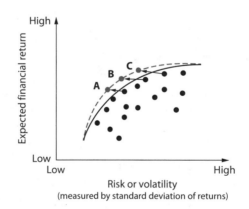

*Figure 10.2* The boundary of the efficient frontier can shift when mixing in concessionary investments by way of cross-sector partnerships. Consider that portfolios may fall beyond a given frontier when blending nontraditional forms of capital into project finance, such as charitable contributions or instruments comprised of philanthropic dollars. This is illustrated by portfolio configurations A, B, and C. The distance and direction of movement for these portfolio configurations is fictitious and for illustrative purposes only (figure is adapted from multiple sources and does not represent actual financial analysis). For a detailed discussion regarding calculations of the efficient frontier, see Robert Merton, "An Analytic Derivation of the Efficient Portfolio Frontier," *Journal of financial and Quantitative Analysis 7*, no. 4 (1972): 1851 -1872.

Philanthropic capital held by private foundations stands apart from traditional investment capital in several important ways. First, it is not subject to the same market demands as finance, and it can be invested over very long time horizons.[17] This is primarily because philanthropic capital is much more flexible. It can range from entirely concessionary allocations (such as grants), to quasi-concessionary vehicles (such as low-interest loans), to more innovative coinvestments (such as social impact bonds). Philanthropic assets, even if deployed through traditional investment instruments, are unbound by the return-maximizing constraints of the markets. Foundations have no shareholders (by the traditional definition) demanding higher profits and no investors pressuring management to make short-term trade-offs for financial gain.[18] Instead, a foundation's obligation is to its charitable mission and the delivery of social good.

The idea of blending capital through cross-sector partnerships aligns with two key ingredients of the social value investing approach. First, it allows for investment over longer time periods than traditional finance. Second, it enables investors and philanthropists to collaborate in ways that unlock hidden or unrecognized intrinsic value. Philanthropic capital can act as an enabler, supporting local community needs and prosperity, which in turn serves the mission of the foundation. An investor can enter a market it otherwise would not enter, increasing economic activity in the region and linking market activity, while at the same time making a financial return. Combining diverse investment tools blends financial and social goals and bridges gaps in the risk/reward calculus where value would otherwise remain locked away by unresolved constraints.[19]

In some cases, a blended cross-sector portfolio approach can be straightforward. We saw this in the Comunitas case study with the public-private partnership Juntos Pelo Desenvolvimento Sustentável (Juntos). Private sector leaders and philanthropic donors contributed to the partnership's general fund by cofinancing projects and services that would improve government processes and reduce bureaucracy. Sometimes outside experts guided planning and program improvements, and the fund partnered with a technology firm to facilitate constituent feedback and input—in line with the *people* and *place* elements of social value investing. Once partners settled on program improvements, the government financed the cost of implementing required changes and communicated this to its citizens. These changes improved the social and business climate around local municipalities and made the governments more accountable to constituents. One study found that for every dollar invested the partnership created ten dollars of return through more efficient government services or increased revenue.[20]

Oftentimes government agencies or municipalities are a primary contributor to a cross-sector blended-capital portfolio. With public financing, all levels of government can play an enabling role, whether through various types of instruments or through changes in regulation. Governments can engage in tax increment financing, provide block grants, offer new market tax credits, or designate business improvement districts, among other things.[21] Some government agencies, such as the Overseas Private Investment Corporation, exist to offset business risks for U.S. companies interested in working in emerging markets.[22] Although some or all of these methods are suitable in our blended cross-sector portfolio approach, government capital can be far more encumbered than philanthropic capital. Therefore, we are limiting the scope of this chapter to the latter.

## HOW PRIVATE AND PHILANTHROPIC CAPITAL MEET

Ultimately, many successful cross-sector partnerships rely on market solutions for long-term success. Some solutions may begin with philanthropic or government grants, but gains for society are more sustainable if these grants catalyze activity supported by a broader economic system. Philanthropic capital can construct the first rungs in a ladder from poverty to prosperity or move social programs from financially infeasible to financially viable, but it cannot complete the journey alone.

For example, philanthropy can provide an impoverished rural community with access to basic resources, training, scientific data, and the supplies necessary to transform barren rural land into productive cropland. As we discussed in the Afghanistan case, local conditions might pose implementation risks and limit prospects for near-term financial return, which would deter private investment. But over time this development might open the door for small-scale food processing and farmer cooperatives. Then the community may gain access to grain marketing and forward contracting. Access to microcredit could provide economies of scale and support more vibrant agribusiness. Eventually this could lead to an environment more conducive to agriculture-related private sector services, such as lending, equipment servicing, and new infrastructure. This is an oversimplification, but many problems remain unsolved for lack of private investment or scaling capital, which relies on market solutions. Using aid or philanthropic funding to offset early stage risk can create opportunities for businesses to support an economic ecosystem and bring in financial products that engage a wide range of potential investors.

Through a blended cross-sector portfolio approach, philanthropists can collaborate with investors using many different types of financial products.[23] Early stage capital may focus on advancing the maturity of a project to reach viability, sustaining it until it is large enough for more traditional forms of investment. This type of philanthropic stacking places grants at one end of a range of options, uses different types of reduced-cost lending in middle layers, and finds market-return-seeking products at the other end.[24]

## FINANCIAL TOOLS IN A BLENDED CROSS-SECTOR CAPITAL PORTFOLIO

A range of blended portfolio tools is described in this section, and figure 10.3 outlines ten types of capital allocations available to philanthropic organizations. The furthest left end of the range represents allocations with no requirement for financial return or payback. These types of allocations have high overall flexibility and the potential to significantly affect the risk/reward profile of a given project. At the right end of the

*Figure 10.3* A blended cross-sector portfolio approach may draw from many types of philanthropically oriented financial tools. This chart illustrates ten types of various capital allocations ranging from completely concessionary grants at the left end to more traditional return-seeking investments at the right end.

range are investments with an increasing requirement for financial return and constraints over how the funding can be allocated.[25]

## Traditional Grants

Through traditional grant-making—at the furthest left end of the range—a foundation typically transfers capital to an implementer who completes a project, advancing mutual goals to improve society. This is similar to what we saw in the Comunitas case, where the Juntos program relied extensively on foundations and private donors to finance operations and program services. While grant-making is fairly common, Juntos represents an innovative program design, including funder participation going well beyond just giving a gift. At the city level, grants funded strategic planning in Pelotas, Brazil, for a network of clinics, called Rede Bem Cuidar.[26] Partners engaged the community to gather input on how to deliver improved services to meet their needs.[27] Grant funding was used to finance project design support by Comunitas staff, rebuild two clinics, and renovate three basic healthcare units. The use of philanthropic capital significantly offset program and implementation risk for the city and provided flexibility for its elected officials to make decisions guided by the community's input.

In a broad sense, the landscape of traditional grant-making is undergoing change. Until recently, few intentional links between grants and private sector strategies would be found. Typically, uptake into private markets from a grant would be considered an added benefit, not a function of the grant itself. The Afghanistan case, however, contrasts this by illustrating small scale grants that financed market-enabling expenditures.[28] As the availability of philanthropic capital has increased generally, and as NGOs become more significant market actors and cross-sector partnerships proliferate, this will continue to shift.[29]

## Program-Related Investments

The U.S. Internal Revenue Service requires private nonoperating foundations to give away, on average, at least 5 percent of their assets to charitable causes every year (or face penalties).[30] Foundations generally use the remaining funds to generate profits to grow their assets, leaving considerable resources locked away from charitable activity. Historically, foundations tend to build large financial corpuses. Assets held by all foundations in 2014 in the United States totaled over $865 billion;[31] assets held by private nonoperating foundations alone comprised more than 80 percent of that total.[32] Generally, foundations think of their assets in a compartmentalized way: 95 percent dedicated to growing assets and 5 percent allocated to grants or charity. Innovative capital allocation strategies (namely, program-related investments and mission-related investments, discussed later) can bridge the two.

As a classification of investment approaches subject to specific eligibility requirements, program-related investments (PRIs) can include many of the financial instruments outlined here. PRIs allow foundations to use dollars from their traditional grant-making allocation to make low-yield investments in support of the foundation's philanthropic mission. Among other things, this broadens the financial and impact analysis used to allocate the capital and opens interesting cross-sector partnership opportunities.

In 2012, the White House updated its description of PRIs in the U.S. Code as "an investment made by a foundation, which, although it may generate income, is made primarily to accomplish charitable purposes."[33] Accordingly, a foundation can make qualified investments (such as those indicated in figure 10.3) that count toward its minimum 5 percent annual charitable distribution requirements. Furthermore, this class of investments is exempt from a number of taxes imposed on other types of investments made by a foundation. But, as the definition says, the purpose of a PRI must be to serve the foundation's charitable mission rather than to focus on a potential financial return.[34]

## Pioneering PRIs: Profile of the Ford Foundation

The Ford Foundation was established in 1936 by Henry Ford, founder of the Ford Motor Company, and his son, Edsel. At one point, the foundation owned nearly 90 percent of the nonvoting shares of the automotive company, making it the largest private foundation in the country.[35] By 1968 the Ford Foundation was grappling with how to increase its social reach beyond the limits of its grant-making resources.[36] In a proposal to the foundation's trustees that year, foundation staff urged them to "re-examine the tradition that limits our philanthropy to a single mode—the outright grant."[37] Shortly thereafter, the foundation began its first program-related investments.[38] Although not technically classified as such then (the Tax Reform Act of 1969 provided the first legal definition for a PRI[39]), it focused on programs for minority business development, affordable housing, and environmental preservation.[40] The foundation has since allocated about $690 million[41] toward PRIs and engages in direct loans, equity investments, and loan guarantees.[42]

The Ford Foundation has a long record of success with PRIs.[43] In 1977, the foundation provided a grant to a new nonprofit lender in Bangladesh for an experimental small-scale credit program.[44] This program sought to provide access to credit, mainly to women who had no collateral (such as land), and it organized debtors into small groups with collective responsibility for loan repayment. The model showed promise, reaching fifteen thousand participants with a 98 percent loan repayment rate within a few years. By 1981, the program sought to expand to one hundred thousand borrowers, increasing its partner commercial banks from twenty-five to one hundred.[45] The Ford Foundation provided a multiyear recoverable grant for $770,000 as a 10 percent loan default guarantee.[46] This guarantee offset the risk of potential loss for new commercial banks interested in joining the program and supported the program's rapid expansion. Funds from the guarantee that were not needed by the end of the term were to be repaid to the foundation.[47] Over time, the foundation increased its support, including financing for a revolving fund for larger enterprises.

Today, this nonprofit lender—Grameen Bank—has more than 2,500 branches and has made over eight million loans totaling more than $20 billion,[48] and it pays dividends to its borrowers.[49] Structured as a cooperative, Grameen's borrowers are also the bank's owners, holding more than 90 percent of the organization. The remainder is owned by the Bangladeshi government.[50] In 2006, Grameen Bank and its founder, Muhammad Yunus, were awarded the Nobel Peace Prize.[51]

The number of foundations and the amount of foundation assets available for PRIs has grown considerably since PRIs began in 1969. The MacArthur Foundation, the David and Lucile Packard Foundation, the Rockefeller Foundation, the W. K. Kellogg Foundation, the F. B. Heron Foundation, to name a few, all use PRIs to unlock their assets and increase social good. More recently, the Bill & Melinda Gates Foundation entered this space.[52] It has made more than sixty PRIs, committing more than $1.8 billion in capital with a total allocation of $2 billion to its PRI strategy.[53]

## Recoverable Grants

Recoverable grants are pools of capital allocated to projects that meet the objectives of a funder but are dedicated to catalyzing longer-term for-profit business development.[54] Similar to traditional grants, they are given without a requirement for financial return. What makes them "recoverable" is that any profits generated from the grant funding, which (as traditional commercially generated profit) would normally be returned to an investor, are instead put back into a capital pool to make future grants. For example, the nonprofit Echoing Green provides cash stipends to for-profit social entrepreneurs who agree to pay back the stipend if their company becomes successful. If the company fails, then it owes no debt.[55]

As one of the most risk-tolerant and inexpensive forms of capital available, recoverable grants act as "convertible note[s] with no time expiration and no liquidation payback rights."[56] Because these products are classified as grants, there is no obligation to the grant-maker if the borrower defaults.[57]

## Zero Interest Short-Term Loans / Zero Interest Long-Term Loans

Another way for a foundation to spur market development is by offering zero-interest loans.[58] For example, a community garden that is expanding operations may need financing for a new greenhouse and the equipment and supplies to grow more food. A community foundation could provide a long-term, no-cost loan for the greenhouse so that a local community development financial institution (CDFI) would be willing to open a line of credit for seed, fertilizer, and tools.

This type of commitment can encourage private sector lenders to loan to individuals or groups they would otherwise find too risky, and it creates credit histories that can be used for future lending considerations. Zero-interest loans provide a substantial subsidy to a loan offering, and it holds a borrower accountable more than grants or recoverable grants do but less than other financial products.

## Forgivable Debt

Forgivable debt is typically a loan structured to incentivize a particular behavior or accomplish a measurable social outcome agreed upon between a philanthropic lender and a borrower.[59] Any portion of the loan may be forgiven if specific conditions are met.

For example, a foundation makes a forgivable loan to a social enterprise running an early morning before-school program with the goal of reducing high school truancy. If the program meets a given target— a 20 percent reduction in student absentees within six months—then the foundation would forgive the loan as though it were a grant. If the target is not met, the foundation could recollect the money as a debt.

## Low-Interest (Concessionary Rate) Long-Term Loans and Low-Interest Short-Term Loans

In other cases, a lender may offer a loan at a rate that the borrower cannot afford but *could* pay back at a reduced interest rate.[60] In these cases, philanthropy can subsidize the lending rate to a level feasible for the borrower but still profitable for the lender. Sometimes these rates can be adjusted over time, with the subsidy gradually removed as a track record is established, the borrower stabilizes, and the lender becomes more confident that the loan will be repaid at favorable terms.

In the community garden example, imagine that the CDFI is providing both the loan and the line of credit. In this case, a foundation could subsidize the interest rate on the loan and line of credit so that it meets the needs of both organizations.

## Social Impact Bonds

Social impact bonds (SIBs) are an innovative financing instrument designed to help governments, foundations, and investors structure prevention programs that achieve social outcomes.[61] These outcomes, if realized, save long-term costs that would otherwise be absorbed by society. Therefore, the government agrees to pass some of those savings along to investors who take the risk to fund the programs. But investors are only repaid if the desired outcomes are met.

SIBs are similar to pay-for-performance contracts, through which service providers are paid for results, not for their work to achieve specific outcomes.[62] In both cases, providers must closely document success and establish meaningful and measurable outcome indicators.[63] For example, a state government agency may want to reduce the number of people receiving compensation through unemployment insurance. Through a pay-for-performance contract, that agency agrees to pay a job training and placement company $5,000 for every person (otherwise on unemployment benefits) they place in a job at a living wage for six months or longer. If the company does not achieve the outcome, they are not reimbursed for their program expenses.

With SIBs, an investor underwrites the cost of a program through a project manager responsible for coordinating the activities. Payment for success goes from the government through the manager to the investors. This payment can include a return on investment, depending on the success of the program. If the program fails, the investors can lose their capital. As a result, the entire up-front investment is at risk because there is no guaranteed payment.[64] So far, as the Rikers Island example shows, SIBs have had a mixed track record.

## Lessons to Learn: Rikers Island Social Impact Bond

In 2012, a coalition of partners launched the first SIB in the United States. It was designed to reduce recidivism of teenagers released from Rikers Island jail in New York. Financed by a $9.6 million loan from Goldman Sachs (insured by a $7.2 million guarantee from Bloomberg Philanthropies), the program delivered cognitive behavioral therapy from the Osborne Association to teenage inmates.[65] MDRC, a nonprofit research center, was the intermediary managing organization, and the Vera Institute of Justice served as an independent evaluator. In the arrangement, Goldman Sachs would be repaid only if the existing recidivism rate of 50 percent was reduced by 8.5 percent, and they would receive a profit of up to $2.1 million if the reduction exceeded 10 percent.[66]

The program encountered a series of operational and contractual challenges, including control group problems and staffing short-falls.[67] In July 2015, the Vera Institute concluded that the program did not reduce recidivism for the 2013 program participants during the twelve months following their release from Rikers, as compared to a historical control group who passed through the jail before the program began.[68]

How much value the program ultimately provided, regardless of its cancellation, depends on who you ask.[69] Supporters argue it was worthwhile for what they learned using an experimental approach. Supporters also point out that the experiment was paid for by investors, not taxpayers,[70] and implementers of the program can document participants who say it helped them stay out of jail.

Bringing a private partner into government social programs can yield efficiency and innovation, and having government as a partner creates opportunities to scale successful experiments more easily. But bringing these two groups together in such a collaboration requires an independent evaluator, especially because financial payment is conditioned on mutually agreed goals. Involving the philanthropic sector diffuses the risk and encourages partners to expand programs if they succeed.

Detractors of the Rikers Island SIB, however, suspect that city officials spent a lot of taxpayer-subsidized time on the project. They also wonder whether the time horizon for investor payouts over a long-term program would have been prohibitive for investors, even if the experiment had run successfully. The same holds true for the payer: significant savings for the government may not occur until, for example, recidivism is dramatically reduced.

Furthermore, SIBs could pressure government to privatize activities that may not benefit from being privatized—prisons are an example. The high transaction costs of adding a managing intermediary, an outside evaluator, and an outside operator may doom some SIBs to failure. Even when successful, SIBs may be too complicated to easily replicate or scale. Finally, critics point to opportunity costs—philanthropic dollars are not unlimited, and they claim spending them on speculative experiments could be wasteful.[71] We believe this type of experimentation is a sweet spot for philanthropic dollars, and regardless of these challenges, SIBs are not likely to go away soon.[72]

The very first SIB is a recent success story. The Peterborough Pilot Social Impact Bond in the UK ran from 2010 to 2015 and had positive results.[73] Similar in goals to the Rikers Island SIB, the Peterborough SIB was designed to reduce the number of prison reoffenders. Of a first cohort population of roughly a thousand participants, the SIB-financed program reduced the reoffending rate by 8.4 percent compared to the control group.[74] An analysis from the results of a second cohort estimated an improved reduction rate of 9.7 percent.[75] These results averaged above the minimum threshold required for success (a 7.5 percent reduction), and the SIB's outcome payment to investors was triggered.[76]

Since this first SIB launched in 2010, over one hundred others have begun, with at least seventy more under development.[77] SIBs are under way around the world: in Australia, Austria, Belgium, Canada, Finland, Germany, Ireland, Israel, Netherlands, Switzerland, the United Kingdom, and the United States, among others.[78] A social impact bond is inherently structured as a cross-sector partnership. According to an OECD study on SIBs, "the combination of partners is part of the innovation."[79] Although still a developing model, the goals and intentions of SIBs embody many of the characteristics of the social value investing framework.[80]

## Restricted Private Equity Stake

In 2016, the U.S. Treasury Department updated and clarified their list of permissible PRI-related activities.[81] As a result, foundations were given more clarity on the use of PRIs for making equity investments in for-profit companies if those investments serve a social purpose (assuming certain conditions are met).[82] For example, the Gates Foundation took an equity stake in a biotech start-up in Cambridge, Massachusetts. Among other things, it encouraged the company to apply its new and pioneering T-cell targeting discovery technology toward the creation of a vaccine against malaria—a major focus of the foundation's global health strategy.[83]

Although not a requirement, the IRS indicated that exit triggers automatically liquidating a foundation's stake in a company, once the company turned profitable, could substantiate the charitable claim of the investment.[84] Furthermore, such equity investments may be combined with grants or loans (from the same foundation or otherwise), enhancing the charitable objectives of the investment even further.[85]

## Mission-Related Investments

In very simple terms, mission-related investments (MRIs) complement PRIs by picking up where they leave off.[86] An MRI strategy either supports social goals (such as actively seeking investments that contribute to a foundation's overall charitable purpose) or avoids contradicting the values or mission of a foundation. However, investments in an MRI portfolio fall outside the scope of PRIs, in part because these investments are intended to generate a market-rate financial return, and because they come from the corpus of the foundation, not the grant-making side.[87] For example, a foundation focused on environmental preservation or air quality could use its corpus to make a significant investment in a large, for-profit solar energy project. Unlike PRIs, a foundation cannot count MRIs toward its 5 percent annual charitable distribution requirement. Although mission-related investments are not a separate legal classification on their own, they must still follow IRS non-jeopardizing rules.[88] Similar to traditional investments, MRIs may be subject to unrelated taxable income (whereas PRIs are not).[89]

An investment strategy led by MRIs is very different from a passive or blind investment strategy, which could have a foundation's endowment investing in companies that are diametrically opposed to its charitable mission. Continuing with the environmentally focused foundation example, that same foundation could have holdings in a coal or oil company under a blind or agnostic investment approach. Therefore, a foundation may use negative screening to avoid broad investment categories antithetical to their charitable mission or values (such as screening out investments in weapons or tobacco). Or it may choose to engage in or support specific company or industry divestment. For example, the Rockefeller Brothers Fund (established by descendants of John D. Rockefeller and financed by the family's success in the oil industry) announced in 2014 that it would divest its endowment's assets from fossil fuels.[90] Shortly thereafter, the fund also signed onto the United Nations–sponsored Principles for Responsible Investment,[91] a voluntary agreement among investors to track and consider environmental, social, and governance metrics in their investment strategies.[92]

The Ford Foundation took a bold step in 2017 when it announced it would allocate up to $1 billion of its endowment, roughly 8 percent, to an active MRI strategy.[93] This was the largest MRI commitment ever for a private foundation, and it is initially focused on "affordable housing in the United States and access to financial services in emerging markets."[94] It is likely we will see more and more foundations making similarly significant commitments in the future.

## ADVANTAGES OF A BLENDED CROSS-SECTOR CAPITAL PORTFOLIO

A blended cross-sector capital portfolio uses innovative and flexible funding, such as philanthropic dollars, to shift the risk frontier for projects in a partnership. It is a critical enabler for other elements in the social value investing framework because it unlocks partnership opportunities with high intrinsic social value, and because it also allows partners to focus on outcomes over a long time horizon. As a result, blending investments for social and financial goals has inherent advantages for everyone involved.

- *It widens the risk/reward profile for investors.* By blending philanthropic and financial products with differing risk appetites and reward requirements, investors can tap into diverse capital pools for financing partnerships that serve the public good.[95]

- *It leverages collective assets.* By adjusting the risk/reward horizon, initiatives can bring together new coalitions of public, private, and philanthropic partners. Using an effective and collaborative partnership process enables collective capital to solve problems that cannot be addressed by any single sector or class of funding.[96]

- *It builds a coalition of people.* By tapping into a broader alliance of participants, the initiative can access an expanded, decentralized network of leaders, experts, teams, and organizations spanning multiple geographic areas and providing for complementary capital allocation needs.[97]

- *It aligns financial and social outcomes.* By integrating traditional finance, social programs can draw from for-profit sector knowledge, experience, and resources to improve the efficacy of grants or charitable activity. These advantages may not typically be available to such programs, which makes this an important approach for partnerships involved in the development of place-based strategies.[98]

Partnerships and projects of all sizes can benefit from a blended-capital portfolio. Long-term systems-based solutions, in particular, require significant and diverse capital to finance program expenditures, infrastructure, and services. By engaging an array of capital types, partnerships can provide new solutions or accomplish collectively what would otherwise be impossible individually. This is especially important in parts of the world that face chronic poverty, conflict, or economic downturns, as we saw in the Juntos case. In places where government aid or market forces alone have not built prosperity for communities, or even whole countries, innovative financing through cross-sector collaboration is an exceedingly important strategy.

# PERFORMANCE

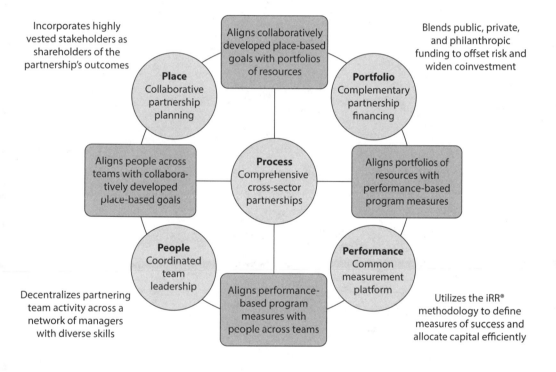

Incorporates highly vested stakeholders as shareholders of the partnership's outcomes

Aligns collaboratively developed place-based goals with portfolios of resources

Blends public, private, and philanthropic funding to offset risk and widen coinvestment

**Place**
Collaborative partnership planning

**Portfolio**
Complementary partnership financing

Aligns people across teams with collaboratively developed place-based goals

**Process**
Comprehensive cross-sector partnerships

Aligns portfolios of resources with performance-based program measures

**People**
Coordinated team leadership

**Performance**
Common measurement platform

Decentralizes partnering team activity across a network of managers with diverse skills

Aligns performance-based program measures with people across teams

Utilizes the iRR® methodology to define measures of success and allocate capital efficiently

# CHAPTER ELEVEN

# The Performance Case

## Using Big Data to Improve City Services— FDNY and Beyond

### WILLIAM B. EIMICKE

In previous chapters we presented cases and analysis to illustrate how the elements of social value investing—process, people, place, and portfolio—contribute to the success of cross-sector partnerships. This chapter focuses on the fifth and final element of the social investing framework, a partnership's *performance*. To illustrate how a focus on performance measurement can produce outcomes that meaningfully impact people's lives, we present several examples from New York City. Over the course of a few decades, New York City transformed from one of the most dangerous cities with the least effective city government in the world to one of the most admired and copied. New York City adopted performance management citywide in 1977, but the effects were limited until 1994 when Police Commissioner Bill Bratton created and implemented the CompStat system, a performance management program focused on crime prevention.[1] CompStat has evolved over the past several decades, but it continues to help keep New Yorkers safe. By the turn of the century, Mayor Michael Bloomberg directed the enhancement of CompStat and the successful application of similar, performance-based management systems for the city's emergency and rescue services, operated by the Fire Department of New York City (FDNY). Over time, FDNY's focus on performance measurement— ranging from response times and lives saved to fires prevented—as well as new performance management systems, led to a transformational change in how it accomplished its mission and served the public.

## PREVENTING CRIME

Everything about performance management in New York City changed on January 10, 1994, when a new mayor, a self-identified crime-fighter named Rudolph Giuliani appointed William J. Bratton commissioner of the New York City Police Department (NYPD). Bratton had a track record of reducing crime in Boston and in the New York City subway system.

Bratton had extraordinary success in transforming New York City from one of the most violent and dangerous big cities in the world into one of the safest, with a multifaceted strategy using techniques that had helped other cities. Bratton's major contribution to policing theory was elegantly simple—policing should be focused on crime prevention first. Before Bratton, NYPD was famous around the world as fearless, relentless, and, occasionally, corrupt. Bratton changed the NYPD for decades to come by harnessing the big data the agency was already collecting and making it available in real time so precinct commanders could predict emerging patterns of crime geographically and focus their resources on "hot spots" before criminals could take over a neighborhood.[2]

The system started with a few dedicated in-house believers, particularly the late Jack Maple,[3] appointed by Bratton as a deputy commissioner for designing the CompStat crime control strategies. In the beginning, CompStat used only elementary desktop computers, a big map of the city, and some colored pushpins. Over time, the NYPD's data and analytics program evolved into a partnership with IBM to create the NYPD Real Time Crime Center and the program known as CompStat, which the city still uses today.

Using FBI's Uniform Crime Reporting categories of serious crimes,[4] CompStat provided weekly reports on the number of these crimes, precinct by precinct, across New York City's seventy-seven precincts (each holding 100,000 or more residents). Precinct commanders, guided by the top brass at headquarters, can deploy their resources to most effectively control and ultimately reduce crime. Bratton chaired weekly (twice weekly in the early years) citywide meetings to hold precinct commanders accountable for their performance. CompStat enabled top NYPD leaders to question lower-level commanders regularly and in person, in front of a large number of their supervisors and peers. Crime dropped by 12 percent in 1994 compared to 1993, whereas the comparable figure nationwide was a drop of 1.1 percent.[5] By the end of the decade, citywide crime was down by 50 percent.[6] CompStat subsequently won the prestigious and highly selective Harvard University Kennedy School Innovations in American Government award and has been copied by cities across the country and around the world.[7]

Based on the extraordinary success of CompStat, the Giuliani administration tried to bring CompStat-style data-driven, predictive performance management to other city agencies—with limited success. FireMarc, the FDNY version of CompStat, failed miserably. It languished without real commitment and suffered from a poor choice of indicators and few incentives or penalties—sticks and carrots—to ensure accountability. In the Department of Parks and Recreation, Parkstat fared somewhat better. Parkstat used inspections and a rating system to grade pass or fail equipment, benches, and leisure areas of each park. But here again resources were limited, and there was no effective accountability system.

The Central Park Conservancy (CPC) under the leadership of Doug Blonsky developed an effective system for parks, using CompStat-like zone management and performance standards and accountability, comprehensive manuals, standard operating procedures, and detailed handbooks for horticulture management, turf management, and trash management and recycling (see chapter 5). Partnering first with Mayor Michael Bloomberg and more recently with Mayor Bill de Blasio, CPC is now training City Parks Department managers to deploy the same accountability system in other city parks throughout New York City.

## MAKING NEW YORK'S BRAVEST EVEN BETTER—FROM TACTICS TO STRATEGY

Businessman Michael Bloomberg faced daunting challenges when he became the first new mayor elected post-9/11. Major areas of lower Manhattan had been completely destroyed or severely damaged, the city's economy was depressed, the government's budget had a large and growing deficit, and even though crime was still dropping, the city faced a very real and imminent threat of terrorism as well. Bloomberg was committed to running the city like a business, which meant belt-tightening and fiscal discipline. But Bloomberg also understood that serving customers (in this case city residents and visitors) was at least as important. Bloomberg used performance-based accountability and partnerships to do both extremely well.

Despite the fiscal constraints, Bloomberg continued to invest in CompStat and the impact-based approach to policing, and he worked aggressively and effectively to bring CompStat-style performance management to other New York City agencies, particularly the FDNY.

FDNY, New York City's fire and emergency medical services agency, has always been one of the world's best. On September 11, 2001, FDNY personnel became America's heroes as they evacuated 13,000 to 15,000 people[8] from the two World Trade Center towers in the 102 minutes between American Airlines Flight 11 hitting the north tower and when the tower collapsed at 10:28 AM.[9] This extraordinary success came at a very high price—343 FDNY personnel died,[10] a staggering nearly one-third of the total number of 1,172 FDNY deaths from the very first firefighter to die while on duty in 1865.[11]

With so many deaths and the subsequent realization that FDNY initially had serious difficulty determining who was at the site and who was not, it was clear to the department and incoming mayor Bloomberg that FDNY needed to improve its systems management. The Mayor's Office commissioned the well-respected consulting firm McKinsey & Company to conduct a pro bono management review of FDNY and NYPD, focused on how both agencies could be better prepared for future major events, whether it be terrorism, fire, epidemic, or natural disaster. McKinsey's key recommendations included that FDNY should "improve accountability and discipline" through "enhanced planning and management."[12] To accomplish this, McKinsey recommended increasing the number of personnel in management positions, enhancing the planning and analytical skills of those managers, and focusing more on "explicit metrics and milestones" to monitor the overall performance of the FDNY.[13]

To implement the McKinsey Report recommendations, the FDNY recognized that the vast majority of its senior managers came from the field—that is, firefighting—and had little training in management, analysis, planning, and organizational communication. This leadership and management challenge was acute given FDNY's size—an annual operating budget exceeding $1.8 billion, 1.7 million incidents annually, and a workforce of over seventeen thousand spread over 250 locations.[14] To overcome this training gap, Mayor Bloomberg and Fire Commissioner Nicholas Scoppetta engaged Columbia University to partner with the FDNY to develop an executive leadership and management training certificate program, modeled on the core curriculum of Columbia's MPA and MBA degrees.[15]

Every year since 2002, mixed cohorts of sixteen[16] of the FDNY senior management (and those the department viewed as the next generation of leaders) from both the fire and EMS divisions have completed the FDNY Officers Management Institute (FOMI), including a program-long team project.[17] Sessions are taught at GE's state of the art John F. Welch Leadership Development Center, a 59 acre corporate university campus founded in 1956 and named after legendary former GE CEO Jack Welch. As one GE employee selected to attend a program at the Welch Center described the experience, "this is where you go to get promoted."[18]

GE's president and CEO at the time, Jeff Immelt, was one of the first people to contribute to 9/11 charities after the attacks on the World Trade Center, and from the very beginning Immelt and GE have been full partners in FOMI. GE has donated the full cost of housing, food, classrooms, support, and recreation for all FOMI participants and Columbia University and FDNY faculty since the beginning in the fall of 2002. Given the all-day, every-day nature of FDNY, getting managers off site to a full-service learning center is an essential element in the success of the program. Participants continue to be paid during the training time but are taken off line by the FDNY and live and study at the Welch Center, an hour train ride north of New York City. Immelt and other GE leaders have addressed every FOMI cohort. Receptions and meeting opportunities allow FOMI and GE managers in programs at the center to get to know each other and share best practices.

Mayor Bloomberg and Commissioner Scoppetta recognized that partnering with Columbia University and GE could teach practical management skills and problem-solving techniques that FDNY participants would use to significantly improve FDNY performance. Over the past fifteen years, the FDNY-Columbia-GE partnership has prepared well over two hundred participants for senior management positions, and most of the top jobs at FDNY have been filled by FOMI graduates for more than a decade. A FOMI certificate has almost become a requirement for promotion to senior management. The quality and effectiveness of FOMI has been recognized by Harvard University's Innovations in American Government annual competition, selecting FOMI as a "Top 50" program in both 2008 and 2009.

FOMI has played a major part in bridging the divide between FDNY's fire and EMS divisions.[19] FDNY leadership credits FOMI's mixed cohorts of the next generation of fire and EMS leaders with creating more of a unified FDNY culture; this has resulted in much safer and more effective emergency services agencies, particularly as the number of fires has declined over the past decade and medical and other emergency calls have increased dramatically. Today, it is more likely that FDNY will save a life through a medical intervention than a rescue from a burning building.

In 2004, FOMI graduate Chief Joseph Pfeifer led the effort to create the first formal FDNY Strategic Plan in the department's then nearly 140-year history.[20] Over the past decade, the plan dramatically increased the FDNY's success in securing federal grants from the U.S. Department of Homeland Security and others for equipment, including new fireboats, advanced technology, and grants for natural disaster and many other types of training programs. The plan also led to major improvements in emergency response operations, health and safety initiatives benefiting FDNY members, increased diversity, enhanced fire prevention and education initiatives, and a much stronger and more effective management and organizational system. The Strategic Plans also led to a $17 million upgrade of the Fire Department Operations Center (FDOC) in 2006[21] and a new FDNY Terrorism and Disaster Preparedness Strategy to be implemented by Chief Pfeifer, who then became the director of the FDNY Center for Terrorism and Disaster Preparedness.[22]

FOMI created a stronger learning culture at FDNY. The department probably has the best-equipped emergency services training center of any U.S. city, and a wide array of educational programs operate year-round, primarily focused on tactics and field operations. FOMI has encouraged management degrees at major universities across the country including Harvard's Kennedy School, the School of International and Public Affairs at Columbia University (SIPA) and the Naval Postgraduate School, and a certificate in Counter Terrorism from West Point. Chief Pfeifer now holds a Master's in Public Administration from the Kennedy School and a Master's in Security Studies from the Naval Postgraduate School.[23] FOMI graduate Assistant Chief of Fire Prevention and Citywide Command Chief Richard Tobin, a leader of FDNY's risk-based inspection innovation, went on to earn his MPA from SIPA. Several other FOMI graduates went on to earn degrees from the Naval Postgraduate School. Currently, FOMI graduate Battalion Chief for Times Square Mike Meyers is pursuing his Master's in Public Administration at SIPA. Partners FDNY, Columbia University, and GE all benefit from the shared learning happening at the Welch Center among current and future leaders from the public (FDNY), private (GE), and nonprofit sectors (Columbia University); and the public benefits from this sharing of best practices, which enables the FDNY to better save and protect lives and property in New York City, today and for decades to come.

## PREVENTING FIRES

Former fire commissioner Nicholas Scoppetta once said, "Inspections are not firefighters' favorite activity" (firefighters carry hoses, an ax, someone in need of rescue, not a clipboard and pencil, or even an iPad).[24] Those who relish running into burning buildings do not enjoy walking around stores and office buildings issuing violations for overloaded electrical sockets or bicycles cluttering hallways. Firefighters previously disliked inspection activities enough that their unions negotiated contracts to limit inspection periods to two days a week and only when weather conditions were moderate.

The importance of effective inspections (figure 11.1) for saving lives became very clear in the aftermath of a major fire at the vacant Deutsche Bank building in Lower Manhattan (adjacent to the World

*Figure 11.1* A Fire Department of New York firefighter carrying out an inspection before the new prevention-based priority process was developed by the NYC FDNY-IBM cross-sector partnership. Photo by Richard Numeroff, courtesy of SIPA Case Collection.

Trade Center site) on August 18, 2007, which took the lives of two firefighters. The building was severely damaged on 9/11 but was still under slow deconstruction because of the presence of asbestos, toxic materials, and possibly human remains. Firefighters went into the building to put out the fire because of the environmental dangers so close to nearby occupied buildings.[25]

The investigations that followed the incident discovered that a test of a standpipe that had been noted as breached earlier that year was never completed, and an even larger break in the basement was completely missed.[26] The fallen firefighters were unable to escape because there was no water coming from the cut standpipe to fight the fire, and the primary escape route down the staircase was improperly blocked. Fire officers at several levels failed to carry out the rule that buildings under construction or demolition must be inspected every fifteen days. Inspectors at the Department of Buildings also failed to properly train inspectors and conduct proper inspections, and they did not communicate important information to other city agencies, including the FDNY.[27] FDNY executives were forced to confront the reality that in 2007 inspection records were not digitized in easily accessible databases. Rather, many were kept on index cards, written in pencil, and stored in local FDNY captain's firehouse offices (of which there were over two hundred and twenty). Accessing inspection information or monitoring the inspection program from FDNY headquarters was virtually impossible.[28]

A team of FDNY members, civilian and uniformed, were charged by the Mayor's Office with developing a comprehensive solution to the obviously flawed inspection system. The team quickly concluded that the decentralized, paper-based program was outdated; cyclical inspections in such a large city were wasteful and ineffective; and prioritizing by catastrophic risk (such as schools and hospitals) had led to multiple annual inspections of the city's safest buildings and infrequent inspections of buildings most likely to have a fire, explosion, or structural collapse. With a workload of three hundred thousand buildings, fewer than four hundred civilian inspectors, and limited inspection time for uniformed firefighters, the team concluded that a radical reform of the current system was in order. However, the city government did not have the in-house knowledge of technology and global best practices to build a new system on its own.[29] After careful consideration of multiple options, FDNY turned to IBM (NYPD's long-time partner on the Real Time Crime Center and on CompStat) for help.

Claudia Gerola, an experienced IBM business strategy and development consultant, and a team from IBM worked closely with the FDNY team to map out the inspection process and interview the people who actually did the work, from the firefighters on the truck, to the captain in the firehouse, to the IT system managers, and throughout headquarters to the decision makers who needed the information.[30] The two teams conducted a gap analysis to determine what data were needed to build a predictive inspection prioritization model, what data were already being collected, and what data needed to be collected or found. They explored solutions to close those gaps and then began to build a system with the primary goal of preventing as many fires and building-based emergencies as possible—for fires that did occur, they hoped to make them less dangerous and damaging.

As FDNY Deputy Chief Richard Tobin (figure 11.2) described it,

> We saw all of the successes the police department had with CompStat. We saw where they were targeting their resources to where the crime was occurring. The whole idea was to get there before the crime occurred, saturate the area. And we wanted to duplicate the same thing with our inspection process. We didn't want to wait for a fire to hit, we wanted to be out there proactively inspecting these buildings, eliminating their hazards before they had a fire there.[31]

*Figure 11.2* FDNY Chief Richard Tobin reviews paper files with previously inaccessible data for setting inspection priorities. Photo by Richard Numeroff, courtesy of SIPA Case Collection.

The FDNY needed a system like CompStat that could analyze all the inspection information available (from FDNY and from other city, state, and federal agencies) and use a learning algorithm to prioritize the most dangerous buildings in their area for the inspection teams for each inspection period. That way, even with limited inspection resources, the opportunity to prevent damage and death before it happened would be greatest.

The first step in creating a new system was to digitize the existing inspection database. Then, to create a process for collecting new inspection information digitally, and to identify and track key performance indicators tied directly to program success. Digitizing the data required close cooperation among IBM, FDNY headquarters, the FDNY IT unit, and the firehouses. It was slow and challenging because firefighters in the field were not particularly interested in inspections in the first place. But some firehouses were more interested than others, and the team picked them to pilot the system. As the new system began to take shape, cooperation across the field operations increased. By 2009, there was a computer in every firehouse—replacing the index cards and pencils of 2007—connected to the FDNY Metrotech Center headquarters in Brooklyn, so senior management could review, analyze, and monitor the entire inspection program for the first time.[32] As Commissioner Scoppetta said in 2009 after the Deutsche Bank fire investigations, "I think that if there is a silver lining to this cloud, it is that there is not an officer or a firefighter in the FDNY who does not recognize how important inspections are, how it saves lives and sometimes it will be the lives of our own members responding."[33]

By 2010, FDNY and IBM were testing a new system that provided captains in the pilot-tested neighborhoods with a list of the most dangerous buildings in their area in real time at the beginning of each inspection period. The local captain could override recommendations based on experience or local knowledge, but the variation in buildings inspected would have to be explained and entered in the computer database. Pilot-testing made clear that a truly predictive inspection system would require data from multiple city agencies: the Department of Buildings, the Department of Environmental Protection, the Finance Department, Sanitation Department, Health Department, and even NYPD. Violations issued by these other agencies could also indicate a higher risk of fire. Failure to pay taxes could indicate neglected building maintenance. Police activity in a building might indicate dangerous chemicals being used in making illegal drugs or explosives used by terrorists. State and federal agency databases could provide similar information to make the predictive model even more robust.

Mayor Bloomberg created a citywide fire response task force almost immediately after the Deutsche Bank incident. Directed by Caswell Holloway IV of the Mayor's Office (one of Mayor Bloomberg's most trusted advisors, particularly in crisis situations),[34] the task force identified the interagency nature of risk-based inspections and initiated the data sharing that would make the new system predictive. Although most city agencies were well on the way to digitizing their data, most used different platforms and many were using outdated legacy equipment. As Chief Tobin told us, "Sharing that data across [agency] lines was very difficult, really difficult."[35] Fortunately, the mayor was working on a parallel track to share and publish as much city data as possible through his commitment to open government and citizen engagement.

Beginning in December 2009, Mayor Bloomberg charged a few young analysts led by a charismatic, hard-driving former federal lawyer named Mike Flowers (who had worked on the Saddam Hussein trial in Iraq) to find a way to share data that could mitigate city problems before they spun out of control. Flowers knew the city had a tremendous amount of publicly accessible but agency-siloed data that could be better used to improve the quality and efficiency of government services. Flowers also knew that the more than forty city agencies could not change their systems, procedures, platforms, and identifiers for years, even if they wanted to (which they didn't). Even if there was a will, he and his team of six did not have access to the money and technology, much less the time, to get it done. In any case, Bloomberg wanted results—and he wanted them yesterday.

Rather than go to war with agency heads, his team, dubbed the "Geek Squad,"[36] recognized that technology had advanced so that data from different platforms and systems could be synthesized for problem solving in their present form. With this insight, Flowers and team set up the system that incorporated information from the Buildings Department, Department of Finance, and other agencies into the FDNY platform, which improved the accuracy in identifying the most dangerous buildings so FDNY could inspect those buildings first. In May 2013, the FDNY Risk-Based Assessment System was officially launched. During its development and after its official launch, the number of serious violations issued by FDNY inspectors has risen significantly, and fatal fires since 2009 have held at historically low numbers.[37]

Flowers and the Geek Squad went on to other data-matching triumphs, including identifying and preventing mortgage fraud, uncovering Medicaid fraud to access OxyContin and oxycodone, and tracking down restaurants that were illegally dumping cooking oil into city sewers. Harvard professor and former mayor Stephen Goldsmith would later describe them as "the best city data team in the United States, and one of the best in the world."[38] Goldsmith served as a deputy mayor under Mayor Bloomberg and was a major force in establishing the Mayor's Office of Data Analytics (MODA), led by Flowers, and in leading Bloomberg's efforts to share 311 and other city data with the public, organized geographically, so citizens could find out easily what the city was doing in their neighborhood, good and bad.[39]

Reflecting on his experience as the senior New York City official overseeing the risk-based fire inspection innovation, Goldsmith described it as an iterative process. FDNY was hampered by an underpowered internal technology system and limited staff support, but it had the on-the-ground personnel. IBM brought vast processing capacity, but perhaps too broad of an approach. And the Geek Squad brought knowledge of the entire New York City data system with insight on what could be accomplished rather quickly using cross-agency collaboration and the ever-increasing power of algorithms. This led Goldsmith to initiate a major innovation of his own—creating teams of Building Department and FDNY inspectors to work jointly on buildings identified by the algorithm as presenting the greatest risk of fire.[40]

The evolving partnership of FDNY, IBM, New York City Department of Buildings, and the Mayor's Office illustrates how rethinking a program—fire inspections—to deliver quantitatively better results was made possible through a cross-sector, multiorganization partnership. Accessing the more sophisticated technology and analytic skills of IBM and City Hall's Geek Squad enabled the application of advanced algorithms to actually prevent fires and building-related emergencies. Given the chronic and long-standing underfunding of IT equipment and staff in most city government agencies, this innovative breakthrough would not have happened without a partnership focused on performance measurement and analysis.

## "IN GOD WE TRUST. EVERYONE ELSE, BRING DATA."[41]

Mike Bloomberg became one of the richest people in the world by figuring out how to get the best information to Wall Street traders and managers before anyone else realized how important and profitable that might be. For twelve years, from 2002 through 2013, he used data-driven accountability systems to make the New York City government more effective than it had ever been. He often chose partnerships to accomplish complex challenges, sometimes private companies such as IBM and GE, sometimes nonprofits, and sometimes philanthropic organizations, including his own foundation. (He used his foundation to facilitate implementation of some of his most creative and risky innovations because he did not want to experiment with taxpayer dollars, such as the Rikers Island Social Impact Bond program described in chapter 10). His reliance on partnerships and performance contributed significantly to his overall success; in 2013, an independent panel of historians and political scientists rated Bloomberg second only to Fiorello La Guardia as the best mayor in the city's very long history dating back to 1665 (and several rated him first, even though he was still in his third term at the time).[42]

## BLOOMBERG'S LEGACY FOR SOCIAL IMPACT MEASUREMENT AND MANAGEMENT

Through Bloomberg's performance-based approach, his administration partnered with a wide range of large and small for-profit and nonprofit organizations to drive improved outcomes and an ever-better city for twelve years.[43] Many of these examples proved that impact-based partnerships can make a real, positive difference in people's lives. While limits to performance measurement in its current practice remain, it has great potential for improving public programs and services, as highlighted by the comprehensive management programs in New York City.[44]

Data-driven performance management did not originate with Mike Bloomberg; in fact, CompStat began under Rudy Giuliani, but Bloomberg recognized that city activities could be dramatically improved by following a CompStat-style performance-based model. The process: first, carefully think through the mission and goals (prevent crime and prevent fires rather than catch criminals or put out fires); second, designate key impact indicators that enable senior managers to measure how well their organizations are doing in achieving their mission (cut serious crimes in half or eliminate fire-related deaths); and third, hold all members accountable for success.

At a general level, this approach to performance management is applicable to a broad range of social missions. In chapter 12 we discuss a variety of impact measurement tools and outline how a predictive based methodology might apply to many of the cross-sector partnerships profiled in this book. We explore specific questions such as: How might the FDNY score new fire prevention programs and choose which to fund? We also detail the new Impact Rate of Return (iRR) formula, which helps partners compare potential program options or strategies to achieve a desired positive social impact.

# CHAPTER TWELVE

# The Performance Framework

## Predicting the Social Value of a Partnership

### HOWARD W. BUFFETT

When organizations spanning multiple sectors decide to collaborate, they often enter the partnership with different ideas about what they hope to accomplish. As discussed in previous chapters, they may use dissimilar terminology to describe their objectives and intended outcomes.[1] In addition, their respective preferences and priorities will drive the metrics they choose to analyze programs against a partnership's goals (see chapter 8). Even when partners determine mutual measures of success, it can be difficult to predict which programs will be best at creating social value. This chapter discusses a standardized approach for doing so. Called Impact Rate of Return (iRR), it provides organizations in a cross-sector partnership with a common platform to forecast a project's or a program's *performance* and calculate an assumed intrinsic value for society.[2] Using this methodology, partners can estimate which programs will yield the greatest social return per dollar expended, based on how they collaboratively define success.

Organizations *measure* success based on how they *define* it. In the private sector, the universality of currency allows firms to define success using straightforward financial measures, such as an investment's total gain or its dollar-in per dollar-out rate of return. Making capital allocation decisions in finance requires context and a comparative analysis of projected return across investment alternatives.[3] Organizations in a cross-sector partnership should think about capital allocation for social improvement in a similar way. However, program selection is more challenging without a universal unit of measure for public benefit.[4] How might the Fire Department of New York City (see chapter 11) compare different program options to reduce the number of fire-related deaths? In the Afghanistan case (see chapter 7), how might partners compare the social good created by providing irrigation to one set of farmers over another?

There is no right or wrong answer, but the Impact Rate of Return methodology helps to overcome some of these comparative challenges. Using a formula that mirrors traditional financial models, it translates a program's potential performance into a uniform output.[5] By comparing the iRR output of similar programs against an appropriately established goal for social improvement, partners can make more efficient and better informed capital allocation decisions. Using iRR is very much a starting point, but we believe this method will develop into a set of tools that provides rigor, reliability, and comparability similar to the methods available for analysis of financial investments. This chapter outlines a number of measurement approaches and their applicability to cross-sector partnerships before introducing the full iRR methodology. Comparative examples across four areas—fire safety, renewable energy, smallholder agriculture, and sustainable mixed-use real estate development—are then analyzed.

## DEFINING MEASURES OF SOCIAL IMPACT

Scholars and practitioners have yet to agree universally on terminology or measurements for calculating a program's or capital allocation's potential costs or benefits to society (often referred to as *social impact*).[6] The evolving field of social impact measurement has made tremendous progress in recent years, including newly developed frameworks such as the Impact Reporting and Investment Standards (IRIS) discussed later in this chapter. Governments, foundations, and other partners are constantly looking for ways to apply improved thinking around measurement, especially for significant collaborative efforts such as the Sustainable Development Goals (discussed in chapter 1). Numerous approaches to measuring results and wide-ranging measurement tools have emerged over the past few decades, but a lack of consensus hampers the ability of organizations to assess the performance of programs in a cross-sector partnership.[7] Having a positive or negative social impact on something means different things, even in similar contexts, and is measurable in many different ways.[8] Positive impact, for instance, may include improvements in standards of living, increases in life expectancy, decreases in carbon emissions, additional students graduating, and so on. As a result, the field has many examples of tools, approaches, or programs related to social impact measurement that are diverse in their scopes, methodologies, and purposes. The next section looks at a few notable examples and discusses their limitations and applications to the types of cross-sector partnerships profiled in this book.

## Disability-Adjusted Life Year

The United Nations World Health Organization uses a technique that quantifies the negative social impact of an individual's poor health and disease.[9] The Disability-Adjusted Life Year (DALY) measures both mortality (as years of life lost due to early or premature death) and morbidity (as nonfatal health problems).[10] Programs that reduce or avoid the highest number of DALYs accomplish the most social good. DALY is useful because it combines these factors into a single output, which organizations can use to compare the cost-effectiveness of various relevant programs.[11] However, the approach is not without drawbacks (critics argue there are flaws in its design and validation), and it has limited applicability for cross-sector partnerships outside of health-related fields.[12]

## Best Available Charitable Option

Acumen is a nonprofit organization that applies entrepreneurial principles through venture funding to address global poverty issues. They have invested over $100 million in more than one hundred companies across thirteen countries in areas such as agriculture, education, and health.[13] In 2007, Acumen detailed a social impact measurement methodology comparing a potential investment for social good against the "best available charitable option" (BACO).[14] They sought to understand how much social good they could create per dollar invested over the lifetime of an investment compared to a traditional philanthropic grant with similar goals. Acumen provided a comparative analysis by examining which of two options were likely to create more good for society: for example, a loan to a manufacturer of malaria-preventing bed nets or a "sunk cost" grant in the same amount to an international NGO to procure and distribute bed nets.[15] The resulting analysis showed that the loan option could be fifty-two times more effective.[16] The BACO methodology is a useful approach for thinking through the cost effectiveness per unit of defined social impact. However, as Acumen points out, it requires careful selection of a "right" charitable alternative for comparison. Similar to monetization approaches discussed later in the chapter, BACO focuses mainly on financially based cost-effectiveness comparisons.[17] As originally presented by Acumen, this does not necessarily account for important aspects of varying impact quality or program delivery between alternatives.

## Social Internal Rate of Return

Another example is a method used by the intergovernmental Organisation for Economic Co-operation and Development (OECD), called social internal rate of return.[18] The OECD initially used it to compare the social costs and benefits of education at a countrywide level. Among other things, the calculation captures various aspects of related economic activity in addition to numerous positive externalities resulting from a country's investment in education (such as reduced crime, improved health, and increased productivity).[19] Others have applied the social internal rate of return calculus to fields outside of education, such as infrastructure investment.[20] Overall, the method focuses mainly on economic evaluation and the aggregate output of public investments from the societal perspective. It has little or no focus on program quality or organizational or stakeholder preferences, which are critical design elements in cross-sector partnerships.

## Social Progress Index

A broader methodology, also at a countrywide level (but increasingly at subnational levels as well), is the Social Progress Index.[21] This index aggregates social and environmental indicators from 128 countries, and across three aspects of social progress: basic human needs (such as nutrition and shelter), foundations of well-being (such as access to information and a sustainable environment), and opportunity (such as freedom of expression and access to higher education).[22] The index purposely excludes economic indicators so that others can use its data to "rigorously and systematically analyze the relationship between economic development (measured for example by GDP per capita) and social development."[23] By design, the index does not provide a rate of return output, an impact measurement, or assessment at a programmatic level. However, the data are useful in guiding program priorities or coordinating program activities across numerous cross-sector partnerships.[24]

## B Impact Assessment

Another tool, B Impact Assessment, standardizes and indexes the measure of benefit created by corporations that undergo its evaluation.[25] It provides comparative, organization-level impact scores in areas such as corporate governance, workforce advancement, and effects the company has on the community and the environment.[26] The tool does not assess collaborative programs or cross-sector partnerships, but it does perform an important benchmarking function for participating groups. Moreover, establishing "social impact" baselines is helpful for comparing relative performance measurement regardless of the sector. The nonprofit B Lab operates the tool and certifies companies that meet minimum levels of social and environmental performance, transparency, and legal accountability.[27]

## DEVELOPING INDUSTRY STANDARDS

Perhaps the most widely known work to establish industry standards for social impact measurement is that of the Global Impact Investing Network (GIIN). Originated by the Rockefeller Foundation (among others) in 2007, GIIN is a self-described "nonprofit organization dedicated to increasing the scale and effectiveness of impact investing."[28] Impact investing, a developing category of finance, attempts to combine social improvement and profitability, with an expectation that results are quantifiable.[29] GIIN defines impact investments as those "made into companies, organizations, and funds with the intention to generate social and environmental impact alongside a financial return."[30] A number of the financial tools discussed in chapter 10, including some program-related investments and most mission-related investments, qualify under this definition.

GIIN argues that the practice of impact investing has the following characteristics:[31]

1. An "intention to have a positive social or environmental impact;"[32]
2. An "expectation of generating a financial return;"[33]
3. A "range of return expectations and asset classes targeted;"[34] and
4. A "commitment to measure and report the social and environmental performance of investments."[35]

To further the practice of impact investing, GIIN, the U.S. Agency for International Development, the Rockefeller Foundation, and JP Morgan Chase launched a joint initiative in 2009.[36] This cross-sector partnership focused on developing a broad catalog of impact performance measurements, which are likely the most widely accepted in the field of impact investing.[37] The Impact Reporting and Investment Standards (IRIS) provide more than five hundred metrics to define and track social change, and GIIN updates it with some frequency.[38] These social impact measurements range from the number of part-time employee jobs created, to the amount of waste reduced, to the number of forest rangers trained for conservation initiatives.

One of the catalog's most direct applications to social value investing relates to the program analysis framework (or the Impact Balance Sheet) outlined in chapter 8. Partners can use the metrics in IRIS to guide development of their program evaluation criteria, which also helps them differentiate between low- and high-quality impact. This, in turn, informs iRR's *Impact Multiplier* variable, discussed later in this chapter. Given its expansive size, the catalog has many metrics relevant to performance measurement for the types of cross-sector partnerships described in this book.[39]

IRIS is, therefore, a valuable resource, even if the breadth of its scope can be intimidating. This scope illustrates the extensive number of items partners may want to consider when defining social impact, as well as the complexity of social issues and their associated indicators. Moreover, the catalog is useful for articulating a program's or partnership's social impact goals to practitioners from other industries. IRIS is free and open to all, and the metrics can be easily simplified and adapted to other platforms to support streamlined reporting.[40]

## BENEFITS OF A FORWARD-LOOKING APPROACH

Many social impact organizations outline broad intended or hoped-for outcomes from a program, and then they examine what took place in retrospect. This *ex-post* or after-the-fact analysis is particularly important for understanding what aspects of program design and implementation worked and which did not work. This process also supports progressive or milestone-based monitoring, which is especially useful for programs implemented over long time periods.

Some organizations, such as the Robin Hood Foundation, have developed impact assessments that take a forward-looking or predictive-based approach. Robin Hood very clearly defines its mission: poverty fighting in New York City.[41] They fund what they consider the most effective poverty fighting programs; efforts that reduce poverty or increase future earnings for low-income New Yorkers fall within their mission's purview.[42] To assist in this, Robin Hood uses an approach called "relentless monetization," which computes the dollar value of social benefits created by a grant.[43]

To analyze program effectiveness relative to its mission, Robin Hood developed an extensive set of metrics—as well as 163 formulas spelled out across 168 pages—to assist their team in monetizing the particular outcomes of a program.[44] Robin Hood then compares the outcomes of a given program to what they predict would have happened in the absence of their funding; in this way, they are developing counterfactual estimates of the true value created due to their support. By dividing the total estimated benefit created from the program by investment in the program (the size of the grant), Robin Hood calculates a benefit-cost ratio.[45]

For example, Robin Hood estimates that a low-income adult who attends a dental health care program can, through a variety of dependent factors, expect an approximately 1 percent increase in future earnings. They base this claim on research and available data cited in their metrics manual. On average, they estimate that every low-income adult who receives such dental work will have roughly an additional $20,000 of future lifetime earnings because of the program.[46] By multiplying the future earnings by the number of individuals who receive the treatment and then dividing by Robin Hood's investment in the program, the organization calculates its benefit-cost ratio.

Another example looks at the benefit-cost ratio of a program designed to increase the number of high school graduates at a particular school. With a $400,000 grant, Robin Hood estimates that a hypothetical program would lead to twenty-five more students graduating than would have absent the program. Furthermore, twenty of those students would go on to attend some college who otherwise would not have done so. In monetizing the outcomes, Robin Hood estimates that each of the high school graduates will have a $6,500 earnings boost per year, and each will live a healthier and longer life (which itself carries a benefit of $90,000 over an individual's lifetime). Furthermore, by attending some college, twenty of the students increase their future earnings by an additional $2,000 per year. Robin Hood estimates that this adds up to just over $6 million in benefits to low-income individuals participating in the program, and by dividing the benefits by the initial investment of $400,000, this leads to a 15:1 benefit-cost ratio. That is, for every dollar invested, Robin Hood can forecast that low-income participants will receive lifetime benefits equivalent to $15.[47]

The Robin Hood Foundation's assessment philosophy articulates a social return on investment for its programs and illustrates how economic benefit and anticipated outcomes combine into a uniform and straightforward monetary output.[48] This allows the organization to distill a wide variety of poverty fighting programs into a simple benefit-cost ratio that is informative and broadly applicable. It also illustrates a very effective method for conducting social impact performance measurement at the programmatic level.[49]

The monetization approach, and other cost-benefit calculations, are well suited for programs that define success in terms of economic benefit created or monetary value added.[50] However, many cross-sector partnerships (including some profiled in this book) use measures of a different kind, or ones that cannot be monetized.[51] Substituting monetary value in place of certain outcomes runs the risk of leaving out important information or relevant program factors that cannot, or should not, be captured in dollars.[52] Because of this, groups such as Robin Hood may choose to incorporate additional, non-monetary measures into their evaluation for a more comprehensive analysis.[53] Measuring performance may need to consider subjective viewpoints, cultural nuance, or design aspects of program delivery. For instance, think back to the Digital India case (chapter 3) and imagine that the government and Apollo Telemedicine are considering new healthcare services for eUrban Primary Health Centers. What happens if they evaluate two dental care programs that yield nearly identical benefit-cost ratios but differ in the quality of care, customer satisfaction, or the experience and credentials of the dental care practitioners?[54] Comparing programs in a case such as this is an area where the iRR approach has some advantages.

## OUTLINING THE iRR METHODOLOGY

Social impact means something different to everyone, so quantifying it requires a customizable approach that can take into account partners' various preferences and priorities. Despite the difficulties inherent in impact measurement models, Impact Rate of Return shows promise because it incorporates flexibility yet maintains a standardized framework. By doing so, organizations in a cross-sector partnership can compare relative social impact performance between programs against specific goals to improve society. Organizations can do this in a manner that is uniform regardless of the type of impact they choose to measure. In effect, iRR allows organizations to estimate how much future impact they can expect to achieve per dollar expended in comparison to projects of a similar type, and to do so consistently.

Similar to financial analysis for Net Present Value (NPV), which calculates the time value of money, iRR estimates the *impact value of money*. The formula divides future (or expected) impact from an investment by the effectiveness and quality of that impact over time. Doing so solves for a program's potential rate of impact. For the sake of comparison, we represent Net Present Value as:

$$\text{Net Present Value} = \frac{\text{Future Value}}{(1 + \text{Interest Rate})^{\text{Number of Time Periods}}}$$

$$\textit{Simplified}: \text{NPV} = \frac{\text{FV}}{(1+r)^n}$$

In comparing the variables of the Net Present Value formula to the iRR formula (below), we find that iRR replaces "Future Value" with "Future Impact." Instead of calculating an "Interest Rate," as NPV does, the denominator of iRR calculates a "Net Impact Rate"—a product of a program's "Impact Multiplier" and "Impact Efficiency." Finally, the "Number of Time Periods" represents the same in both formulas. Therefore, we represent iRR as:

$$\text{iRR} = \frac{\text{Future Impact}}{[(1-\text{Impact Multiplier})\times(\text{Impact Efficiency})]\times \text{Number of Time Periods}}$$

We further simplify the iRR formula by representing the "Impact Multiplier" and "Impact Efficiency" variables as "Net Impact Rate" as follows:

$$\text{iRR} = \frac{\text{Future Impact}}{(\text{Net Impact Rate})\times n} \quad \textit{or further simplified: } \text{iRR} = \frac{\text{FI}}{(\text{NIR})\times n}$$

## Customizing the iRR Formula

To set up the iRR formula, organizations in a cross-sector partnership must do the following:

1. *Determine the impact theme*: this is a categorical type of impact related to the desired outcome of the cross-sector partnership (e.g., fire safety, renewable energy, smallholder agriculture). This categorization guides the formula's customization.

2. *Establish a Key Impact Indicator*: this is a unit of measurement for the type of positive social impact delivered by programs or projects in the cross-sector partnership's theme.

   For example, indicators could include the number of lives lost that were prevented by a new fire department safety program, the megawatt hours generated by a solar power energy project, acres of farmland improved, or the number of square feet developed for a sustainable real estate project. In each case, the Key Impact

Indicator is a clearly defined and straightforward metric directly tied to the social impact goals of the organization or partnership.[55] The greater the number of Key Impact Indicator units, the greater the potential social impact of the program.

3. *Set an impact goal for the theme*: this establishes desired impact in terms of the theme's Key Impact Indicator and creates a comparative baseline for any programs evaluated in that theme.

   For the purpose of the iRR formula, an organization's impact goal is the number of Key Impact Indicator units it hopes to reach within a theme (e.g., forty-eight lives lost will be prevented, 150 MWs will be generated, 10,000 acres of farmland will be improved).

4. *Define a uniform scale for quality of impact*: this is iRR's Impact Multiplier, and it outlines the qualifications or attributes a project must meet or adhere to in order to achieve a given rating within an impact theme.

The Impact Multiplier rating is a numeric scale ranging from "highest-quality impact" (measuring a 0.99) down to "lowest-quality impact" (as low as 0). Quality of impact may be based on existing and widely accepted standards, such as LEED Certification for sustainable construction, which uses ratings classified as "Platinum" (highest), "Gold" (second highest), "Silver," and so on.[56]

In many cross-sector partnerships, the Impact Multiplier will be custom defined by partners based on their preferences and priorities. Partners may choose to use a program analysis framework (such as the Impact Balance Sheet), outlined in chapter 8, to determine weighted points-based evaluation criteria. Alternatively, a simpler scale may be used. For example, a project meeting twelve out of fourteen specific impact qualifications might be considered "very high quality" and earn a 0.86 (which is twelve divided by fourteen). A project meeting eleven out of fourteen qualifications might earn a 0.79, and so on.

This is a critical component of the tool because organizations will have different ways of defining what qualifies as high-quality impact, as well as which metrics should factor into the rating system. Organizations should use the same rating framework (whether customized or based on existing standards) to compare all projects within a given theme.

Once the formula is set, organizations must calculate two figures to determine the iRR for a given project or program:

1. *Estimate the project's Future Impact*: this is the percentage of an organization's or partnership's thematic impact goal it expects to achieve with a given project. For example, if a project is expected to prevent six fire-related deaths out of a goal of forty-eight, its Future Impact is represented as 0.125 (or 12.5 percent).

2. *Calculate the project's Impact Efficiency*: this variable combines the measure of dollars expended per Key Impact Indicator (KII) unit reached with a standard logarithmic scale (using a uniform log base of 100 for the examples in this chapter). This merits further explanation:

Because the cost per unit of impact can vary significantly between comparable projects—and quite dramatically between different types of thematic impact—a logarithmic function allows us to normalize the value into a more consistent output.

For example, cost per KII unit may range from millions or hundreds of thousands of dollars per solar MW, to thousands of dollars per acre of farmland, to hundreds of dollars per square foot of mixed-use real estate developed. The resulting logarithmic output provides a useful and structured scale regardless of the cost expended per KII unit. As one might expect, the lower the cost per unit of projected impact, the more cost efficient that impact will be. The Impact Efficiency figure reflects this inverse relationship by showing a lower value for greater cost efficiency.[57]

In general, the information required for these two calculations is available through due diligence or is provided in a grant application, project proposal, or program prospectus. The following sections illustrate iRR's customization and calculation process across four thematic examples.

## iRR and the FDNY

iRR's predictive, goal-based approach is an important aspect of its formulation. As discussed in chapter 11, the Fire Department of New York City (FDNY) uses predictive methodologies to determine the most effective allocation of its resources. Through risk-based fire inspections, the department redesigned operations based on clearly established goals and the way in which it measures success.[58]

Here we consider an application of the iRR formula using an impact goal relevant to the department.[59] The FDNY may use the *number of fire-related deaths prevented* as their Key Impact Indicator, and we can assume that they have a goal of preventing *all* fire-related deaths. In 2016, the number of fire-related deaths was a historically low forty-eight (despite responding to more than 26,000 structural fires across the city).[60] To calculate iRR's Future Impact quantity in this example, we use the percent of the expected impact goal achieved (fire-related deaths prevented) by a given project.

For the sake of illustration, say that the FDNY is evaluating a number of similar projects to deploy new "smart" home smoke detectors in the highest risk areas of the city (faulty detectors are a contributing factor to in-home fire-related deaths).[61] The first project the FDNY evaluates costs $8 million to develop and deploy, will take three years to test and implement, and is expected to reduce annual fire-related deaths by twelve. In reducing fire-related deaths by twelve, the project would accomplish 12/48ths, or 25 percent of the FDNY's overall impact goal. This number represents the amount of Future Impact expected by this project, and three years is the number of time periods. We enter these amounts into the formula as follows:

$$\text{Example iRR calculation:} \frac{.25}{[(1 - \text{Impact Multiplier}) \times (\text{Impact Efficiency})] \times 3}$$

At this point, we have established our measurement units (deaths prevented), our goal (forty-eight), and the expected amount of the goal accomplished by the first proposed project (twelve, or 25 percent). We also know the project's cost ($8 million) and the number of time periods required for implementation (three years).

The next step in the iRR process is to determine the project's Impact Multiplier. In this hypothetical case, the FDNY uses a customized program analysis framework to establish a number of straightforward impact qualifications for its smart detector program. This includes variables such as the complexity of user installation, the type of failsafe system (such as a low-battery warning), the frequency of safety inspections required, previous successful deployments of similar programs, overall efficacy of the detectors, and so forth. Upon analysis by the FDNY, the first smart detector project meets sixteen out of twenty qualifications, and scores an Impact Multiplier rating of 0.80. We enter that value into the formula as follows:

$$\text{Example iRR calculation:} \frac{.25}{[(1-0.80)\times(\text{Impact Efficiency})]\times 3}$$

Our final calculation is the Impact Efficiency of the project. In the case of this first smart detector project, the cost per KII unit (fire-related death prevented) is $666,667. The logarithm base 100 of 666,667, written $\log_{100}$ (666,667), equals 2.9120. Entering this value into the formula results in the following:

$$\text{Example iRR calculation:} \frac{.25}{[(1-0.80)\times(2.9120)]\times 3} = 0.1431$$

Therefore, the Impact Rate of Return for this example project is 14.31 percent (table 12.1).

Given this outline, the FDNY can easily compare the iRR of this project to any other potential smart detector project. For example, it can compare a similar project that costs $10 million to implement over four years, and prevents fourteen deaths with a similar quality of impact rating.

The formula and corresponding outputs are as follows:

$$\text{Example iRR calculation:} \frac{.2917}{[(1-0.80)\times(2.9269)]\times 4} = 0.1246$$

The Impact Rate of Return for this second example project is 12.46 percent, slightly lower than the first example. Although estimated future impact is higher (fourteen versus twelve), the "quality" of impact is the same (both score a 0.80), the cost per KII is higher, and the time to implement the project is longer.

In a third similar project example, we evaluate an option that costs $15 million over five years, will prevent seventeen fire-related deaths, and achieves a higher impact rating. The corresponding outputs are as follows:

$$\text{Example iRR calculation:} \frac{.3542}{[(1-0.90)\times(2.9728)]\times 5} = 0.2383$$

The Impact Rate of Return for this third project example is 23.83 percent. The significant increase in iRR is due mainly to the "quality" of impact in the Impact Multiplier evaluation. In this case, the project receives such a high rating because end-user installation is much simpler than the other two projects and because it has an effective failsafe system that actively communicates with FDNY's central command. Further, the smart detectors in this project do not require ongoing in-person safety inspections due to their design. This project takes more up-front time compared to the first two examples (and organizations may want to factor in opportunity cost), and it cost more per KII, but it has a greater longer-term impact and a higher likelihood of success.

Had this example only achieved a 0.80 rating, similar to the previous two project examples, it would have received the lowest iRR of the group. This illustrates the importance of the impact rating system used in the iRR calculation.

In the following pages, three additional sets of examples illustrate the diverse applicability of the iRR formula and the potential utility of the tool for a variety of calculations.

TABLE 12.1 Fire Safety

| Example | Impact Goal (deaths prevented) | Projected KII | % Impact Goal | Impact Multiplier | Cost ($ million) | Cost per KII | Time (Yrs) | iRR |
|---|---|---|---|---|---|---|---|---|
| 1 | 48 | 12 | 25.00 | 0.80 | $8 | $666,667 | 3 | 14.31% |
| 2 | 48 | 14 | 29.17 | 0.80 | $10 | $714,286 | 4 | 12.46% |
| 3 | 48 | 17 | 35.42 | 0.90 | $15 | $882,353 | 5 | 23.83% |

## Renewable Energy iRR

In 2007, New York City mayor Michael Bloomberg launched PlaNYC,[62] a city-wide effort that included a series of large-scale sustainability initiatives.[63] With an initial goal of improving quality of life in the city and reducing carbon emissions by 30 percent by 2030, PlaNYC kicked off a number of new programs.[64] For example, the New York City Department of Parks and Recreation led an effort to plant a million new trees within ten years (MillionTreesNYC).[65] More than two hundred miles of bike lanes were added in the city between 2007 and 2009,[66] and major bike-sharing programs launched through new cross-sector partnerships.[67] In 2010, New York City Parks Commissioner Adrian Benepe started an expansive citywide Sustainable Parks initiative,[68] including performance scorecards with detailed metrics and measurement methodologies.[69]

The city's commitment to sustainability continued under Mayor Bill de Blasio. In 2014, Mayor de Blasio announced New York City's goal to reduce greenhouse gas emissions by 80 percent by 2050.[70] His plan also included major goals for renewable energy production, with targets for home and commercial solar power generation.[71] Similar trends took place at the state level as well. In 2016, New York Governor Andrew Cuomo announced an ambitious plan mandating that half of the state's electricity would come from renewable sources by 2030, including solar, to reduce carbon emissions and protect the environment.[72]

As cities and states plan for sustainability commitments and increase renewable energy production to meet growing demands, they will have to collaborate across sectors and stakeholder interests.[73] In this section, we examine a scenario where a city and state government plan to cofinance a large solar power project in partnership with private sector developers and a non-profit economic development corporation.

To begin, the partners establish an impact goal of replacing 150 megawatts (MW) of fossil-based energy capacity through new solar-based production. With the KII measurement units (megawatts) and goal (150 MW capacity) established, we are able to calculate the Future Impact figure for any potential solar project. An example three-year, $80 million project with production capacity of 46 MW would accomplish 30.67 percent of our previously established 150 MW goal.[74] The cost per KII for this example rounds to $1.739 million, which equals

3.1202 on the logarithmic scale. This project scores the equivalent of a 0.80 rating when taking into account variables such as its energy output efficiency, power grid availability, transmission disruption, net carbon offset, and constraints in project construction.[75]

The following formula illustrates this example and the corresponding iRR output:

$$\text{Example iRR calculation:} \frac{.3067}{[(1-0.80)\times(3.1202)]\times 3} = 0.1638$$

Therefore, the Impact Rate of Return for this example project is 16.38 percent (table 12.2).

Understandably, that output in isolation has limited value. There is benefit in going through the process of establishing a well-defined social impact goal and the exercise of defining and applying a multiplier rating for that impact. However, comparable iRR outputs are required to evaluate which resource allocation has the greatest potential relative impact.

Here we examine a second three-year solar project, assuming the same partnering organizations with the same Impact Goal and Multiplier Rating system. In this example, the project is slightly smaller (roughly $76 million), with a capacity of 42 MW, and achieves a similar 0.80 rating.

The following formula illustrates this example and the corresponding iRR output:

$$\text{Example iRR calculation:} \frac{.28}{[(1-0.80)\times(3.1276)]\times 3} = 0.1492$$

The calculated Impact Rate of Return for this second solar example is 14.92 percent. We can expect this slightly lower output because the project yields fewer MWs of sustainably produced energy and costs more per KII in comparison to the first.

Our third example evaluates another three-year solar project, again with the same Impact Goal and Multiplier Rating system. This solar project has a 44 MW capacity for the same roughly $76 million cost as the previous project. However, this project's profile only scored a 0.70 rating.

The following formula illustrates this example and the corresponding iRR output:

$$\text{Example iRR calculation:}\frac{.2933}{[(1-0.70)\times(3.1175)]\times3}=0.1045$$

Therefore, the iRR for this third solar example is 10.45 percent. Although the project's cost per KII was the lowest of all three examples, the fact that its Impact Multiplier was lower had an understandably dramatic effect on this project's overall projected iRR performance.

TABLE 12.2  Renewable Energy

| Example | Impact Goal (MW) | Projected KII | % Impact Goal | Impact Multiplier | Cost ($ million) | Cost per KII | Time (Yrs) | iRR |
|---|---|---|---|---|---|---|---|---|
| 1 | 150 | 46 | 30.67 | 0.80 | $80 | $1,739,130 | 3 | 16.38% |
| 2 | 150 | 42 | 28.00 | 0.80 | $75.6 | $1,800,000 | 3 | 14.92% |
| 3 | 150 | 44 | 29.33 | 0.70 | $75.6 | $1,718,182 | 3 | 10.45% |

## Smallholder Agriculture iRR

Social value investing guides organizations in the development of place-based, or regionally focused cross-sector partnerships (see chapter 8). In addition to important aspects of stakeholder engagement, it outlines collaborative planning through a scoping exercise and a program analysis framework. We examined a detailed example of this in the Afghanistan case (chapter 7), specifically related to smallholder farmers and increases in farm productivity through investments in irrigation and agricultural cooperatives.

Using a similar scenario, imagine a local NGO in Rwanda that engages a foundation and a university to develop a cross-sector partnership focused on goals analogous to the programs in Afghanistan[76] (agriculture employs roughly the same percentage of people in each country).[77] The group begins by surveying numerous communities to learn residents' preferences and priorities regarding improved agricultural practices and needs. Partners draft initial plans with ongoing community participation while conducting a value-chain analysis across regions. They also involve the Rwandan government, which in 2010 established an ambitious ten-year goal to increase domestic agricultural production by 8.5 percent annually.[78] Collaboratively the group develops the partnership's program analysis framework, and settles on a place-based strategy in a regional area of approximately 10,000 acres (this size based on the administrative locality in Rwanda where the NGO has the most experience).[79] As a result, the partners use land area (acres) for their iRR Key Impact Indicator, and set an impact goal of improving 10,000 acres of farmland using economically and ecologically sustainable production practices.[80]

The group plans to evaluate clusters of cooperative-sized development projects (ranging from a few hundred acres to over a thousand acres, depending on location) and will then cross-compare consolidated, averaged iRR outputs between clusters in similarly sized regions. Factors that contribute to the partnership's Impact Multiplier rating include the number of farming households reached by a given project, the gender demographic of project participants,[81] whether a given approach is conducive to the needs of farmers with uneven plots of land (82 percent of farmland in Rwanda is on hillsides[82]), opportunities for mechanization,[83] and an evaluation of what other developments are already underway in the area. The evaluation also takes into account how well a project addresses gaps in surrounding agricultural value chains (discussed in chapter 4), such as logistical constraints, access to local markets, availability of crop inputs, and so on.

In this scenario, the first set of evaluations consider three similar opportunities, each with comparable size, cost, time required, and impact profiles. One is a four-year, $4 million agricultural development project consisting of 823 acres, which is just over 8 percent of the partnership's 10,000 acre goal. In this case, project evaluation against the program analysis framework results in a fairly high impact multiplier rating of 0.89. The project is well suited for the topography of the area, represents a model easily replicated to other regions, reaches a significant number of female farmers, and meets many of the impact requirements outlined in the program analysis framework.

Calculating this project's Impact Efficiency shows that it costs $4,860 per Key Impact Indicator (acre), which converts to 1.8433 on the logarithmic scale. Combining these various components, the corresponding iRR output is:

$$\text{Example iRR calculation:} \frac{.0823}{[(1-0.89)\times(1.8433)]\times 4} = 0.1015$$

Therefore, the Impact Rate of Return for this example project is 10.15 percent (table 12.3).

The second project opportunity evaluated by the group covers more area (985 acres), accounting for 9.85 percent of the partnership's Impact Goal. Its total cost is slightly higher ($4.05 million), but the implementation per KII is lower than that of the first example ($4,112). Partners, however, do not expect the project to adequately address soil erosion challenges, and its participants comprise a less diverse gender profile than the first project opportunity. Despite these limitations, the project still meets many of the other qualifications outlined in the program analysis framework, and scores an Impact Multiplier rating of 0.85.

$$\text{Example iRR calculation:} \frac{.0985}{[(1-0.85)\times(1.8070)]\times 4} = 0.0908$$

Therefore, the iRR for this example project is 9.08 percent.

In the final example the partners evaluate a project proposal costing $4.15 million, and reaching the most number of acres (1,282). Its cost per KII is the lowest ($3,237) and, like the others, is expected to require four years for implementation. This project provides less access to mechanization, and is less effective in how it prepares farmers for market-readiness—important components of Rwanda's Vision 2020 plan. Because aspects of its program design are somewhat less comprehensive than the others, it is limited in its program analysis score. Although, this particular project includes intercropping for high intensity agroforestry plots, which the others do not.[84] Overall, it scores an Impact Multiplier rating of 0.82.

$$\text{Example iRR calculation:} \frac{.1282}{[(1-0.82)\times(1.7551)]\times 4} = 0.1015$$

The iRR for this project is 10.15 percent, which is the same as the first example.

The identical results between the first and third projects underscore a difficult trade-off organizations face when planning cross-sector partnerships: depth of impact versus breadth of impact (which we discussed in the scoping exercise in chapter 8). The first project covers less area than the third, but it does so with a higher quality of impact as defined by the organizations and stakeholders in the partnership.

In practice, these types of project opportunities would not likely be as similar in size, cost, and projected impact as they are in this scenario. However, this example illustrates how partners can combine a program analysis framework and the iRR methodology into place-based partnership planning.

TABLE 12.3 Smallholder Agriculture

| Example | Impact Goal (acres) | Projected KII | % Impact Goal | Impact Multiplier | Cost ($ million) | Cost per KII | Time (Yrs) | iRR |
|---------|---------------------|---------------|---------------|-------------------|------------------|--------------|------------|--------|
| 1 | 10,000 | 823 | 8.23 | 0.89 | $4 | $4,860 | 4 | 10.15% |
| 2 | 10,000 | 985 | 9.85 | 0.85 | $4.05 | $4,112 | 4 | 9.08% |
| 3 | 10,000 | 1,282 | 12.82 | 0.82 | $4.15 | $3,237 | 4 | 10.15% |

## Sustainable Mixed-Use Real Estate Development iRR

In chapter 9 we learned about Comunitas and its Juntos program in Brazil. In addition to working with municipal governments to improve the effectiveness of city services, Comunitas is also committed to advancing sustainable development through partnerships with businesses and communities.[85] The Comunitas headquarters is in São Paulo, where our final iRR scenario takes place.

In this scenario, Comunitas partners with a newly formed, university-led urban development coalition focused on a major, environmentally sustainable mixed-use real estate initiative.[86] In addition to commercial, university, and residential tenants, the initiative aims to pilot a newly designed government services center, as well as a state-of-the-art community health clinic.

The primary organizing principle of the coalition is environmentally sustainable development, which defines this partnership's overall impact theme. The partners use square feet as their Key Impact Indicator, and establish an impact goal of developing 3,000,000 square feet in a highly sustainable manner over a multi-year period. In the beginning phase of the project, the coalition analyzes three similar development opportunities. The first is a four-year project consisting of 500,000 square feet, which would accomplish 16.67 percent of the 3,000,000 square feet goal.[87]

In determining this project's Impact Multiplier, it accomplishes a rating of 0.90 by implementing the requirements for LEED Platinum certification and compliance with specific environmental, social, and governance (ESG) measures—two factors adopted by the partners considering this project.[88] Finally, the cost of development is equal to $300 per Key Impact Indicator (square foot), which equals 1.2386 on the logarithmic scale. In this case, the iRR output is as follows:

$$\text{Example iRR calculation:} \frac{.1667}{[(1-0.90)\times(1.2386)]\times 4} = 0.3364$$

The resulting iRR for this example project is 33.64 percent (table 12.4).

The second example illustrates a similarly sized opportunity, and assumes the same Impact Goal and Multiplier Rating system. This hypothetical project costs less ($115.5 million), and taking into account build-out restrictions, only meets a LEED Gold standard. It therefore receives a lower Multiplier Rating, which significantly affects its Impact Rate of Return.

The overall square footage developed is the same, as is the time horizon for the project:

$$\text{Example iRR calculation:} \frac{.1667}{[(1-0.80)\times(1.1818)]\times 4} = 0.1763$$

The resulting iRR for this example project is only 17.63 percent, despite having a lower up-front cost and lower dollar per KII than the first example. Like the examples in the previous themes, this further illustrates the importance of the Impact Multiplier in the overall framework.

The final example is a nearly identical project opportunity. The calculation uses the same formula customization, and the project's profile differs only in that it has a marginally lower cost ($112 million) and, therefore, better (lower) impact efficiency value:

$$\text{Example iRR calculation:} \frac{.1667}{[(1-0.80)\times(1.1751)]\times 4} = 0.1773$$

Due to the lower cost per KII ($224), the iRR for this project is slightly better than the previous one, yielding 17.73 percent. The second and third examples illustrate how the formula responds when cost differs but all other factors are the same.

With the analysis framework established, and the partnership's iRR formula customized, partners in this scenario will be able to calculate and compare the iRR of future project opportunities throughout the phases of development.

TABLE 12.4 Sustainable Mixed-Use Real Estate Development

| Example | Impact Goal (sq ft) | Projected KII | % Impact Goal | Impact Multiplier | Cost ($ million) | Cost per KII | Time (Yrs) | iRR |
|---|---|---|---|---|---|---|---|---|
| 1 | 3,000,000 | 500,000 | 16.67 | 0.90 | $150 | $300 | 4 | 33.64% |
| 2 | 3,000,000 | 500,000 | 16.67 | 0.80 | $115.5 | $231 | 4 | 17.63% |
| 3 | 3,000,000 | 500,000 | 16.67 | 0.80 | $112 | $224 | 4 | 17.73% |

## CONSIDERATIONS ABOUT THE MODEL

The iRR model has both advantages and disadvantages. It lends itself well to situations that can use clear Key Impact Indicator units as a basis for defining projected impact. Furthermore, in situations where it is desirable to use multiple indicator units (or where the partners do not want to roll secondary units into a rating system), the formula can be easily modified for additional KII calculations, and the outputs averaged or weighted depending on partner preferences.[89]

In cases where profitability is a consideration, such as impact- or mission-related investments, groups can apply a combined financial and

impact analysis. For instance, partners may analyze particular investments or projects within a partnership and average scores based on
weighted values assigned to both the financial internal rate of return
(IRR) and the iRR—depending on their preferences. In this way, the
iRR model can combine goals for financial return with discrete goals
to improve society when such goals are not mutually exclusive.

Moreover, iRR is not limited to *ex-ante* analysis. Partners may
wish to establish escalating target iRR values across time periods
and compare or average delivered iRR throughout the life cycle
of a partnership. Partners also can conduct a retrospective evaluation following a program's completion to determine the actual iRR
achieved. Comparing program outputs to initial projections allows
partners to measure the variance between predicted and actual
impact accomplished on a per-dollar basis, resulting in a powerful
assessment tool.[90]

## Disadvantages of the Model

One of the greatest strengths of the Impact Rate of Return model—
its customizability—is also the source of its greatest vulnerability.
The model relies on the expertise and judgment of those who customize it. If an evaluator poorly defines or haphazardly selects its subjective
qualities of impact, its output may result in wasted resources. Worse
yet, it may direct resources toward programs that have unintended
negative consequences, or that cause societal harm.

This is where the combined knowledge and experience of teams
becomes so important. Inclusive planning is critical. Engaging stakeholders in the model's design and analysis helps reduce the risk that
uninformed assumptions will affect its output. Partners can further
mitigate risk by conducting program or partnership evaluation within
a broader, comprehensive value-chain analysis.

Another drawback to iRR is that some partners may find it time
consuming or impractical to gather required data, or to integrate qualitative attributes into the formula. For example, it may be prohibitively
costly to design and thoroughly test a uniquely customized impact
rating scale, especially in a new field or area that has limited reliable
research. Some organizations may find it easier to use or improve on
the model if they have a budget for monitoring and evaluation or have

experience with other similar tools. This is an area where flexible funding in a partnership, such as philanthropic capital, can offset programmatic or project impact–evaluation costs.

Finally, the success of the model's predictability depends on certainty related to program output. For example, in the sustainable real estate scenario, a proven developer with a successful track record can project, with a reasonably high degree of certainty, that $150 million will in fact result in 500,000 square feet developed. Or in the smallholder agriculture example, there is fair certainty that a $4 million project will in fact result in expected farmland improvements. If we use measures such as the number of students projected to graduate from high school, our certainty could fall. In such cases, it may help to integrate discount factors in addition to the confidence levels discussed in the program analysis framework in chapter 8.

## CONCLUSION

All impact performance models have limitations—including iRR, even with the flexibility of its Impact Multiplier rating system. Many programs carry complexities, or partners may have preferences, that are difficult to capture in any model's format. Furthermore, some qualitative attributes are simply too complex to capture in any formula.[91]

The Impact Rate of Return methodology is simply a first step. We hope it will lead to new ways of thinking about social impact performance and encourage standardized formulae by which to describe the impact effectiveness of various programs in a cross-sector partnership. The methodology lends itself well to many of the financial tools discussed in chapter 10, and it has the potential to begin influencing an expanding pool of impact-oriented capital. As the breadth and number of partnerships grow and expand, we hope that the Impact Rate of Return methodology may lead some organizations to reconsider how they measure their performance and, therefore, how they define success.

# THE RISKS AND
# PROMISE OF
# PARTNERSHIPS

# CHAPTER THIRTEEN

# The Cautionary Case

## The Risks of Large-Scale Partnerships and the Rio Olympics

### WILLIAM B. EIMICKE

As we discussed in chapter 9, a massive corruption scandal plunged the Brazilian economy into one of its worst recessions in decades. Since 2004, Brazil had been among the rapidly growing BRIC economies (along with Russia, India, and China). Brazil developed and instituted important and interesting innovations in the application of the public-private partnership model. Prior to the rapidly unfolding economic and political crises of 2012, Brazil had been the darling of international investors and enjoyed an average growth rate of 4.4 percent from 2004 to 2010, peaking at 7.5 percent in 2010, a time when many other major world economies were in deep recession.[1]

A key figure in the rise and fall of Brazil's economic fortunes and international reputation was the controversial mayor of Rio de Janeiro, Eduardo Paes. Elected in 2008, Paes championed Rio's successful bid in 2009 to host the 2016 Olympic Games over strong competing bids from Chicago, Tokyo, and Madrid. The mayor rode the winning bid to national and international attention and fame, delivering a widely viewed TED Talk in 2012[2] and succeeding Michael Bloomberg as chair of the C40, an international organization of cities advocating for urban solutions to climate change.[3] Paes's strategic plan was based on a vision to create a twenty-first-century Rio to debut when the Olympic Games arrived in the summer of 2016.

Using the approaching Olympics as a driving force, Paes developed a set of projects to launch his vision for the future of the city. The mayor laid out his plan between 2010 and 2012, and we can see reflections of a cross-sector partnership approach in it. For example, he articulated a long-term investment strategy realized through several related development projects. These projects were designed to unlock intrinsic community value—in this case, the revitalization of a deteriorated city neighborhood, creation of new public spaces, commercial building construction, and projects such as new schools and clinics and major upgrades to the mass transit system intended to create better opportunities for all of Rio's residents. Some limited aspects of a comprehensive cross-sector partnership model were used to accomplish the projects, leveraging private investment with improved public infrastructure, and financing the projects with a mix of capital. These collaborations, however, ended up more reminiscent of the twentieth century public-private partnership (PPP) model discussed in chapter 1.

As with some of our other case studies, the long-term successes and failures of the Olympic-based revitalization of Rio cannot yet be determined. At present, the results are mixed, and the process is under a cloud of investigations. In this chapter, we examine how the city of Rio used a number of PPPs to develop and modernize the city to handle the 2016 Summer Olympic Games, including the redevelopment of the derelict and dangerous Porto Maravilha neighborhood in the downtown area near the original seaport. The city also built an edgy, environmentally themed Museum of Tomorrow in that same neighborhood, along with an Olympian participant housing project, transportation upgrades, and the Olympic Park itself.

Although these partnerships were successful in the sense that the Rio Olympic Games themselves took place without any major catastrophe, it subsequently became clear that there had been widespread corruption with private sector payoffs to public officials. Corruption in public contracting is all too common in Brazil, and large public-private partnership projects are clearly vulnerable. Failure to follow some key aspects of collaborative and inclusive partnership planning may explain how these problems developed.

As you will see, the Rio process did not include enough transparency, and there was almost no community participation in decision making. The government of Rio and the private developers worked independently with limited mutually developed operations or collaboration. There was an established strategic plan, but the focus was on getting done what needed to be done in time for the Olympic Games. The short-term goal was achieved, but the long-term planned objectives have languished since the games concluded and Paes's term in office ended.

Paes's driving style and complete commitment to the project helped meet the Olympic deadlines, but his lack of inclusive leadership was damaging. He refused to welcome community participation in the process, and he did not engage those critical of his approach. He also failed to operate in an open manner, and his lack of respect for many key stakeholders likely contributed to the overall controversy regarding the wisdom of some of the developments. Further controversy over charges of corruption marred the image of the Rio Olympics, as well as the city of Rio and the entire country of Brazil.

## RIO OF TOMORROW?

Rio de Janeiro's modern history dates back to January 1, 1502, when Portuguese explorers landed on the shores of Guanabara Bay. The bay lies at the opening of a river, which in English is called the "River of January."[4] Prior to its independence in 1822, Rio's economy was based on agriculture, gold, diamonds, and coffee exports. After independence, Rio became its nation's capital, busiest port, and the political, cultural, and economic center of Brazil. After World War II, Rio transitioned into an industrial economy, headquarters for domestic and international businesses, and a major population center, including a large group of low-income families concentrated in what are now widely known as *favelas*.

In 1960, the nation's political capital was moved inland to the new planned city of Brasília. The 1960s and 1970s saw São Paulo's rise as the new center for Brazilian business and industry. With a population of more than twelve million in its metro area, against Rio's six million, São Paulo is South America's largest city and the undisputed leader for Brazilian industry and finance.

Today, Rio, like many global cities, has focused on its role as a service center. It is home to international businesses and a cultural center. It is the hometown of the bossa nova and its most famous song "The Girl from Ipanema," was a global hit in the 1960s and a theme song for the 2016 Rio Summer Olympic Games. Rio is a major tourist destination and an emerging technology hub with university-business joint research ventures. For people around the world, Rio is synonymous with a complex mix of Carnival, crime, creativity, beautiful beaches, and corruption. Rio's famous landmarks include *Cristo Redentor*; the nearly hundred-foot-tall statute is the largest Art Deco–style sculpture anywhere[5] and was voted one of the New Seven Wonders of the World. It overlooks Rio from the top of Corcovado Mountain amid the Tijuca forest preserve.[6]

Rio, indeed all of Brazil, has been going through difficult times. A major corruption scandal at the country's oil giant Petrobras,[7] declining oil prices, impeachment of the nation's president in a related corruption scandal, exchange rate depreciation, and inflation have combined to dig a deep recession since 2015.[8] Gross national product declined for six consecutive quarters, and 2.8 million jobs were lost (7 percent of total employment).[9] But these recent troubles followed a period of significant economic and social progress. According to the World Bank, between 2003 and 2014, approximately twenty-nine million Brazilians moved above the poverty line, and Brazil's inequality index rating improved by 11 percent.[10] Brazil has been a leader in international negotiations for climate change, including the successful 2015 COP 21, and voluntarily committed to reduce greenhouse gas emissions by at least 36.1 percent by 2020.[11] Brazil remains committed to universal coverage in primary education, although the quality and outcomes of the system leave much to be desired.[12]

## RIO OLYMPICS—SUCCESS OR FAILURE OF A PARTNERSHIP MODEL?

Few things in Brazil remain as controversial as the Rio Olympics. Will they be remembered as a great example of the success of the partnership model, or did the partnership model open the gates to corruption and misappropriations? Just eight months after taking office in January 2009, Mayor Paes became an international figure when Rio was chosen to host the 2016 Olympics. Paes used the World Cup and Olympic Games as a catalyst to redevelop dilapidated areas of the city, particularly Porto Maravilha—the city's port area and central business district—modernizing its public transportation system and making Rio a "smart city" modeled after the innovations of New York City mayor Michael Bloomberg. In partnership with IBM, Rio opened its state of the art Operations Centre in 2010, which coordinates emergency response, traffic management, and weather information, and connects city workers from thirty different agencies to utility companies and transit operators, at all hours of the day, similar to New York City's 911 and 311 systems and open data portals.[13] Similar to Bloomberg, Paes chose to share data on city operations with the public, accessible on mobile devices and through social networks, so citizens could learn what was going on in their neighborhoods and alert the government to issues in their communities in real time.[14]

Under the pressure of long days and nights working on the World Cup, the Olympics, and their renewal projects, the mayor was known to throw things at staffers, insult other elected officials, and once even punched a citizen in the face.[15] Elected in 2008, and reelected with 65 percent of the vote in 2012, Paes nevertheless faced ongoing criticism for his vision of a modern and efficient Rio for the twenty-first century: street protests, accusations of favorable deals for developers, construction delays, and battles between police (run by the state government) and street gangs (and residents) over renewal in the favelas.[16]

Paes sought progress at almost any cost, never retreating in the face of protesters, whom he called "morons."[17] As he said in a 2015 interview, "if you look at Rio now, at least we are looking toward the future. The discussion in Rio was about what governments are not doing. Now people are complaining about things that we are doing. So, I love that."[18] Early on, the Olympic excitement was a unifying force, providing a sense of pride and general optimism about how Olympic-driven investments and tourism would benefit Brazil. Unfortunately, each individual Olympic project involved winners and losers, at least in the short run. Unlike Narendra Modi, who planned Digital India to be in everyone's interests, Paes often dismissed or fought his opponents, and did not stress enough the convergence of interests between all parties, as well as shared risk and potential rewards.

When we consider this case through our definition of successful cross-sector partnerships, we can see signs of trouble. Successful partnerships rely on strong leadership from the *people* involved, and Paes did not possess the collaborative mind-set required to inspire and coordinate with private partners, community representatives, and advocates for affordable housing. Nor did he follow important *place*-based principles and engage the relatively large and vocal group of Rio's citizens and members of the local community affected by the partnership's projects. The partnership *process* appeared to be seriously flawed. There was almost no opportunity for true collaboration, and the absence of transparency in the contracting negotiations allowed the now apparent corruption to go undetected until the projects were completed and the games were over. Presumably to meet the extremely tight schedule required by the International Olympic Committee, the city chose a closed process with minimal comprehensive planning and little opportunity for citizen participation. And with few official *performance* measures other than on-time completion and functionality while the Olympics were under way, assessing success and holding partners accountable became very difficult.

## PORTO MARAVILHA: PARTNERSHIP FOR THE FUTURE

In the downtown port area is a project, some say the largest of its type in Brazil,[19] to revitalize deteriorated buildings and vacant land in a Rio neighborhood called Porto Maravilha. The city managed the partnership through a port development authority that engaged private companies to prepare the site, develop the projects, and manage many of the public services in the area, including street lighting, garbage collection, and landscaping. The largest private partner was a consortium headed by Brazil's construction giant Odebrecht Infraestrutura and Carioca Engenharia.[20] Much of the land was previously under an elevated highway that the mayor tore down to create over fifty million square feet of new office, retail, residential, and cultural space—not dissimilar to Battery Park City in lower Manhattan.[21] If the project is completed between 2020 and 2025, as called for in the plan, it is expected to reach $2.9 billion in investment. The development has achieved some significant effects, although there is still much work to be done.[22]

For example, the project demolished three miles of elevated highway called the Perimetral and replaced it with a pedestrian walkway now open to the bay (figure 13.1). The area's heavy, deadlocked traffic is now rerouted through two tunnels. New roads, sidewalks, electric, sewage, drainage, and fiber optic cable will bring the entire area up to twenty-first-century standards. Under the current plan, a private

*Figure 13.1* People gather to observe the Perimetral overpass, after its partial demolition as part of Rio's Porto Maravilha (Marvelous Port) urbanization project, in Rio de Janeiro April 20, 2014. The project was for the city's redevelopment ahead of the 2016 Olympic Games. REUTERS/Ricardo Moraes

consortium known as Porto Novo is managing the development until 2025.[23] The project design met a number of aspects of our definition of a cross-sector partnership. The city entered a formal agreement with one of the country's most successful development companies. They brought in experienced teams to lead the revitalization and maintain public spaces and amenities in return for private development rights. And there was some degree of accountability for partner performance by requiring the private consortium to maintain the public services and spaces for fifteen years into the future.[24]

Initially, thirty-two commercial projects committed to the site, including Nissan Motor Company and L'Oreal SA. The infrastructure improvements and prime location are designed to lure major private companies, and the city is planning to pay for those improvements primarily with fees received from an auction of the rights to build higher than the existing zoning limits.[25] Paes argued that the PPP approach—a public plan and infrastructure with private financing and management—would enable Rio to redevelop much quicker and more cheaply than either the public sector alone or private development (which generally occurs site by site and negotiation by negotiation, without a comprehensive vision for the neighborhood).[26]

In the early phases of the project, this approach worked quite well—private contractors funded by the city quickly removed the antiquated, elevated highway that divided and blocked sunlight from the area. They also installed the modern infrastructure necessary to attract new office space for international and large domestic companies. But failure to guard against corruption by using a transparent and rigorous public bidding process has led to several ongoing investigations.

In addition, the project's progress has been slowed by the very large Petrobras scandal and its damage to the nation's economy, political stability, and international reputation. Petrobras is a huge, government controlled petroleum company that controls most of the country's oil, all of its refineries, wholesale distribution, and pipelines, and the nation's largest chain of service stations.[27] The company was rocked by charges of massive corruption uncovered by a police investigation now widely known in Brazil as Operation Car Wash. In essence, executives from Petrobras and its many subcontractors overbilled the company and then used the excess cash to pay bribes to elected and appointed government officials.

In 2015, economists estimated that Petrobras and its subcontractors accounted for as much as 10 percent of the entire nation's output, and cuts in their spending as a result of the scandal might reduce the nation's growth rate by three-quarters of a percent.[28] In 2015 alone, Petrobras wrote off about $20 billion related to the corruption scandal and reduced its investment spending by $25 billion compared to 2013.[29] The corruption scandal continued to unfold in 2016, and Brazil reported its worst economic performance in twenty-five years.[30]

Nevertheless, the work at Porto Maravilha continued despite the scandal due to the pressure of the start of the Olympic Games in the late summer of 2016. Both vehicle tunnels are operating, buildings are going up, and more than thirteen hundred units of private housing are built or under construction. The city's goal is to bring at least sixty thousand new residents to the area, up from the thirty thousand living in the port area in 2010.[31] At the same time, one of the most spectacular components of the Porto Maravilha is open and already attracting local and international praise and criticism: the Museum of Tomorrow.[32]

## MUSEU DO AMANHA—A DIFFERENT
## KIND OF MUSEUM

Designed by world-renowned Spanish architect Santiago Calatrava (who also designed the subway station at the rebuilt World Trade Center in New York City), the Museum of Tomorrow (figure 13.2) opened in December 2015. Already it is attracting a great deal of positive attention in the media, in Brazil, and internationally. For example, "Rio de Janeiro's new museum, focusing on ideas rather than objects, ecology more than technology, is a little trippy, a little hippy, very worthy, but rarely dull,"[33] and "its design is bold—it looks like the exoskeleton of a pre-historic fish. Its aim is ambitious: to raise consciousness on the future of our planet."[34]

The museum's theme is sustainability and the consequences of ignoring climate change. Its exhibits are designed to advocate for immediate sustainability efforts, which is the reason it is called the Museum of Tomorrow instead of the Museum of the Future.[35] The main exhibition is digital and asks visitors to ponder where we came from, where we are, and where we might go as a society. It includes audio, visual,

*Figure 13.2* The Museum of Tomorrow, funded in partnership with philanthropists, is a major tourist attraction and educates the public and raises awareness about global climate challenges. Photo by Cesar Barreto, courtesy of Alexandre Fernandes.

film, and data describing the origins of the planet, through evolution, and into the present and future of climate change, including burning forests, melting ice caps, choking auto emissions, growing population and consumption, acidification, and rising greenhouse gas concentrations. It also includes interactive games that enable visitors to evaluate a variety of future scenarios depending on how humans behave. The exhibits are constructed and maintained with data and analysis flowing in from Brazil's best universities, global scientists, international space agencies, the United Nations, and a wide array of expert consultants.[36] The museum also raises awareness about the urgency of adopting sustainable practices, creating pressure on other developments in the neighborhood and around the city. The museum building itself is said to use 40 percent less energy than a conventional building and is powered by solar and cooled by water from the adjacent Guanabara Bay.[37]

The museum's beautiful appearance, provocative presentations, and location in the newly developing Porto Maravilha neighborhood has made it a must-see destination for visitors and local residents alike; it is already the most visited museum in Brazil.[38]

Financed with public money and philanthropic contributions, particularly from the Roberto Marinho Foundation, and some well-known international corporate sponsors, the museum pooled funding from various sources for its development and exhibits. Philanthropic support helped develop the plan for the museum, provided the initial risk capital, and added prestige and gravitas to the project. This helped justify and leverage public and private investment in the museum and the surrounding neighborhood, turning around what was a dangerous and dilapidated area in the heart of downtown Rio. Each of the partners made substantial, tangible contributions, and without public sector–financed infrastructure, the developments would not have been possible.

The museum project illustrates the important effects of blending different types of capital for social good. It is a joint initiative of the city of Rio de Janeiro, the Marinho Foundation, Banco Santander, and other corporate supporters. It has received financing from the state government of Rio and the federal FINEP program. It is part of a museum network that receives funding from the Rio Local Cultural Office, and support for the project's administration is provided by the Institute of Development and Management (IDG), a nonprofit cultural organization.[39]

The museum has attracted rave reviews and won numerous awards, including the Leading Culture Destinations of the Year Award from the UK and the International Design & Communication Award in Canada.[40] However, community activists have criticized the museum's cost (estimated to be about USD $100 million) and other new developments in the port area for using scarce public dollars during a deep national recession. They say that the museum ignores the area's important history,[41] and claim the developments are gentrifying the surrounding neighborhood and pricing the current poor residents out.[42] Criticisms aside, the grand scale and beauty of the museum and its early popularity as a destination for tourists and locals foretell a future icon that may one day rival Christ the Redeemer as a global identifier for Rio.[43] In its first year of operation, the Museum of Tomorrow attracted around 1.4 million visitors.[44]

## THE RIO OLYMPICS: UNLOCKING INTRINSIC VALUE?

It will be years if not decades before anyone can accurately assess whether the award of the Olympic Games to Rio de Janeiro ignited a process that helped make Rio a twenty-first-century, world-class city (as former mayor Paes dreamed it would be), or whether it wasted city money on projects that made the city's rich richer, exacerbated the already extreme inequality, and gentrified favelas, as its critics now say. Future generations will likely look back at it as somewhere in between. Six months after the games ended, reports profiled abandoned "White Elephant" projects in the Olympic Park—stadium entrances boarded up, an empty pool filled with dirt and garbage, and arenas promised to be converted into schools still vacant and untouched.[45] City and state officials maintain that numerous improvements to the city's infrastructure and transport systems as part of the Olympic project are already benefiting all residents and promised that reuse of the so-called White Elephants would happen.

The international media forecast just before the Rio Olympics opening ceremony in August 2016 was universally negative. As a writer for *Forbes* predicted, "a few things are hard to imagine about Brazil right now. One is that the Olympics in Rio can possibly be anything but horrible judging by the headlines."[46] The months, weeks, and

*Figure 13.3* Residents in Rio take to the streets to express frustration and make their voices heard. Citizens frequently protested over their disenfranchisement and exclusion from the Olympic planning process. *Source*: Getty Images.

days leading up to the Rio Olympics were dominated by media headlines and stories about unfinished facilities, the dangerously polluted Guanabara Bay, street protests (figure 13.3), violent confrontations between protestors and the state police, and top athletes canceling because they feared what the media characterized as an out-of-control outbreak of the mosquito-borne Zika virus.[47]

Worse, in May 2016, Brazil's president Dilma Rousseff was suspended by the federal Senate on charges that she manipulated the federal budget to conceal the country's rapidly deteriorating economy, in part as a result of the growing Petrobras scandal and associated Operation Car Wash investigation.[48] On August 31, 2016, ten days after the closing ceremonies of 2016 Rio Games, the federal Senate voted 61–20 to convict Ms. Rousseff, and she was impeached and removed from office.[49] The Petrobras scandal (Rousseff had been chairman of the Petrobras board before being elected president of Brazil) also implicated several of the country's largest construction companies under contract to build much of the Olympic infrastructure and facilities. The promises of Brazil's Olympic bid-book to clean up Guanabara Bay and improve life in Rio's favelas were dramatically scaled back.[50]

## Olympic Participant Housing

A good example of why it may be too soon to tell who will benefit from the Olympics is the reuse of the Olympic participant housing. A total of 3,604 apartments in thirty-one buildings built by a private real estate company were originally expected to transition to upper-middle income residences. However, with the multiyear recession depressing the real estate market, in early 2017 Rio's newly elected mayor, Marcelo Crivella, reached an agreement with the government-owned Caixa Economica financial company to provide low-cost mortgages to civil servants, enabling them to purchase the apartments. The same report indicates that similar programs are under way for members of the Navy and other government agencies and state-owned enterprises, including the Army, Banco do Brasil, Caixa Econômica Federal (CEF), the Brazilian Development Bank (BNDES), Furnas, Eletrobras, Vale, and Petrobras. Prices will be somewhat below market value and may include long-term leases with an option to buy. The Olympic subsidy covering the construction loan interest is expiring, so the owner of the buildings has a strong incentive to sell quickly and might even make a small profit if negotiations lead to a large number of purchases.[51]

This new reuse of the Olympic participant housing could serve as a positive example of project adaptation for post-Olympic, post-Paes Rio. The city of Rio, the private housing developer, government employers, and a finance company are collaborating to find a financially sound and socially beneficial purpose for the site. These new partners are seeking to offset financial risks and are leveraging each other's resources to make affordable workforce housing financially viable since the intended high-end market-rate housing plan failed. Without all four partners, the new plan could not work.

## Improvements in Rio's Transit System

There has been much criticism of the high cost and possible corruption in the transportation improvements financed as part of the Olympics project. In addition to highway improvements, Rio added several new bus rapid transit lines and a new light rail line that opened in time for the games. The government reports mass transit use went from 18 percent in 2009 (when Rio won the bid for the games) to 63 percent at the time of the Olympics (not counting the recently opened light rail). Cost overruns accompanied many of the projects, but roughly 40 percent of the infrastructure projects were PPPs, spreading the cost and the risk.[52] Rio's Olympic plan focused on connecting more than 60 percent of its residents to mass transit, but critics note that the city still faces major challenges in making jobs a manageable commute for the large population of low-income residents living in the many favelas cut off by geographic barriers or distance.[53]

Some observers are more positive in their assessment of the Olympic "effect" on public transit in Rio. The mass transit system is now twice the length promised for the games (from 47 to 97 miles), there is a metro line extension from 2.5 to 10 miles, and a new light rail line, which was not part of the Olympic promise.[54] Rider surveys indicate travel time has decreased significantly, and transit costs have declined or remained the same; however, the entire system must still be fully integrated.[55]

## Use of the Olympic Park

The current state of the Olympic Park is much less promising. According to local reports, the park hosted its first sports event six months after the games, and visitors described it as "beautiful" but "abandoned."[56] Federal and city officials acknowledge the slow start of programming but maintain that a full agenda of training, competition, and social programs for children and young people are forthcoming. Current Rio mayor Marcelo Crivella has committed to partner with the federal government to ensure that "every weekend we can have an event." In September 2017, the Olympic Park hosted a seven-day rock spectacle (called Rock in Rio 2017), with a follow-up concert not scheduled until 2019.[57] Some reuse is happening, but the pace thus far is slow.

## TAKEAWAYS FROM RIO

The estimated costs of the Olympic games range widely, from $3 billion to $20 billion.[58] The budget is a major issue, even if it ends up being lower than the estimated $15 billion spent by the previous summer games in London.[59] The cost is not generally offset by the revenues generated from the games, where again, estimates range widely, with some as high as $9 billion.[60] Supporters of the games also see the funds that were spent on rapid bus, light rail, and highway projects as long-term investments in the future of Rio. They stress that Rio used PPPs for most of the projects, with 60 percent of all costs paid for with private funds.[61]

Others see the Olympics as ultimately bad for Brazil. In *Circus Maximus: The Economic Gamble Behind Hosting the Olympics and the World Cup*, Andrew Zimbalist was very negative in his assessment of the value of the World Cup to Brazil and only slightly less pessimistic about the long-term impact of the Olympic Games on Rio.[62] His book was published before the games actually took place, and many of the disasters he anticipated did not occur. He also predicted that, ultimately, the games themselves would be "delivered with few blemishes" but without improving the lives of the average Rio citizen.[63]

In a *New York Times* op-ed following the games, Brazilian journalist Vanessa Barbara wrote about how she was attacked in social media for criticizing the Rio Olympics. She called the Olympics "a public calamity for many citizens, especially those affected by the evictions, by police brutality and by the antidemocratic shakedown of an unequal and segregated city." She concluded, "after the final ceremonies, when the last fireworks have been launched and all the foreign journalists have returned home, a bankrupt state of Rio will be left to pick up the pieces. And neither patriotism nor the love of sports will entitle us to overlook our reality."[64]

Failure to clean up Guanabara Bay, crime, low-paid and unpaid government teachers and doctors, little improvement in the favelas, and unabated inequality are major negative results from the Rio Olympics. At the same time, the number of tourists exceeded the plan's goal, sales targets were met, Zika fears proved to be exaggerated, and the housing, transportation, and facilities were up to par and without serious incident.[65] Writing in the *New York Times*, reporter Andrew Jacobs said, "But the criticism aside, the 2016 Summer Olympics in Rio have profoundly altered this city of six million, yielding a revitalized port; a new subway line; and a flush of municipal projects, big and small, that had long been on the wish list of city planners."[66] Jonathan Watts of *The Guardian* wrote of Mayor Paes, "His proudest boast was the Olympic Boulevard near Praca Maua—the revamped port area, which thronged with visitors, food trucks and street artists. It was a remarkable transformation from the ugly overhead expressway that once dominated a district known for crime."[67]

A strong argument can be made that the Olympic Games catalyzed a public-private partnership process that completed important infrastructure projects that would have otherwise taken decades.[68] There seems to be agreement that the Porto Maravilha renovation, on the drawing board since the 1980s, was perhaps the most important achievement of the Olympic-related investments. Currently estimated at $2.5 billion, much of the financing came from the city's sale of air rights and tax incentives to private developers, embodying some limited aspects of a cross-sector approach.[69] The port project and its centerpiece, the Museu do Amanha, are already crowded with locals and tourists day and night. Once derelict and dangerous, the area is now "a must-see tourist destination for its historical landmarks, sophisticated cultural activities, charming squares and waterfront views."[70] And even five hundred affordable residential apartments to house those living in a nearby favela are in the plan.[71]

In April 2017, stunning allegations that Mayor Eduardo Paes himself pocketed millions of dollars in kickbacks cast a dark shadow over the potential benefits of the 2016 Olympic Games to Rio. The investigation of the Petrobras oil giant that began in 2014 expanded into both the World Cup and the Olympic Games. Brazil's supreme court subsequently opened investigations into nearly three hundred politicians,[72] including Paes, based on the testimony of executives from the construction giant Odebrecht, the firm contracted to build many of the Olympic-related projects.[73] A separate police investigation opened into possible fraud in the construction of the new subway line.[74] As part of a plea bargain, the chairman and the chief executive of Odebrecht suggested that two former presidents of Brazil and a former speaker of the parliament colluded with potential bidders in the pay-to-play contract award process during the build-out of the World Cup and Olympic projects.[75]

## A CAUTIONARY TALE—PARTNERSHIPS INVOLVE RISK

While researching for this book, it was first thought the Olympic-driven revitalization of Rio de Janeiro might become a case illustrating the successful implementation of numerous cross-sector partnerships.

At the time, it seemed Mayor Paes was working to form a robust series of partnerships, driven by the Olympic Games, to bring Rio up to twenty-first-century standards. In fact, the mayor's written plan tracked some aspects of a comprehensive cross-sector partnership approach, including the use of a mixed portfolio of public and private capital. By using partnerships to accomplish most projects, Rio planned to leverage substantial private investment with improved public infrastructure, and it involved the philanthropic community to create the iconic Museum of Tomorrow. Aspects of the museum partnership seem most successful, and it is one of the few projects to be achieving the high hopes of the original Olympic-driven promises.

Some of the partnerships associated with the Rio Olympics may have helped fuel corruption between willing public officials and greedy private companies. It is difficult to determine whether the corruption originated from those leading organizations in the private sector, the public sector, or both. As discussed in chapter 5, successful leadership requires not only vision and drive but also integrity, respect for stakeholders, and admirable ambition. Unlike leaders from our other cases (Doug Blonsky and Betsy Rogers of New York's Central Park Conservancy, former NYC mayor Bloomberg, and India's Prime Minster Modi), leadership in Rio was unable to maintain the commitment to collaboration, engagement, and integrity partnerships require to achieve success, both financially and in terms of social value.

Perhaps the conditions in Rio were at least partially to blame. Similar types of corruption associated with the Porto Maravilha and the Olympic Park projects were happening at Petrobras, involving many other partnerships and leaders. Another major corruption scandal broke in 2017, indicating that Brazil's president Michel Temer (the former vice president who succeeded impeached President Rousseff) took $4.6 million in illegal campaign contributions from executives of JBS SA, one of the world's largest food companies.[76] Temer ultimately avoided trial,[77] but in 2018, he remained under investigation by police for separate corruption allegations.[78] A national poll showed his approval rating at just three percent—the lowest in Brazil's modern history.[79]

Unlike our cases in India and Afghanistan, Rio's Olympic projects did not follow the principles of a *place*-based approach. Rio's leaders failed to engage the vast majority of people affected by the projects and did not give them adequate voice in the development process. Without transparency and public participation in the revitalization of Rio, we believe the success of its projects in the long run will be severely limited. We can learn from a careful assessment of what took place, and upon review of our cross-sector partnership checklist (outlined in the Conclusion), it is clear that the Rio implementation plan was missing many elements of the social value investing framework. It is a cautionary tale, presented with the belief that we often learn more from our failures than from our successes.

# Conclusion

## Partnering for a Better Tomorrow

HOWARD W. BUFFETT AND WILLIAM B. EIMICKE

Cross-sector partnerships are based on the idea that more is accomplished when organizations collaborate and share in their success. These partnerships are not only important but will be necessary if society is to overcome its most complex challenges.[1] Some of these partnerships are already taking place, and we looked at a number of them in this book—Digital India, place-based development in Afghanistan, and emergency response in New York City, to name a few.

We wrote this book because we believe the world can be much improved from where it is today. Not only can we do better—we must do better. We must set aside individualistic and short-term thinking and work together to realize a world that is more equitable, inclusive, and responsible to the needs of all. Leaders of organizations who think and act in isolation are constrained in what they can accomplish over the long term and ultimately, may end up doing more harm to society than good.

We must also rethink our assumptions about the role of organizations *in* society. We generally expect too much from government, do not hold the private sector accountable enough for its negative externalities, and rely too heavily on the social sector to close the gap.[2] We know there are opportunities to improve how society approaches collective problem solving in the world.[3] We also know that partnerships between public, private, and philanthropic organizations are better equipped to act upon society's interests than any organization can on its own.[4]

As we have detailed in the preceding chapters, we envision a strategy for cross-sector partnerships based on a framework called *social value investing*. This framework is inspired by one of history's most successful investment paradigms—value investing—developed by Columbia University professors Benjamin Graham and David Dodd in the 1920s.[5] As Columbia University professors ourselves, we find special meaning in building from these and other past successes.

Similar to value investing, social value investing focuses on a long-term time horizon. It presents a strategy for unlocking intrinsic social value for individuals, communities, and organizations, with a framework spanning five elements: *process, people, place, portfolio,* and *performance.* We have provided case studies illustrating how partnerships with similar approaches—most developed independent of our framework—are improving conditions around the world. Our hope is that future partnerships will benefit from our analysis of these successful collaborations and improve on the framework. Although the work has just begun, our experience tells us there is good reason to be optimistic.

Digital India, for example, is already a positive force in the lives of millions of Indians. Its implementation rests on a *process* that starts with the national government, works through the nation's leading for-profit technology companies, and is driven by local entrepreneurs.[6] These entrepreneurs operate access points to a system of services providing government benefits, medical care, banking, and insurance. Citizens also can access secure electronic records of important documents such as driver's licenses and birth certificates. Led by a strong prime minister, the process has evolved to deal with legal, bureaucratic, political, and technological challenges. Digital India continues because it delivers valuable benefits to the country's citizens, whether they are rich or poor, urban or rural, and therefore it retains popular support.

Our Central Park and High Line cases illustrate how, with the right focus on *people*, social sector organizations can take the lead in partnering with government to transform public spaces. Betsy Rogers, Doug Blonsky, and Ira Millstein provided critical leadership for the Central Park Conservancy.[7] City Parks Department leaders, particularly Gordon Davis, Adrian Benepe, and Mitchell Silver, as well as five strongly supportive mayors (Koch, Dinkins, Giuliani, Bloomberg, and de Blasio), illustrated the important enabling role of the public sector. And an army of dedicated and generous donors, including John A. Paulson and Richard Gilder, saved Central Park's budget, leading to a model for twenty-first-century urban spaces.[8] Collaborative experts who can navigate across the organizational boundaries of all three sectors are critical to establishing effective partnerships.

The public sector was key in rebuilding parts of Afghanistan, but so were universities and private companies. Without a strong government peace-keeping presence, it would have been impossible to do much at all. In our view, the essential ingredient to the measured success in these projects was a *place*-based strategy, created in close collaboration with farming communities such as the Rabāṭ-e Pīrzādah village. Local entrepreneurs including Zainab Sufizada helped design facilities and operating processes so that the resources and expertise from the other partners could make a significant, positive, and lasting impact on the ground.[9]

In Brazil, a consortium of many of the most successful corporate leaders in the nation came together to establish Comunitas, a nonprofit dedicated to restoring the public's faith in the efficacy and honesty of local government. Under the leadership of its board and Comunitas director and president Regina Siqueira, Juntos used a *portfolio* approach, blending public, private, and philanthropic investment into programs to improve municipal services.[10] This allowed local governments to acquire the best financial, technology, architecture, and engineering consultants in the country, and at no cost to taxpayers. The program also created a platform that illuminated the activities of local government to citizens and gave those citizens significant influence on the priorities of their locality.

We saw how New York City Mayor Michael Bloomberg based his administration on *performance* management. This data-driven approach helped New York City's emergency response system, and by 2016 it had the fewest fire-related deaths in its history.[11] Key indicators of public health, environmental quality, and economic development also improved significantly during Bloomberg's twelve years in office. Similar performance measures led the city to experiment with new methods of preventing recidivism among recently released inmates from Rikers Island. Overall, this case illustrated the positive effects of orienting programs in a cross-sector partnership around performance-based measurements.

Finally, our case study profiling the development of partnerships for the 2016 Summer Olympics in Rio de Janeiro outlines some risks and consequences of not planning collaboratively. Among other problems were leadership challenges and a lack of transparency and stakeholder inclusion. This fueled an environment ripe for corruption and led to anger on the part of local residents.[12] Although the games themselves succeeded, we believe the partnership process would have benefited significantly from following many of the key elements of the social value investing framework, including the partnership checklist outlined in the next section.

## THE SOCIAL VALUE INVESTING PARTNERSHIP CHECKLIST

It is too soon to tell how successful some of these high-risk but potentially high-reward partnership initiatives will be, but we can analyze them all through the social value investing framework. We recognize that partnerships are not the easiest organizational structure to accomplish critical social objectives. It can be hard enough to get things done within one organization, let alone two or more. Succeeding by coordinating across multiple parties, often from different sectors, is complicated.[13] Therefore, as organizations develop new cross-sector partnerships, we recommend that partners consider the following checklist.[14] Here we categorize important lessons and takeaways from each of the five elements of the social value investing framework.

⎯⎯ ⌇⌇⌇ ⎯⎯

*Process:* Successful cross-sector partnerships comprise diverse yet complementary organizations that collectively contribute to the creation of long-term value. Through a well-structured operating *process*, partners expand and align their efforts and draw on comparative strengths.

### 1. Formalize Partnership Structures

The management compatibility challenges of cross-sector partnerships can be diminished through a *formal partnership structure*.[15] Organizations must work from common definitions and use formal agreements such as letters of intent or memorandums of understanding (as discussed in chapter 4). Still there may be downsides or difficulties in formalizing a partnership, which we saw in the Central Park case (chapter 5). New York City Parks Commissioner Gordon Davis and Central Park Conservancy CEO and Central Park Administrator Betsy Rogers recognized early on that they were operating a virtual cross-sector partnership. But they also believed that a formal partnership for a large public park was an idea ahead of its time in the late 1970s. They moved slowly but methodically toward that objective and, in 1998, the time was right. They signed a formal eight-year partnership agreement. The partnership contract was renewed in 2006 for a second eight years, and again in 2013 for what will be at least twenty-four years of partnership operation under a formal contract.

## 2. Establish Mutual Operations

Successful partnerships typically establish and synchronize *mutual operations* to guide collaborative programs. For example, partners may create a project charter, develop a work plan, or follow a coordinated communications strategy.[16] In the case of Digital India (chapter 3), cooperative yet distributed program delivery allowed the government, Apollo Telemedicine, the common service centers, and village-level entrepreneurs to execute joint work efficiently. In the case of preventing fires (chapter 11), the IBM team colocated at FDNY headquarters with the FDNY project team.[17] They spent significant time in firehouses throughout the city and rode with firefighter inspection teams so they could fully understand fire inspection procedures before the partners jointly designed a new, more effective set of them. Through understanding and the establishment of new procedures, FDNY, IBM, and others were better equipped to develop the partnership's long-term strategy.

## 3. Develop a Comprehensive Strategy

Addressing a complex challenge requires a *comprehensive strategy* that enables and benefits from the cooperative and coordinated activities of a group of partners.[18] This was evident in many of our partnership examples, and especially in Afghanistan (chapter 7). In this case, partners invested considerable time researching and analyzing their program strategy's complete value chain throughout the Herat area. Alongside community stakeholders, they developed a thorough logic model for the resources and activities required to address economic and social gaps and to support the outcomes all partners desired. The funders relied on formal agreements with locally focused NGOs and with Herat University and put operating procedures in place for coordinating program development and resource deployment between the communities.

⌘⌘⌘

*People:* Cross-sector partnerships thrive through a network of decentralized leaders and managers who operate independent programs and organizations. These leaders and their teams comprise a range of varied strengths but are aligned toward shared goals. By focusing on and empowering the *people* involved, partnering organizations can support their teams' collective ability to lead and succeed.

## 4. Emphasize Collaborative Leadership

To achieve success, partnerships must *emphasize collaborative leadership* between teams.[19] Experience tells us that management by committee seldom works. At the same time, it is virtually impossible to sustain success by ordering people around, many of whom may not even work for you. In 1999, New York City was ready to tear down the elevated train tracks of the High Line (chapter 5) when the local community, led by residents Joshua David and Robert Hammond, came together with a better idea.[20] Partnering with nationally known real estate expert John Alschuler (who later became the organization's board chair), Friends of the High Line reached out and learned from Betsy Rogers's success at Central Park. They also built a strong partnership with key members of the Bloomberg administration, particularly with the city planning commissioner, the parks commissioner, the deputy mayor, and Mayor Bloomberg himself. Early on they were able to engage major philanthropists to support the effort, and they worked collaboratively with many others to build the High Line. It is now one of the most visited and admired urban parks in the world, freely accessible to anyone, and primarily operated with private funds.[21]

In a starkly different example, we learned that the absence of collaborative leadership can have seriously detrimental effects on the results of a partnership. In the 2016 Olympics case (chapter 13), the failure of government officials to collaboratively engage partners and the community was a contributing factor to the significant problems and corruption that surfaced after the games concluded.[22]

## 5. Maintain Integrity and Respect

Partners may come from different sectors, and may be from different parts of the world, with different histories and cultures. They may be small or new organizations, or ones that are well known, large, and powerful. We see excellent examples of partners overcoming these differences in the High Line case, in which a new community-based organization (Friends of the High Line) partnered with the very large and powerful Bloomberg administration (chapter 5). This was also reflected in how participants interacted between local communities, NGOs, and the international partners in the Afghanistan case (chapter 7). Partners must *act with integrity and treat each other with respect* according to widely accepted social norms, no matter with whom they are partnered.[23] In the case of the Rio Olympics, however, it appears that the mayor's administration failed to do this. They did not engage community-level partners adequately enough in the planning phases of development. The mayor also dismissed critics and public opponents in the face of sometimes violent street protests, which took place as the implementation process moved forward.[24]

## 6. Build Diverse Teams

Successful partnerships rely on varying sets of leadership skills and experiences across organizations and the people running them.[25] Leaders must *build diverse teams* that account for the skills-based capital necessary for achieving the partnership's goals. In the Juntos case in Brazil (chapter 9), the Comunitas partnership did more than bring together a portfolio of financial capital. It also built a network of accomplished and capable leaders from organizations across sectors to meet its objectives. Only through this inclusive approach could the partnership draw on the combined knowledge and expertise of its participants for the broad array of necessary programs. This way, partnering teams improved local government programs, reformed financial practices, increased public outreach, conducted economic development, and expanded critical community services.

---

*Place:* By employing a place-based strategy, cross-sector partnerships incorporate stakeholders as true shareholders rather than just beneficiaries of a partnership's investment. This typically requires time and effort to build trust and requires intentionality around prioritizing stakeholders' best interests. Working collaboratively with a sense of permanent community, what we call *place*-based co-ownership, reinforces important long-term relationships between partners.

## 7. Recognize Interdependence

Partnership strategies that are effectively place-based bring together many different participants comprehensively, with goals that rely on unique partner strengths, attributes, and contributions.[26] To support often difficult and lengthy partnership engagements, partners benefit from mutual reliance established by a commitment to work together. Before agreeing to formalize a partnership, partners should decide individually and agree collectively that they are *interdependent*—they need each other to achieve the partnership's shared goals.[27] This recognition of and reliance on interdependence was clearly true in the Afghanistan case (chapter 7). Partners depended on the actions of one another—from the philanthropic and NGO investments, to the commitments by local entrepreneurs, to the academic and private sector expertise, and even to the security provided by the coalition forces—all of which were essential for the projects to be feasible and successful.

## 8. Broaden Public Participation

By definition, comprehensive, place-based partnership strategies require *broad public participation* to succeed. More and more frequently, partnerships are using technology and communication platforms to enable civic engagement, as we saw in the Juntos case.[28] The Comunitas initiatives were transformative in large part because they invited citizens to participate in setting the Campinas budget priorities and in Curitiba's strategic planning process (chapter 9). Public participation was similarly important for Digital India and the Telemedicine program (chapter 3). In some cases, participation platforms can serve multiple purposes, as we saw in New York City's partnerships to transform public safety through cutting edge technology and open data (chapter 11). In contrast, being unwilling to give local communities enough voice in planning and implementation can be damaging. This was the case with the Rio Olympics projects; lack of public engagement contributed to increasing opposition and protests throughout project development. From an implementation standpoint alone, such public opposition can delay project construction, increase costs, or even result in a partnership's cancellation.[29]

## 9. Codify Common Values

Cross-sector partnerships typically involve a range of organizations and stakeholders, all of whom must align their missions, program time lines, and priorities in collaboration. Discovering and *codifying common values* between partners is necessary if they are to understand organizational norms and establish operational expectations.[30] Partners may choose to establish a set of cooperative principles and measures for mutual accountability that guide the partnership's ongoing collaboration. Participants will also benefit from a common framework to analyze program options and support coordinated decision making. This was evident in many of our cases, including New York City's parks. In developing the High Line collaboration, for example (chapter 5), common values helped partners work past the cumbersome process of five separate sign-offs for decisions of all sizes. As a result of their mutual trust, they broke ground and began construction for the project at the same time they were finalizing the official partnership agreement.

---

*Portfolio:* Cross-sector partnerships can draw from and combine various financial tools and investments. This enables partners to diversify risk and expand the pool of capital available to carry out the partnership's programs and deliver its outcomes. By blending financial capital from different sources, including philanthropic capital (which can take significant risks),[31] programs can be funded by a versatile and coordinated *portfolio* of investments.

## 10. Make Substantial Commitments

Organizations must *make substantial commitments* to the partnership, not just at the beginning of the effort but throughout its duration.[32] We saw this in the economic development projects in Herat Province, Afghanistan (chapter 7). The U.S. government made significant up-front investments in research, data discovery, and construction. The Afghan provincial government invested in electricity infrastructure to better enable new agricultural processing capacity, and a philanthropic partner financed irrigation equipment. Such up-front investments by partners typically reflect broad consensus that the projects are important and worthwhile. We also saw this in the Juntos case in Brazil (chapter 9), where the Comunitas group provided up-front investments for financial, architectural, and technology consultants. Local governments provided human capital and infrastructure, the federal government supplied annual intergovernmental revenue sharing, and the technological advancements gave residents a voice in city decisions.

## 11. Agree on Complementary Contributions

As partners consider options for program financing, it is essential that they develop a coinvestment strategy agreed to and based on *complementary contributions*, not an effort to disguise or mitigate individual weaknesses or a lack of funding.[33] This allows partners to share both risk and potential reward, and to leverage their assets, financial or otherwise. As we discussed in chapter 4, such collaborations go beyond typical fee-for-service or product procurement between the partnering groups, with contributed assets that may have both tangible and intrinsic value. We saw this in the performance case (chapter 11), where FDNY and IBM each invested organizational resources and time, and provided access to their unique systems, operations, and capabilities. This was also the case with Comunitas (chapter 9) and the cities of

Campinas, Pelotas, and Curitiba, where the partners combined financial capital, including private and philanthropic funding, to open program opportunities not otherwise possible.

## 12. Use Innovative Financing

*Innovative financing* can be the cornerstone of a cross-sector partnership. This is especially true for partnerships that develop and deploy new, untested, or creative methods for addressing challenging problems.[34] In such cases, partners can access and leverage private-sector financing and direct it toward public good. We see this with the relatively new financial structure called a social impact bond (SIB), which brings together and takes advantage of the respective strengths and flexibility of public, private, and philanthropic sector partners. Partnerships can benefit from risk offsetting through program-related investments (PRIs), which are well-established but underused opportunities for incentivizing inventive collaboration (SIBs and PRIs are both outlined in chapter 10). In many respects, combining a broad suite of financial tools can result in an expanded network of organizations working toward common goals, and with better alignment of financial and social outcomes.

*Performance:* Partners must work together to identify and select collaborative programs with comparatively high intrinsic values—programs that are in line with partners' principles and the partnership's overall objectives. By predicting the relative *performance* of a given set of program options using the Impact Rate of Return formula, partners can allocate capital based on specific priorities and goals.

## 13. Determine Measurable Indicators

Without clearly defined and mutually accepted *measurable indicators*, partners cannot know whether they have succeeded, much less determine whether programs are on track or performing well.[35] Former New York City mayor Michael Bloomberg led the recovery of

New York City after September 11, 2001, anchored on a consensus of the most accurate metrics of success, a relentless quest for more and better data, and the development and refinement of operational strategies around those factors. In public safety and emergency response, as discussed in chapter 11, Bloomberg-era partnerships (and previously existing programs) relied heavily on transparent, well-defined, and generally accepted performance measures that were agreed to by all partners. As we learned with the Impact Rate of Return formula (chapter 12), one of the first steps in customizing the iRR measurement platform is determining the partnership's Key Impact Indicators. Equally important is determining the formula's specific metrics that define the partnership's quality of impact (see the Impact Balance Sheet tool outlined in chapter 8).

## 14. Share Data and Information

To measure progress against established indicators, partners must *share data and information* across organizational boundaries.[36] This is not natural for competitive organizations, particularly because for-profit businesses are accustomed to aggressively hiding trade secrets, strategy, and proprietary data. But such sources of protected information may not be required for a partnership's performance measurement and monitoring. In some cases, information-sharing is a main purpose of the partnership, as it was in the case of Digital India (chapter 3). In other situations, it is simply a matter of making otherwise public data more readily accessible or searchable. In New York City, Mayor Bloomberg put virtually all of the important information and performance measures for their partnerships on the city's open data page,[37] allowing others to leverage the value of that data freely (see chapter 11).[38]

## 15. Redefine Success

The hallmark of the Impact Rate of Return formula is that it provides a measurement framework for translating a partnership's diverse objectives into a common language (see chapter 12). Simply stated, it allows many different partners to come together and *redefine success* around

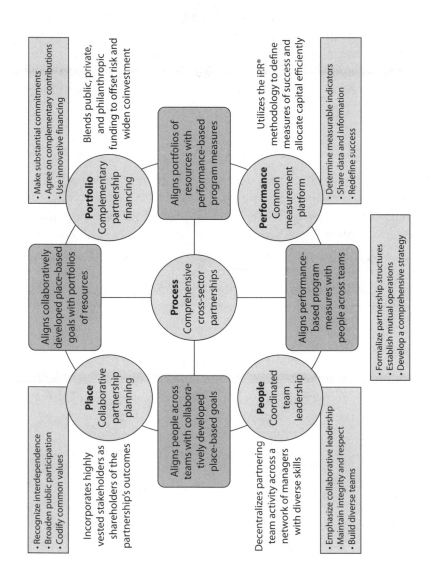

- Make substantial commitments
- Agree on complementary contributions
- Use innovative financing

Blends public, private, and philanthropic funding to offset risk and widen coinvestment

**Portfolio**
Complementary partnership financing

Aligns portfolios of resources with performance-based program measures

**Performance**
Common measurement platform

Utilizes the iRR® methodology to define measures of success and allocate capital efficiently

- Determine measurable indicators
- Share data and information
- Redefine success

Aligns collaboratively developed place-based goals with portfolios of resources

**Process**
Comprehensive cross-sector partnerships

Aligns performance-based program measures with people across teams

- Formalize partnership structures
- Establish mutual operations
- Develop a comprehensive strategy

- Recognize interdependence
- Broaden public participation
- Codify common values

Incorporates highly vested stakeholders as shareholders of the partnership's outcomes

**Place**
Collaborative partnership planning

Aligns people across teams with collaboratively developed place-based goals

**People**
Coordinated team leadership

Decentralizes partnering team activity across a network of managers with diverse skills

- Emphasize collaborative leadership
- Maintain integrity and respect
- Build diverse teams

their mutually shared goals. The formula predicts the social impact performance of a given project and combines important measureable indicators with program-related data into a platform for partners to make more informed decisions about capital allocation. All partners, including individual and community stakeholders, should participate in determining what aspects or qualities of impact will guide program evaluation (as discussed in chapter 8). As a result, the partnership's measures of success will be more inclusive and allow for solutions that are more effective over the long term.

———— ∞∞∞∞ ————

This fifteen-point checklist covers many of the most important aspects of cross-sector partnership development and management as discussed throughout the book. These points represent lessons and observations from the successful cases we present and analyze. Furthermore, we believe this list will be useful to organizations as they prepare and implement new partnerships—especially when combined with a sense of optimism that the goals are achievable and will result in better outcomes for stakeholders and society.

## WHY WE ARE OPTIMISTIC

Chapter 1 documents the long and evolving history of collaboration between sectors, including the expansive role of large-scale public-private partnerships during the twentieth century. A World Bank study of recent public-private partnerships found that they have been on the rise for decades, exist in more than 130 countries, and account for more than 15 percent of overall infrastructure development.[39] The report indicates that over two-thirds of the projects studied (more than a hundred) achieved their development outcomes. The evaluators of these projects identified the need for, and the significant potential benefit of, more public works partnerships in the future to improve infrastructure and promote economic growth.[40]

Using partnerships to develop and implement new solutions to complex social, economic, and environmental policy problems is different and more difficult, however, particularly because we are only beginning to establish accurate and reliable measures of social impact.[41] As Peter Drucker often said, you cannot manage effectively unless you are clear on what you are trying to accomplish and can measure your progress toward achieving your goals.[42] We have made great progress in measuring the financial impact of improved management practices, but we can and should judge the success of all organizations, no matter the sector, beyond their mission statement and financial performance.[43] We should also evaluate whether they harm or improve their local communities, as well as society as a whole.[44] We are already seeing shifts to this effect, and we believe new management and measurement standards may eventually lead to marked improvements in how financial assets are directed.[45] For example, imagine unlocking the value of many trillions of dollars held in endowments, retirement accounts, sovereign wealth funds, and private investments by deploying them not just for financial return but also for measurably improving our society.[46]

## BUILDING ON MOMENTUM

We mentioned the work of economist Steven Radelet in the introduction. Radelet argues that we are in the midst of the greatest improvement in the lives of the world's poor, measured by reduced poverty, increased incomes, improvement in health care, fewer wars and conflicts, and the spread of democracy.[47] Although economic conditions for the poor have improved substantially, society continues to grapple with growing global inequality.[48] Fortunately, we can take steps to address this while also accelerating economic growth. As Nobel laureate Joseph Stiglitz writes, "policies are available that would simultaneously increase growth and equality—creating a shared prosperity."[49] Stiglitz recommends a set of policies, including ones to reach full employment, at least in part by increasing public investments in infrastructure, education, innovation, and the environment. He writes that such government "investments will expand the economy and make private investments even more attractive."[50] Historically, he notes, periods of high productivity growth are strongly related to public-sector investment.[51] As we argue throughout this book, partnerships can be an extremely effective vehicle for implementing this type of inequality-reducing and pro-growth strategy.

## A TIME FOR MORE EFFECTIVE PARTNERSHIPS

Cross-sector partnerships—especially those that share the principles of social value investing—are not just a good idea, they are essential for overcoming society's most critical challenges.[52] To succeed, we need groups of all kinds to come together, share their learning, and promote best practices for a partnership management and delivery system that maximizes positive social impact. Peter Drucker was right when he observed that leadership and management contribute as much or more to progress as technological innovation does.[53]

Such management, though, must be both effective and strategic, and it must focus on goals that improve society—goals that promote a safe, healthy, prosperous, and thriving world for everyone. Idealistic as this sounds, partnerships based on these principles can lead to more equitable, inclusive, and responsible solutions. But society must be willing to account for the negative externalities of our actions and stop exploitation by certain industries and economic practices.[54] By doing so, organizations of all types will be better positioned to serve the important needs of communities everywhere.

We make clear how important measurement is to good management throughout this book. Even more important than how we *measure* success is how we *define* success to begin with, because that dramatically affects our intentions, our actions, and our results.

Society is in the process of rediscovering what it means to succeed.[55] As that discovery evolves we remain incredibly optimistic, and we ask you to take the observations, frameworks, and lessons in this book, use them for social good, and also improve upon them. We hope this brings together organizations, individuals, and local communities in an inclusive and collective problem solving process to overcome our most intractable challenges. Finally, we hope this work supports transformational change in the way we all collaborate—so that everyone can participate in making the world a far better place.

# Acknowledgments

Few—if any—important tasks are accomplished by one individual working alone. We hope that over time this book will be considered a useful and important work. If our hope becomes reality, there are many people who share in the credit.

———— ⌬ ————

## HWB

Numerous friends, colleagues, and mentors contributed in some way to my understanding of the world, and to my ability to author this work. Bill Eimicke is not only my coauthor but my dear friend and supporter. He embodies the true sense of the word partner. There are also many in the world of academia who helped make this book possible. First, thank you to Steve Cohen and the team at the Earth Institute. Steve is a long-time advisor, and someone I will never stop learning from. I have also had tremendous support from the team at the University of Nebraska, especially Hank Bounds, Ronnie Green, Jeff Gold, Steve Waller, and Tiffany Heng-Moss. I must also thank professor Mike Roloff, Beth Buske, and N. P. Das, as well as the many other professors and teachers who guided my thinking and development over the years.

There are those who contributed by reviewing this work and by providing feedback, suggestions, or corrections. Thank you to Matthew Bishop and Ruma Bose, Jerry Hirsch and the Collaboration Prize team, Andrew Kassoy, Christine Looney and the Ford Foundation,

Wes Moore and the team at the Robin Hood Foundation, Mark Newberg (who continues to challenge my thinking), and Brian Trelstad. Steven Radelet provided early and helpful counsel on this work, as did Daniel Shapiro and the team at Harvard University's International Negotiation Program. Also, thank you to Adam Stepan for your ongoing support of this project, and Chrissy Garton and Padma Tata for your dedicated research and review of the framework portion of the manuscript.

I have had the wonderful opportunity to learn from many who have mentored me or included me in their work. Thank you Amir and Tas Dossal and the entire team at the United Nations Office for Partnerships. A further thank you to Admiral Cecil Haney and the many individuals serving the mission of U.S. Strategic Command. Additionally, thank you Mogens Bay, Dan Glickman, Jane Goodall, Alexis Herman, Don and Mickie Keough, Tom Mangelsen, Patricia Rosenfield, Pete Rouse, Suzanne and Walter Scott Jr., Raj Shah, Josette Sheeran, and Gail and Mike Yanney—all for your many years of guidance and support.

Also, thank you to Nick Batter, Allen Beermann, Susan Bell, Julie Borlaug, J. D. Bryant, Mike Culver, Elliott Donnelley II, Peggy Dulany, Alan H. Fleischmann, Ellen Gustafson, Jacob Harold, Adam Hitchcock, Ajit, Tinku, Akshay, and Ajay Jain, Laura and Gary Lauder, Lauren Bush Lauren, Marco Lopez, John McNaught, Dmitri Mehlhorn, Clay Mitchell, Rob Myers, Trevor Neilson, Doug Oller, Ron and Jane Olson, Robert Reffkin, Kate Roberts, Nishant Roy, Robert Schutt, Klaus Schwab, Christine Sherry, David Slattery Jr., Darian Swig, Jack Vrett, and Mike Walter. I also benefited from ideas and feedback from participants in the White House Next Generation Leadership initiative and at the Global Impact Institute convening.

The importance of teamwork is discussed throughout this book, and the social value investing framework itself would not exist without three team efforts in particular. At the origin of the framework is the value investing paradigm. Its principles and rigor are thanks to the important work of Benjamin Graham and David Dodd at Columbia University from nearly a century ago. The management theory for the framework is inspired by and modeled after the structure and success of Berkshire Hathaway. For this, I want to thank the entire Berkshire team and acknowledge the leadership and hard work of Berkshire's managers and its board of directors—all of whom I greatly respect, and many of whom are friends. Finally, the adaptation of the management theory to its present framework for cross-sector partnerships is a result of the work and the programs of the Howard G. Buffett Foundation. I would like to thank the entire HGBF team, including Trisha Cook, Ann Kelly Bolten, Paula Goedert, its board, its staff, and its many partners from throughout the years.

A special thank you to Bill and Melinda Gates for including me in the work of your foundation, for your dedication to improving the world, and for your commitment to good stewardship. Further thank you to Mark Suzman, Bridgitt Arnold, and Ryan Kreitzer for your assistance with the manuscript. Important aspects of the social value investing framework were inspired by work with a special projects team at the Bill & Melinda Gates Foundation. Thank you to Patty Stonesifer, Cheryl Scott, Alex Friedman, Lowell Weiss, Olivia Leland, Greg Cain, and others from that group. Also, thank you to the teams supporting the Goalkeepers initiative and the Giving Pledge for your excellent work, including Robert Rosen and Adrienne DiCasparro.

An incredible team contributed to the development and success of the White House Office of Social Innovation and Civic Participation, from which many of my observations and lessons about cross-sector partnerships were drawn. This included Michele Jolin, Carlos Monje, Marta Urquilla, Paul Schmitz, Jonathan Greenblatt, Cheryl Dorsey, Charlie Anderson, and many others. We were all inspired by President Barack Obama and the leadership of Sonal Shah, for whom I feel profound gratitude.

A rather large team at the Defense Department and many DoD partners made the work in the Afghanistan case possible. I would like to thank President Ashraf Ghani, Admiral Michael Mullen, Secretary Robert Gates, General David Petraeus, Paul Brinkley, Stan Lumish, Eric Clark, Gerry Brown, Christine Rafiekian, many others from the C and A rings, as well as the many civilians and individuals in uniform serving our country. Also, thank you to Roya Mahboob, Lou Pierce, Eric Crowley, as well as the entire Norman Borlaug Institute team, including Mark Q. Smith, Glen Shinn, Richard Ford, Rahmat Attaie, and David Quarles. And a special thank you to Dr. Ed Price, who serves as a mentor and friend to many—myself included.

Some of my dearest and closest friends have invested countless hours supporting me and the development of many ideas found throughout this book. I would not be who I am today without Zecki Dossal, Luis A. Renta, Jorge Cervantes, Katherine Lorenz, and Rob Lalka.

I must also acknowledge the numerous and significant contributions Rob made specifically to this manuscript, for which I express my sincere gratitude.

The book is dedicated to my son and wife because of their profound impact on my life, and the inspiration they provide. Without Lili's support and the dedication of *her* time and energy, this project would have never been completed. For this I am indebted, and I express my deepest appreciation.

I also appreciate the love and guidance from everyone in my family throughout the years. Thank you Doris, Bertie, Astrid, Pam, Susie, Allen, Em, Mike and Joe, Alex and Mimi, as well as Jenn and Peter— for teaching me things I did not know I could learn. A special thank you to each of my sisters, Megan, Chelsea, Heather, and Erin, as well as your families. You all make up a bedrock of support.

A very special acknowledgment of appreciation to my mother and father, to whom I owe a great many things. My mother never ceased to care for or nurture me along, and continues to do so today—she exudes limitless empathy and love. My father had the foresight, fortitude, and patience to take his young son along with him on his many travels—experiencing the best and the worst of the world together. I could not ask for a better mom or dad.

I also would like to acknowledge my grandmother, who serves as a beacon of light for our family; she embodied endless and unconditional generosity, which continues to inspire us all.

And to my grandfather: there is much for which to thank you. Not least for the incredible amount of time you invested reviewing my drafts, and for your invaluable feedback, guidance, and encouragement throughout my writing process. I am incredibly grateful for your powerful example of what a single individual can accomplish in one lifetime. Your approach to business, and to life, serves as an inspiration for this work, as does your boundless sense of optimism.

---

## WBE

First and foremost, I would like to thank my coauthor, colleague, and close friend, Howard W. Buffett. We teach together, we learn together, we write together and, I believe, we continue to make each other better. Second, my dear friend and perennial coauthor Steven Cohen has collaborated with me for more than thirty years to discover how to best help make tomorrow's public leaders and managers even better than those of today and yesterday.

For this book specifically, those contributing critical influence over my thinking on cross-sector partnerships include Adam Stepan, his father Al Stepan, Thomas Trebat, Jagdish Bhagwati, Arvind Panagariya, Krishnan Ganapathy, Doug Blonsky, John Alschuler, Rodrigo Soares, Regina Siqueira, Jose Roberto Marinho, Carlos Jereissati, FDNY Chief Richard Tobin, FDNY Chief Joseph Pfeifer, the legendary NYPD police commissioner Bill Bratton, Ester Fuchs, and too many others to name here. Former NYS Senator John Dunne, NYC Mayor Ed Koch, NYS Governor Mario Cuomo, former mayor and Professor Stephen Goldsmith, and Mayor Mike Bloomberg are my role models for all that can be achieved by government, ethically and with economic and social justice always in mind. David Osborne, researcher, friend, and brilliant thinker wrote one of the most influential books of the twentieth century, *Reinventing Government*, on how to achieve the public interest more effectively and more inclusively; his work always inspires me to think bigger and write better.

I am grateful to our team at Columbia's Picker Center, particularly Arvid Lukauskas, Valerie Zimmer, Aleschia Johnson, Bruna Santos, and Nitasha Nair, who have helped make our center a place where faculty, students, working professionals, and other academic centers come to learn about best practices in management innovation, social value, and cross-sector partnerships.

Finally, without Karen Murphy, Annemarie Eimicke, Balsam Murphy, and Sugar Ray Murphy, my contribution to this book would not have been possible.

---

We would both like to express our appreciation to the remarkable team at Columbia University Press. Myles Thompson and Stephen Wesley were truly our partners in the creation of this book. We would also like to thank Eric Schwartz, Meredith Howard, Marielle Poss, Ben Kolstad, Bill Hawley, and the entire production team. Further, we also benefited from invaluable feedback from our peer reviewers, and the Columbia University Press editorial board and Publications Committee—all of whom helped us improve our work and thinking considerably.

We are also incredibly grateful to Columbia President Lee Bollinger, Provost John Coatsworth, and SIPA Dean Merit Janow for giving us the opportunity to work at Columbia University and the freedom to follow our passions for making the world a better place for all.

# Notes

## INTRODUCTION

1. Trust for Public Land, "2017 City Park Facts," April 2017, 33. https://www
   .tpl.org/sites/default/files/files_upload/CityParkFacts_2017.4_7_17
   .FIN_.LO_.pdf.
2. Total visitors calculated by multiplying the average visitors per acre
   (1,129,272) times the number of acres for the park (7). The Trust for
   Public Land. "2017 City park facts," April 2017, 33.
3. Columbia University School of International and Public Affairs, 2017–
   2018 SIPA Bulletin, http://bulletin.columbia.edu/sipa/.
4. Neil Hood and Stephen Young, eds. *The Globalization of Multinational
   Enterprise Activity and Economic Development.* (London: Palgrave
   Macmillan, 2000).
5. For a detailed analysis of this point, see Andreas Bergh and Therese
   Nilsson, "Is Globalization Reducing Absolute Poverty?." *World Development* 62 (2014): 42–61.
6. Eric Helleiner, "Understanding the 2007–2008 Global Financial Crisis:
   Lessons for Scholars of International Political Economy." *Annual Review
   of Political Science* 14 (2011): 67–87.
7. Erik Brynjolfsson and Andrew McAfee, *The Second Machine Age*
   (New York: Norton, 2014).
8. For more information regarding this sentiment, see the polling data
   from the 2017 Edelman Trust Barometer Global Report: www.edelman
   .com/global-results/.
9. Steven Radelet, *The Great Surge: the Ascent of the Developing World*
   (New York: Simon and Schuster, 2015), 5.

10. The WHO defines clean water as access to improved water sources, both piped and nonpiped. Joint Monitoring Programme for Water Supply, Sanitation and Hygiene, *Progress on Drinking Water, Sanitation and Hygiene: 2017 Update and SDG Baselines* (Geneva: World Health Organization and the United Nations Children's Fund, 2017), 12, fig. 16. License: CC BY-NC-SA 3.0 IGO.

11. World Health Organization, "Children: Reducing Mortality" (Factsheet), October 2017, www.who.int/mediacentre/factsheets/fs178/en/.

12. United States Census Bureau, "Millennials Outnumber Baby Boomers and Are Far More Diverse, Census Bureau Reports." June 25, 2015. Release Number: CB15-113, https://www.census.gov/newsroom/press-releases/2015/cb15-113.html.

13. John J. Havens and Paul G. Schervish, "A Golden Age of Philanthropy Still Beckons: National Wealth Transfer and Potential for Philanthropy," Boston College Center on Wealth and Philanthropy, 2014, www.bc.edu/content/dam/files/research_sites/cwp/pdf/A%20Golden%20Age%20of%20Philanthropy%20Still%20Bekons.pdf.

14. Sustainable investing is defined by the Morgan Stanley Institute for Sustainable Investing as "the practice of making investments in companies or funds which aim to achieve market-rate financial returns while pursuing positive social and/or environmental impact," 3. Morgan Stanley Institute for Sustainable Investing, "Sustainable Signals: New Data from the Individual Investor," August 7, 2017, www.eenews.net/assets/2017/08/11/document_cw_01.pdf.

15. Morgan Stanley Institute for Sustainable Investing, "Sustainable Signals: New Data from the Individual Investor," 5. August 7, 2017, www.eenews.net/assets/2017/08/11/document_cw_01.pdf.

16. More than 4,500 individuals globally, born after January 1982, stated the primary purpose of business was to "improve society." Deloitte. "Millennial Innovation Survey," January 2013, www2.deloitte.com/content/dam/Deloitte/global/Documents/About-Deloitte/dttl-crs-millennial-innovation-survey-2013.pdf.

17. Forum for Sustainable and Responsible Investment, "Report on US Sustainable, Responsible and Impact Investing Trends," 2014, www.ussif.org/trends.

18. The Boston Consulting Group, "Total Societal Impact; A New Lens for Strategy," October 2017, 7, http://3blmedia.com/sites/www.3blmedia.com/files/other/BCG_Total_Societal_Impact.pdf.

19. Darshan Groux, "Millennial in the Workplace," Center for Women & Business, Bentley University, 4, www.bentley.edu/centers/center-for-women-and-business/millennials-workplace.

20. Joseph E. Stiglitz, *The Price of Inequality* (New York: Norton, 2013), xxi.

21. Stiglitz, *The Price of Inequality*, xxix.
22. Robert J. Gordon, *The Rise and Fall of American Growth* (Princeton, NJ: Princeton University Press, 2016).
23. Peter F. Drucker, *Management: Tasks, Responsibilities, Practices* (New York: HarperCollins, 1974), 807.
24. 2017 Deloitte Millennial Survey, https://www2.deloitte.com/global /en/pages/about-deloitte/articles/millennialsurvey.html.
25. Peter F. Drucker, *The Age of Discontinuity* (Brunswick, NJ: Transaction, 2008), 234–241.
26. John Casey, "Comparing Nonprofit Sectors Around the World," *Journal of Nonprofit Education and Leadership* 6, no. 3 (2016): 187–223, http:// dx.doi.org/10.18666/JNEL-2016-V6-13-7583.
27. Speech by Howard W. Buffett, United Nations Social Innovation Summit, May 31, 2012. New York.
28. See, for example, Elliot D. Sclar, *You Don't Always Get What You Pay For: The Economics of Privatization* (Ithaca, NY: Cornell University Press, 2000).
29. Inspired by John F. Kennedy's quote: "Our problems are man-made—therefore, they can be solved by man." Commencement Speech at American University, June 10, 1963, www.jfklibrary.org/Asset-Viewer /BWC7I4C9QUmLG9J6I8oy8w.aspx.
30. For example, people fifteen to twenty-nine years old exceed 30 percent of the working-age population in most Middle East and North Africa countries. For more information, see Organization for Economic Co-operation and Development, "Youth in the MENA Region: How to Bring Them In" (Paris: OECD, 2016), http://dx.doi.org/10.1787 /9789264265721-en.

# 1. THE EVOLUTION OF CROSS-SECTOR PARTNERSHIPS

1. Tony Bovaird, "Public-Private Partnerships: From Contested Concepts to Prevalent Practice," *International Review of Administrative Sciences* 70, no. 2 (2004): 199–215.
2. Bovaird, "Public-Private Partnerships," 199.
3. David Maurrasse, *Strategic Public Private Partnerships—Innovation and Development* (Cheltenham, UK: Edward Elgar, 2013), 10–41.
4. Valerie Wildridge, Sue Childs, Lynette Cawthra, and Bruce Madge, "How to Create Successful Partnerships—a Review of the Literature," *Health Information & Libraries Journal* 21 (2004): 3–19. https://doi .org/10.1111/j.1740-3324.2004.00497.x.

5. For more on socially valuable activities, see Luigi Guiso, Paola Sapienza, and Luigi Zingales, "Civic Capital as the Missing Link: Handbooks in Economics," in *Social Economics, Volume 1A: Handbooks in Economics*, ed. Jess Benhabib, Mathew O. Jackson, and Alberta Bisin (San Diego, Calif.: North-Holland, 2011), 417–80.

6. For a discussion and analysis of overcoming collective action problems related to sustainable development objectives, see Yvonne Rydin and Nancy Holman, "Re-evaluating the Contribution of Social Capital in Achieving Sustainable Development," *Local Environment* 9, no. 2 (April 2004): 117–133, particularly 127–131, https://doi.org/10.1080 /1354983042000199561.

7. Ronald W. McQuaid, "Theory of Organisational Partnerships—Partnership Advantages, Disadvantages and Success Factors," in *The New Public Governance: Critical Perspectives and Future Directions*, ed. Stephen P. Osborne (London: Routledge, 2010), 125–46.

8. For more on this, see Andrés Rodríguez-Pose and Michael Storper, "Better Rules or Stronger Communities? On the Social Foundations of Institutional Change and Its Economic Effects," *Economic Geography* 82 (2006): 1–25. https://doi.org/10.1111/j.1944-8287.2006.tb00286.x.

9. For a discussion of challenges associated with establishing and managing cross-sector partnerships, see Kathy Babiak and Lucie Thibault, "Challenges in Multiple Cross-Sector Partnerships," *Nonprofit and Voluntary Sector Quarterly* 38, no. 1 (December 2007): 117–43. https:// doi.org/ 10.1177/0899764008316054.

10. Thomas G. Pittz and Terry R. Adler, "An Exemplar of Open Strategy: Decision-Making Within Multi-Sector Collaborations," *Management Decision* 54, no. 7 (2016):1595–1614.

11. David Maurrasse, *Strategic Public Private Partnerships*, 3.

12. United Nations, "Transforming Our World: The 2030 Agenda for Sustainable Development," United Nations A/Res/70/1, adopted September 27, 2015. For additional information, see https://sustainable development.un.org/.

13. For more about the Goalkeepers Initiative, see www.globalgoals.org /goalkeepers/.

14. Maurrasse, *Strategic Public Private Partnerships*, 17.

15. National Park Service, U.S. Department of the Interior, *About the Homestead Act*, www.nps.gov/home/learn/historyculture/abouthome steadactlaw.htm.

16. Robert D. Launius, *Historical Analogs for the Stimulation of Space Commerce*, Monographs in Aerospace History, no. 54 (Washington, D.C.: NASA, 2014).

17. Robert Gordon, *The Rise and Fall of American Growth* (Princeton, N.J.: Princeton University Press, 2016).

18. Mario Cuomo speech at the Democratic National Convention, July 16, 1984, San Francisco, California.

19. Arthur M Schlesinger Jr., *The Coming of the New Deal* (New York: Houghton Mifflin, 1958), 299–301.

20. While the U.S. economy has led to some 75 million owner-occupied homes, much homeownership has been financed through debt. This topic is discussed on pages 5–6 of the Berkshire Hathaway Inc., *2016 Annual Report*, berkshirehathaway.com/2016ar/2016ar.pdf.

21. The authors converted costs to 2018 dollars using data from the U.S. Bureau of Labor Statistics. For original figures, see the U.S. Department of Transportation, Federal Highway Administration, reprint of: Richard F. Weingroff, "Federal-Aid Highway Act of 1956: Creating The Interstate System," *Highway History* 60, no. 1, Summer 1996, https://www.fhwa.dot.gov/publications/publicroads/96summer/p96su10.cfm.

22. The authors converted costs to 2018 dollars using data from the U.S. Bureau of Labor Statistics. For original figures, see U.S. Department of Transportation, Federal Highway Administration, *Highway History*, www.fhwa.dot.gov/interstate/faq.cfm#question6.

23. U.S. Department of Transportation, Federal Highway Administration, *Highway History*, www.fhwa.dot.gov/interstate/faq.

24. Andrew J. Bacevich, "The Tyranny of Defense Inc.," *The Atlantic*, January 2011, http://theatlantic.com/magazine/archive/2011/01/the-tyranny-of-defense-inc/308342/.

25. John F. Kennedy, *Historic Speeches*, John F. Kennedy Presidential Library and Museum, www.jfklibrary.org/JFK/Historic-Speeches.aspx.

26. Frank Holeman, "President Kennedy Announces He Wants to Put a Man on the Moon," *New York Daily News*, May 26, 1961, www.nydailynews.com/news/national/jfk-announces-1961-put-man-moon-article-1.2648222.

27. Michio Kaku, "The Cost of Space Exploration," *Forbes*, July 16, 2009, www.forbes.com/2009/07/16/apollo-moon-landing-anniversary-opinions-contributors-cost-money.html.

28. The exact cost of the program has been estimated at $21 billion to $30 billion, depending on what is included in the total. See, for example, Paul D. Lowman Jr., *Our First Lunar Program: What Did We Get from Apollo?* September 6, 2007, www.nasa.gov/centers/goddard/news/series/moon/first_lunar_program.html; and Telegraph Media Group, *Apollo 11 Moon Landing; Ten Facts About Armstrong, Aldrin and Collins' Mission*, July 18, 2009, www.telegraph.co.uk/news/science/space/5852237/Apollo-11-Moon-landing-ten-facts-about-Armstrong-Aldrin-and-Collins-mission.html.

29. NASA, *Public-Private Partnerships for Space Capability Development*, April 2014, www.nasa.gov/sites/default/files/files/NASA_Partnership _Report_LR_20140429.pdf.

30. Miriam Kramer, *Public-Private Partnerships Key to US Spaceflight Future, Experts Say*, May 14, 2014, www.space.com/25880-government-private -partnerships-us-spaceflight-future.html; Anthony Velocci, *Commercialization in Space*, March 30, 2012, http://hr.harvard.edu/article/?a=2921.

31. NASA, "Europa: Overview: Ingredients for Life?," solarsystem.nasa .gov/planets/europa.

32. See the following NASA sources: *Apollo I, The Fire, 27 January 1967*, www.history.nasa.gov/SP-4029/Apollo_01a_Summary.htm; *Challenger STS 51-L Accident, January 28, 1986*, www.history.nasa.gov/sts51l.html; and *Report of Columbia Accident Investigation Board, Vol. 1*, www.nasa .gov/columbia/home/CAIB_Vol1.html.

33. Peter Drucker, *The Age of Discontinuity* (Brunswick, N.J.: Transaction, 2008).

34. Drucker, *The Age of Discontinuity*, 101.

35. Drucker, *The Age of Discontinuity*, 212–33.

36. Drucker, *The Age of Discontinuity*, 234.

37. Drucker, *The Age of Discontinuity*, 241.

38. Ronald Regan, *Inaugural Address*, January 20, 1981, Ronald Regan, Presidential Library & Museum, www.reaganlibrary.archives.gov/archives /speeches/1981/12081a.htm.

39. Lester Salamon, *Beyond Privatization: The Tools of Government Action* (Washington, D.C.: Urban Institute Press, 1989), 245.

40. Geoffrey Smith, *Reagan & Thatcher: The Balance Sheet*, The Eighties Club, 1991, http:/eightiesclub.tripod.com/id133.htm.

41. Michael Grant, "Financing Eurotunnel," *Japan Railway & Transport Review* 47, April 1997, http://www.jrtr.net/jrtr11/pdf/f46_gra.pdf.

42. David Osborne, *Laboratories of Democracy* (Brighton, Mass.: Harvard Business School Press, 1988).

43. David Osborne and Ted Gaebler, *Reinventing Government* (Boston, Mass.: Addison-Wesley, 1992).

44. David Osborne and Ted Gaebler, *Reinventing Government*, ix–x.

45. William Eimicke was selected to work with Osborne as a volunteer expert and focused on reinvention opportunities in the federal agencies related to housing.

46. Stephen Goldsmith, *The Twenty-First Century City* (Washington, D.C.: Regnery, 1997). Goldsmith is currently the Daniel Paul Professor of the Practice of Government and the Director of the Innovations in American Government Program at Harvard's Kennedy School of Government. He previously served as deputy mayor of New York City under Mayor

Michael Bloomberg and was chair of the Corporation for National and Community Service under President George W. Bush.

47. Emanuel S. Savas, *Privatization in the City* (Washington, D.C.: CQ Press, 2005).

48. Faith-Based And Community Initiative, United States Government Accountability Office. *Improvements in Monitoring Grantees and Measuring Performance Could Enhance Accountability.* (Washington, D.C.: U.S. G.A.O., 2006).

49. Daniel F. Runde, with Aaron Milner and Jena Santoro, *The Millennium Challenge Corporation in the Trump Era* (Washington, D.C.: Center for Strategic and International Studies, 2017), 1.

50. Runde, *The Millennium Challenge Corporation*, 7.

51. See Howard W. Buffett, *MCC's Impact Evaluations Challenge Us All to Do Better*, December 6, 2012, www.mcc.gov/blog/entry/entry-120612 -howard-w-buffett-on-impact-evaluations.

52. Sarah Rose and Franck Wiebe, *Defining the Next Ten Years of the Millennium Challenge Corporation*, Center for Global Development, 2016, 4, www.cgdev.org/sites/default/files/whw-mcc.pdf.

53. U.S. Department of State, Secretary's Office of Global Partnerships, *About Us*, www.state.gov/s/partnerships/mission/index.htm.

54. Deputy Secretary of Defense Ashton Carter and Vice Chairman of the Joint Chiefs of Staff Admiral James Winnefeld, "Public-Private Partnerships Supporting the DoD Mission," DoD Memorandum, April 25, 2013.

55. See *US Pacific Command's J92 Partnering Division*, http://www.pacom .mil/Contact/Directory/J9/Strategic-Partnerships; and *US Southern Command's J7/9 Coalition Affairs Directorate* statement on partnership, http://www.southcom.mil/Focus-Areas/Partner-of-Choice/.

56. National Intelligence Council, *Global Trends: Paradox of Progress*, January 3, 2017, www.dni.gov/files/documents/nic/GT-Full-Report.pdf.

57. National Intelligence Council. *Global Trends*, 28.

58. This was a key theme in a set of managment recommendations prepared for U.S. Strategic Command regarding the adaptation of social value investing principles to U.S. nuclear command and control operations. See more in "Innovating U.S. Strategic Command's Deterrence and Assurance Operations," Columbia University School of International and Public Affairs, ed. Howard W. Buffett, Spring 2017. Available at: stratcom.mil/Portals/8/Documents/Columbia University SIPA USSTRATCOM Final Report.pdf.

59. For an editorial on this subject, see Tom Watson, "Philanthropy in a Time of Turmoil: 3 Cheers for the Establishment," *The Chronicle of Philanthropy* (June 28, 2016): Opinion, www.philanthropy.com/article /Opinion-3-Cheers-for-the/236937/.

## 2. SOCIAL VALUE INVESTING

1. Joel L. Fleishman, *The Foundation: A Great American Secret; How Private Wealth Is Changing the World* (New York: PublicAffairs, 2007).
2. Joel L. Fleishman, *Putting Wealth to Work: Philanthropy for Today or Investing for Tomorrow?* (New York: PublicAffairs, 2017).
3. Timothy O'Brien and Stephanie Saul, "Buffett to Give Bulk of His Fortune to Gates Charity," *New York Times*, June 26, 2006.
4. Karen Richardson, "Warren Buffett Gives $30 Billion to Gates Foundation," *Wall Street Journal*, June 26, 2006.
5. Columbia Business School, the Heilbrunn Center for Graham & Dodd Investing, *Value Investing History*, https://www8.gsb.columbia.edu/valueinvesting/about/history.
6. Bruce Greenwald and Paul Johnson, "Value Investing," in *A Century of Ideas*, ed. Brian Thomas (New York: Columbia University Press, 2016), chapter 2.
7. Benjamin Graham and David Dodd co-authored *Security Analysis*; Benjamin Graham authored *The Intelligent Investor*.
8. Benjamin Graham, *The Intelligent Investor*, 4th rev. ed. (New York: Harper & Row, 1973).
9. Dealbook, "Buffett Beats Gates to Become World's Richest Person," *New York Times*, March 6, 2008.
10. BBC News, "Buffett donates $37bn to charity," June 26, 2006, http://news.bbc.co.uk/2/hi/5115920.stm.
11. Each letter is available on Berkshire Hathaway's website at http://berkshirehathaway.com/donate/webdonat.html.
12. See, for example, the letter to Howard G. Buffett from Warren E. Buffett, June 26, 2006, at www.berkshirehathaway.com/donate/hgbltr.pdf.
13. Howard G. Buffett Foundation, *2006 Annual Report*, www.thehowardgbuffettfoundation.org/.
14. Data compiled from various Howard G. Buffett Foundation annual reports and confirmed by foundation staff on August 31, 2016.
15. Data compiled from various Howard G. Buffett Foundation annual reports and confirmed by foundation staff on August 31, 2016.
16. For more detailed information on the Global Water Initiative, visit http://globalwaterinitiative.org/.
17. This initial gathering took place in Omaha, Nebraska, on September 25–26, 2006.
18. Although less common in the philanthropic sector, these types of collaboration occur in the private sector frequently. For instance, see the discussion of "Networks" and "Consortia" in Bruce R. Barringer

and Jeffrey S. Harrison, "Walking a Tightrope: Creating Value Through Interorganizational Relationships," *Journal of Management* 26, no. 3 (2000): 367–403, at 387–91, https://doi.org/10.1177 /014920630002600302.

19. For a narrative of this process, including challenges faced, see Howard G. Buffett, with Howard W. Buffett, *40 Chances: Finding Hope in a Hungry World* (New York: Simon & Schuster, 2013), chapter 26, "Less Than Sparkling".

20. For an additional example of this approach, see Howard W. Buffett and Adam Stepan, "Aid or Investment? Post-Conflict Development in DRC and Rwanda," Columbia University School of International and Public Affairs Case Consortium, SIPA-18-0016.0, 2018.

21. Principle #4, "Owner-Related Business Principles," in *Berkshire Hathaway's Owner's Manual*, June 1996, updated February 25, 2012, www.berkshirehathaway.com/ownman.pdf.

22. Section on "The Managing of Berkshire," in *Berkshire Hathaway's Owner's Manual*.

23. See also David F. Larcker and Brian Tayan, *Trust and Consequences: A Survey of Berkshire Hathaway Operating Managers*, Stanford University Closer Look Series, CGRP52, October 20, 2015, www.gsb.stanford.edu /faculty-research/publications/trust-consequences-survey-berkshire-hathaway-operating-managers.

24. Principle #1, Principle #12, and Principle #14, in *Berkshire Hathaway's Owner's Manual*.

25. For instance, the company's leadership engages in open and honest communication with a propensity to point out mistakes, failures, and missed opportunities. My grandfather's annual letter to shareholders is written as though shareholders were themselves family members. And the annual shareholder's meeting in Omaha, Nebraska, instills its own sense of community and comradery. Many consider these attributes unique for an organization the size and complexity of Berkshire Hathaway, and we believe they are important aspects of its shareholder focus, and critical to its overall success.

26. Principle #7 (discussion of deferred taxes and "float") and Principle #14, in *Berkshire Hathaway's Owner's Manual*.

27. Principle #3, Principle #6, and Section on "Intrinsic Value," in *Berkshire Hathaway's Owner's Manual*.

28. For instance, in 2007 the Rockefeller Foundation convened a small group of philanthropists and investors to discuss the emerging practices of impact investing. This led to the creation of the Global Impact Investing Network (GIIN), discussed in chapter 12. More information is available at https://thegiin.org/giin/history.

29. Impact Rate of Return is a federally registered trademark of Global Impact LLC and all rights are reserved.

30. For information on the current work of the UNOP, visit www.un.org /partnerships/.

31. "Report of the Secretary-General, United Nations Office for Partnerships," A/64/91, United Nations General Assembly, August 12, 2009.

32. "Organization of the United Nations Office for Partnerships," Secretary-General's bulletin, ST/SGB/2009/14, United Nations Secretariat, December 18, 2009.

33. For a list of projects and funds balances across UNOP program areas, see "Report of the Secretary-General, United Nations Office for Partnerships," A/64/91, United Nations General Assembly, August 12, 2009.

34. These priorities informed development of the White House Domestic Policy Council "Partnerships" perspective, with contributions or coauthored by Howard W. Buffett, https://obamawhitehouse.archives.gov /administration/eop/sicp/initiatives/partnerships.

35. See more at *Recovery Act*, Department of the Treasury, www.treasury .gov/initiatives/recovery/Pages/recovery-act.aspx.

36. For instance, the TIGR team organized significant outreach and engagement activities with diverse nongovernmental stakeholders to better inform its partnership strategies. These engagements spanned the areas of technology, philanthropy, social innovation, and mission-driven businesses, among others.

37. *White House Officials Discuss Plans for Social-Innovation Office*, The Chronicle of Philanthropy, May 28, 2009, www.philanthropy.com /article/White-House-Officials-Discuss/162587.

38. President Barack Obama signed into law the Edward M. Kennedy Serve America Act on April 22, 2009, creating the Social Innovation Fund.

39. Howard W. Buffett, *Promoting Partnerships for Innovation in Energy*, The White House, May 10, 2010, www.whitehouse.gov/blog/2010/05/10 /promoting-partnerships-innovation-energy; and Howard W. Buffett, *Partnerships for Regional Energy Innovation in Omaha, Nebraska*, The White House, June 17, 2010, www.whitehouse.gov/blog/2010/06/17 /partnerships-regional-energy-innovation-omaha-nebraska.

40. Howard W. Buffett, *Conference on Next Generation Leadership*, The White House, July 28, 2010, www.whitehouse.gov/blog/2010/07/28 /conference-next-generation-leadership.

41. Robert M. Gates, Secretary of Defense, *Continuation of Task Force for Business and Stability Operations* (Memorandum), March 25, 2010 (Washington, D.C.: U.S. Department of Defense).

42. For instance, see the section titled "Rebuilding Afghanistan's Agriculture Sector" in Department of State, Office of the Special Representative for Afghanistan and Pakistan, "Afghanistan and Pakistan Regional Stabilization Strategy," February 2010.

43. This was done in alignment with the U.S. Government Counterinsurgency Guide, issued January 2009 by the U.S. Agency for International Development, the U.S. Department of Defense, and the U.S. Department of State.

44. Nongovernmental program supporters included the Norman Borlaug Foundation, the Howard G. Buffett Foundation, the United Nations World Food Program, and others.

45. See the section on "Advocacy and Awareness" in Howard G. Buffett Foundation, *2011 Annual Report*, www.thehowardgbuffettfoundation .org/.

46. For example, see Buffett, *40 Chances*, chapter 29, "Chains That Unlock Potential."

47. Howard G. Buffett Foundation, *Ag Leaders Announce Partnership to Promote Conservation Agriculture Adoption*, October 17, 2013, www .prnewswire.com/news-releases/ag-leaders-announce-partnership-to -promote-conservation-agriculture-adoption-228166511.html.

48. World Bank Group, *World Bank Group Agriculture Action Plan, 2013– 2015*, July 25, 2012, siteresources.worldbank.org/.../WBG_Agriculture ActionPlan-FY13-15-7-25-2012[1]. For additional, frequently updated information on the subject, visit www.worldbank.org/en/topic/agriculture /overview.

49. Robert Townsend, *Ending Poverty and Hunger by 2030: An Agenda for the Global Food System* (Washington, D.C.: World Bank Group, 2015), http:// documents.worldbank.org/curated/en/700061468334490682/Ending -poverty-and-hunger-by-2030-an-agenda-for-the-global-food-system.

50. UN FAO, *Contribution of Agricultural Growth to Reduction of Poverty, Hunger and Malnutrition*, 2012, www.fao.org/docrep/016/i3027e /i3027e04.pdf.

51. For more information on this partnership, see Howard W. Buffett and Adam Stepan, "Saved by the Soil? Africa's Frontier for Conservation-Based Agriculture," Columbia University School of International and Public Affairs Case Consortium, SIPA-17-0011.01, 2017.

52. See Warren Buffett's letter to his children, August 30, 2012, http:// berkshirehathaway.com/donate/shpltr.pdf.

53. See Howard G. Buffett Foundation, *2014 Annual Report*, www.thehowar dgbuffettfoundation.org/.

54. For access to the book's supplementary material, visit www.socialvalue investing.com.

# 3. THE PROCESS CASE

1. For a wonderful history of this period, see Lawrence James, *Raj, The Making and Unmaking of British India* (New York: St. Martin's Griffin, 1997).
2. James, *Raj*, 642–47.
3. A great insight into the promise and contradictions of modern India is provided in Sunil Khilannai, *The Idea of India* (New York: Farrar, Straus and Giroux, 1999).
4. World Bank, *Overview of India*, October 17, 2016, www.worldbank.org /en/country/india.
5. Central Intelligence Agency, *The World Factbook*, Gini Index, www.cia.gov /library/publications/the-world-factbook/rankorder/2172rank.html.
6. Central Intelligence Agency, *The World Factbook*, October 17, 2016, www .cia.gov/library/publications/the-world-factbook/rankorder/2172rank .html; see also World Bank, *Poverty & Equity Data*, October 17, 2016, http://povertydata.worldbank.org/poverty/country/IND.
7. World Bank, *Overview of India*.
8. USDA Foreign Agricultural Service, *India's Agricultural Exports Climb to Record High*, August 2014, www.fas.usda.gov/sites/default /files/2015-02/india_iatr_august_2014.pdf.
9. USDA Foreign Agricultural Service, *India's Agricultural Exports Climb*.
10. See also Columbia University's SIPA short case study film, *Digital India*, Picker Center, 2015.
11. Government of India, *About the Digital India Programme*, October 11, 2016, http://digitalindia.gov.in/print/node/2.
12. Government of India, *About the Digital India Programme*.
13. Indian tech billionaire Nardan Nilekani is credited with the original idea for a universal India ID, and he served as the chairman of UIDAI between 2009 and 2014. For more information, see Ted Smalley Bowen and Adam Stepan, "Digital India," Picker Center for Executive Education at Columbia University's School of International and Public Affairs (SIPA) Case Study, SIPA-15-0009.0, 2015.
14. UIDAI, *About Aadhaar*, October 11, 2016, https://uidai.gov.in/beta /your-aahaar/about-aadhaar.html.
15. UIDAI, *About Aadhaar*.
16. David Lalmalswama, "India Speaks 780 Languages, 220 Lost in Last 50 Years," *Thomson Reuters*, September 7, 2013, http://blogs.reuters .com/india/2013/09/07/india-speaks-780-languages-220-lost-in-last -50-years-survey/.
17. Bowen and Stepan, "Digital India," 6.

18. "Aadhaar Now Most Widely Held ID with 92cr [920 Million] Holders," *Times of India*, October 2, 2015.

19. "92 Percent of India's Adult Population Has Aadhaar Card," *Times of India*, January 21, 2016.

20. World Bank, *WDR16 Spotlight on Digital Identity*, May 2015, http://pubdocs.worldbank.org/en/959381434483205387/WDR16-Spotlight-on-Digital-ID-May-2015-Mariana-Dahan.pdf.

21. UIDAI, *About UIDAI*, February 3, 2017, UIDIA.gov.in.

22. UIDAI, *About UIDAI*.

23. Department of Information Technology, *National Population Register*, accessed February 2, 2017, http://ditnpr.in/faqs.aspx.

24. Rohin Dharmakumar, Seema Singh, and N. S. Ramnath, "How Nandan Nilekani Took Aadharr Past the Tipping Point," October 8, 2013, www.forbesindia.com/article/big-bet/how-nandan-nilekani-took-aadhaar-past-the-tipping-point/36259/1.

25. Shweta Punj, "How the UID Project Can Transform India," *Business Today*, February 22, 2012, www.businesstoday.in/storyprint/22288; see also Bowen and Stepan, "Digital India," 6.

26. Bowen and Stepan, "Digital India," 7–8; ET Bureau, *HCL Infosystems Bags Rs 2,200 cr Aadhaar Contract from UIDAI*, March 2, 2012, www.gadgetsnow.com/it-services/HCL-Infosystems-bags-Rs-2200-cr-Aadhaar-contract-from-UIDAI/articleshowprint/12108328.cms?null.

27. Prabhat Barnwal, *Curbing Leakage in Public Programs with Biometric Identification Systems: Evidence from India's Fuel Subsidies*, May 2015, www.med.uio.no/helsam/english/research/news-and-events/events/conferences/2015/vedlegg-warsaw/subsidy-leakage-uid.pdf.

28. Siddharth George and Arvind Subramamian, "Transforming the Fight Against Poverty in India," *New York Times*, July 22, 2015.

29. Shweta S. Banerjee, "From Cash to Digital Transfers in India: The Story So Far," *CGAP Brief*, February 2015, www.cgap.org/sites/default/files/Brief-From-Cash-to-Digital-Transfers-in India-Feb-2015_0.pdf.

30. Jhagdish Bhagwati and Arvind Panagariya, *Why Growth Matters: How Economic Growth in India Reduced Poverty and the Lessons for Other Developing Countries* (New York: PublicAffairs, 2013).

31. George and Subramamian, "Transforming the Fight Against Poverty in India."

32. George and Subramamian, "Transforming the Fight Against Poverty in India."

33. Vishwanath Nair, "Over 70 Percent of Accounts Opened Under Jan Dhan Are Now Active," *live Mint*, February 29, 2016, www.livemint.com/Politics/uhXJMepfwvOsWDHuRhhj6l/Over-70-accounts-opened-under-Jan-Dhan-are-now-active.html.

34. Aadhaar Dashboard, October 11, 2016, https://portal.uidai.gov.in/uid webportal/dashboard.do.

35. Karn Chauhan, "Indian Smartphone Premium Segment Grew 180% Annually in Q3 2017," Counterpoint Research. November 14, 2017, https://www.counterpointresearch.com/three-brands-control-indias -premium-smartphone-segment/.

36. Mark Scott, "In the Battle for Digital India, Vodafone Teams Up with Idea Cellular," *New York Times*, March 20, 2017.

37. "What Is the Impact of Mobile Telephone on Economic Growth?," A report to the GSM Association by Deloitte and CISCO, November, 2012.

38. *live Mint*, "Govt Launches 22 New Schemes Under Digital India Programme," December 29, 2015, http://www.livemint.com/Home-Page/QgFspv8UzykQP99AukcSjI/Govt-launches-22-new-schemes-under-Digital-India-programme.html.

39. Narayan Lakshman, "Modi Boots Up 'Digital India' with High-Profile Silicon Valley Show," *The Hindu*, September 27, 2015.

40. Communications Minister Ravi Shankar Prasad, quoted in *live Mint*, "Govt Launches 22 New Schemes Under Digital India Programme."

41. Aman Shah and Nivedita Bhattarcharjee, "After WiFi at the Taj, Modi Revives Campaign for 'Digital India'," *Reuters*, July 1, 2015.

42. "It is a reliable and safe platform," said Sidharth Vishwanath, partner at Pricewaterhouse Coopers, quoted in Mansi Taneja, "India to Set Up Digital Locker Authority for e-Governance," *VCCIRCLE*, www.vccircle.com/iinfracircle/india/india-set-digital-locker-authority -e-governance/.

43. *live Mint*, "How DigiLocker Can Make Driving Without Documents Easy," www.livemint.com/Leisure/SjclOod37q9km216iirtWJ/How-can -DigiLocker-make-driving-without-documents-easy-html.

44. DigiLocker, *FAQs & Customer Support*, accessed February 8, 2017, https://digilocker.gov.in/faq.php.

45. DigiLocker National Statistics,2016, https://digilocker.gov.in/.

46. Anja Manuel, "Tackling Graft in India," *New York Times*, April 19, 2016.

47. Manuel, "Tackling Graft in India."

48. Manuel, "Tackling Graft in India."

49. Bowen and Stepan, "Digital India," 14.

50. Duncan Grahan Rowe, "Ageing Eyes Hinder Biometric Scans," *Nature*, May 2012.

51. UIDAI's Central Identities Data Repository is comprised of three automated biometric identity subsystems running in parallel, which increases accuracy and enabled UIDAI to limit the risk of relying on only one private partner/vendor.

52. Bowen and Stepan, "Digital India," 14.

53. Neha Pandey Deonas, "Endgame Aadhaar? The SC's Latest Order May Put Paid to the 'One Identity Number for All Transactions' Vision for the Card," *Business Standard*, March 24, 2014.

54. Aknksha Jain, "Use Aadhaar to Identify Accident Victims," *The Hindu*, May 10, 2015.

55. Bowen and Stepan, "Digital India," 16.

56. Dheeraj Tiwar, "Government Asks Central Public Sector Enterprises to Enroll Employees Under Aadhaar," *Economic Times*, May 5, 2015.

57. In 2015, BJP dropped from ninety-one seats to fifty-three seats in the Bihar Assembly, and from thirty-two seats to three seats in the Delhi Assembly, www.elections.in/bihar/#info_id2 and www.elections.in/delhi/#info _id2. In 2016, BJP won only 3 of 294 seats in the West Bengal Assembly, www.elections.in/west-bengal/assembly-constituencies/2016-election -results.html.

58. Geeta Anand, "Modi's Party Wins Big in India's Largest State," *New York Times*, March 12, 2017.

59. Nida Najar, "Modi Retains Broad Support in India Despite Criticism, Poll Finds," *New York Times*, September 19, 2016.

60. Najar, "Modi Retains Broad Support."

61. Ted Smalley Bowen and Adam Stepan, "eDoctors: Primary Care Innovation in Brazil and India," School of International and Public Affairs, Picker Center for Executive Education, SIPA-15-0008.0 (New York: Columbia University, 2015).

62. Apollo Hospitals, *Company Overview*, October 26, 2016, www.apollo hospitals.com/corporate/company-overview.

63. Ministry of Electronic and Information Technology, *Common Service Centers*, www.Meity.gov.in.

64. Digital India, *Common Services Centers*, October 26, 2016, www.digital india.gov.in/content/common-service-centers.

65. Interviews with Dr. Prathap Reddy, founding Chairman of Apollo Hospitals and Dr. Krishnan Ganapathy of Apollo Telemedicine Networking Foundation conducted in Chennai, India, and New York City during 2014 and 2015 by members of the SIPA's Picker Center Case Study team and quoted in Bowen and Stepan, "eDoctors: Primary Care Innovation in Brazil and India," 10–11.

66. Bowen and Stepan, "eDoctors," 12. The government requires Apollo to treat patients who seek care but cannot afford even the minimal fees.

67. Bowen and Stepan, "eDoctors," 12.

68. Bowen and Stepan, "eDoctors,"13.

69. India Ministry of Health & Family Welfare, *Telemedicine Division*, accessed October 26, 2016, http://mohfw.nic.in/index1.php?lang =1&level=4&sublinkid=6165&lid=4006.

70. PTI, "Government, Apollo Hospitals Partner to Launch Telemedicine Services," *Economic Times*, August 23, 2015.

71. FP staff, "LS Passes Aadhaar Bill, Rejects RS Recommendations; All You Need to Know About the Law," *First Post*, March 17, 2016.

## 4. THE PROCESS FRAMEWORK

1. Sandra A. Waddock, "Building Successful Social Partnerships," *Sloan Management Review* 29, no. 4 (1988): 22.

2. Colin Armistead, Paul Pettigrew, and Sally Aves, "Exploring Leadership in Multi-Sectoral Partnerships," *Leadership* 3, no. 2 (August 2016): 211–30, https://doi.org/ 10.1177/1742715007076214.

3. Emanuela Todeva and David Knoke, "Strategic Alliances and Models of Collaboration," *Management Decision*, 43, no. 1 (2005): 123–25.

4. Todeva and Knoke, "Strategic Alliances."

5. A discussion of this question is brought forward from the perspective of private sector companies operating in low-income or "base of the pyramid" markets in Tassilo Schuster, "Benefits of Cross-Sector Partnerships in Markets at the Base of the Pyramid," *Business Strategy and the Environment* 23 (2014): 188–203, https://doi.org/ 10.1002/bse.1780.

6. PTI, "Government, Apollo Hospitals Partner to Launch Telemedicine Services," *Economic Times*, August 23, 2015.

7. Armistead, Pettigrew, and Aves, "Exploring Leadership in Multi-Sectoral Partnerships."

8. These differences are inherent to concerns raised by the increasing role of the private sector in multilateral governance. See Benedicte Bull et al., "Private Sector Influence in the Multilateral System: A Changing Structure of World Governance?" *Global Governance* 10, no. 4 (2004): 481–98.

9. Letter from Warren Buffett to Bill and Melinda Gates, December 12, 2016, www.gatesnotes.com/2017-Annual-Letter.

10. Samuel Bendett, "Defense Partnerships: Documenting Trends and Emerging Topics for Action," *Defense Horizons* 78 (2015): 1–12.

11. A multitude of definitions for the term "partnership" exist; for an extensive literature review concerning the topic, including definitions, see Valerie Wildridge, Sue Childs, Lynette Cawthra, and Bruce Madge, "How to Create Successful Partnerships—A Review of the Literature," *Health Information & Libraries Journal* 21 (2004): 3–19, https://doi .org/10.1111/j.1740-3324.2004.00497.x.

12. Internal Revenue Service, *Partnerships*, October 24, 2016, www.irs.gov /businesses/small-businesses-self-employed/partnerships.

13. See section on "Joint Ventures" in Bruce R. Barringer and Jeffrey S. Harrison, "Walking a Tightrope: Creating Value Through Interorganizational

Relationships," *Journal of Management* 26, no. 3 (June 2000): 367–403, at 384, https://doi.org/10.1177/014920630002600302.

14. The lack of consistency is discussed in Linton Wells II and Samuel Bendett, "Public-Private Cooperation in the Department of Defense: A Framework for Analysis and Recommendations for Action," *Defense Horizons*, October 2012, http://ndupress.ndu.edu/Portals/68/Documents/defensehorizon/DH-74.pdf?ver=2014-03-06-114916-250.

15. Basic description adapted from the White House Domestic Policy Council "Partnerships" perspective, with contributions from or coauthored by Howard W. Buffett, https://obamawhitehouse.archives.gov/administration/eop/sicp/initiatives/partnerships.

16. Many of the partnerships that informed our definition share characteristics with the concept of "collective impact"; however, we disagree with the delineation between "technical" and "adaptive" problems described by John Kania and Mark Kramer, "Collective Impact," *Stanford Social Innovation Review* (Winter 2011), https://ssir.org/articles/entry/collective_impact.

17. Adapted from Ashton Carter and Admiral James Winnefeld, *Public-Private Partnerships Supporting the DoD Mission*, United States Department of Defense, 2013, www.defensecommunities.org/wp-content/uploads/2011/.../OSD004391-13-RES.pdf.

18. For simple guidelines on language related to nonbinding agreements, see U.S. Department of State, *Guidance on Non-Binding Documents*, www.state.gov/s/l/treaty/guidance/.

19. For a series of relevant templates and example agreements, see "Policy Framework and Legal Guidelines for Partnerships," U.S. Department of State, February 2011, 21–71.

20. For a discussion of public-private partnerships, see the white paper on partnerships prepared by the National Council for Public-Private Partnerships, "For the Good of the People: Using Public-Private Partnerships To Meet America's Essential Needs," (4), 2002, https://www.ncppp.org/wp-content/uploads/2013/03/WPFortheGoodofthePeople.pdf.

21. Seitanidi, M. May, and Andrew Crane, eds. *Social Partnerships and Responsible Business: A Research Handbook* (New York: Routledge, 2013), 1–12, 36, 60–85.

22. Skills-based capital is categorically similar to, yet more broadly defined than, "skill-based capital" found in: Lester Taylor, *Capital, Accumulation, and Money: An Integration of Capital, Growth, and Monetary Theory* (Boston, Mass.: Springer Verlag, 2010), 12.

23. Brett M. Frischmann, "Environmental Infrastructure," *Ecology Law Quarterly* 35, no. 2 (2008): 151–78, http://scholarship.law.berkeley.edu/elq/vol35/iss2/1.

24. This is a central aspect of the definition of a cross-sector partnership: "a cross-sector, inter-organizational group, working together under some form of recognized governance, towards common goals which would be extremely difficult, if not impossible, to achieve if tackled by any single organization": Colin Armistead, Paul Pettigrew, and Sally Aves, "Exploring Leadership in Multi-Sectoral Partnerships," *Leadership* 3, no. 2 (August 2016): 211–30, at 212, https://doi.org/10.1177/1742715007076214.

25. See the discussion of measurement methodologies relevant to the social sector in Nino Antadze and Frances R. Westley, "Impact Metrics for Social Innovation: Barriers or Bridges to Radical Change?," *Journal of Social Entrepreneurship* 3, no. 2 (2012): 133–150.

26. For example, Sandra Waddock characterized social partnerships as "the voluntary collaborative efforts of actors from organizations in two or more economic sectors in a forum in which they cooperatively attempt to solve a problem or issue of mutual concern that is in some way identified with a public policy agenda item": Sandra Waddock, "A Typology of Social Partnership Organizations," *Administration & Society* 22, no. 4 (1991): 480–516, at 481–82.

27. Overlapping characteristics of cross-sector partnerships include "1) they have formal autonomous actors, each with . . . objectives and resources, decid[ing] whether . . . to provide certain services in exchange with other actors. 2) Interactions between the participants are framed by . . . contractual or informal organization—[whereby] complementary resources are combined to serve jointly defined functions. 3) Participating actors are tied into different institutional arrangements roughly described by the generic terms 'government,' 'market,' and 'society'": Maria Oppen, Detlef Sack, and Alexander Wegener, "German Public-Private Partnerships in Personal Social Services: New Directions in a Corporatist Environment," in *The Challenge of Public-Private Partnerships: Learning from International Experience*, ed. Graeme Hodge and Carsten Greve (Cheltenham, UK: Edward Elgar, 2005), 269–89, at 270.

28. These characteristics are adapted from the White House Domestic Policy Council "Partnerships" perspective, with contributions from or coauthored by Howard W. Buffett, https://obamawhitehouse.archives.gov/administration/eop/sicp/initiatives/partnerships.

29. This characteristic is similar to how organizations engage in "mutually reinforcing activities" as described by John Kania and Mark Kramer, "Collective Impact," *Stanford Social Innovation Review* (Winter 2011), https://ssir.org/articles/entry/collective_impact.

30. See the concept of shared investment risk discussed in the "cooperation perspective" (6) as well as "mutual incremental reinforcement" (52), in Ranjay Gulati, Franz Wohlgezogen, and Pavel Zhelyazkov,

*The Two Facets of Collaboration: Cooperation and Coordination in Strategic Alliances,* 2012, http://nrs.harvard.edu/urn-3:HUL.Inst Repos:10996795.

31. This characteristic is similar to the "integrative stage" of the cross-sector collaboration continuum as described in James Austin, "Connecting With Non-Profits," *Working Knowledge: Business Research for Business Leaders* (October 2001), hbswk.hbs.edu/item/connecting -with-nonprofits.

32. These advantages are adapted from the White House Domestic Policy Council "Partnerships" perspective, with contributions from or coauthored by Howard W. Buffett, https://obamawhitehouse.archives.gov /administration/eop/sicp/initiatives/partnerships.

33. James E. Austin and Maria May Seitanidi, "Collaborative Value Creation: A Review of Partnering Between Nonprofits and Businesses. Part 2: Partnership Processes and Outcomes," *Nonprofit and Voluntary Sector Quarterly* 41, no. 6 (2012): 929–68, journals.sagepub.com/doi /pdf/10.1177/0899764012454685.

34. John A. Pearce II and Jonathan P. Doh, "The High Impact of Collaborative Social Initiatives," *MIT Sloan Management Review* 46, no. 3 (2005): 30, www.researchgate.net/profile/John_Pearce4/publication /242424545_The_High_Impact_of_Collaborative_Social/links /02e7e529bc6e5b3450000000.pdf.

35. Adapted from Department of State, *Quadrennial Diplomacy and Development Review, Leading Through Civilian Power,* December 15, 2010, 68, www.state.gov/documents/organization/153108.pdf.

36. Donna J. Wood and Barbara Gray, "Toward a Comprehensive Theory of Collaboration," *Journal of Applied Behavioral Science* 27, no. 2 (1991): 139–62, https://doi.org/ 10.1177/0021886391272001.

37. Pearce and Doh, "The High Impact of Collaborative Social Initiatives."

38. Janine Nahapiet and Sumantra Ghoshal, "Social Capital, Intellectual Capital, and the Organizational Advantage," *Academy of Management Review* 23, no. 2 (1998): 242–66, http://eli.johogo.com/Class/p18 .pdf.

39. These functions are adapted from U.S. Department of State's Policy Framework and Legal Guidelines for Partnerships, February 2011.

40. Julia Streets, "Partnerships for Sustainable Development: On the Road to Implementation," *The Seed Initiative Partnerships Report 2006,* Global Public Policy Institute, 2006, www.gppi.net/fileadmin/user_upload /media/pub/2006/Steets_2006_Partnerships.pdf.

41. Sandra A. Waddock and James E. Post, "Catalytic Alliances for Social Problem Solving," *Human Relations* 48, no. 8 (August 1995): 951–73, https://doi.org/10.1177/001872679504800807.

42. See discussion of the "Social Issues Platform," in John W. Selsky and Barbara Parker, "Cross-Sector Partnerships to Address Social Issues: Challenges to Theory and Practice," *Journal of Management* 31, no. 6 (December 2005): 849–73, at 852.

43. Nancy C. Roberts and Raymond Trevor Bradley, "Stakeholder Collaboration and Innovation: A Study of Public Policy Initiation at the State Level," *Journal of Applied Behavioral Science* 27, no. 2 (June 1991): 209–27.

44. Beth Eschenfelder, "Funder-Initiated Integration," *Nonprofit Management and Leadership* 21, no. 3 (Spring 2011): 273–88. https://doi .org/10.1002/nml.20025.

45. See the discussion of implementation roles in the section titled "The Developmental Process of Successful Partnership Working," in Sue Childs and Sharon Dobbins, "The Research-Practice Spiral," *VINE* 33, no. 2 (2003): 51–64, https://doi.org/10.1108/03055720310509073.

46. Ronald McQuaid, "The Theory of Partnerships—Why Have Partnerships?" in *Managing Public-Private Partnerships for Public Services: An International Perspective*, ed. S. P. Osborne (London: Routledge, 2000), 9–35.

47. One formal definition of stakeholder is given by Herman Brouwer and Jim Woodhill: "someone who can affect, or is affected by, decisions about an issue that concerns him or her." In Brouwer and Woodhill, *The MSP Guide: How to Design and Facilitate Multi-Stakeholder Partnerships* (Rugby, UK: Wageningen University and Research, 2015), 18. Because this is an extremely broad classification, delineating a vested interest is important for defining the scope of active stakeholder engagement. For a further discussion on this subject and strategies for stakeholder identification and mapping, see Brouwer and Woodhill.

48. Gulati, Wohlgezogen, and Zhelyazkov, "The Two Facets of Collaboration."

49. Howard W. Buffett served as a final round judge for the prize. For more information, see Mark A. Hager and Tyler Curry, *Models of Collaboration; Nonprofit Organizations Working Together*, The Collaboration Prize, ASU Lodestar Center, https://lodestar.asu.edu/sites/default/files/coll _models_report-2009.pdf.

50. In Hager and Curry, *Models of Collaboration*, this model is titled a "Joint Program Office," 4.

51. This model was one of the more common across the approximately 600 partnerships submitted to the Collaboration Prize. It is referred to as a "Joint Partnership with Affiliated Programming" in Hager and Curry, *Models of Collaboration*, 5.

52. This may be a useful structure when organizations engage in lobbying activity. The model is referred to as a "Joint Partnership for Issue Advocacy" in Hager and Curry, *Models of Collaboration*, 6.

53. Model 6 is otherwise called a "Joint Partnership with the Birth of a New Formal Organization" in Hager and Curry, *Models of Collaboration*, 7.

54. This model is similar in nature to the Affiliated Programming model but centered on organizational administration. It is referred to as "Joint Administrative Office and Back Office Operations" in Hager and Curry, *Models of Collaboration*, 8.

55. Described simply as a "Confederation" in Hager and Curry, *Models of Collaboration*, 8. An example type organization is the Independent Sector, a national membership organization for philanthropic organizations. See more at http://independentsector.org/.

56. This is referred to as a "Partially-Integrated Merger" in Hager and Curry, *Models of Collaboration*, 3.

57. For additional related resources, visit the Collaboration Hub hosted by the Foundation Center's GrantSpace at http://grantspace.org /collaboration.

58. Carol Hirschon Weiss, "Nothing as Practical as Good Theory: Exploring Theory-Based Evaluation for Comprehensive Community Initiatives for Children and Families," in *New Approaches to Evaluating Community Initiatives: Concepts, Methods, and Contexts*, ed. James Connell et al. (Washington, D.C.: Aspen Institute, 1995).

59. Andrea Anderson, "An Introduction to Theory of Change," *The Evaluation Exchange* 11, no. 2 (2005), www.hfrp.org/evaluation /the-evaluation-exchange/issue-archive/evaluation-methodology /an-introduction-to-theory-of-change.

60. For more details on conducting a theory of change analysis, see James P. Connell and Anne C. Kubisch, "Applying a Theory of Change Approach to the Evaluation of Comprehensive Community Initiatives: Progress, Prospects and Problems," in *New Approaches to Evaluating Community Initiatives, Vol. 2, Theory, Measurement and Analysis* ed. K. Fullbright-Anderson, Anne C. Kubisch, and James P. Connell (Washington, D.C.: Aspen Institute, 1998).

61. Centers for Disease Control and Prevention, *A Structured Approach to Effective Partnering; Lessons Learned from Public and Private Sector Leaders*, www.cdc.gov/phpr/partnerships/documents/a_structured_approach _to_effective_partnering.pdf.

62. Institute for Strategy and Competitiveness, *The Value Chain*, www.isc .hbs.edu/strategy/business-strategy/pages/the-value-chain.aspx.

63. Description adapted from the United Nations Global Compact, *Unchaining Value; Innovative Approaches to Sustainable Supply*, www .unglobalcompact.org/library/99.

64. Hallie Preskill and Srik Gopal, "Evaluating Complexity Propositions for Improving Practice." *FSG*, www.thecapacitygroup.org/uploads /2/0/9/3/20932388/evaluating_complexity.pdf.

65. Srik Gopal, "Evaluating Complex Social Initiatives," *Stanford Social Innovation Project Review* 4 (March 2015), ssir.org/articles/entry /evaluating_complex_social_initiatives.

66. John Kania and Mark Kramer, "Collective Impact," *Stanford Social Innovation Review* (2011), ssir.org/articles/entry/collective_impact.

67. Dwayne Spradlin, "Are You Solving the Right Problem?" *Harvard Business Review* (September 2012), hbr.org/2012/09/are-you-solving -the-right-problem.

68. For additional related discussion in the context of humanitarian response supply chains, see Jérôme Chandes and Gilles Paché, "Investigating Humanitarian Logistics Issues: From Operations Management to Strategic Action," *Journal of Manufacturing Technology Management* 21, no. 3 (2010): 320–40, http://dx.doi.org.ezproxy.cul.columbia.edu/10.1108 /17410381011024313.

69. Of the 2.5 billion people in poor countries living directly from the food and agriculture sector, 1.5 billion of them live in households that operate smallholder farms. UN FAO, *Smallholders* (fact sheet), www.fao .org/fileadmin/templates/nr/sustainability_pathways/docs/Factsheet _SMALLHOLDERS.pdf.

70. For additional discussion on this subject, see Howard W. Buffett, Erik Chavez, and Gordon Conway, "How Partnerships Can Create Resilient Food Supply Chains," *The Aspen Institute Journal of Ideas* (October 31, 2016), www.aspeninstitute.org/aspen-journal-of-ideas /partnerships-create-resilient-food-supply-chains/.

71. For a discussion and study of similar challenges in the context of NGO and government collaboration in response to health service delivery needs in Sudan, see: I A Yagub A, "Collaboration Between Government and Non-Governmental Organizations (NGOs) in Delivering Curative Health Services in North Darfur State, Sudan—a National Report," *Iranian Journal of Public Health* 43, no. 5 (2014): 561–71.

72. Eva Sorensen and Jacob Torfing, "Introduction: Collaborative Innovation in the Public Sector," *Innovation Journal* 17, no. 1 (2012): 1–14, www.innovation.cc/volumes-issues/intro_eva_sorensen_torfing_17v1i1 .pdf.

73. Emmanuel Lazega and Lise Mounier, "Interdependent Entrepreneurs and the Social Discipline of Their Cooperation: A Research Programme

for Structural Economic Sociology in a Society of Organizations," in *Conventions and Structures in Economic Organization: Markets, Networks, and Hierarchies* (Cheltenham, UK: Edward Elgar, 2002).

# 5. THE PEOPLE CASE

1. Central Park, *Visitor Information*, http://www.centralparknyc.org/visit/faq.html#visit.
2. Sara Ceder Miller, *Seeing Central Park* (New York: Abrams, 2009), 10.
3. Ted Smalley Bowen and Adam Stepan, "Public-Private Partnerships for Green Space in NYC," 2014, School of International and Public Affairs, Columbia University, Case Study, SIPA-14-0005.4.
4. Miller, *Seeing Central Park*, 26.
5. Tammany Hall was the common nickname for the Democratic Party corruption machine that ran the government in New York City in the post–Civil War period until well into the early decades of the twentieth century. Its rise coincided with the waves of Irish Catholic immigrants coming into the city during that period. For many, the cartoons of Thomas Nast depicting Tammany Boss William M. Tweed symbolizes the graft, corruption, and election fraud associated with the machine. The progressive era reform movement, led by the Bureau of Municipal Research and the Citizens Union, began the decline of Tammany Hall with the election of Columbia University President Seth Low as mayor in 1902, but Tammany took City Hall back two years later. Tammany's power was basically usurped by the New Deal programs of Franklyn Roosevelt. Nevertheless, the machine limped along, primarily at the borough and community levels, into the 1960s.

   For a brief history of Tammany Hall and the reform of the New York City Democratic Party, see Vincent J. Cannato, "Big Blue Machine," *The Weekly Standard*, April 14, 2014.
6. New York City Department of Parks and Recreation, "Olmstead—Designed New York City Parks," accessed March 15, 2017, at https://www.nycparks.org/about/history/olmstead-parks.
7. New York City Department of Parks and Recreation, "Olmstead."
8. Miller, *Seeing Central Park*, 27.
9. Robert Caro, *The Power Broker* (New York: Alfred A. Knopf, 1974), 331.
10. Caro, *The Power Broker*, 331.
11. Caro, *The Power Broker*, 335.
12. Caro, *The Power Broker*, 336.
13. Caro, *The Power Broker*, 356–63.

14. The Living New Deal, *Central Park Improvements—New York NY*, July 23, 2015, https://livingnewdeal.org/projects/central-park-improvements-new-york-ny/.

15. Caro, *The Power Broker*, 378–79. According to Caro, Moses was in the New York papers in 1934 even more than J. Edgar Hoover and his "Public Enemies" campaign.

16. Miller, *Seeing Central Park*, 28.

17. Miller, *Seeing Central Park*, 28.

18. Caro, *The Power Broker*, 1026–39.

19. The World's Fair position gave Moses global recognition and power, and the salary and fourteen-year contract gave him the financial resources he needed to care for his very ill wife, equally sick daughter, and the college tuitions of his grandson and granddaughter. Caro, *The Power Broker*, 1040–66. For an excellent summary of the World's Fair, see Lisa L. Colangelo, "1964 World's Fair: When the World Came to Queens," *New York Daily News*, accessed March 29, 2017, http://creative.nydailynews.com/worldsfair.

20. American Planning Association, "Central Park: New York, New York," *Great Places in America: Public Spaces*, accessed March 28, 2017, www.planning.org/greatplaces/spaces/2008/centralpark.htm.

21. Kim Phillips-Fein, "The Legacy of the 1970s Fiscal Crisis," *The Nation*, April 16, 2013.

22. Phillips-Fein, "The Legacy of the 1970s Fiscal Crisis."

23. The New York Preservation Archive Project, *Central Park*, accessed March 29, 2017, www.nypap.org/preservation-history/central-park/.

24. Bowen and Stepan, "Public-Private Partnerships for Green Space in NYC," 2.

25. Franklin E. Zimring, *The City That Became Safe* (New York: Oxford University Press, 2012), 116, 232, 125–32; James Q. Wilson and George Keiling, "Broken Windows, the Police and Neighborhood Safety," *Atlantic Monthly*, March 1982.

26. *Public Private Partnerships for Parks*, School of International and Public Affairs Video Case Study, SIPA-14-0005.4, 2014.

27. Central Park Conservancy, *History*, http://centralparknyc.org/about/history.html.

28. "Central Park Jogger Case (1989)," *New York Times*, July 6, 2017, www.nytimes.com/topic/subject/central-park-jogger-case-1989.

29. George James, "New York Killings Set a Record, While Other Crimes Fell in 1990," *New York Times*, April 23, 1991.

30. Haeyoun Park and Josh Katz, "Murder Rates Rose in a Quarter of the Nation's 100 Largest Cities," *New York Times*, September 8, 2016.

31. More than half a million people live within a ten-minute walk from the park and over 1.1 million can reach it in less than thirty minutes via

public transportation. Central Park Conservancy, *2014 Press Kit*, http://www.centralparknyc.org.

32. A comprehensive guide to what Central Park means to New York is Miller, *Seeing Central Park*.

33. E. S. Savas et al., *A Study of Central Park* (New York: Columbia University, 1976).

34. Savas et al., *A Study of Central Park*, 3–45.

35. Eimicke served in the Koch administration from 1978 to 1982 in the Office of Management and Budget and then as Deputy Commissioner for Property Management in the Department of Housing Preservation and Development. Similar to Gordon Davis, Eimicke realized the only way to do significantly more with fewer city funds was to find partners. In housing, the partners included community-based housing groups, banks, foundations, private developers, and federal Community Development Block Grant funds.

36. *Public Private Partnerships for Parks*, School of International and Public Affairs.

37. Bowen and Stepan, "Public-Private Partnerships for Green Space in NYC," 3.

38. Bowen and Stepan, "Public-Private Partnerships for Green Space in NYC," 3–4.

39. *Public Private Partnerships for Parks*, School of International and Public Affairs.

40. *Public Private Partnerships for Parks*, School of International and Public Affairs.

41. Bowen and Stepan, "Public-Private Partnerships for Green Space in NYC," 4.

42. Bowen and Stepan, "Public-Private Partnerships for Green Space in NYC," 4.

43. Interview with Doug Blonsky, March 28, 2017.

44. Interview with Doug Blonsky, December 1, 2016.

45. Bowen and Stepan, "Public-Private Partnerships for Green Space in NYC," 5.

46. Bowen and Stepan, "Public-Private Partnerships for Green Space in NYC."

47. Bowen and Stepan, "Public-Private Partnerships for Green Space in NYC," 6.

48. Andrew L. Yarrow, "In New York's Parks, More Litter and Less Money," *New York Times*, August 13, 1990.

49. Interview with Douglas Blonsky, December 1, 2016.

50. Douglas Martin, "Private Group Signs Central Park Deal to Be Its Manager," *New York Times*, February 12, 1998.

51. Martin, "Private Group Signs Central Park Deal," 7.
52. CPC, *Financial and Legal Info*, accessed September 14, 2016, www .centralparknyc.org/about/about-cpc/financial-legal-information. html; and Interview with Doug Blonsky, April 5, 2017.
53. Interview with Doug Blonsky, December 1, 2016.
54. Central Park Conservancy, *History*.
55. Lisa W. Foderaro, "A $100 Million Thank-You for a Lifetime's Central Park Memories," *New York Times*, October 23, 2012.
56. Robin Pogrebin, "Central Park, Bucolic but Aging, Is in a Quest for $300 Million," *New York Times*, July 13, 2016.
57. Interview with Doug Blonsky, March 29, 2017.
58. Central Park Conservancy, *Institute for Urban Parks* (booklet), 2015.
59. Appleseed, *The Central Park Effect*, November 2015, 10, http://assets .centralparknyc.org/pdfs/about/The_Central_Park_Effect.pdf.
60. EMPA Capstone Class, "The Certified Urban Park Manager," *SIPA, Columbia University*, April 2016.
61. Appleseed, *Valuing Central Park's Contribution to New York's Economy*, 2009, http://landscapeperformance.org/fast-fact-library/property-value -premium-within-3-blocks-of-central-park.
62. Interview with Doug Blonsky, January 30, 2018.
63. Appleseed, *The Central Park Effect*, 10; and Interview with Doug Blonsky, April 5, 2017.
64. Appleseed, *The Central Park Effect*, 9.
65. Central Park Conservancy, *History*.
66. On December 12, 2017, the Central Park Conservancy announced that Elizabeth Smith, former Assistant NYC Parks Commissioner under Mike Bloomberg and Institute for Urban Parks board member would succeed the retiring Doug Blonsky as CEO of CPC. She indicated she would remain on the Institute board, signaling the importance of CPC's expanding role in education and sharing best practices to improve urban parks throughout New York City and around the world. James Barron, "A New Leader for Central Park," *New York Times*, December 12, 2017.
67. Joshua David and Robert Hammond, *High Line: The Inside Story of New York City's Park in the Sky* (New York: Farrar, Straus and Giroux, 2011), vii.
68. Christopher Gray, "As High Line Park Rises, a Time Capsule Remains," *New York Times*, May 28, 2008.
69. Initially known as just an elevated track when built in 1930s, David and Hammond say the High Line nickname came into use in the late 1980s. See David and Hammond, *High Line*, ix.
70. John Alschuler, former chair, Friends of the High Line, email comments received May 1, 2017.

71. In 1983, Congress passed the National Trails System Act, allowing rail lines to be "banked" for future rail use; in the interim they can be used for pedestrian or bike trails. The tracks are not "abandoned," so they can be sold, leased, or donated. CSX assumed control of Conrail in 1999. See David and Hammond, *High Line*, x.

72. Bowen and Stepan, "Public-Private Partnerships for Green Space in NYC," 8.

73. Bowen and Stepan, "Public-Private Partnerships for Green Space in NYC," 70–71.

74. Bowen and Stepan, "Public-Private Partnerships for Green Space in NYC," 8.

75. David and Hammond, *High Line*, 46.

76. Alan Tate with Marcella Eaton, *Great City Parks*, 2nd ed. (New York: Routledge, 2015), 45.

77. David and Hammond, *High Line*, 8.

78. David and Hammond, *High Line*, 38–42.

79. David and Hammond, *High Line*, 54, 69, 71, 78.

80. Comment by Lisa Switkin, principal at James Corner urban designers, in the film *Public Private Partnerships for Parks*, School of International and Public Affairs Video Case Study, SIPA-14-0005.4, 2014.

81. Bowen and Stepan, "Public-Private Partnerships for Green Space in NYC," 9.

82. Kaid Benfield, "The Original High Line: La Promenade Plantee in Paris," *The Atlantic*, July 14, 2011.

83. Benfield, "The Original High Line."

84. Bowen and Stepan, "Public-Private Partnerships for Green Space in NYC," 9.

85. Matt Chaban, "Good News and Bad News for the High Line as Chelsea Market Approved by City Planning," *New York Observer*, September 5, 2012.

86. *High Line Fact Sheet*, www.thehighline.org/about.

87. NYC Parks, *City Acquires Third Section of the High Line*, accessed May 2, 2017, www.nycgovparks.org/parks/the-high-line/dailyplant/22715; see also NYC, "Mayor Bloomberg, Speaker Quinn and Friends of the High Line Announce Opening of First Section of New York City's Newest Park," June 8, 2009, www1.nyc.gov/office-of-the-mayor/news/257-09 /mayor-bloomberg-speaker-quinn-friends-the-high-line-opening-first -section-of; and David and Hammond, *High Line*. 116–17.

88. David and Hammond, *High Line*. 71.

89. *The High Line*, New York City Economic Development Corporation, updated September 12, 2016, https://www.nycedc.com/project /high-line.

90. NYC Mayor's Office, "Mayor Bloomberg, Speaker Quinn and Friends of the High Line Break Ground on the Third and Final Section of the High Line at the Rail Yards," Press release, September 20, 2012.

91. Anne Raver, "Upstairs, a Walk on the Wild Side," *New York Times*, September 3, 2014.

92. Michael Kimmelman, "The Climax in a Tale of Green and Gritty," *New York Times*, September 19, 2014.

93. Kimmelman, "The Climax in a Tale of Green and Gritty."

94. Lisa Foderaro, "Record $20 Million Gift to Help Finish the High Line Park," *New York Times*, October 26, 2011. See also David and Hammond, *High Line*, 91, 93, 94.

95. David and Hammond, *High Line*, 115.

96. David and Hammond, *High Line*, 93–94.

97. David and Hammond, *High Line*, 114–15.

98. Kate Taylor, "After High Line's Success, Other Cities Look Up," *New York Times*, July 14, 2010.

99. Bowen and Stepan, "Public-Private Partnerships for Green Space in NYC," 11.

100. Statistics provided by Friends of the High Line, www.highline.org /about/high-line-food.

101. Foderaro, "Record $20 Million Gift to Help Finish the High Line Park."

102. Josh Barbanel, "The High Line's 'Halo Effect' on Property: Residential Values Along the Park Appreciate Faster Than Those Farther Away," *Wall Street Journal*, August 7, 2016.

103. Barbanel, "The High Line's 'Halo Effect' on Property."

104. Barbanel, "The High Line's 'Halo Effect' on Property."

105. Julie Satow, "Home on the High Line," *New York Times*, May 17, 2013.

106. Bowen and Stepan, "Public-Private Partnerships for Green Space in NYC," 12.

107. My NYCHA Development Portal, http://my.nycha.info/DevPortal /Portal.

108. Mireya Navarro, "In Chelsea, a Great Wealth Divide," *New York Times*, October 23, 2015.

109. Navarro, "In Chelsea, a Great Wealth Divide."

110. United Nations, *World Urbanization Prospects, 2014 Revision* (New York: United Nations, 2014).

111. Some people criticize conservancies as elitist and only interested in the high-profile parks in wealthy neighborhoods. In New York City, legislation has been proposed to tax conservancies and send some of their donor funds to parks with fewer resources. See Michael Powell, "Parks Department Takes a Seat Behind Nonprofit Conservancies," *New York Times*, February 3, 2014. But as Friends of the High Line Chair Emeritus John

Alshuler points out, discouraging or eliminating conservancies would only make the funding shortfalls for poorer parks worse. See Bowen and Stepan, "Public-Private Partnerships for Green Space in NYC," 13.

112. William Neuman, "5 Neglected New York City Parks to Get $150 Million for Upgrades," *New York Times*, August 18, 2016.

113. Neuman, "5 Neglected New York City Parks to Get $150 Million for Upgrades."

# 6. THE PEOPLE FRAMEWORK

1. Colin Armistead, Paul Pettigrew, and Sally Aves, "Exploring Leadership in Multi-Sectoral Partnerships," *Leadership* 3, no. 2 (August 2016): 211–30, https://doi.org/10.1177/1742715007076214.

2. Peter Drucker, *Management Challenges for the 21st Century* (New York: HarperBusiness, 1999), 9–17.

3. The scope of this chapter does not include a review of leadership theory or history. For a comprehensive analysis on those subjects, see Richard Bolden et al., *A Review of Leadership Theory and Competency Frameworks*, Centre for Leadership Studies, University of Exeter, 2003, www .researchgate.net/publication/29810623_A_Review_of_Leadership _Theory_and_Competency_Frameworks.

4. For a discussion on decentralization as well as how it relates to corporate social performance, see Elaine M. Wong et al., "The Effects of Top Management Team Integrative Complexity and Decentralized Decision Making on Corporate Social Performance," *Academy of Management Journal* 54, no. 6 (2011): 1207–28.

5. See Principle 1. Focus Collaboration on Achieving Business Results, in Michael M. Beyerlein, Sue Freedman, Craig McGee, and Linda Moran, "The Ten Principles of Collaborative Organizations," *Journal of Organizational Excellence* 22, no. 2 (2003): 51–63.

6. K. Anbuvelan, *Principles of Management* (Boston: Firewall Media, 2007), 108.

7. Wong et al., "The Effects of Top Management Team Integrative Complexity," 1211.

8. The benefits listed here are also discussed in Thomas W. Malone, *The Future of Work: How the New Order of Business Will Shape Your Organization, Your Management Style, and Your Life* (Brighton, Mass.: Harvard Business School Press, 2004).

9. Lisa Foderaro, "With 843 Acres Buffed, Central Park Leader Will Step Down," *New York Times*, June 6, 2017.

10. Shelley A. Kirkpatrick and Edwin A. Locke, "Leadership: Do Traits Matter?" *The Executive* 5, no. 2 (May 1991): 48–60.

11. Lisa Gardner and Con Stough, "Examining the Relationship Between Leadership and Emotional Intelligence in Senior Level Managers," *Leadership & Organization Development Journal* 23, no. 2 (2002): 68–78.

12. For example, many of these characteristics are found across the five themes of collaborative leadership analyzed in Jeffery A. Alexander, Maureen E. Comfort, Bryan J. Weiner, and Richard Bogue, "Leadership in Collaborative Community Health Partnerships," *Nonprofit Management and Leadership* 12 (2001): 159–75, https://doi.org/10.1002/nml.12203.

13. These characteristics are similar in nature to a "shared leadership" style, which contrasts with forms of "traditional leadership." For a study on this topic, see Michael Shane Wood, "Determinants of Shared Leadership in Management Teams," *International Journal of Leadership Studies* 1, no. 1 (2005): 64–85.

14. This is similar in concept to the idea of "creating the space for change," as discussed in Peter Senge, Hal Hamilton, and John Kania, "The Dawn of System Leadership," *Stanford Social Innovation Review* (Winter 2015), https://ssir.org/articles/entry/the_dawn_of_system_leadership.

15. For a discussion about challenges and recommendations related to decentralized team management, see Preston G. Smith and Emily L. Blanck, "From Experience: Leading Dispersed Teams," *Journal of Product Innovation Management* 19 (2002): 294–304, https://doi.org/10.1111/1540-5885.1940294.

16. For example, see McKinsey & Company, *Organizational Capacity Assessment Tool*, http://mckinseyonsociety.com/ocat/; or McKinsey & Company, *Social Impact Assessment Portal*, http://mckinseyonsociety.com/social-impact-assessment/. Social enterprises can use B-Lab's Impact Assessment platform, http://bimpactassessment.net/.

17. In the case of the High Line, the city government instituted a zoning fee of $50 per square foot for new construction above zoning height limits to help finance the partnership.

18. For example, see Laura Albareda, Josep Maria Lozano, Antonio Tencati, Atle Midttun, and Francesco Perrini, "The Changing Role of Governments in Corporate Social Responsibility: Drivers and Responses," *Business Ethics: A European Review* 17 (2008): 347–63, https://doi.org/10.1111/j.1467-8608.2008.00539.x.

19. See example in section 4.2.2 and discussion in 4.2.4 in Alyson Warhurst, "Future Roles of Business in Society: The Expanding Boundaries of Corporate Responsibility and a Compelling Case for Partnership," *Futures* 37, no. 2 (2005): 151–68, at 161–62, 163–64.

20. For example, technology business leader Nandan Nilekani brought these skills to the Digital India programs (see chapter 3).

21. For a discussion on this topic, focused on research-related cross-sector partnerships, see Henry R. Hertzfeld, Albert N. Link, Nicholas S. Vonortas, "Intellectual Property Protection Mechanisms in Research Partnerships," *Research Policy* 35, no. 6, 2006: 825–38, https://doi .org/10.1016/j.respol.2006.04.006.

22. We see this in the brief example of the Global Water Initiative led by the Howard G. Buffett Foundation (see chapter 2).

23. For a further discussion on this subject, see: "Making Markets Work for the Poor; How the Bill & Melinda Gates Foundation Uses Program-Related Investments," *Stanford Social Innovation Review* (Summer 2016), www .omidyar.com/sites/default/files/file_archive/Pdfs/MakingMarkets WorkforthePoor.pdf.

24. Joel L. Fleishman, *The Foundation: A Great American Secret; How Private Wealth Is Changing the World* (New York: PublicAffairs, 2007).

25. In the Juntos program in Brazil described in chapter 9, we see this in the work of the nonprofit organization Comunitas and their team's ability to work effectively across cities and partners.

26. For information on the role of nonprofits in cross-sector partnerships, particularly in relation to the public sector, as well as four country-specific examples, see Dennis R. Young, "Alternative Models of Government-Nonprofit Sector Relations: Theoretical and International Perspectives," *Nonprofit and Voluntary Sector Quarterly* 29, no. 1 (2000): 149–72.

27. For a discussion and case study on university partnerships, see Linda Silka et al., "Community-University Partnerships: Achieving the Promise in the Face of Changing Goals, Changing Funding Patterns, and Competing Priorities," *New Solutions: A Journal of Environmental and Occupational Health Policy* 18, no. 2 (2008): 161–75.

28. In the Afghanistan case in chapter 7, Herat University's Agriculture Faculty were critical partners in developing that area's regional projects.

29. For an applicable discussion, see Joseph Friedman and Jonathan Silberman, "University Technology Transfer: Do Incentives, Management, and Location Matter?" *Journal of Technology Transfer* 28, no. 1 (2003): 17–30.

30. See Principle 2. Leadership System, in Beyerlein, Freedman, McGee, and Moran, "The Ten Principles of Collaborative Organizations."

31. For a literature review and study on collaborative leadership qualities, including five leadership configuration types, see Helen Sullivan, Paul Williams, and Stephen Jeffares, "Leadership for Collaboration," *Public Management Review*, 14, no. 1 (2012): 41–66, at 52–55, https://doi.org /10.1080/14719037.2011.589617.

32. Skills-based capital is categorically similar to, yet more broadly defined than, "skill-based capital" found in: Lester Taylor, *Capital, Accumulation, and Money: An Integration of Capital, Growth, and Monetary Theory* (Boston: Springer Verlag 2010), 12.

33. We consider this distinct from the type of skills-based capital described in Gerard McElwee and Robert Smith, "Researching Rural Enterprise," in *Handbook of Research on Entrepreneurship: What We Know and What We Need to Know*, ed. Alain Fayolle (Northampton, Mass.: Edward Elgar, 2014), 322.

34. The importance of intellectual, or knowledge-based capital (particularly for organizational innovation) is discussed in Mohan Subramaniam and Mark A. Youndt, "The Influence of Intellectual Capital on the Types of Innovative Capabilities," *Academy of Management Journal* 48, no. 3 (2005): 450–63.

35. There are some similarities in concept to the type of leadership capital discussed in Mark Bennister, Paul 't Hart, and Ben Worthy, "Assessing the Authority of Political Office-Holders: The Leadership Capital Index," *West European Politics* 38, no. 3 (2015): 417–40, https://doi.org/10.1080/01402382.2014.954778.

36. For an alternative view on representative leadership, providing an interorganization analysis, see Martin Clarke, "A Study of the Role of 'Representative' Leadership in Stimulating Organization Democracy," *Leadership* 2, no. 4 (2006): 427–50.

37. A traditional view of transactional leadership is discussed in contrast to transforming leadership James MacGregor Burns, *Transforming Leadership* (New York: Grove Press, 2003), 22–25, 43, 48, 136, 171, 176, 180.

38. See NYC Parks, *The High Line*, www.nycgovparks.org/parks/the-high-line.

39. This carries similarities to "transformative leadership" as described by Warren Bennis and Burt Nanus, *Leaders: Strategies for Taking Charge* (New York: HarperCollins, 2007), 200–217.

40. For an in-depth discussion of social capital, see Edward L. Glaeser, David Laibson, and Bruce Sacerdote, "An Economic Approach to Social Capital," *The Economic Journal* 112 (2002): F437–F458, https://doi.org/10.1111/1468-0297.00078.

41. For additional information, see Boas Shamir et al., "The Motivational Effects of Charismatic Leadership: A Self-Concept Based Theory," *Organization Science* 4, no. 4 (1993): 577–94.

42. For a discussion of related leadership attributes, also see Drucker, *Management Challenges for the 21st Century*, 33–40.

43. A good basic discussion of organizational leadership through team management, and how to use it effectively, can be found in Steven Cohen,

William Eimicke, and Tanya Heikkula, *The Effective Public Manager*, 5th ed. (San Francisco, Calif.: Jossey-Bass, 2013), 130–39.

44. Central Park Conservancy, "Park History," http://www.centralparknyc .org/visit/park-history.html.

45. Based on analysis and interviews, McKinsey & Company, *A Guide to Measuring Advocacy and Policy*, Annie E. Casey Foundation by Organizational Research Services, http://mckinseyonsociety.com/downloads /tools/LSI/McKinsey_Learning_for_Social_Impact_white_paper.pdf.

46. See exhibits 2 and 4, in McKinsey & Company, *A Guide to Measuring Advocacy and Policy*, 10–11.

47. Experience with knowledge development often aligns with intellectual leadership skills as well as intellectual or knowledge-based capital, each described earlier in the chapter.

48. For a broader view of knowledge-based capital, see Giovanni Schiuma and Antonio Lerro, "Knowledge-Based Capital in Building Regional Innovation Capacity," *Journal of Knowledge Management* 12, no. 5 (2008): 121–36, http://dx.doi.org.ezproxy.cul.columbia.edu/10.1108 /13673270810902984.

49. E. S. Savas et al., *A Study of Central Park* (New York: Columbia University, 1976).

50. Adapted from Policy Development and Implementation, exhibits 2 and 4, McKinsey & Company, *A Guide to Measuring Advocacy and Policy*, 10–11.

51. As an example, see the joint work of the Indiana University Lilly Family School of Philanthropy and the Independent Sector, Patrick M. Rooney, Una Osili, Xiaonan Kou, Sasha Zarins, and Jonathan Bergdoll, *Tax Policy and Charitable Giving Results*, May 2017, https://scholarworks.iupui .edu/bitstream/handle/1805/12599/tax-policy170518.pdf.

52. Leaders with experience in policy development and implementation often carry representative leadership skills and have well-established political-based capital.

53. Adapted from the category Enabling Systems and Infrastructure Development, exhibits 2 and 4, McKinsey & Company, *A Guide to Measuring Advocacy and Policy*, 10–11.

54. As an example, see the work profiled in Howard W. Buffett and Adam Stepan, "Aid or Investment? Post-Conflict Development in DRC and Rwanda," Columbia University School of International and Public Affairs Case Consortium, 2018, SIPA-18-0016.0.

55. Experience with enabling systems and infrastructure development may align with a combination of skills and capital previously described, including transactional leadership skills from a systems or infrastructure financing perspective.

56. Presentation, "Central Park Conservancy Institute for Urban Parks; Programming in Central Park," section titled "A Look Into The Future," 30, October 16, 2014.

57. Adapted from the combined categories of Capacity Enhancement and Skills Development and Behavior Change Programs, exhibits 2 and 4, McKinsey & Company, *A Guide to Measuring Advocacy and Policy*, 10–11.

58. As an example, see Nikki Shechtman, Louise Yarnall, Regie Stites, and Britte Haugan Cheng, *Empowering Adults to Thrive at Work: Personal Success Skills for 21st Century Jobs. A Report on Promising Research and Practice* (Chicago, Ill.: Joyce Foundation, 2016).

59. Programmatic experience in this category is often associated with the types of inspirational leadership skills and social capital described in the previous section.

60. Adapted from the category Service / Product Development and Delivery, exhibits 2 and 4, McKinsey & Company, *A Guide to Measuring Advocacy and Policy*, 10–11.

61. For an example of these types of services, see Feeding America, *Hunger in America 2014*, http://help.feedingamerica.org/HungerInAmerica/hunger-in-america-2014-full-report.pdf.

62. Experience with service and product development or delivery often aligns with organizational leadership skills, such as the effective sequencing and planning of activities in a partnership.

63. Vanessa Urch Druskat and Steven B. Wolff, *Building the Emotional Intelligence of Groups*, March 2001, https://hbr.org/2001/03/building-the-emotional-intelligence-of-groups.

64. *Public Private Partnerships for Parks*, School of International and Public Affairs Video Case Study, SIPA-14-0005.4, 2014.

65. Daniel Shapiro, *Negotiating the Nonnegotiable; How to Resolve Your Most Emotionally Charged Conflicts* (New York: Viking, 2016), 13.

66. Shapiro, *Negotiating the Nonnegotiable*, 15.

67. Shapiro, *Negotiating the Nonnegotiable*, 15.

68. In *Negotiating the Nonnegotiable*, Shapiro refers to this as "allegiances," 15.

69. In *Negotiating the Nonnegotiable*, Shapiro refers to this as "emotionally meaningful experiences," 15.

70. See the discussion of "emergent reciprocal influence" as it relates to distributed leadership in a collaborative context, Sheldon T. Watson and Jay Paredes Scribner, "Beyond Distributed Leadership: Collaboration, Interaction, and Emergent Reciprocal Influence," *Journal of School Leadership* 17, no. 4 (2007): 443–68, at 461.

71. Bryan Walker and Sarah Soule, "Changing Company Culture Requires a Movement, Not a Mandate," *Harvard Business Review* (June 20, 2017), https://hbr.org/2017/06/changing-company-culture-requires-a-movement-not-a-mandate.

72. Ted Smalley Bowen and Adam Stepan, "Public-Private Partnerships for Green Space in NYC," 3, 2014, School of International and Public Affairs, Columbia University, Case Study, SIPA-14-0005.4.

73. This was done under the federal Comprehensive Employment and Training Act. For more information, see "The Labor Department in The Carter Administration: A Summary Report—January 14, 1981," U.S. Department of Labor, www.dol.gov/oasam/programs/history/carter-eta .htm.

74. The Urban Park Rangers also served as an important uniformed and visible presence to help monitor activities in the park. For more information, see "Urban Park Rangers," New York City Department of Parks & Recreation, www.nycgovparks.org/programs/rangers.

75. Some of these strategies, including items one and two, overlap with or reinforce those identified by John P. Kotter, *Leading Change* (Brighton, Mass.: Harvard Business Review Press, 2012).

76. See principles of collaborative leadership and the discussion on the leader's role in building broad-based involvement, David D. Chrislip and Carl E. Larson, *Collaborative Leadership: How Citizens and Civic Leaders Make a Difference* (San Francisco, Calif.: Jossey-Bass, 1994), 138–46.

77. See Principle 6. Standards for Discussions, Dialogue, and Information Sharing, Beyerlein, Freedman, McGee, and Moran, "The Ten Principles of Collaborative Organizations," 51–63.

78. See Principle 9. Treat Collaboration as a Disciplined Process, Beyerlein, Freedman, McGee, and Moran, "The Ten Principles of Collaborative Organizations," 51–63.

79. An example of this took place in the High Line partnership when Joshua David and Robert Hammond organized and led their community in the fight to preserve the High Line and overcome challenges presented by City Hall.

80. See principles of collaborative leadership and discussion on the leader's role in sustaining hope and participation among team members, Chrislip and Larson, *Collaborative Leadership*, 138–46.

81. Perhaps the most visible supporter of the High Line partnership was Mayor Michael Bloomberg, who dedicated time and energy to recognize significant progress (for example, by announcing major gifts to the partnership). He also publicly recognized the quality of work and the importance of the partnership (seen in 2010 when he presented the Freedman Award to Friends of the High Line). See "Mayor Bloomberg Presents 2010 Doris C. Freedman Award to Friends of the High Line," City of New York, June 16, 2010, www1.nyc.gov/office-of-the-mayor /news/270-10/mayor-bloomberg-presents-2010-doris-c-freedman -award-friends-the-high-line#/6.

82. For further information, see David A. Buchanan et al., "No Going Back: A Review of the Literature on Sustaining Organizational Change," *International Journal of Management Reviews* 7 (2005): 189–205, https://doi.org/10.1111/j.1468-2370.2005.00111.x.

83. However, leaders should be aware of the risks of escalating commitment. For more information, see Joel Brockner, "The Escalation of Commitment to a Failing Course of Action: Toward Theoretical Progress," *Academy of Management Review* 17, no. 1 (1992): 39–61.

84. This does not speak to a partnership's brand story per se, but it is a useful perspective on the topic of brand narrative and longevity. Terry Smith, "Brand Salience Not Brand Science: A Brand Narrative Approach to Sustaining Brand Longevity," *The Marketing Review* 11, no. 1 (Spring 2011): 25–40, https://doi.org/10.1362/146934711X565279.

85. This is a further adaptation from the discussion in Shapiro, *Negotiating the Nonnegotiable*.

86. Bowen and Stepan, *Public-Private Partnerships for Green Space in NYC.*

87. James Barron, "A New Leader for Central Park," *New York Times*, December 12, 2017.

88. Howard W. Buffett worked with Daniel Shapiro to adapt ideas from his book, *Negotiating the Nonnegotiable*, and from the work of the Harvard International Negotiation Program (see: http://inp.harvard.edu/). The concept of *cross-sector team identity* resulted from numerous discussions and interviews, including a day-long session in Cambridge, Mass., on November 30, 2017.

89. Anbuvelan, *Principles of Management*, 105.

90. For example, there are statutory limits on the number and composition of staff in offices and departments of the White House. See "3 U.S. Code § 107—Domestic Policy Staff and Office of Administration; Personnel," Cornell Law School, Legal Information Institute: www.law.cornell.edu /uscode/pdf/uscode03/lii_usc_TI_03_CH_2_SE_107.pdf.

91. Developed as the Certified Urban Park Manager (CUPM) education, training, examination, and certification program through the Institute for Urban Parks. CPC is now using the curricula it developed and its practitioner "faculty" for in-house training in horticulture, turf management, zone management, and waste management to train Parks Department personnel working in the smaller public parks throughout the city.

92. Mark L. Davison, *The Challenges We Face Managing Those External (and Internal) Consultants!* Paper presented at PMI® Global Congress, 2009, Orlando, Florida, www.pmi.org/learning/library/challenges -managing-external-internal-consultants-6670.

93. The Convene, Coordinate, and Catalyze construct is adapted from Robert Lalka, "Tilting the Balance Away from a Multi-Polar World and

Toward a Multi-Partner World," U.S. Department of State Global Partnership Initiative, *UN-Business Focal Point* 12 (August 2009): 57.

94. Siv Vangen and Chris Huxham, "Enacting Leadership for Collaborative Advantage: Dilemmas of Ideology and Pragmatism in the Activities of Partnership Managers," *British Journal of Management* 14 (December 2003): S61–S76.


# 7. THE PLACE CASE

1. Interagency Counterinsurgency Initiative, *U.S. Government Counterinsurgency Guide*, January 2009, www.state.gov/documents/organization/119629.pdf.
2. Robert M. Gates, Secretary of Defense, "Continuation of Task Force for Business and Stability Operations," Memorandum (Washington, D.C.: U.S. Department of Defense, March 25, 2010).
3. David J. Berteau, Hardin Lang, Ashley Chandler, Matthew Zlatnik, Tara Callahan, and Thomas Patterson, *Final Report on Lessons Learned: Department of Defense Task Force for Business and Stability Operations*, Center for Strategic and International Studies, June 14, 2010, www.csis.org/analysis/final-report-lessons-learned.
4. Interagency Counterinsurgency Initiative, *U.S. Government Counterinsurgency Guide*.
5. Ashraf Ghani and Clare Lockhart, *Fixing Failed States: A Framework for Rebuilding a Fractured World* (Oxford, England: Oxford University Press, 2008), 48.
6. S. Rebecca Zimmerman, Daniel Egel, and Ilana Blum, *Task Force for Business and Stability Operations: Lessons from Afghanistan* (Santa Monica, Calif.: RAND Corporation, 2016).
7. Based on various discussions with General David Petraeus between February 24, 2010, and September 28, 2016. General Petraeus served as the Combatant Commander in charge of U.S. Central Command during the early development of the DoD team's agricultural sector strategy.
8. Some adaptation of social value investing principles to conflict-related environments resulted from a White House convening regarding a proposed working group, "A Working Group for Coordinating Stability," June 22, 2010, which was joined by attendees from more than twenty federal agencies or offices.
9. CIA World Factbook, *Afghanistan Country Profile*, www.cia.gov/library/publications/the-world-factbook/geos/af.html.

10. UNESCO, *Afghanistan Country Profile*, www.uis.unesco.org/DataCentre /Pages/country-profile.aspx?code=AFG&regioncode=40535.
11. CIA World Factbook, *Afghanistan Country Profile*.
12. U.S. Department of Agriculture, Foreign Agricultural Service, "2011 Afghan Agricultural Economy Update," 4, July 9, 2011.
13. World Bank, *Afghanistan—Agricultural Sector Review: Revitalizing Agriculture for Economic Growth, Job Creation, and Food Security* (Washington, D.C.: World Bank Group, 2014), http://documents.worldbank.org /curated/en/245541467973233146/Afghanistan-Agricultural-sector -review-revitalizing-agriculture-for-economic-growth-job-creation-and -food-security.
14. Christopher Ward, David Mansfield, Peter Oldham, and William Byrd, *Afghanistan: Economic Incentives and Development Initiatives to Reduce Opium Production* (Washington, D.C.: DFID and World Bank, 2008), http://documents.worldbank.org/curated/en/992981467996725814 /pdf/424010fullrepo1mIncentives01PUBLIC1.pdf.
15. World Bank, *Afghanistan–State Building, Sustaining Growth, and Reducing Poverty*, A World Bank Country Study (Washington, D.C.: The World Bank, 2005), 92. Also see *Revitalizing Agriculture for Growth, Jobs, and Food Security in Afghanistan*, 2015, www.worldbank .org/en/country/afghanistan/publication/revitalizing-agriculture-for -growth-jobs-and-food-security-in-afghanistan.
16. World Bank, *Islamic Republic of Afghanistan Agricultural Sector Review*, June 2014, http://documents.worldbank.org/curated/en /245541467973233146/pdf/AUS9779-REVISED-WP-PUBLIC -Box391431B-Final-Afghanistan-ASR-web-October-31-2014.pdf.
17. Norman Borlaug Institute research estimate citing data from the Ministry of Rural Rehabilitation and Development, Government of Afghanistan, 2009.
18. Vinicius J. B. Martins et al., "Long-Lasting Effects of Undernutrition," *International Journal of Environmental Research and Public Health* 8, no 6 (2011): 1817–46, https://doi.org/10.3390/ijerph8061817.
19. United Nations World Food Program, "Purchase for Progress," Afghanistan Implementation Plan, August 31, 2009.
20. Paul Collier, *The Bottom Billion: Why the Poorest Countries Are Failing and What Can Be Done About It* (Oxford, England: Oxford University Press, 2007).
21. Ashley Jackson, *The Cost of War; Afghan Experiences of Conflict, 1978–2009*, November 2009, https://www.oxfam.org/sites/www.oxfam.org /files/afghanistan-the-cost-of-war.pdf.
22. Saswati Bopra, Iride Ceccacci, Christopher Delgado, and Robert Townsend, "Food Security and Conflict," World Development Report

2011, October 22, 2010, https://openknowledge.worldbank.org /bitstream/handle/10986/9107/WDR2011_0031.pdf;sequence=1.

23. e-Afghan Ag, *Afghan Agriculture*, accessed October 6, 2017, http:// afghanag.ucdavis.edu/.

24. Provincial employment estimated based on 2008 MRRD population and employment figures scaled up to 2010 using World Bank and CIA national growth projections, "A Strategy for Herat's Economic Development," Unpublished report, February 2011.

25. Norman Borlaug Institute research estimate, 2010.

26. Norman Borlaug Institute research estimate, 2010.

27. Income extrapolated from data provided in "Randomized Impact Evaluation of Afghanistan's National Solidarity Programme," World Bank's Trust Fund for Environmental and Socially Sustainable Development, et al. July 1, 2013.

28. Ministry of Rural Rehabilitation and Development, Government of Afghanistan.

29. For a discussion of instability in the Guzara district, see Jennifer Brick Murtazashvili, *Informal Order and the State in Afghanistan* (New York: Cambridge University Press, 2016), 237–39.

30. The scale defined risk ranging from green (safe) to amber (caution) to red (dangerous).

31. More information on the subject can be found at World Food Programme, *Women and Hunger: 10 Facts*, www.wfp.org/our-work /preventing-hunger/focus-women/women-hunger-facts.

32. Agnes Quisumbing and Lauren Pandolfelli, *Promising Approaches to Address the Needs of Poor Female Farmers: Resources, Constraints, and Interventions*, Science Direct, 2009, www.sciencedirect.com/science /article/pii/S0305750X09001806.

33. *UN Expert Calls on Countries to Empower Women to Tackle Hunger and Malnutrition*, UN News Centre, March 4, 2013, www.un.org /apps/news/story.asp?NewsID=44270#.WfAIDmiPJ3g.

34. Afghanistan Ministry of Agriculture, Irrigation and Livestock, "National Strategy on Women in Agriculture" (September 29, 2015), 7. http:// extwprlegs1.fao.org/docs/pdf/afg156955.pdf.

35. Dirk J. Bezemer and Derek Headey, "Agriculture, Development and Urban Bias," MPRA Paper 7026, (Munich, Germany: University Library of Munich, 2007).

36. *The Value Chain*, Institute for Strategy and Competitiveness, Harvard Business School, www.isc.hbs.edu/strategy/business-strategy/pages /the-value-chain.aspx. This description is adapted from the United Nations Global Compact definition found in *Unchaining Value; Innovative Approaches to Sustainable Supply*,, www.unglobalcompact.org/library/99.

37. "Healthy Food for a Healthy World: Leveraging Agriculture and Food to Improve Global Nutrition," Chicago Council on Global Affairs, April 16, 2015.
38. The Norman Borlaug Institute Team conducted in-country assessments throughout eight provinces in Afghanistan during 2010.
39. USAID Afghanistan, *Accelerating Sustainable Agriculture Program, Herat Province Agricultural Profile 2008*, http://afghanag.ucdavis.edu /country-info/Province-agriculture-profiles/reports-usaid-nais /Ag_brief_2008_Herat_rev1.doc.
40. Norman Borlaug Institute research estimate, 2010.
41. Frank G. Hoffman, "Neo-Classical Counterinsurgency?," *Parameters*, 11, Summer 2007, http://ssi.armywarcollege.edu/pubs/parameters/articles /2011winter/hoffman.pdf.
42. Detailed agricultural assessments spanned the provinces of Herat, Kabul, Nangarhar, and Balkh, with program analysis conducted in additional provinces, such as Bamyan.
43. The Borlaug Team referred to this as an "Integrated Commercial Produce Production Model."
44. Hector Maletta and Raphy Favre, *Agriculture and Food Production in Post-War Afghanistan: A Report on the Winter Agricultural Survey 2002–2003* (Kabul: FAO, 2003).
45. "A Strategy for Herat's Economic Development," Unpublished research report, February 2011.
46. See section titled "Rebuilding Afghanistan's Agriculture Sector" in *Afghanistan and Pakistan Regional Stabilization Strategy*, Department of State, Office of the Special Representative for Afghanistan and Pakistan, February 2010.
47. Description adapted from USDA's National Institute of Food and Agriculture, https://nifa.usda.gov/extension.
48. This included a pilot program to provide Defense Department Agribusiness Development Teams (ADT) with direct access to University of Nebraska-Lincoln cooperative extension knowledge, as well as an embedded cooperative extension agent assigned to an ADT on an exploratory basis.
49. For more information on the Center on Conflict and Development, visit http://condevcenter.org/.
50. For more information, see *Local Governance and Community Development* (Fact Sheet), U.S. Agency for International Development, www.usaid.gov/sites/default/files/documents/1871/Fact%20sheet %20LGCD%20FINAL%20June%202011.pdf.
51. Mark Martins, "The Commander's Emergency Response Program," *Joint Forces Quarterly* 37, no. 2 (2005): 46–52, www.dtic.mil/dtic/tr /fulltext/u2/a523853.pdf.

52. UN Food and Agriculture Organization, *Irrigation Water Management: Irrigation Water Needs*, Training Manual no. 3, 1986, www.fao.org/docrep/S2022E/s2022e06.htm.

53. Paul Kelso, "Taliban Secret Weapon: Ancient Irrigation Trenches," *National Geographic News*, November 5, 2001, http://news.national geographic.com/news/2001/11/1105_wirekarez.html.

54. U.S. Geological Survey, *Irrigation Techniques*, December 2, 2016, https://water.usgs.gov/edu/irmethods.html.

55. Valley Irrigation, *Choosing the Right Irrigation System; A Comparison of Center Pivot Irrigation and Flood Irrigation*, http://ww2.valmont.com/valley-irrigation/us/irrigation-management/irrigation-comparisons/center-pivot-vs-flood.

56. Spelling for the village varies. This use is according to the U.S. Board on Geographic Names. Information provided by Scott A. Zillmer, Senior Research Editor, Maps and Graphics at National Geographic.

57. Glen C. Shinn, Richard K. Ford, Rahmat Attaie, and Gary E. Briers, "Understanding Afghan Opinion Leaders' Viewpoints About Post-Conflict Foreign Agricultural Development: A Case Study in Herāt Province, Afghanistan," *Journal of International Agricultural & Extension Education* 19, no. 2 (Summer 2012): 27–38, https://www.aiacc.org/attachments/article/1475/Shinn-1.pdf.

58. A Herat construction and drilling company provided an initial well drilling quote on May 9, 2011, for a maximum drilling depth of 394 feet.

59. Team member field interviews and research, 2011.

60. Post-project interviews with Ghulam Jalani, head of Rabāṭ-e Pīrzādah shura, August 2013 (by Elaha Mahboob) and July 2017 (by Masoud Soheili), Herat, Afghanistan. Translations by Roya Mahboob.

61. For additional information, see the Agricultural Research Institute of Afghanistan, *Urdu Khah Research Farm*, 2017, http://aria.gov.af/?page_id=190.

62. Post-project interview with Habibullah Sabiri, head of Urdu Khan Research Farm, August 2013 (by Elaha Mahboob), Herat, Afghanistan. Translations by Roya Mahboob.

63. "Request for Expressions of Interest," Afghanistan Agricultural Inputs Project (AAIP), Afghanistan Ministry of Agriculture, Irrigation, and Livestock, http://mail.gov.af/en/tender/arm-lands-irrigation-systems-and-buildings.

64. "Procurement of Works for Construction of West Farms (Herat Urdo Agricultural Farm)-MAIL/WB/AAIP/ICB-006/W.006.1," Afghanistan Ministry of Agriculture, Irrigation, and Livestock, http://mail.gov.af/en/tender/procurement-of-works-for-construction-of-west-farms-herat-urdo-agricultural-farm-mailwbaaipicb-006w0061.

65. Food loss and spoilage is a persistent problem on a global basis. For more information, see *Global Food Losses and Food Waste* (New York: UN FAO, 2011), www.fao.org/docrep/014/mb060e/mb060e00.pdf.

66. Team member field interviews and research, 2011.

67. Postproject interviews with Zainab Sufizada, head of the Ziaratja Food Processing Center, August 2013 (by Elaha Mahboob) and July 2017 (by Masoud Soheili), Herat, Afghanistan. Translations by Roya Mahboob.

68. Norman Borlaug Institute research estimate, 2010.

69. Norman Borlaug Institute provincial assessments, Herat Province.

70. Norman Borlaug Institute research estimate, 2010.

71. Team member field interviews and research, 2011.

72. Postproject interview with Glen Shinn, former member of Norman Borlaug Institute for International Agriculture team, July 2017 (by Adam Stepan), College Station, Texas.

73. Norman Borlaug Institute research estimate, 2010.

74. Norman Borlaug Institute research estimate, 2010–11.

75. Based on interviews with Herat University Agriculture staff, February 2010.

76. "Ag College Groundbreaking Plants Seeds for Afghan Agriculture," *AgriLife TODAY*, December 8, 2010, https://today.agrilife.org/2010/12/08/ag-college-afghan-agriculture/.

77. Postproject interview with Dr. Abdullah Faiz, Dean of Herat University Agriculture Faculty, July 2017 (by Masoud Soheili), Herat, Afghanistan. Translations by Roya Mahboob.

78. Postproject interview with M. Yousof Amini, faculty member of Herat University Agriculture program, August 2013 (by Elaha Mahboob), Herat, Afghanistan. Translations by Roya Mahboob.

79. According to a postproject field report by a member of the Norman Borlaug Institute.

80. Team member field interviews and research, 2011.

81. Data provided by Herat University, 2012, including a "Herat Basic Laboratory Training and Course Syllabus."

82. Data provided by Herat University, "Basic Laboratory Training Report, DAIL & AG Faculty," May 2012.

83. Based on research and knowledge of the DoD team's efforts across program areas and throughout Afghanistan.

84. For instance, in 2011, the DoD team went through the practice of cataloging interagency meetings and collaboration. The agriculture development program alone had interacted with or briefed more than twenty distinct government and intergovernmental agencies in the course of five months between October 2010 and February 2011.

85. Zimmerman, Egel, and Blum, *Task Force for Business and Stability Operations.*

86. For example, see Ans Kolk and François Lenfant, "Business–NGO Collaboration in a Conflict Setting," *Business & Society* 51, no. 3 (June 6, 2012): 478–511, https://doi.org/10.1177/0007650312446474.

87. For example, see Howard W. Buffett, Erik Chavez, and Gordon Conway, "How Partnerships Can Create Resilient Food Supply Chains," *Aspen Institute Journal of Ideas*, October 31, 2016, www.aspeninstitute.org /aspen-journal-of-ideas/partnerships-create-resilient-food-supply-chains/.

88. According to a 2010 interview with Din Mohammed, vice president of a Guzara tomato growers association.

89. Two contributing researchers and editors for a pre-publication draft of this case were Gerry Brown and Robert Lalka.

## 8. THE PLACE FRAMEWORK

1. Fabrizio Barca, Philip McCann, and Andrés Rodríguez-Pose, "The Case for Regional Development Intervention: Place-Based Versus Place-Neutral Approaches," *Journal of Regional Science* 52 (2012): 134–52. https://doi.org/10.1111/j.1467-9787.2011.00756.x.

2. Organisation for Economic Co-Operation and Development, *How Regions Grow*, Policy Brief, March 2009, www.oecd.org/regional/searf2009 /42576934.pdf.

3. See the place-based initiative in Detroit, Michigan, Kresge Foundation, *Detroit*, http://kresge.org/programs/detroit.

4. White House, *Developing Effective Place-Based Policies for the FY 2011 Budget*, August 11, 2009, https://obamawhitehouse.archives.gov/sites /default/files/omb/assets/memoranda_fy2009/m09-28.pdf.

5. World Bank, *World Development Report 2009: Reshaping Economic Geography* (Washington, D.C.: World Bank, 2009), http://siteresources. worldbank.org/EXTAR2009/Resources/6223977-1252950831873/ AR09_Complete.pdf.

6. Aspen Institute Forum for Community Solutions and the Neighborhood Funders Group, *Towards a Better Place: A Conversation About Promising Practice in Place-Based Philanthropy*, September 8–10, 2014, http://aspencommunitysolutions.org/wp-content/uploads/2015/03 /Towards_a_Better_Place_Conference_Report.pdf.

7. Elwood M. Hopkis and James M. Ferris, Eds., *Place-Based Initiatives in the Context of Public Policy and Markets: Moving to Higher Ground*, March, 2015, http://emergingmarkets.us/wp-content/uploads/2015/03/Moving ToHigherGround.pdf .

8. For a more detailed discussion regarding geographic locality, see Andy Pike, Andrés Rodríguez-Pose, and John Tomaney, *Local and Regional Development* (London: Routledge, 2006), 35–39.

9. Description adapted from Laura Choi, "Place-Based Initiatives," *Community Investments* 22, no. 1 (Spring 2010), www.frbsf.org/community -development/files/Spring_CI_2010a.pdf.

10. Description adapted from Larkin Tackett, *Impact in Place: A Progress Report on the Department of Education's Place-Based Strategy*, June 2012, https://obamawhitehouse.archives.gov/blog/2012/06/08/impact -place-ed-releases-report-place-based-strategy.

11. See Katelyn Mack, Hallile Preskill, James Keddy, and Moninder-Mona K. Jhawar, "Redefining Expectations for Place-Based Philanthropy," *The Foundation Review* 6, no. 4 (2014): Article 6, http://scholarworks. gvsu.edu/cgi/viewcontent.cgi?article=1224&context=tfr.

12. For further discussion regarding "sense of place" and its economic value, see Roger Bolton, " 'Place Prosperity vs People Prosperity' Revisited: An Old Issue with a New Angle," *Urban Studies* 29, no. 2 (1992): 185–203.

13. S. Rebecca Zimmerman, Daniel Egel, and Ilana Blum, *Task Force for Business and Stability Operations: Lessons from Afghanistan* (Santa Monica, Calif.: RAND Corporation, 2016).

14. For discussion of a partnership life cycle, see Vivien Lowndes and Chris Skelcher, "The Dynamics of Multi-Organizational Partnerships: An Analysis of Changing Modes of Governance," *Public Administration* 76 (Summer 1998): 313–33, at 320–330.

15. John J. Forrer, *Global Governance Enterprises: Creating Multisector Collaborations* (New York: Taylor & Francis, 2016): 44.

16. There are notable examples, however, such as the "Partnerships and Partnership Management" guidelines, in World Wildlife Fund, "Resources for Implementing the WWF Project & Programme Standards," April 2007, www.panda.org/standards/3_4_partnerships_and_partner_management.

17. For definitions, tools, and a discussion on stakeholder inclusion, see the section titled "Who Is Involved in an MSP?" in Herman Brouwer and Jim Woodhill, *The MSP Guide: How to Design and Facilitate Multi-Stakeholder Partnerships*, 2nd ed. (Wageningen, The Netherlands: Wageningen University & Research, 2015), 18, http://www.mspguide.org.

18. Karin Bäckstrand, "Multi-Stakeholder Partnerships for Sustainable Development: Rethinking Legitimacy, Accountability and Effectiveness," *European Environment* 16 (2006): 290–306. https://doi.org/10.1002 /eet.425.

19. For instance, consider the implications of the findings in William Easterly, "Can Foreign Aid Buy Growth?," *Journal of Economic Perspectives* 17, no. 3 (2003): 23–48.

20. Elise R. Irwin and Kathryn D. Mickett Kennedy, "Engaging Stakeholders for Adaptive Management Using Structured Decision Analysis," in *Planning for an Uncertain Future-Monitoring, Integration, and Adaptation*, ed. Richard M. T. Webb and Darius J. Semmens, Scientific Investigations Report No. 2009–5049 (Washington, D.C.: U.S. Geological Survey, 2009).

21. Eva Schiffer and Douglas Waale, "Tracing Power and Influence in Networks," the International Food Policy Research Institute (IFPRI) Discussion Paper 00772, June 2008, 3.

22. See the discussion of "Resources Count" and "Partner Alignment & Power" in Simon Zadek and Sasha Radovich, "Governing Collaborative Governance: Enhancing Development Outcomes by Improving Partnership Governance and Accountability," AccountAbility and the Corporate Social Responsibility Initiative, Working Paper No. 23 (Cambridge, Mass.: John F. Kennedy School of Government, Harvard University, 2006), 11–16.

23. Andy Pike, Andrés Rodríguez-Pose, and John Tomaney, "What Kind of Local and Regional Development and for Whom?" *Regional Studies* 41, no. 9 (2007): 1253–69, at 1260.

24. Barca, McCann, and Rodríguez-Pose, "The Case for Regional Development Intervention."

25. For detailed, firsthand discussions on the topic, see Howard G. Buffett with Howard W. Buffett, *40 Chances: Finding Hope in a Hungry World* (New York: Simon & Schuster, 2013).

26. Fabrizio Barca, "An Agenda for a Reformed Cohesion Policy: A Place-Based Approach to Meeting European Union Challenges and Expectations," Independent Report, Prepared at the Request of the European Commissioner for Regional Policy (Brussels: European Commission, 2009).

27. Julia Steets, "The Seed Initiative Partnerships Report 2006; Partnerships for Sustainable Development: On the Road to Implementation," Global Public Policy Institute, 2006, www.gppi.net/fileadmin/user_upload /media/pub/2006/Steets_2006_Partnerships.pdf.

28. Thomas G. Pittz and Terry Adler, "An Exemplar of Open Strategy: Decision-Making Within Multi-Sector Collaborations," *Management Decision* 54, no. 7 (2016): 1595–1614.

29. Andrés Rodríguez-Pose and Michael Storper, "Better Rules or Stronger Communities? On the Social Foundations of Institutional Change and Its Economic Effects," *Economic Geography* 82, no. 1 (2006): 1–25.

30. Team core identities are adapted from Daniel Shapiro, *Negotiating the Nonnegotiable; How to Resolve Your Most Emotionally Charged Conflicts* (New York: Viking, 2016).

31. Many example lists of principles exist. For instance, see "Eight Factors for Effective Partnerships," in KPMG International, *Unlocking the Power of Partnership—A Framework for Effective Cross-Sector Collaboration to Advance the Global Goals for Sustainable Development*, 2016, 12–18, https://home.kpmg.com/content/dam/kpmg/pdf/2016/01/unlocking -power-of-partnership.pdf.

32. Brouwer and Woodhill, *The MSP Guide*, 14.

33. U.S. Department of Interior, *What Are the Keys to Creating and Managing a Successful Partnership?* accessed January 9, 2015, www.doi .gov/partnerships/keys-to-successful-partnerships.cfm.

34. Ros Tennyson, *The Partnering Toolbook; An Essential Guide to Cross-Sector Partnering*, The Partnering Initiative (IBLF), 2011, 17, https:// thepartneringinitiative.org/wp-content/uploads/2014/08/Partnering -Toolbook-en-20113.pdf.

35. John Kotter, *Leading Change* (Brighton Watertown, Mass.: Harvard Business Review Press, 2012).

36. Carmen Malena, "Strategic Partnership: Challenges and Best Practices in the Management and Governance of Multi-Stakeholder Partnerships Involving UN and Civil Society Actors," Background paper for the Multi-Stakeholder Workshop on Partnerships and UN-Civil Society Relations, Pocantico, New York, February 2004, 9.

37. Valerie Wildridge, Sue Childs, Lynette Cawthra, and Bruce Madge, "How to Create Successful Partnerships—A Review of the Literature," *Health Information & Libraries Journal* 21 (2004): 3–19, at 9, https:// doi.org/10.1111/j.1740-3324.2004.00497.x.

38. Ricardo Ramirez, "Stakeholder Analysis and Conflict Management," in *Cultivating Peace: Conflict and Collaboration in Natural Resource Management*, ed. Daniel Buckles (Ottawa, Ontario: International Development Research Center, 1999), chapter 5.

39. See the section on "Setting Ground Rules for Partnerships: Accountability, Capacity Building, and Evaluation," in Jan Martin Witte, Charlotte Streck, and Thorsten Benner, "The Road from Johannesburg: What Future for Partnerships in Global Environmental Governance?" in *Progress or Peril? Networks and Partnerships in Global Environmental Governance. The Post-Johannesburg Agenda*, ed. Thorsten Benner, Charlotte Streck, and Jan Martin Witte (Berlin: Global Public Policy Institute, 2003).

40. Pittz and Adler, "An Exemplar of Open Strategy."

41. See section on "Building GGEs," in John J. Forrer, *Global Governance Enterprises: Creating Multisector Collaborations* (New York: Taylor & Francis, 2016), 244.

42. Brouwer and Woodhill, *The MSP Guide*, 84.

43. See the type of *external accountability* discussed in Karin Bäckstrand, "Multi-Stakeholder Partnerships for Sustainable Development: Rethinking Legitimacy, Accountability and Effectiveness," *European Environment*, 16 (2006): 295, https://doi.org/10.1002/eet.425.

44. See the discussion of organizations collaborating through a "strategic alliance" (195–96) and reaching points of mutual accountability along the Collaboration Continuum (197) in Fred Mayhew, "Aligning for Impact: The Influence of the Funder–Fundee Relationship on Evaluation Utilization," *Nonprofit Management and Leadership* 23, no. 2 (2012): 193–217, https://doi.org/10.1002/nml.21045.

45. Witte, Streck, and Benner, "The Road from Johannesburg."

46. See section on "Allow Self-Determination," in Carol Reade, Anne Marie Todd, Asbjorn Osland, and Joyce Osland, "Poverty and the Multiple Stakeholder Challenge for Global Leaders," *Journal of Management Education* (2008): 820–40, https://doi.org/10.1177/1052562908317445.

47. In some cases, cross-sector partnerships use an independent entity dedicated to organizing and managing partnership activities (sometimes referred to as a backbone organization or secretariat). For example, see "The Aspen Institute Partners for a New Beginning Secretariat," a collaborative effort established by the Aspen Institute in support of the U.S. State Department, https://2009-2017.state.gov/s/partnerships/newbeginning/.

48. See section on "Resources Count" in Zadek and Radovich, "Governing Collaborative Governance," 11.

49. This is similar in concept to "Strategic Guidance," discussed in Brouwer and Woodhill, *The MSP Guide*, 129.

50. See *Developing Local Knowledge to Inform Action*, Building Neighborhood Capacity Program Practice Brief, https://www.cssp.org/community/neighborhood-investment/place-based-initiatives/body/Developing-Local-Knowledge-to-Inform-Action-Practice-Brief.pdf.

51. Bäckstrand, "Multi-Stakeholder Partnerships for Sustainable Development."

52. For a discussion of the advantages of gaining access to particular resources in a cross-sector partnership, see Bruce R. Barringer and Jeffrey S. Harrison, "Walking a Tightrope: Creating Value Through Interorganizational Relationships," *Journal of Management* 26, no. 3 (June 2000): 367–403, at table 3.

53. Barca, McCann, and Rodríguez-Pose, "The Case for Regional Development Intervention."

54. This aspect of participatory planning and decision making is discussed in Pittz and Adler, "An Exemplar of Open Strategy," 1604.

55. See *BNCP Toolkit—Resident Engagement*, December 2014, www.cssp .org/community/neighborhood-investment/place-based-initiatives /building-neighborhood-capacity.

56. Shapiro, *Negotiating the Nonnegotiable*.

57. Pike, Rodríguez-Pose, and Tomaney, *Local and Regional Development*.

58. In this instance, Zainab Sufizada provided guidance on project redesign.

59. Geoffrey Hamilton, *United Nations Economic Commission for Europe's Guidebook on Promoting Good Governance in Public-Private Partnerships* (Geneva, 2008).

60. For a brief summary of various participatory decision-making tools, see Timothy Lynam, Wil de Jong, Douglas Sheil, Trikurnianti Kusumanto, and Kirsen Evans, "A Review of Tools for Incorporating Community Knowledge, Preferences, and Values Into Decision Making in Natural Resources Management," *Ecology and Society* 12, no. 1 (2007): article 5, www.ecologyandsociety.org/vol12/iss1/art5/.

61. Multiattribute utility theory helps decision makers specify variable conditions or weighting of a set of preferences and facilitates measurement of those preferences or other values. See Rakesh K. Sarin, "Multi-Attribute Utility Theory," in *Encyclopedia of Operations Research and Management Science*, ed. Saul I. Gass and Michael C. Fu (Boston, Mass.: Springer, 2013): 1004–6.

62. For an applied example of a traditional Pugh matrix analysis, see H. Frank Cervone, "Applied Digital Library Project Management," *OCLC Systems & Services* 25, no. 4 (2009): 228–32, doi.org/10.1108/10650750911001815.

63. Ramaswamy Ramesh and Stanley Zionts, "Multiple Criteria Decision Making," *Encyclopedia of Operations Research and Management Science*, ed. Saul I. Gass and Michael C. Fu (Boston, Mass.: Springer, 2016), 1007–13.

64. Mayhew, "Aligning for Impact."

65. Developed in 2007–2008 as part of a Bill & Melinda Gates Foundation Special Initiatives team project. The team worked under the leadership of former foundation staff, including Patty Stonesifer (CEO), and included Cheryl Scott (COO), Alex Friedman (CFO), Lowell Weiss (Senior Policy and Advocacy Officer), Olivia Leland, Greg Cain, and others in the project working group.

66. Framework description is based on and adapted from an unpublished project overview, with contributions from Howard W. Buffett, August 31, 2007.

67. Framework categories based on and adapted from an unpublished project overview, with contributions from Howard W. Buffett, August 31, 2007.

68. Creech, Heather, Leslie Paas, and Miruna Oana. *Typologies for Partnerships for Sustainable Development and for Social and Environmental Enterprises: Exploring SEED Winners Through Two Lenses*, Report for the

SEED Initiative Research Program, International Institute for Sustainable Development, 2008.

69. Pittz and Adler, "An Exemplar of Open Strategy," 1601.
70. Barca, "An Agenda for a Reformed Cohesion Policy."
71. Reade, Todd, Osland, and Osland, "Poverty and the Multiple Stakeholder Challenge for Global Leaders."
72. Stephan Haggard, Andrew MacIntyre, and Lydia Tiede, "The Rule of Law and Economic Development," *Annual Review of Political Science* 11 (2008): 205–34.
73. Howard W. Buffett and Adam Stepan, "Aid or Investment? Post-Conflict Development in DRC and Rwanda," Columbia University School of International and Public Affairs Case Consortium, 2018, SIPA-18-0016.0.
74. See section on "Some Negative Aspects of Partnerships" in Leslie R. Boydell and Jorun Rugkåsa, "Benefits of Working in Partnership: A Model," *Critical Public Health* 17, no. 3 (2007): 217–228, at 224–25.

## 9. THE PORTFOLIO CASE

1. The foundation of this case comes from research conducted by Bruna Santos, Nora Shannon, Adam Stepan, Thomas Trebat and William B. Eimicke in developing a short documentary film, academic case study, and white paper on Comunitas and Juntos for SIPA's Picker Center Case Study Program at Columbia University.
2. Interview with Columbia Professor Rodrigo Soares, Columbia University Lemann Professor of Brazilian Public Policy and International and Public Affairs, quoted in Bruna Santos, Nora Shannon, and Adam Stepan, "Juntos: Mentoring Cities in Brazil," School of International and Public Affairs, Case Consortium@Columbia, Columbia University, 2017, 2, SIPA-17-0013.1.
3. Santos, Shannon, and Stepan, "Juntos," 2.
4. PricewaterhouseCoopers and World Bank, *Paying Taxes 2014: The Global Picture*, http://documents.worldbank.org/curated/en/143331468313829830/Paying-taxes-2014-the-global-picture.
5. PricewaterhouseCoopers and World Bank, *Paying Taxes 2014*, 21.
6. World Bank Group, *Doing Business 2017: Equal Opportunity for All, Economy Profile Brazil*, 2, www.doingbusiness.org/data/exploreeconomies/brazil.
7. World Bank Group, *Doing Business 2017*, 2.
8. Anderson Antunes, *The 20 Companies That Own Brazil*, Forbes.com, January 23, 2014, www.forbes.com/sites/andersonantunes/2014/01/23/the-20-companies-that-own-brazil/#37235ea82ec9.

9. Comunitas, Mission, http://www.comunitas.org/portal/?s=mission.
10. Comunitas, *Benchmarking Report on Corporate Social Investment (BISC)*, 2014, www.comunitas.org.
11. Interview with Comunitas President Regina Celia Esteves de Siqueria, quoted in Santos, Shannon, and Stepan, "Juntos," 3.
12. See Comunitas website for more details on membership at www.comunitas.org/portal/parceiros-2/.
13. Interview with Juntos board member and business leader Pedro Jereissati, in Santos, Shannon, and Stepan, "Juntos," 4.
14. Interview with Dr. Thomas Trebat, in Santos, Shannon, and Stepan, "Juntos," 5.
15. Interview with Pedro Jereissati, in Santos, Shannon, and Stepan, "Juntos," 5–6.
16. Santos, Shannon, and Stepan, "Juntos," 6–9.
17. Santos, Shannon, and Stepan, "Juntos," 7.
18. Interview with Campinas Secretary of Administration Silvio Roberto Bernardin, quoted in Santos, Shannon, and Stepan, "Juntos," 7.
19. Santos, Shannon, and Stepan, "Juntos," 7.
20. Santos, Shannon, and Stepan, "Juntos," 8.
21. Santos, Shannon, and Stepan, "Juntos," 9.
22. In January 2016, Bill Eimicke visited Campinas at the invitation of Professor Thomas Trebat, director of the Columbia University Global Center in Rio de Janeiro; Regina Celia Esteves de Siqueira, president and CEO of Comunitas; and Mayor Jonas Donizette of Campinas to see the innovations taking place in the city and speak to them about the benefits of developing a strategic plan as the next step in modernization.
23. Interview with Pelotas former mayor Eduardo Leite on May 31, 2017. Comunitas sponsored Leite to be a visiting scholar at SIPA during the spring semester of 2017 after his term as mayor.
24. "Quero Ser Um Prefeito Amigo, Diz Eduardo Leite Apos Vitoria Em Pelotas," *Eleicoes 2012 No Rio Grande Do Sul*, October 28, 2012.
25. Bruna Santos, "Juntos: Building Governance for the 21st Century: Public Private Coalition to Reform Local Government in Brazil," Picker Center Case Collection White Paper, SIPA, Columbia University, January 2017, 16–17.
26. Interview with former Mayor Eduardo Leite, May 31, 2017.
27. Santos, "Juntos: Building Governance for the 21st Century," 17.
28. Robin Banerji, "Niemeyer's Brasilia: Does It Work as a City?" *BBC Magazine*, December 7, 2012.
29. David Adler, "Story of Cities, #37: How Radical Ideas Turned Curitiba Into Brazil's 'Green Capital'," *The Guardian*, May 6, 2016.

30. Drew Reed, "How Curitiba's BRT Stations Sparked a Transport Revolution—A History of Cities in 50 Buildings, Day 43," *The Guardian*, May 26, 2015.

31. Reed, "How Curitiba's BRT Stations Sparked a Transport Revolution," 4.

32. Santos, "Juntos: Building Governance for the 21st Century," 11–12.

33. Santos, "Juntos: Building Governance for the 21st Century," 12.

34. See Simon Romero, "Michel Timer Government in Brazil Reels as Dozens Face New Graft Investigations," *New York Times*, April 11, 2017; and Amanda Taub, "How Fighting Corruption Could Imperil Brazil's Political Stability," *New York Times*, May 28, 2017.

35. Jesus Rios and Julie Ray, *Brazilians' Trust in Country's Leadership at Record Low*, Gallup News, April 7, 2016, www.gallup.com/poll/190481 /brazilians-trust-country-leadership-record-low.aspx.

36. Dom Phillips, "Brazil President Endorsed Businessman's Bribes in Secret Tape, Newspaper Says," *New York Times*, May 17, 2017.

37. "Eduardo Leite Leads the Dispute in Pelotas, Says Research," *Correio do Povo*, December 21, 2017, www.correiodopovo.com.br/Noticias/Pol %C3%ADtica/2016/5/587418/Eduardo-Leite-lidera-disputa-em -Pelotas,-aponta-pesquisa.

38. See Gregory Scruggs, "Latin America's New Superstar," *Next City*, March 31, 2014, https://nextcity.org/features/view/medellins-eternal- spring-social-urbanism-transforms-latin-america; Ashoka, "The Transfor- mation of Medellin, and the Surprising Company Behind It," *Forbes*, Jan- uary 27, 2014; and "McBains Cooper Wins PPP Consultancy Contract in Medellin, Colombia," September 20, 2017, http://www.worldhighways .com/categories/auctions-equipment-supply-servicing-finance/news /mcbains-cooper-wins-ppp-consultancy-contract-in-medellin-colombia/.

39. Santos, Shannon, and Stepan, "Juntos," 11–12.

40. Santos, Shannon, and Stepan, "Juntos," 17.

41. Pan Kwan Yuk, "Brazil's Economy Shrinks 3.6% in 2016," *Financial Times* (online), March 7, 2017, www.ft.com/content/e1c89278-c33c-3fbe -83ae-985497365cf6.

42. *Comunitas lança Cartilha de Replicabilidade de equilíbrio fiscal*, Comu- nitas.org, accessed June 21, 2017, http://www.comunitas.org/portal /comunitas-lanca-cartilha-de-replicabilidade-de-equilibrio-fiscal-2/.

## 10. THE PORTFOLIO FRAMEWORK

1. Modern portfolio theory was developed by American economist Harry Markowitz, who later won the Nobel Prize in Economics in 1990. Harry Markowitz, "Portfolio Selection," *Journal of Finance* 7, no. 1 (1952): 77–91.

2. Ian Shipway, "Modern Portfolio Theory," *Trusts & Trustees*, 15, no. 2 (2009): 66–71, https://doi.org/10.1093/tandt/ttn129.

3. To indicate his views on the subject, Markowitz stated, "a rule of behavior which does not imply the superiority of diversification must be rejected both as a hypothesis and as a maxim." Harry Markowitz, "Portfolio Selection," 77.

4. Edwin J. Elton, Martin J. Gruber, and Manfred W. Padberg, "Simple Criteria for Optimal Portfolio Selection: Tracing Out the Efficient Frontier," *Journal of Finance* 33 (1978): 296–302, https://doi.org /10.1111/j.1540-6261.1978.tb03407.x.

5. Some example types of allocations are discussed in the section on "Concessionary Investments" in Paul Brest and Kelly Born, "When Can Impact Investing Create Real Impact?" *Stanford Social Innovation Review* (Fall 2013), https://ssir.org/index_dev.php/up_for_debate /article/impact_investing.

6. This is part of the World Economic Forum's System Initiatives, *Shaping the Future of Long-Term Investing, Infrastructure and Development*, www.weforum.org/system-initiatives/shaping-the-future-of-long-term -investing-infrastructure-and-development.

7. World Economic Forum, *Overview: ReDesigning Development Finance*, www3.weforum.org/docs/WEF_ReDesigningDevelopmentFinance _Overview.pdf.

8. For a context specific discussion, see *Addis Ababa Action Agenda of the Third International Conference; Financing for Development* (New York, N.Y.: United Nations. July 13–16, 2015), 22, 24–25.

9. World Economic Forum, *Blended Finance Vol. 1: A Primer for Development Finance and Philanthropic Funders*, September 2015, www3 .weforum.org/docs/WEF_Blended_Finance_A_Primer_Development _Finance_Philanthropic_Funders_report_2015.pdf.

10. OECD, "Blended Finance; Mobilising resources for sustainable development and climate action in developing countries," October, 2017.

11. World Economic Forum and the OECD, *A How-To Guide for Blended Finance*, September 2015, www3.weforum.org/docs/WEF_Blended _Finance_How_To_Guide.pdf.

12. Brian Dunn discusses the role of the philanthropist in creating a "new efficient frontier." We disagree with some of his interpretations about the limitations of philanthropic capital as it applies to his thesis. However, the overall premise of the white paper is relevant. Brian Dunn, *Modern Portfolio Theory—With a Twist*, August 2006, www.americansforcommunity development.org/downloads/NewEfficientFrontier.pdf.

13. For additional discussion on this topic, see Michael McCreless, "Toward the Efficient Impact Frontier," *Stanford Social Innovation Review*

(Winter 2017), https://ssir.org/articles/entry/toward_the_efficient _impact_frontier.

14. The Global Impact Investing Network, *Catalytic First-Loss Capital*, October 2013, https://thegiin.org/assets/documents/pub/Catalytic FirstLossCapital.pdf.

15. This example is analogous to the partnership profiled in Howard W. Buffett and Adam Stepan, "Saved by the Soil? Africa's Frontier for Conservation-Based Agriculture," Columbia University School of International and Public Affairs Case Consortium, SIPA-17-0011.01, 2017.

16. Nicole Systrom, Sarah Kearney, and Fiona Murray, *Foundations: Exploring the Emerging Practice of Philanthropic Investing to Support Innovation in Science and Engineering*, Practice Briefing, June 2017, 3, https:// innovation.mit.edu/assets/MIT-PRIME_Foundations.pdf.

17. J. Gregory Dees, "Philanthropy and Enterprise: Harnessing the Power of Business and Social Entrepreneurship for Development," *Innovations* 3, no. 3 (2008): 119–32.

18. This is not to say that foundations can be reckless with their investment strategies or are free from all limits. Foundations cannot jeopardize their charitable mission with certain high-risk investments. IRS regulations on the subject can be found at www.irs.gov/charities-non-profits/private -foundations/private-foundation-jeopardizing-investments-defined.

19. For a more detailed description, see Sara Olson, Aislinn Betancourt, and Courtney Kemp, *The Pulse of Impact Management*, Middlebury Institute of International Studies at Monterey, February 24, 2017, https://drive .google.com/file/d/0B1vHuHdX1l33ejJzakZfVzJVWEU/view.

20. For a discussion of various public financing tools and theory, see: Lester M. Salamon, "The New Governance and the Tools of Public Action: An Introduction," *Fordham Urban Law Journal* 28, no. 5 (June 2001): 1611–1674.

21. Comunitas, *Comunitas lança Cartilha de Replicabilidade de equilíbrio fiscal*, accessed June 21, 2017, http://www.comunitas.org/portal /comunitas-lanca-cartilha-de-replicabilidade-de-equilibrio-fiscal-2/.

22. "Overseas Private Investment Corporation." *Issue: A Journal of Opinion* 8, no. 2/3 (1978): 101–03, https://doi.org/10.2307/1166668.

23. For examples and additional analysis, see charts in Jed Emerson, "The Blended Value Proposition: Integrating Social and Financial Returns," *California Management Review* 45, no. 4 (2003): 35–51, at 37–39.

24. Also see J. Gregory Dees, "Enterprising Nonprofits," *Harvard Business Review* (January-February 1998): 55–67.

25. The following is a subset of available instruments and is not meant to represent the full universe of allocation options.

26. Paper presented to Comunitas, Juntos Pelo Desenvolvimento Sustentavel, Pelotas–RS, March, 2016, 13–15.

27. Bruna Santos, Knowledge Manager, Comunitas, email comments received January 3, 2018.

28. For example, private donors underwrote financing for irrigation infrastructure that communities would not have otherwise been able to afford. This increased farmers' incomes and expanded raw commodity production enough to support local food processing enterprises. The technical assistance, training, and knowledge-sharing—all activities that would not have commercial market support in rural western Afghanistan—were financed through grants to Herat University. Taken together, these contributions created an environment for private sector participation and improved the likelihood that the rest of the cross-sector partnership would succeed.

29. For example, see the discussion of using an intermediary partner to this end in: Prime Coalition and MIT Sloan School of Management, section titled "Option B—Issue a Grant That Qualifies as Charitable to a Non-Profit Intermediary That Supports Market-Based Solutions," in *Foundations: exploring the emerging practice of philanthropic investing to support innovation in science and engineering*, Practice Briefing (June 2017): 8.

30. Internal Revenue Service, *Taxes on Failure to Distribute Income—Private Foundations*, updated August 3, 2017, www.irs.gov/charities -non-profits/private-foundations/taxes-on-failure-to-distribute-income -private-foundations.

31. The Foundation Center, *Aggregate Fiscal Data of Foundations in the U.S.*, 2014, http://data.foundationcenter.org/; see also The Foundation Center, *Foundation Research*, 2017, http://foundationcenter.org /gain-knowledge/foundation-research.

32. For comparison, $865 billion is roughly equivalent to the combined GDP of the world's ninety-six lowest producing countries. Data analyzed from the International Monetary Fund, *World Economic Outlook Database*, October 2017, www.imf.org/external/pubs/ft/weo/2017/02 /weodata/download.aspx.

33. Jonathan Greenblatt, *Opening the Door for Program Related Investments*, May 4, 2012, www.whitehouse.gov/blog/2012/05/04/opening-door -program-related-investments.

34. K. Martin Worthy, "The Tax Reform Act of 1969: Consequences for Private Foundations," *Law and Contemporary Problems* 39, no. 4 (1975): 232–54.

35. Patricia L. Rosenfield and Rachel Wimpee, "The Ford Foundation: Themes 1936–2001," The Rockefeller Archive Center, 2015, rockarch. org/publications/resrep/niedfeldt.pdf.

36. Ford Foundation, *Program-Related Investments:A Different Approach to Philanthropy*, October 1974, https://community-wealth.org/sites /clone.community-wealth.org/files/downloads/report-ford74.pdf.
37. Ford Foundation, *New Opinions in the Philanthropic Process*, A Ford Foundation Statement of Policy (New York, N.Y.: Ford Foundation, 1968).
38. Ford Foundation, *Investing for Social Gain: Reflections on Two Decades of Program-Related Investments* (New York, N.Y.: Ford Foundation, 1991), 7.
39. Worthy, "The Tax Reform Act of 1969."
40. Ford Foundation, *Investing for Social Gain.*
41. Christine Looney, *Inclusive Economies*, Ford Foundation, November 3, 2017.
42. Global Impact Investing Network, *Ford Foundation—PRI Fund IRIS Profile*, https://iris.thegiin.org/users/profile/the-ford-foundation-pri-fund.
43. Phone interview with Christine Looney, Senior Program Investment Officer, Inclusive Economies, the Ford Foundation, June 22, 2017.
44. Ford Foundation, *Investing for Social Gain*, 34.
45. Robert Mark Silverman, Ed., *Community-Based Organizations: The Intersection of Social Capital and Local Context in Contemporary Urban Society* (Detroit, Mich.: Wayne State University Press, 2004), 40.
46. Christine Looney, email message to Howard W. Buffett. November 9, 2017.
47. Ford Foundation, *Investing for Social Gain*, 35.
48. Grameen Bank, *Monthly Report: 2017–09*, Issue 453 in USD, www .grameen.com/monthly-report-2016/.
49. Grameen Bank, *About Us*, www.grameen-bank.net/about-us/.
50. Grameen Bank, *FAQ*, www.grameen-bank.net/faq/.
51. The Nobel Peace Prize for 2006, The Norwegian Nobel Committee, www.nobelprize.org/nobel_prizes/peace/laureates/2006/press.html.
52. For additional information, including detailed examples from the Gates Foundation PRI strategy, see "Making Markets Work for the Poor: How the Bill & Melinda Gates Foundation Uses Program-Related Investments," *Stanford Social Innovation Review* (Summer 2016).
53. Discussion with Ryan Kreitzer, Principal, Program-Related Investments, and others at the Bill & Melinda Gates Foundation, July 21, 2017, with follow-up on November 8, 2017.
54. Prime Coalition and MIT Sloan School of Management, "Option C— Issue a Recoverable Grant or Loan That Qualifies as Charitable to a Non-Profit Intermediary That Supports Market-Based Solutions," *Practice Briefing* (June 2017): 8.
55. Echoing Green, *Deviation from the Standard: Funding and Supporting Emerging Social Entrepreneurs*, 2015, www.echoinggreen.org/pubs /Echoing-Green-Deviation-Standard-Impact-Investing.pdf.

56. John Walker, *Introducing Recoverable Grants*, www.echoinggreen.org /ideas/introduction-to-recoverable-grants.

57. Christie Baxter, "A Basic Guide to Program-Related Investments," *The Grantsmanship Center Magazine* (Fall 1997).

58. Christie Baxter, *Program-Related Investments: A Technical Manual for Foundations* (Hoboken, N.J.: Wiley, 1997).

59. Alex Nicholls and Cathy Pharoah, *The Landscape of Social Investment: A Holistic Topology of Opportunities and Challenges*, 2008, http://eureka .sbs.ox.ac.uk/760/1/Landscape_of_Social_Investment.pdf.

60. Baxter, *Program-Related Investments*.

61. Social Finance, *Social Impact Bonds: The Early Years*, July 2016, www .socialfinance.org.uk/wp-content/uploads/2016/07/SIBs-Early-Years _Social-Finance_2016_Final-003.pdf.

62. For more information, see Nonprofit Finance Fund, *Pay for Success Scorecard: Lessons from the Vanguard of the Outcomes Movement*, September 2017, www.nff.org/sites/default/files/paragraphs/file /download/Pay%20for%20Success%20Scorecard_0.pdf.

63. Alex Nicholls and Emma Tomkinson, "The Peterborough Pilot Social Impact Bond," *Said Business School University of Oxford Case Study* (October 2013): 39.

64. See "overview" in the Rockefeller Foundation, "Social Impact Bonds: Helping State and local Governments Fund Critical Social Programs," www.rockefellerfoundation.org/our-work/initiatives/social -impact-bonds/.

65. Jennifer Maloney, "Goldman to Invest in Rikers Program," *Wall Street Journal*, August 2, 2012.

66. Donald Cohen and Jennifer Zelnick, "What We Learned from the Failure of the Rikers Island Social Impact Bond," *Nonprofit Quarterly*, August 7, 2015.

67. Eduardo Porter, "Wall Street Money Meets Social Policy at Rikers Island," *New York Times*, July 28, 2015.

68. *Impact Evaluation of the Adolescent Behavioral Learning Experience (ABLE) Program at Rikers Island. Summary of Findings*, July 2015, http:// archive.vera.org/sites/default/files/resources/downloads/adolescent -behavioral-learning-experience-evaluation-rikers-island-summary.pdf.

69. Michael R. Bloomberg, *Bringing Social Impact Bonds to New York City*, https://emmatomkinson.com/2015/07/30/rikers-island-sib-success -or-failure/.

70. Eduardo Porter, "Wall Street Money Meets Social Policy at Rikers Island," *New York Times*, July 28, 2015.

71. Nicholls and Tomkinson, "The Peterborough Pilot Social Impact Bond," 28–29.

72. To learn more about Social Impact Bonds, see Emily Gustafsson-Wright, Sophie Gardiner, and Vidya Putcha, *The Potential and Limitations of Impact Bonds: Lessons from the First Five Years of Experience Worldwide* (Washington, D.C.: Brookings Institute, July 2015).

73. RAND Corporation, *Evaluating the World's First Social Impact Bond*, www.rand.org/randeurope/research/projects/social-impact-bonds.html.

74. Emma Disley, Chris Giacomantonio, Kristy Kruithof, and Megan Sim, *The Payment by Results Social Impact Bond Pilot at HMP Peterborough: Final Process Evaluation Report*, RAND Europe and the Ministry of Justice Analytical Series, 2015, www.gov.uk/government/uploads /system/uploads/attachment_data/file/486512/social-impact-bond -pilot-peterborough-report.pdf.

75. Jake Anders and Richard Dorsett, *HMP Peterborough Social Impact Bond—Cohort 2 and Final Cohort Impact Evaluation*, National Institute of Economic and Social Research, June 11, 2017, www.gov.uk /government/uploads/system/uploads/attachment_data/file/633243/ peterborough-social-impact-bond-cohort-2-results-report.pdf.

76. Social Finance, "World's 1st Social Impact Bond Shown to Cut Reoffending and to Make Impact Investors a Return," Press Release, July 27, 2017, www.socialfinance.org.uk/sites/default/files/news/final-press -release-pb-july-2017.pdf.

77. Social Finance Impact Bond Global Database, accessed February 26, 2018, http://sibdatabase.socialfinance.org.uk/.

78. Instiglio, *Social Impact Bonds and Development Bonds Worldwide*, http://instiglio.org/en/sibs-worldwide/.

79. Peter Ramsden, *Social Impact Bonds: State of Play & Lessons Learnt*, OECD, 2016, www.oecd.org/cfe/leed/SIBs-State-Play-Lessons-Final.pdf.

80. Daniel Edmiston and Alex Nicholls, "Social Impact Bonds: The Role of Private Capital in Outcome-Based Commissioning," *Journal of Social Policy* 47, no. 1 (2017): 57–76, https://doi.org/10.1017/S0047279417000125.

81. "Examples of Program-Related Investments: A Rule by the Internal Revenue Service on 04/25/2016," *The Federal Register* 81: 24014–19, www.federalregister.gov/documents/2016/04/25/2016-09396 /examples-of-program-related-investments.

82. Council on Foundations, *New Examples of Permissible Program-Related Investments*, www.cof.org/page/new-examples-permissible-program-related -investments.

83. "Making Markets Work for the Poor: How the Bill & Melinda Gates Foundation Uses Program-Related Investments," *Stanford Social Innovation Review* (Summer 2016): 8.

84. Council on Foundations, *New Examples of Permissible Program-Related Investments*.

85. Internal Revenue Service, *Program-Related Investments*, updated September 29, 2017, www.irs.gov/charities-non-profits/private-foundations /program-related-investments.
86. This is in terms of the range of blended cross-sector financial tools presented in this chapter.
87. The investment priorities of foundations vary significantly. Simply to illustrate, a foundation may hypothetically target 0–3 percent returns for PRIs, and 4–10 percent returns (or more) for MRIs, depending on the asset class.
88. See IRS regulations on the subject. Internal Revenue Service, *Private Foundation—Jeopardizing Investments*, www.irs.gov/charities-non-profits /private-foundations/private-foundation-jeopardizing-investments -defined.
89. No information in this publication is intended as, nor does it constitute, investment advice, legal advice, or tax advice. Nor is it an offer to sell any securities to any person or a solicitation or offer to purchase any securities. Information and included references are not recommendations, sponsorships, or endorsements by the authors of any company, organization, or security.
90. Rockefeller Brothers Fund, *Fund Announces Plans to Divest from Fossil Fuels*, September 22, 2014, www.rbf.org/news/fund-announces-plans -divest-fossil-fuels.
91. For more information, see the *Principles for Responsible Investment*, PRI Association, www.unpri.org/.
92. Rockefeller Brothers Fund, *The Fund Joins as a Signatory to the United Nations-Supported Principles for Responsible Investment*, March 6, 2017, www.rbf.org/news/fund-joins-signatory-united-nations-supported -principles-responsible-investment.
93. Phone interview with Christine Looney, Senior Program Investment Officer, Inclusive Economies, the Ford Foundation, June 22, 2017.
94. Ford Foundation, *Ford Foundation Commits $1 Billion from Endowment to Mission-Related Investments*, April 5, 2017, www.fordfoundation.org /the-latest/news/ford-foundation-commits-1-billion-from-endowment -to-mission-related-investments/.
95. A survey by the World Economic Forum's ReDesigning Development Finance Initiative identified ten types of associated risk. World Economic Forum and the OECD, *Insights from Blended Finance Investment Vehicles & Facilities*, January 2016, 25, www3.weforum.org/docs/WEF _Blended_Finance_Insights_Investments_Vehicles_Facilities_report_2016 .pdf.
96. This is adapted from the guiding principle "Leverage Collective Action," from the White House Domestic Policy Council "Partnerships"

perspective, with contributions from or coauthored by Howard W. Buffett, https://obamawhitehouse.archives.gov/administration/eop/sicp /initiatives/partnerships.

97. This is adapted from the guiding principle "Involve a Broad Spectrum of Actors," from the White House Domestic Policy Council "Partnerships" perspective, with contributions from or coauthored by Howard W. Buffett, https://obamawhitehouse.archives.gov/administration/eop/sicp /initiatives/partnerships.

98. This is similar to "Enhancing Impact," in World Economic Forum and the OECD, *A How-To Guide for Blended Finance*, September 2015, 4, www3.weforum.org/docs/WEF_Blended_Finance_How_To_Guide .pdf.

# 11. THE PERFORMANCE CASE

1. The New York City mayor's Office of Operations was created by Executive Order of Mayor Edward I. Koch in 1977. Now mandated by local law and additional executive orders to perform a number of functions, the office is best known for the Mayor's Management Report (MMR), issued twice yearly. The report was initially based on a relatively simple performance management system with primarily process and output measures, seeking to hold government agencies accountable to the mayor and the public for how much work they were doing and how efficiently they were managing the resources given to them. The impact of the report was limited by the fact that it was not connected to the city budget process (the method through which resources were allocated) or connected to formal strategic planning (which would specify the goals, expected outcomes, and time horizon for each agency). Nevertheless, the report continues to this day, expanded from a few dozen pages to more than few hundred pages by the dawn of the twenty-first century. Although there was some communication and collaboration between the mayor's Office of Operations, which was responsible for the MMR, and the government agencies that gathered the information and reported on the indicators (quarterly and annually), New York City's agency commissioners generally viewed the report as unnecessary paperwork and an effort by City Hall to micromanage them. It was the city budget process, run by the mayor's Office of Management and Budget (OMB), that agency officials focused on because that process determined their level of funding for the coming fiscal year. The media gives the MMR only moderate attention when the annual report is released, and their

coverage is generally focused on measures they find curious or silly or on unexpected "big misses"—such as significant shortfalls in inspections expected to be done, or the number of housing units built.

2. For an analysis of why and how Bratton's system worked, see Franklin E. Zimring, *The City That Became Safe* (New York: Oxford University Press, 2012).

3. Jack Maple was a colorful "New York City" character who always wore a homburg hat, two-tone expensive shoes, and a bow tie. He was a regular at the storied "Elaine's" restaurant and bar where political and entertainment celebrities hung out until the wee hours to see each other and be seen by the gossip columnists and tabloid writers. Maples connected with Bratton at the New York City Transit Police when Bratton was appointed to head that organization in 1990. Even as a lieutenant there, Maple was already experimenting with mapping crime patterns to get ahead of what might be the next wave of crime. See Douglas Martin, "Jack Maple, 48, a Designer of City Crime Control Strategies," *New York Times*, August 6, 2001.

4. NYPD Compstat Unit, *City Wide Crime Statistics Weekly*, http://www1.nyc.gov/site/nypd/stats/crime-statistics/crime-statistics-landing.page.

5. John Buntin, "Assertive Policing, Plummeting Crime: The NYPD Takes on Crime in New York City," Harvard Kennedy School of Government Case Study, August 9, 1999, 22.

6. Dennis Smith and William J. Bratton, "Performance Management in New York City: Compstat and the Revolution in Police Management," in *Quicker, Better, Cheaper? Managing Performance in American Government*, ed. Dall Forsythe (New York: Rockefeller Institute Press, October 2001), 455.

7. Smith and Bratton, "Performance Management in New York City."

8. CDC, *Preliminary Results from the World Trade Center Evacuation Study—New York City, 2003*, www.cdc.gov/mmwr/preview/mmwrhtml/mm5335a3.htm.

9. CNN.com/U.S., *September 11: Chronology of Terror*, September 12, 2001, http://edition.cnn.com/2001/US/09/11/chronology.attack/.

10. Rosa Prince, "9/11 Death Toll Rises as Cancer Cases Soar Among Emergency Workers," *The Telegraph*, July 27, 2014, www.telegraph.co.uk/news/worldnews/northamerica/usa/10994227/911-death-toll-rises-as-cancer-cases-soar-among-emergency-workers.html.

11. Uniformed Firefighters Association of Greater New York, *FDNY Line of Duty Deaths*, accessed March 15, 2017. www.ufanyc.org/lodd/.

12. The McKinsey Report, *Increasing FDNY's Preparedness*, 13, 16–17.

13. The McKinsey Report, *Increasing FDNY's Preparedness*.

14. FDNY, *Vital Statistics 2014*, www1.nyc.gov/site/fdny/about/resources/vital-statistics/vital-statistics.page; FDNY, *Strategic Plan 2015–2017*,

2015, 39, www.nyc.gov/html/fdny/pdf/ofc/FDNY_strategic_plan_2015 _2017.pdf.

15. This program was developed by William Eimicke at the SIPA Picker Center for Executive Education of Columbia University and FDNY First Deputy Fire Commissioner Don Shacknai, in partnership with many senior uniformed officers from the fire and EMS divisions.

16. To enable all of the FDNY senior leaders in 2002 to benefit from FOMI, there were two cohorts of sixteen in the first year of 2002–03.

17. The cohorts attend the offsite program one week a month for six months, completing a program-long team project in addition to management and leadership courses. Some examples of projects subsequently implemented by the FDNY include the department's strategic planning process (2003), the purchase of multiple RAC units (Rehabilitation and Care) for use at emergencies to treat fire and EMS personnel operating in extreme environments (2009), and altered EMS response protocols for low-priority calls (segment 7, 8, and 9, for things like broken ankles where it is clear that no one's life is in danger) to no lights and sirens, where the risk posed by longer response times is outweighed by the risk of accident/injury by full on lights and sirens—full speed response (2010).

18. Seth Stevenson, "How Do You Make Better Managers?" *Slate*, June 9, 2014, http://www.slate.com/articles/business/psychology_of_management /2014/06/ge_s_crotonville_management_campus_where_future_company _leaders_are_trained.html.

19. In 1995, former mayor Giuliani transferred the slow responding, low morale, EMS from a similarly troubled New York City Health and Hospitals Corporation to the world class FDNY, in hopes of improving EMS response times and overall performance. Instead, both FDNY and EMS privately opposed the merger, and prior to FOMI, the two organizations functioned as essentially two separate agencies, with very different recruitment and promotion procedures, very few colocation houses/stations, and even different unions.

20. William Eimicke taught the strategic planning course beginning in the first year of FOMI, and Chief Pfeiffer subsequently worked closely with Eimicke and a core group of FDNY senior managers to create the first plan and help institutionalize it in the department. The FDNY Strategic Plan 2015–2017 is guiding the department today.

21. News Report, *New York Unveils New Fire Department Operations Center*, September 25, 2006, www.governing.com/templates/gov_print _article?id=99391429.

22. FireRescue1, *FDNY Announces Citywide Disaster Preparedness Plan*, April 25, 2007, www.firerescue1.com/terrorism-wmd-response/articles /284459-FDNY-commissioner-announces-city-wide-disaster-preparedness -plan/.

23. During his career, Chief Pfeifer commanded response to some of the largest fires and emergencies in New York City's history. On the morning of September 11, 2001, he was the first chief to arrive at the World Trade Center following the attacks.

24. Interview of Fire Commissioner Nicholas Scoppetta, in Al Baker, "7 Fire Dept. Officers Censured in Bank Blaze Inquiry," *New York Times*, June 25, 2009.

25. Ray Rivera, "2 Firefighters Are Dead in Deutsche Bank Fire," *New York Times*, August 18, 2007.

26. Al Baker, "City Agencies Faulted in Deutsche Bank Fire," *New York Times*, June 19, 2009.

27. Baker, "City Agencies Faulted in Deutsche Bank Fire."

28. Baker, "City Agencies Faulted in Deutsche Bank Fire."

29. Kathleen Gilsinan and Adam Stepan, "From Compstat to Gov 2.0: Big Data in New York City Management," SIPA Case Study, Columbia University, SIPA-14-0004.4, 2014.

30. Gerola has since moved on to Microsoft and is working on similar big data and communications projects for the NYPD.

31. Gilsinan and Stepan, "From Compstat to Gov 2.0," 7.

32. Baker, "City Agencies Faulted in Deutsche Bank Fire."

33. Interview of Fire Commissioner Nicholas Scoppetta, in Al Baker, "7 Fire Dept. Officers Censured in Bank Blaze Inquiry."

34. A graduate of Harvard University and the University of Chicago Law School, Holloway served as chief of staff and counsel to Bloomberg's deputy mayor for operations Edward Skyler (now an executive at Citibank), then as commissioner of the New York City Department of Environmental Protection (NYC DEP), and finally as deputy mayor for operations (2011–2013). Holloway left city service in December 2013 when he was appointed deputy chief operating officer of Bloomberg LP. He was forty years old at the time. See Mara Gay, "Bloomberg LP Taps Mayor's Deputy," *Wall Street Journal*, December 29, 2013.

35. Gilsinan and Stepan, "From Compstat to Gov 2.0," 7.

36. Alan Feuer, "The Mayor's Geek Squad," *New York Times Magazine*, March 23, 2013.

37. Michael Gartland, "City Deaths Caused by Fires Hits Record Low in 2016, *New York Post*, January 10, 2017, https://nypost.com/2017/01/10/city-deaths-caused-by-fires-hits-record-low-in-2016/; Gigi Georges, Tim Glynn-Burke, and Andrea McGrath, "Improving the Local Landscape for Innovation (Part 3): Assessment and Implementation," November 1, 2013, http://www.socialinnovationsjournal.org/social-issues/100-human-services/1668-improving-the-local-landscape-for-innovation-part-3-assessment-and-implementation.

38. Stephen Goldsmith and Susan Crawford, *The Responsive City* (San Francisco, Calif.: Jossey-Bass, 2014), 119.

39. Gilsinan and Stepan, "From Compstat to Gov 2.0," 11–12.

40. Interview and email exchange between Stephen Goldsmith and William Eimicke, April 21, 2017.

41. Sam Roberts, "Statistics, Beloved by Mayor, Show a Slump in City Services," *New York Times,* August 29, 2011.

42. Nick Powell, "Three Years Later, It's Still Michael Bloomberg's New York," *City and State,* September 26, 2016, http://http://cityandstateny .com/articles/politics/new-york-city/its-still-his-new-york-why -michael-bloomberg-is-the-runner-up-for-newsmaker-of-the-decade .html#.WmXxaq6nGUk.

43. Mayor Bloomberg also created the New York City Center for Economic Opportunity Innovation Fund, which financed performance-driven programs to reduce poverty. The city provided funding, as did private foundations, with projects chosen through a competitive process that emphasized partnerships among government agencies and philanthropies. Impact measures were applied and external evaluations were conducted. The initiatives were experimental, often controversial, and were not always successful. Efforts to apply similar performance-based criteria to the city's large social service contracts were limited due to challenges connecting actions to results and limited analytic tools and personnel at the time. For more information about NYC Opportunity, visit http:// www1.nyc.gov/site/opportunity/about/about-nyc-opportunity .page. See also "Project on Social Innovation," *NYC Center for Economic Opportunity*, accessed April 24, 2017, www.social innovation.ash .harvard.edu/featured-profile/nyc-ceo-innovation-fund.html.

44. For example, Deputy Mayor Goldsmith told us he was often struck by the large number of indicators included in performance reports that had little or no impact on outcomes. Even when the measures were directly connected to outcomes, it was extremely difficult to improve performance, in part because New York City had difficulty connecting improved outcomes to employee compensation. Interview and email exchange between Stephen Goldsmith and William Eimicke, April 21, 2017.

# 12. THE PERFORMANCE FRAMEWORK

1. John W. Selsky and Barbara Parker, "Cross-Sector Partnerships to Address Social Issues: Challenges to Theory and Practice," *Journal of Management* 31, no. 6 (December 2005): 849–73, at 851.

2. Impact Rate of Return and iRR are federally registered trademarks of Global Impact LLC and all rights are reserved.

3. For a discussion of how firms of varying sizes and organizational structures approach this, see Jeremy C. Stein, "Information Production and Capital Allocation: Decentralized Versus Hierarchical Firms," *Journal of Finance* 57, no. 5 (2002): 1891–1921.

4. In the absence of such a measure, many observers judge organizations in the philanthropic sector by the percentage of their budget spent on operating expenses versus programmatic expenses. For further discussion, see Woods Bowman, "Should Donors Care About Overhead Costs? Do They Care?" *Nonprofit and Voluntary Sector Quarterly* 35, no. 2 (2006): 288–310.

5. Discussed later in this chapter, iRR's uniform output differs from other similar efforts, such as the calculation for a social return on investment or a monetization approach. This is because it does not estimate the value of social good created. Rather, it estimates relative performance of a given program against an established goal for social good, using comparative analysis. In effect, this results in a calculation for an impact value of a dollar, which is somewhat the opposite of monetization.

6. For reference, one broad definition of social impact assessment is "the process of identifying the future consequences of a current or proposed action which are related to individuals, organizations and social macrosystems." Heck Becker, "Social Impact Assessment," *European Journal of Operational Research* 128, no. 2 (January 16, 2001): 311–21, https://doi.org/10.1016/S0377-2217(00)00074-6.

7. Geoff Mulgan, "Measuring Social Value," *Stanford Social Innovation Review* (Summer 2010), https://ssir.org/articles/entry/measuring_social_value.

8. We do not wish to diminish the many previous or ongoing attempts to provide common definitions or consolidate the field's work. For example, the International Association for Impact Assessment (IAIA) has been operating since the 1980s. IAIA has adopted the following definition: "Social Impact Assessment includes the processes of analysing, monitoring and managing the intended and unintended social consequences, both positive and negative, of planned interventions (policies, programs, plans, projects) and any social change processes invoked by those interventions." The definition also includes a goal statement: "Its primary purpose is to bring about a more sustainable and equitable biophysical and human environment." For more information, see Frank Vanclay, "International Principles for Social Impact Assessment," *Impact Assessment and Project Appraisal* 21, no. 1 (2003): 5–12, https://doi.org/10.3152/147154603781766491.

9. See the description in World Health Organization, *Metrics: Disability-Adjusted Life Year (DALY): Quantifying the Burden of Disease from Mortality and Morbidity*, www.who.int/healthinfo/global_burden_disease/metrics_daly/en/.

10. For additional information about the related quality-adjusted life years (QALYs) calculation, see Franco Sassi, "Calculating QALYs, Comparing QALY and DALY Calculations," *Health Policy and Planning* 21, no. 5 (September 1, 2006): 402–8, https://doi.org/10.1093/heapol/czl018.

11. For additional discussion of DALY, see *Interpreting the Disability-Adjusted Life-Year (DALY) Metric*, GiveWell, www.givewell.org/research/DALY.

12. Veronica Li, "The Rise, Critique and Persistence of the DALY in Global Health," *Journal of Global Health* (2014), www.ghjournal.org/the-rise-critique-and-persistence-of-the-daly-in-global-health/.

13. Acumen, *Who We Are*, 2017, https://acumen.org/wp-content/uploads/2017/10/About-Acumen-One-Pager-Q2-2017.pdf.

14. Acumen Fund, *The Best Available Charitable Option*, January 2007, https://acumen.org/wp-content/uploads/2013/03/BACO-Concept-Paper-final.pdf.

15. "Sunk cost" is the term used by the Acumen Fund, *The Best Available Charitable Option*, 1.

16. Acumen's scenario illustrated how their loan (after appropriate discounts) would cost less than $0.02 to prevent malaria for one individual over a year. This is versus a cost of $0.84 for the same results through what they call the best available charitable option. Acumen Fund, *The Best Available Charitable Option*, 2–4.

17. See discussion of BACO in Michael Moran, *Private Foundations and Development Partnerships: American Philanthropy and Global Development Agendas* (New York: Routledge, 2014), 127–28.

18. OECD, *Education at a Glance 2005: OECD Indicators* (Paris: OECD Publishing, 2005), 126, http://dx.doi.org/10.1787/eag-2005-en.

19. OECD, *Education at a Glance 2005: OECD Indicators, Glossary*, 13, www.oecd.org/edu/skills-beyond-school/35325710.pdf.

20. David Canning and Esra Bennathan, "The Social Rate of Return on Infrastructure Investments," World Bank Policy Research Working Paper No. 2390, 2000, https://openknowledge.worldbank.org/handle/10986/19820.

21. Matthew Bishop, email message to Howard W. Buffett, November 14, 2017. Bishop is a member of the board of directors of the Social Progress Imperative, which publishes the Social Progress Index.

22. For additional information, visit the Social Progress Index website at www.socialprogressindex.com/.

23. See an overview of the Social Progress Index Methodology at www .socialprogressindex.com/methodology.

24. See Social Progress Index, *Exclusively Social and Environmental Indicators*, section on "Key Design Principles," www.socialprogressindex.com /methodology.

25. Andrew Kassoy, email message to Howard W. Buffett, November 10, 2017. Kassoy is the cofounder of B Lab.

26. For more information about the B Impact Assessment, including the assessment methodology itself, visit www.bimpactassessment.net.

27. For additional information about B Lab, visit www.bcorporation.net /what-are-b-corps/about-b-lab.

28. For more about the history of the Global Impact Investing Network, visit https://thegiin.org/giin/history.

29. Antony Bugg-Levine and Jed Emerson, "Impact Investing: Transforming How We Make Money While Making a Difference," *Innovations* 6, no. 3 (2011): 9–18.

30. Global Impact Investing Network, "The Business Value of Impact Measurement," Issue Brief, August 2016, https://thegiin.org/assets/GIIN _ImpactMeasurementReport_webfile.pdf.

31. Global Impact Investing Network, "The Business Value of Impact Measurement."

32. Because "positive social or environmental impact" is undefined and not quantified, this precondition is open to wide interpretation. However, the most significant aspect is that the investor must have established intentions to make a positive impact with the investment. The notion of intentionality is an important one because it is a key element separating what could otherwise be two identical investments. For a further discussion on this subject, see Paul Brest and Kelly Born, "When Can Impact Investing Create Real Impact?" *Stanford Social Innovation Review* (Fall 2013).

33. Many investors today associate the concept of concessionary or below-market returns with the goal of social impact. This follows a somewhat traditional school of thinking (sometimes called the "trade-off myth") that there are only two ways of allocating capital—to maximize financial return or to maximize social return—with nothing in between. However, nearly all impact investors have some level of expected financial return. In fact, data illustrate that impact investing strategies may outperform comparable traditional investing in specific fields. See "The Financial Performance of Real Assets Impact Investments; Introducing the Timber, Real Estate, and Infrastructure Impact Benchmarks," The GIIN and Cambridge Associates, May 3, 2017, https://thegiin.org/knowledge /publication/real-assets-impact-investments.

34. This precondition speaks directly to the previous point: that there are a variety of investment tools deployable for social impact, many of which do not fit into the traditional return / no return binary. Just as there are a series of financial tools in traditional investing that range in their expected risk/return profile, so too will there be a range in the impact investing space. For example, read more about the Omidyar Network's framework on the subject at Matt Bannick et al., "Across the Returns Continuum," *Stanford Social Innovation Review* (Winter 2017), https://ssir.org/articles/entry/across_the_returns_continuum#.

35. There are a few difficulties inherent to this precondition. Measurement itself may be cost prohibitive for a given investment. Further, a situation may clearly meet the first three preconditions but cannot meet the last due to complexity or lack of information. This is not to argue against measurement as a precondition but rather to acknowledge its challenges within the scope of impact investing as defined here.

36. USAID, "USAID Launches New Public-Private Partnership to Facilitate Impact Investing That Addresses Social and Environmental Challenges," Press release, September 30, 2009, www.usaid.gov/content/usaid-launches-new-public-private-partnership-facilitate-impact-investing-addresses-social.

37. Amit Bouri, "How Standards Emerge: The Role of Investor Leadership in Realizing the Potential of IRIS," *Innovations: Technology, Governance, Globalization* 6, no. 3 (2011): 117–31.

38. As of 2018, the catalog contains 559 entries, available at https://iris.thegiin.org/metrics.

39. For example, sectors of focus span agriculture, education, energy, financial services, health, water, and others. See more at *Getting Started with IRIS*, 2017, https://iris.thegiin.org/guide/getting-started-guide.

40. For example, the iPAR platform provides financial portfolio impact analysis. It is based on the GIIN IRIS catalog but with a reduced overall tracking burden of thirty-nine primary metrics (such as jobs created or energy saved) and an additional 115 submetrics (as of 2018). iPAR focuses on the intersection of theme and geography and uses a highly visual interface to reflect an investment's impact intent, as well as risks or threats to its successful implementation. See iPAR, *Impact Portfolio Allocation Review*, https://iparimpact.com/.

41. See more about the work of Robin Hood at Robin Hood, *What We Do*, 2017, www.robinhood.org/what-we-do/.

42. For information about specific programs and partners, see Robin Hood, *Who We Fund*, www.robinhood.org/programs/who-we-fund/#all.

43. Michael M. Weinstein and Ralph M. Bradburd, *The Robin Hood Rules for Smart Giving* (New York: Columbia University Press, 2013).

44. Robin Hood's "Metrics Equations," September 2014, are available at https://robinhoodorg-production.s3.amazonaws.com/uploads/2017/04/Metrics-Equations-for-Website_Sept-2014.pdf.
45. Weinstein and Bradburd, *The Robin Hood Rules for Smart Giving*.
46. See metric 46, "Dental Care: Impact on Earnings, Adults," September 2014, 50–51, https://robinhoodorg-production.s3.amazonaws.com/uploads/2017/04/Metrics-Equations-for-Website_Sept-2014.pdf.
47. All data for this example are from the Robin Hood Foundation website infographic, accessed October 19, 2016.
48. Note, "social return on investment" can be used to describe a measurement or output, as well as a formal "SROI" process. The latter is defined by Social Value UK (formerly the SROI Network), with more information available at http://www.socialvalueuk.org/.
49. For additional information and tools for cost-based measurement of social value creation, see Melinda Tuan, *Measuring and/or Estimating Social Value Creation: Insights Into Eight Integrated Cost Approaches*, The Bill & Melinda Gates Foundation, Impact Planning and Improvement, December 15, 2008, https://docs.gatesfoundation.org/documents/wwl-report-measuring-estimating-social-value-creation.pdf.
50. Jane Gibbon and Colin Dey, "Developments in Social Impact Measurement in the Third Sector: Scaling Up or Dumbing Down?" *Social and Environmental Accountability Journal* 31, no. 1 (April 12, 2011): 63–72, http://dx.doi.org/10.1080/0969160X.2011.556399.
51. For example, recall the Social Progress Index mentioned earlier. It takes a very different approach from monetization by decoupling many aspects of social development from those of economic development.
52. This also may apply to cases of private sector collaboration. Barringer and Harrison argue that, "in considering the potential for interorganizational relationships to create value, simple cost/benefit analysis is insufficient . . . [with] potential outcomes that are impossible to place a dollar value on." Bruce R. Barringer and Jeffrey S. Harrison, "Walking a Tightrope: Creating Value Through Interorganizational Relationships," *Journal of Management* 26, no. 3 (June 1, 2000): 367–403, at 396.
53. For example, Robin Hood incorporates a program measure for strength of leadership, and includes other variables in the numerator of its benefit-cost ratio calculation. The organization also determines a "Robin Hood factor" to assess what percentage of success can be attributed directly to its involvement, and it can adjust its evaluation depending on Robin Hood's influence over the success of a program being evaluated. Wes Moore, CEO of Robin Hood, email message to Howard W. Buffett, November 28, 2017.

54. In such instances, virtual or shadow pricing may be used. However, this still assumes that measures for such factors are effective when converted into financial terms. For additional information on the subject, see Lynn A. Karoly, *Valuing Benefits in Benefit-Cost Studies of Social Programs* (Santa Monica, Calif.: RAND Corporation, 2008), www.rand.org/pubs /technical_reports/TR643.html.

55. A working group of Dutch financial institutions and companies developed a core set of aggregated impact indicators across the UN Sustainable Development Goals, cross-referenced with the GIIN IRIS catalog, and similar in concept to iRR's Key Impact Indicator approach. See the working document, *SDG Impact Indicators; A Guide for Investors and Companies*, available at www.dnb.nl/en/about-dnb/co-operation /platform-voor-duurzame-financiering/werkgroepen/index.jsp#.

56. For more information about LEED (Leadership in Energy and Environmental Design) certification, visit the U.S. Green Business Council website, https://new.usgbc.org/leed.

57. This may seem counterintuitive at first. A lower number in the Impact Efficiency figure is representing a lower cost per unit. Therefore, a lower figure value is actually reflecting greater (or higher) cost efficiency.

58. Kathleen Gilsinan and Adam Stepan, "From Compstat to Gov 2.0: Big Data in New York City Management," SIPA Case Study, 2014, Columbia University, SIPA-14-0004.4.

59. The iRR FDNY example was developed in consultation with Joseph Pfeifer, Chief of Counterterrorism at FDNY.

60. J. David Goodman, "New York City's Fire Deaths Reach Lowest Point in Over 100 Years," *New York Times*, January 9, 2017.

61. Interview and email exchange with Joseph Pfeifer, Chief of Counterterrorism at FDNY, January 18, 2017.

62. For a timeline of the first few years of the program, see: "PlaNYC Update April 2011; A Greener, Greater New York," City of New York, 12: http://www.nyc.gov/html/planyc/downloads/pdf/publications /planyc_2011_planyc_full_report.pdf.

63. For example, see a list of programs and best practices highlighted in: "Best Practice: PlaNYC: NYC's Long-Term Sustainability Plan," New York City Global Partners: www.nyc.gov/html/ia/gprb/downloads /pdf/NYC_Environment_PlaNYC.pdf.

64. One component of PlaNYC, called GreeNYC, provided public outreach and education in support of the emissions reduction goal. For more, see GreeNYC, NYC Mayor's Office of Sustainability: www.nyc.gov /html/gbee/html/initiatives/greenyc.shtml.

65. MillionTreesNYC recorded its millionth tree planted in 2015, roughly two years ahead of schedule. More information on the initiative can be

found here: www.nycgovparks.org/trees/milliontreesnyc. Furthermore, the Department of Parks and Recreation engages thousands of volunteers in the cataloging and mapping of street trees across the five boroughs of the city. Information about individual trees throughout New York City can be viewed on a dynamic online map. For example, the following web address links to a Japanese Pagoda tree growing outside the School of International and Public Affairs building on Columbia University's campus: https://tree-map.nycgovparks.org/#treeinfo-2129084.

66. New York City's transportation commissioner at the time, Janette Sadik-Khan, led an aggressive effort. She writes about it in the following: Janette Sadik-Khan, "The Bike Wars are Over, and the Bikes Won," *New York Magazine*, March 8, 2016, http://nymag.com/daily/intelligencer/2016/03/bike-wars-are-over-and-the-bikes-won.html.

67. In 2009, New York City conducted a bike share feasibility study containing a substantial outreach effort with over 350 meetings, more than 10,000 suggestions for bike sharing stations, and 60,000 comments from the public. See information about community engagement in planning, and the feasibility study: "NYC Bike Share, Designed by New Yorkers," New York City Department of Transportation, 2013. For a report about the first two years of the program, see: Sarah M. Kaufman, Lily Gordon-Koven, Nolan Leveson and Mitchell L. Moss, *Citi Bike: The First Two Years* (New York: NYU Wagner Rudin Center, June 2015), 7.

68. Benepe launched a Task Force in 2010 and formally announced the program in 2011. See: "A Plan for Sustainable Practices within NYC Parks," 7, NYC Parks Sustainable Parks Task Force, www.nycgovparks.org/sub_about/sustainable_parks/Sustainable_Parks_Plan.pdf.

69. View the scorecard, indicators, and methodology: "A Plan for Sustainable Practices within NYC Parks," 36–38, 50–52, NYC Parks Sustainable Parks Task Force: www.nycgovparks.org/sub_about/sustainable_parks/Sustainable_Parks_Plan.pdf.

70. "Mayor de Blasio Commits to 80 Percent Reduction of Greenhouse Gas Emissions by 2050, Starting with Sweeping Green Buildings Plan," September 21, 2014. www1.nyc.gov/office-of-the-mayor/news/451-14/mayor-de-blasio-commits-80-percent-reduction-greenhouse-gas-emissions-2050-starting-with#/0.

71. Specifically, Mayor de Blasio's plan called for an increase in 100 MW of decentralized solar capacity for city-owned buildings, and an increase in 250 MW of solar power capacity for privately owned properties. See: "One City Built to Last," 14 and 16, The City of New York Mayor's Office of Long-Term Planning and Sustainability. www.nyc.gov/html/builttolast/assets/downloads/pdf/OneCity.pdf.

72. "Governor Cuomo Announces Establishment of Clean Energy Standard that Mandates 50 Percent Renewables by 2030," August 1, 2016. www

.governor.ny.gov/news/governor-cuomo-announces-establishment
-clean-energy-standard-mandates-50-percent-renewables.

73. For a detailed discussion on this topic, see: Steve Cohen, *The Sustainable City* (New York: Columbia University Press, 2017).

74. Cost and financing estimates for solar development projects are based on Bloomberg New Energy Finance, *About,* 2017, https:// about.newenergyfinance.com/about/; and on International Finance Corporation, *Utility-Scale Solar Photovoltaic Power Plants—A Project Developer's Guide,* 2015, www.ifc.org/wps/wcm/connect/f05d3e00498e 0841bb6fbbe54d141794/IFC+Solar+Report_Web+_08+05.pdf? MOD=AJPERES.

75. International Finance Corporation, *Utility-Scale Solar Photovoltaic Power Plants.*

76. For a case study on a similar type of development initiative, see Howard W. Buffett and Adam Stepan, "Aid or Investment? Post-Conflict Development in DRC and Rwanda," Columbia University School of International and Public Affairs Case Consortium, 2018, SIPA-18-0016.

77. Estimates vary. The Rwandan government's Institute of Statistics reports that over 70 percent of the country's population is employed by agriculture. (Seasonal Agricultural Survey 2016, National Institute of Statistics of Rwanda, 7. Kigali: Rwanda, December, 2016.) The UN FAO estimates this amount as 80 percent for Afghanistan. (The FAO Component of the Consolidated Appeals 2012, Afghanistan. The Food and Agriculture Organization of the United Nations, 6. Rome: Italy, 2011.)

78. See *Rwanda Vision 2020*, rev. 2012, Republic of Rwanda, 16; and section on Key Indicators, 25. www.minecofin.gov.rw/fileadmin/templates /documents/NDPR/Vision_2020_.pdf.

79. Rwanda's Simbwa Cell in the Kabarore Sector, Gatsibo District, Eastern Province, covers 10,091 acres, and has considerable area suitable for agroforestry development. Data provided by Scott A. Zillmer, Senior Research Editor, Maps and Graphics at National Geographic, January 8, 2018. An administrative map of the district can be found here: http://gatsibo.gov. rw/fileadmin/templates/document/Map_of_Gatsibo_District.pdf.

80. In projects such as this, an NGO or international development agency may prefer to use the number of farmers or households as the Key Impact Indicator. However, the government of Rwanda, Ministry of Agriculture and Animal Resources often uses hectares of land as a primary metric. Therefore, this scenario uses land area as its KII. See: Rwanda Irrigation Master Plan, The Government of Rwanda, Ministry of Agriculture and Animal Resources, Ebony Enterprises Ltd, and the World Agroforestry Centre. Nairobi: Kenya, 2010. www.amis.minagri.gov.rw/documents /rwanda-irrigation-master-plan.

81. More women than men participate in subsistence agriculture in Rwanda (*Rwanda Vision 2020*, 17). For a discussion paper recommending that development projects focus on female farmers, see Sheron Randolph and Rickie Sanders, "Female Farmers in the Rwandan Farming System: A Study of the Ruhengeri Prefecture." *Agriculture and Human Values* 9, no. 1 (1992): 59–66. https://doi.org/10.1007/BF02226504.

82. National Agricultural Survey 2008, National Institute of Statistics of Rwanda, 2. February 2010. www.statistics.gov.rw/publication/national -agricultural-survey-report-nas-2008.

83. For example, Rwanda's *Vision 2020* established a goal that the percentage of mechanized agricultural operations in the country would increase from a baseline of 7 percent to 40 percent. *Rwanda Vision 2020*, rev. 2012, Republic of Rwanda, see indicator 17 at page 27. www.minecofin .gov.rw/fileadmin/templates/documents/NDPR/Vision_2020_.pdf.

84. For a discussion on the importance of agroforestry to smallholder farmers in Rwanda, see Charles Bucagu, Bernard Vanlauwe, Mark T. Van Wijk, and Ken E. Giller, "Assessing farmers' interest in agroforestry in two contrasting agro-ecological zones of Rwanda." *Agroforestry systems* 87, no. 1 (2013): 141–158.

85. "Comunitas," *Comunitas*, accessed January 9, 2018. www.comunitas .org/portal/comunitas/.

86. For information on a comparable cross-sector development under way, led by the University of Nebraska Medical Center, Med Center Development Corporation, see Cindy Gonzalez, "UNMC plans partnership to create Omaha's next Aksarben Village or Midtown Crossing," *Omaha World Herald* (Omaha: NE), May 24, 2014.

87. Figures for this scenario were calculated from estimates in Turner & Townsend's International Construction Market Survey 2016. Building costs in São Paulo for this iRR scenario are based on a mix of averages across categories (e.g., Business Park, Education, and Hospital) as well as additional costs for building to LEED certification standards. See *International Construction Market Survey 2016*, Turner & Townsend, 24–25, June 2016: www.turnerandtownsend.com/media/1518/international-construction-market-survey-2016.pdf.

88. For example, see the Global ESG Benchmark for Real Assets, Real Estate Assessment overview: https://gresb.com/gresb-real-estate -assessment/.

89. This may be particularly useful in cases such as the aggregated UN Sustainable Development Goal impact indicators referenced earlier.

90. Aggregated insights from this type of analysis, particularly over time and across different organizations and impact themes, could be especially useful for improving the accuracy of iRR in future applications.

91. For example, happiness, pain, or love. However, we recognize that attempts to measure such factors are under way. For instance, see John Helliwell, Richard Layard, and Jeffrey Sachs, *World Happiness Report 2017* (New York: Sustainable Development Solutions Network, 2017).

# 13. THE CAUTIONARY CASE

1. Brian Winter and Stuart Grudgings, "Brazil's Economy Goes from 'Great' to "Good"," *Thomson Reuters*, August 18, 2011, www.reuters.com/article /us-brazil-economy-idUSTRE77H6CQ20110818.
2. TED, "Mayor Eduardo Paes Is on a Mission to Ensure That Rio's Renaissance Creates a Positive Legacy for All of Its Citizens," April 2012, www.ted.com/speakers/mayor_eduardo_paes.
3. C40 Cities, *Chair of the C40: A Strong Advocate for Cities*, accessed October 31, 2016, www.c40.org/leadership.
4. Encyclopedia Britannica, "Rio de Janeiro," https://www.britannica .com/place/Rio-de-Janeiro-Brazil.
5. Lorranine Murray, "Christ the Redeemer," *Encyclopedia Britannica*, accessed October 31, 2016, www.britannica.com/topic/Christ-the -Redeemer.
6. Lacy Edney and Segolene Poirier, "A Visit to Christ the Redeemer in Rio," *The Rio Times*, March 27, 2012.
7. At one time, Petrobras was the sixth largest company in the world by market capitalization and accounted for about 10 percent of the Brazil GDP. In the aftermath of the scandal, the company lost about half of its market value. See David Segal, "Petrobras Oil Scandal Leaves Brazilians Lamenting a Lost Dream," *New York Times*, August 7, 2015.
8. The World Bank, *Brazil Overview*, accessed October 17, 2016, www .worldbank.org/en/country/brazil/overview.
9. BNP Paribas, *Brazil: A Crucial Turning Point Ahead*, 4th quarter 2016 report, www.economic-research.bnpparibas.com/views/lDisplay Publication.aspx?type=document&IdPdf=29170.
10. The World Bank, *Brazil Overview*, accessed October 17, 2016, www .worldbank.org/en/country/brazil/overview.
11. Maria Fernanda Gebara and Alice Thuault, "GHG Mitigation in Brazil's Land Use Sector," World Resources Institute, December 2013.
12. Lindsay Sandoval, "The Effect of Education on Brazil's Economic Development," *Global Majority E-Journal* 3, no. 1 (June 2012): 4–19. See also Columbia University SIPA's short video case study, "Schools of Tomorrow?" Picker Center, 2015.

13. Andrew Stevens, "Mayor of the Month for January 2013: Eduardo Paes, Mayor of Rio de Janeiro," June 4, 2013, www.citymayors.com/mayors /rio-mayor-paes.html.

14. Stevens, "Mayor of the Month for January 2013."

15. Simon Romero, "Shepherd of the City's Rebirth, Rio's Mayor Feels the Strains, Too," *New York Times*, February 28, 2014.

16. Romero, "Shepherd of the City's Rebirth."

17. Romero, "Shepherd of the City's Rebirth."

18. David Biller, "Mayor Bets Big on Rio de Janeiro's Broken-Down Port Area: Cities," *Bloomberg.com*, February 20, 2015.

19. C40 Cities, *Chair of the C40*.

20. Mimi Whitefield, "Porto Maravilha: Reclaiming Rio de Janeiro's Neglected Port," *Miami Herald*, June 3, 2014.

21. Whitefield, "Porto Maravilha."

22. Biller, "Mayor Bets Big on Rio de Janeiro's Broken-Down Port Area."

23. Rio Prefeitura, "The Porto Marvilha Urban Operation," accessed August 22, 2017, http://portomaravilha.com.br/summary.

24. Rio Prefeitura, "The Porto Marvilha Urban Operation."

25. This is similar to the approach used to provide additional revenue in support of the High Line partnership in the parks case, chapter 5.

26. Rio Prefeitura, "The Porto Marvilha Urban Operation."

27. Dan Horch, "Corruption Scandal at Petrobras Threatens Brazil's Economy," *New York Times*, February 11, 2015.

28. Horch, "Corruption Scandal at Petrobras Threatens Brazil's Economy."

29. Horch, "Corruption Scandal at Petrobras Threatens Brazil's Economy."

30. Will Connors, "5 Things to Know About Brazil's Corruption Scandal," *Wall Street Journal*, March 4, 2016.

31. Rio Prefeitura, "Porto Maravilha: Continuities and Changes," accessed February 10, 2017, www.portomaravilha.com.br.

32. Jonathan Watts, "Museum of Tomorrow: A Captivating Invitation to Imagine a Sustainable World," *The Guardian*, December 17, 2015.

33. Watts, "Museum of Tomorrow."

34. Lulu Garcia-Navarro, "What Brazil's Museum of Tomorrow Means to Locals Today," *NPR*, December 26, 2015.

35. Watts, "Museum of Tomorrow."

36. Watts, "Museum of Tomorrow."

37. Watts, "Museum of Tomorrow."

38. "Museum of Tomorrow, Rio de Janeiro, Brazil," *World Architecture News.com*, February 22, 2017, www.worldarchitecturenews.com/project/2017/27600 /santiago-calatrava/museum-of-tomorrow-in-rio-de-janeiro.html.

39. Museu do Amanha, *About the Museum*, accessed August 23, 2017, http://museudoamanha.org.br/en/about-the-museum.

40. Museu do Amanha, *About the Museum*.

41. Garcia-Navarro, "What Brazil's Museum of Tomorrow Means to Locals Today."

42. Luiza Franco, "Após Cinco Anos de obras, Museu do Amanhã Será Inaugurado No Rio," *FOLHA Digital*, December 15, 2015, www1.folha .uol.com.br/ilustrada/2015/12/1719040-apos-cinco-anos-de-obras -museu-do-amanha-sera-inaugurado-no-rio.shtml.

43. Garcia-Navarro, "What Brazil's Museum of Tomorrow Means to Locals Today."

44. Clara Long, "Rio's Museum of Tomorrow Celebrates One Year Anniversary," *Rio Times Online*, December 19, 2016.

45. Anna Jean Kaiser, "Legacy of Rio Olympics So Far Is a Series of Unkept Promises," *New York Times*, February 15, 2017.

46. Kenneth Rapoza, "Short Term, Olympics Might Do Brazil Economy More Harm Than Good," *Forbes*, August 4, 2016.

47. Taylor Barnes, "Rio's Olympic Legacy Largely Falls Short of Bid Promises," *USA Today*, February 9, 2016.

48. Simon Romero, "Dilma Rouseff of Brazil Says She Won't Be Silenced in Impeachment Trial," *New York Times*, August 29, 2016.

49. Simon Romero, "Dilma Rousseff Is Ousted as Brazil's President in Impeachment Vote," *New York Times*, August 31, 2016.

50. Romero, "Dilma Rousseff Is Ousted as Brazil's President in Impeachment Vote."

51. Nelson Belen, "Rio Officials Negotiating Sale of Olympic Apartments to Civil Workers," *Rio Times Online*, February 2, 2017.

52. Alex Jones and Bruce Katz, "What's Next for Rio?" *Brookings Institution*, August 18, 2016, www.brookings.edu/blog/metropolitan-revolution /2016/08/18/whats-next-for-rio.

53. Joseph Kane, "Aligning Olympic Ambitions with Urban-Access Concerns in Rio and Beyond," *Brookings Institution*, August 12, 2016, www.brookings .edu/blog.the-avenue/2016/08/12/aligning-olympic-ambitions-with -urban-access-concerns-in-rio-and-beyond/.

54. Toni Lindau and Bruno Felin, "Rio Olympics' Legacy: Urban Mobility," *World Resources Institute*, August 22, 2016, www.wri.org/blog/2016/08 /rio-olympics-legacy-urban-mobility.

55. Lindau and Felin, "Rio Olympics' Legacy."

56. Nelson Belen, "Visitors Disappointed with Rio's Abandoned Olympic Park," *Rio Times Online*, February 2, 2017.

57. Belen, "Visitors Disappointed with Rio's Abandoned Olympic Park."

58. Calo Saad, "Cost of Rio's 2016 Olympics Rises by Almost $100 Million," *Reuters.com*, January 29, 2016.

59. Mark Phillips, "London Olympics Billions Over Budget, Study Shows," *CBS News*, June 28, 2012, www.cbsnews.com/news/london-olympics -billions-over-budget-study-shows/.

60. Christinia Settimi, "The 2016 Rio Summer Olympics: By the Numbers," *Forbes*, www.forbes.com/sites/christinasettimi/2016/08/05/the-2016 -summer-olympics-in-rio-by-the-numbers/#67e8d710fa18.

61. Joanna S. Kao, "The Cost of Building the 2016 Rio Olympics," *Financial Times*, August 5, 2016; see also Jonathan Watts, "Rio Mayor Eduardo Paes: 'The Olympics Are a Missed Opportunity for Brazil'," *The Guardian*, July 11, 2016.

62. Andrew Zimbalist, *Circus Maximus: The Economic Gamble Behind Hosting the Olympics and the World Cup* (Washington, D.C.: Brookings Institution Press, 2016), 95–113.

63. Zimbalist, *Circus Maximus*, 154.

64. Vanessa Barbara, "I Criticized the Olympics. That Doesn't Make Me a Traitor," *New York Times*, August 20, 2016.

65. Jonathan Watts, "Have the Olympics Been Worth It for Rio?" *The Guardian*, August 21, 2016.

66. Andrew Jacobs, "After Olympics, Rio Is Altered if Not Reborn," *New York Times*, August 21, 2016.

67. Watts, "Have the Olympics Been Worth It for Rio?"

68. Jacobs, "After Olympics, Rio Is Altered if Not Reborn."

69. Jacobs, "After Olympics, Rio Is Altered if Not Reborn."

70. Nelson Belen, "Exploring the New Centro and Port Zone of Rio de Janeiro," *Rio Times Online*, December 9, 2016.

71. Jacobs, "After Olympics, Rio Is Altered if Not Reborn."

72. Matt Sandy, "The Rio Olympics Could Be the Next Victim of Brazil's Corruption Scandal," *Time.com*, March 24, 2016.

73. Jamil Chade, "Stadium Deals, Corruption and Bribery: The Questions at the Heart of Brazil's Olympic and World Cup 'Miracle'," *The Guardian*, April 23, 2017.

74. Chade, "Stadium Deals, Corruption and Bribery."

75. Chade, "Stadium Deals, Corruption and Bribery."

76. Simon Romero, "Scandal in Brazil Raises Fear of Turmoil's Return," *New York Times*, May 19, 2017.

77. BBC News, "Brazil's President Temer Avoids Corruption Trial," October 26, 2017, http://www.bbc.com/news/world-latin-america-41755666.

78. Lisandra Paraguassu and Ricardo Brito, "Brazil Police Request Temer Answer Questions in Alleged Graft Probe," January 5, 2018, https://www .reuters.com/article/us-brazil-corruption-temer/brazil-police-request -temer-answer-questions-in-alleged-graft-probe-idUSKBN1EV01S.

79. *Buenos Aires Times*, "Brazil President Michel Temer's Approval Rating Slumps to Staggering 3% in Poll," September 28, 2017, http://batimes .com.ar/news/latin-america/brazil-presidents-approval-rating-at-just-3 .phtml.

# CONCLUSION

1. See Andrew Carter and Peter Roberts, "Strategy and Partnership in Urban Regeneration," in *Urban Regeneration*, ed. Peter Roberts, Hugh Sykes, and Rachel Granger (Thousand Oaks, Calif.: Sage 2017), 44–67.
2. For a brief discussion on the gap that NGOs fill in the provision of social welfare services, see Carol Reade, Anne Marie Todd, Asbjorn Osland, and Joyce Osland, "Poverty and the Multiple Stakeholder Challenge for Global Leaders," *Journal of Management Education* (2008): 820–40, https://doi.org/10.1177/1052562908317445.
3. Karin Bäckstrand, "Multi-Stakeholder Partnerships for Sustainable Development: Rethinking Legitimacy, Accountability and Effectiveness," *Environmental Policy and Governance* 16, no. 5 (2006): 290–306.
4. Thomas G. Pittz and Terry Adler, "An Exemplar of Open Strategy: Decision-Making Within Multi-Sector Collaborations," *Management Decision* 54, no. 7 (2016): 1595–1614.
5. *Value Investing History*, Columbia Business School, Heilbrunn Center for Graham & Dodd Investing, 2017, www8.gsb.columbia.edu /valueinvesting/about/history.
6. Government of India, Ministry of Electronics & Information Technology, *Vision and Vision Areas*, October 11, 2017, http://digitalindia.gov .in/content/vision-and-vision-areas.
7. Douglas Martin, "Private Group Signs Central Park Deal to Be Its Manager," *New York Times*, February 12, 1998.
8. See "Central Park Conservancy; Institute for Urban Parks," Booklet, http://assets.centralparknyc.org/pdfs/institute/Institute_for_Urban _Parks.pdf.
9. Howard W. Buffett, Nitasha Nair, and Adam Stepan, "Social Value Investing in Afghanistan," Columbia University School of International and Public Affairs Case Consortium, 2018, SIPA-18-0015.0.
10. Bruna Santos, Nora Shannon, and Adam Stepan, "Juntos: Mentoring Cities in Brazil," Columbia University School of International and Public Affairs Case Consortium, 2017, SIPA-17-0013.1.
11. "New York City's Fire Deaths Reach Lowest Point in Over 100 Years," *New York Times*, January 9, 2017.
12. Matt Sandy, "The Rio Olympics Could Be the Next Victim of Brazil's Corruption Scandal," *Time.com*, March 24, 2016, http://time.com /4271376/brazil-corruption-scandal-olympics/.
13. Kathy Babiak and Lucie Thibault, "Challenges in Multiple Cross-Sector Partnerships," *Nonprofit and Voluntary Sector Quarterly* 38, no. 1 (December 12, 2007): 117–43.

14. For a detailed discussion of strategic management and cross-sector partnership implementation from both an organization and partnership perspective, see Amelia Clarke and Mark Fuller, "Collaborative Strategic Management: Strategy Formulation and Implementation by Multi-Organizational Cross-Sector Social Partnerships," *Journal of Business Ethics* 94 (2010): 85–101.

15. For a series of relevant templates and example agreements, see *Policy Framework and Legal Guidelines for Partnerships* (Washington, D.C.: U.S. Department of State, February 2011), 21–71.

16. For examples and guidance on this process, see "Phase 2: Adaptive Planning," in Herman Brouwer and Jim Woodhill, eds., *The MSP Guide; How to Design and Facilitate Multi-Stakeholder Partnerships* (Wageningen, The Netherlands: Wageningen UR, 2016), 28. Also see online resources at http://www.mspguide.org.

17. Salvatore Cassano, *FDNY 2010 Annual Report on CDA Inspections*, 2010, 3, http://www.nyc.gov/html/fdny/pdf/cda/cy_2010_cda_report_123010.pdf.

18. For an outline of various topics that comprise a "comprehensive long-term regeneration strategy" in the context of the chapter's partnership types, see Ronald W. McQuaid, "The Theory of Partnerships—Why Have Partnerships," in *Managing Public-Private Partnerships for Public Services: An International Perspective*, ed. Stephen P. Osborne (London, UK: Routledge, 2000), 9–35.

19. See the discussion and referenced material for "boundary spanners" in Valerie Wildridge, Sue Childs, Lynette Cawthra, and Bruce Madge, "How to Create Successful Partnerships—A Review of the Literature," *Health Information & Libraries Journal* 21 (2004): 3–19, at 7, https://doi.org/10.1111/j.1740-3324.2004.00497.x.

20. Joshua David and Robert Hammond, *High Line: The Inside Story of New York City's Park in the Sky* (New York: Farrar, Straus and Giroux, 2011).

21. The Trust for Public Land, *2017 City Park Facts*, April 2017, www.tpl.org/2017-city-park-facts.

22. Jamil Chade, "Stadium Deals, Corruption and Bribery: The Questions at the Heart of Brazil's Olympic and World Cup 'Miracle'," *The Guardian*, April 23, 2017.

23. In a survey of business leaders, "integrity" was universally cited as a critical operating business principle among a network of related subsidiaries. See David F. Larcker and Brian Tayan, "Trust and Consequences: A Survey of Berkshire Hathaway Operating Managers," Stanford University Closer Look Series, CGRP52, October 20, 2015.

24. Simon Romero, "Shepherd of the City's Rebirth, Rio's Mayor Feels the Strains, Too," *New York Times*, February 28, 2014.

25. Siv Vangen and Chris Huxham, "Enacting Leadership for Collaborative Advantage: Dilemmas of Ideology and Pragmatism in the Activities of Partnership Managers," *British Journal of Management* 14, suppl. 1 (2003): S61–S76.

26. Laura Choi, "Place-Based Initiatives," *Community Investments* 22, no. 1 (Spring 2010), www.frbsf.org/community-development/files/Spring _CI_2010a.pdf.

27. For a discussion of organizational interdependence, see Vivien Lowndes, "The Dynamics of Multi-Organizational Partnerships: An Analysis of Changing Modes of Governance," *Public Administration* 76 (Summer 1998): 313–333, at 315, 319.

28. See Stephen Goldsmith and Susan Crawford, *The Responsive City: Engaging Communities Through Data-Smart Governance* (Hoboken, N.J.: Wiley, 2014).

29. "AP Analysis: Rio de Janeiro Olympics Cost $13.1 billion," *USA Today*, June 14, 2017.

30. See the section on "Implementation" for a discussion and referenced research on the need for "shared values" to implement "common vision among independent actors." John W. Selsky and Barbara Parker, "Cross-Sector Partnerships to Address Social Issues: Challenges to Theory and Practice," *Journal of Management* 31, no. 6 (December 1, 2005): 849–73, at 856.

31. We acknowledge that most private foundation endowments are not invested in a manner that would reasonably be classified as risk-taking or risk-seeking (within the constraints defined by the IRS). However, philanthropic assets have that flexibility, and we hope to see more innovative financial tools in use in the future.

32. This is listed simply as "Investment," indicating a "sign of commitment" among partners in Rosabeth Kanter, "How to Strike Effective Alliances and Partnerships," *Harvard Business Review* (April 13, 2009), https://hbr.org/2009/04/how-to-strike-effective-allian.html.

33. See discussions on "Contribute 'What We Do'" and "Contribute Specialized Services to a Large-Scale Undertaking" in John A. Pearce II and Jonathan P. Doh, "The High Impact of Collaborative Social Initiatives," *MIT Sloan Management Review* 46 no. 3 (2005): 30–39, at 34–35.

34. For a discussion on this topic in the context of social enterprises, see Antony Bugg-Levine, Bruce Kogut, and Nalin Kulatilaka, "A New Approach to Funding Social Enterprises," *Harvard Business Review* 90 no. 1/2 (2012): 118–23.

35. For a detailed and related analysis examining social impact indicators and indicator categories across numerous social return on investment (SROI) studies between 2002 and 2012, see Gorgi Krlev, Robert Münscher, and Katharina Mülbert, "Social Return on Investment (SROI): State-of-the-Art and Perspectives—A Meta-Analysis of Practice in Social Return on Investment (SROI) Studies Published 2002–2012," CSI Advisory Services, 2013, 39–42, www.csi.uni-heidelberg.de/downloads/CSI _SROI_Meta_Analysis_2013.pdf.

36. For a related discussion and two New York State public sector case studies, see Theresa A. Pardo et al., "Knowledge Sharing in Cross-Boundary Information System Development in the Public Sector," *Information Technology and Management 7*, no. 4 (2006): 293–313.

37. Mayor Bloomberg's open data efforts have continued beyond his administration. See "De Blasio Administration Unveils New Open Data Homepage as New York City Celebrates 5 Years of Open Data," Press release, March 7, 2017, www1.nyc.gov/office-of-the-mayor/news/137-17 /de-blasio-administration-new-open-data-homepage-new-york-city -celebrates-5-years-open.

38. For a related public sector case study from the UK, see David Wastell, Peter Kawalek, Peter Langmead-Jones, and Rob Ormerod, "Information Systems and Partnership in Multi-Agency Networks: An Action Research Project in Crime Reduction," *Information and Organization* 14, no. 3 (2004): 189–210, https://doi.org/10.1016/j.infoandorg.2004.01.001.

39. IEG World Bank Group, *World Bank Group Support to Public-Private Part-nerships: Lessons from Experience in Client Countries, F02-12* (Washington, D.C.: International Bank for Reconstruction and Development/The World Bank, 2015), xiii.

40. IEG World Bank Group, *World Bank Group Support to Public-Private Partnerships*, xiii–xix.

41. For a discussion on the importance of social capital in collaborative partnerships aiming to overcome complex social policy challenges, including collective action problems, see section titled "How Social Capital Can Contribute to Sustainable Development," in Yvonne Rydin and Nancy Holman, "Re-Evaluating the Contribution of Social Capital in Achieving Sustainable Development," *Local Environment* 9 no. 2 (2004): 117–33, at 127–31.

42. Peter F. Drucker, *Management: Tasks, Responsibilities, Practices* (New York: HarperCollins, 1974).

43. For further discussion, see Alexander Bassen and Ana Maria Masha Kovacs, "Environmental, Social and Governance Key Performance Indicators from a Capital Market Perspective," *Zeitschrift für Wirtschafts—und Unternehmensethik* 9, no. 2 (2008): 182–92.

44. Consider the United Nations Global Compact, an initiative to promote sustainable and ethical business practices, mainly focused on the private sector. As a voluntary regulatory program, it has certain limitations; however, it has grown to approximately 13,000 committed organizations (of which over 9,000 are corporate) spanning 170 countries. Its signatories agree to "responsible business practices, combined with collaboration and innovation," through a commitment to ten principles in the areas of human rights, labor, the environment, and anticorruption. For more detailed information, see "2017 United Nations Global Compact Progress Report; Business Solutions to Sustainable Development," United Nations Global Compact, September 2017, www.unglobal compact.org/library/5431.

45. Take, for instance, a working group of European financial institutions and companies directing investments and activities in support of the United Nations Sustainable Development Goals. Among other things, this group has defined specific, socially focused, key performance indicators and submetrics for advancing many of the sustainable development goals. Further, the institutional investors in the group committed to "support the generation of positive social and/or environmental impact through their products and services." These groups also have committed to "actively collaborate with other like-minded investors to accelerate investments into a more sustainable world." This statement is available at www.pggm.nl/wie-zijn-we/pers/Documents/Institutional-investment -into-the-Sustainable-Development-Goals-statement.pdf.

46. Pension funds in OECD countries alone, for example, have more than $30 trillion in assets. *Annual Survey of Large Pension Funds*, OECD, 2014, www.oecd.org/g20/topics/financing-for-investment/survey-large -pension-funds.htm.

47. Steven Radelet, *The Great Surge: The Ascent of the Developing World* (New York: Simon and Schuster, 2015), 3–42.

48. See Thomas Piketty, *Capitalism in the Twenty-First Century* (Cambridge, Mass.: Harvard College, 2014); also, see section on "Distribution of wealth across individuals and wealth inequality," 9, in: "Global Wealth Report 2017," Research Institute, CreditSuisse, November 2017. http://publications.credit-suisse.com/tasks/render/file/index.cfm?fileid =168E2808-9ED4-5A5E-19E43EA2A731A4ED.

49. Joseph E. Stiglitz, *The Price of Inequality* (New York: Norton, 2013), xxix.

50. Stiglitz, *The Price of Inequality*, 336–55.

51. Stiglitz, *The Price of Inequality*, 354.

52. See section on "'New Governance' and 'New Public Management'" in McQuaid, "Theory of Organisational Partnerships," 125–46.

53. Drucker, *Management: Tasks, Responsibilities, Practice.*

54. See the discussion of the evolving roles and expectations of business in society in Alyson Warhurst, "Future Roles of Business in Society: The Expanding Boundaries of Corporate Responsibility and a Compelling Case for Partnership," *Futures* 37 no. 2 (2005): 151–68.

55. In addition to changing social norms and the distinct perspectives of the millennial generation, consider the relatively recent Giving Pledge effort. Launched in 2010, the Giving Pledge asks billionaires to commit at least half of their wealth to philanthropic causes rather than amass it for maximizing generational wealth transfers. Nearly two hundred billionaires from across the world have taken the pledge, representing approximately $1 trillion in assets. For more information, visit the Giving Pledge website at http://givingpledge.org/.

# Index

Page numbers in italics indicate figures or tables.